THE
DEFAULT
LINE

Faisal Islam is the Economics Editor of the UK's *Channel 4 News*. His broadcast and written journalism has received a dozen honours for reporting in Britain and across the world.

THE
DEFAULT
LINE

FAISAL ISLAM

HEAD
of ZEUS

First published in 2013 by Head of Zeus Ltd.

Copyright © Faisal Islam 2013

1 3 5 7 9 10 8 6 4 2

A CIP catalogue record for this book is available
from the British Library.

ISBN (HB) 9781781854105
(E) 9781781854099

Typeset by Palimpsest Book Production Limited,
Falkirk, Stirlingshire

Printed in Germany

Head of Zeus Ltd.
Clerkenwell House
45–47 Clerkenwell Green
London EC1R 0HT

www.headofzeus.com

I've got hugs for you,
If you were born in the 80s, the 80s.

C. Harris, 2007

And for those born even later than that too,
I dedicate this book to the incompetence of
the generation of European political leaders
born in the 50s and 60s

CONTENTS

INTRODUCTION

Economics is not meteorology. In Britain, and across Europe, the economy is not like the weather. Yet this is precisely what a long list of incompetent politicians would like you to believe. Economic downswings and crises 'befall' helpless nations just as might do a ruinous hurricane, tornado or tidal wave. It is an analogy that denies agency to the key decision-makers. It is an excuse. Economics is about choices. These are choices sometimes made on our behalf by politicians or central bankers. They are also choices made by societies. Most countries still feeling the grim underside of the aftermath of the 2008 crisis are doing so because of choices made a decade or so ago. The choices they are making now will loom over us and Europe's youth in particular for decades to come.

This story, which I have called *The Default Line*, is about those choices. Default is fundamentally about debt: the act of borrowing and not repaying in full. People, companies, banks, nations, currency zones, systems and philosophies have teetered on the edge in this ongoing crisis. But the line of solvency is a thin one. Even when sovereign governments defaulted in the past few years, there have been denials and debates in committees and shades of grey. Debt is much more than a financial or economic phenomenon. Debt has social, political, emotional and religious connotations.

There is a moment in the inevitable descent into bust when boom-time exuberance suddenly flips and becomes an inescapable iceberg. A point when nations, companies, civilisations and people step over the mark. A snow dome in the Dubai desert. A future British finance minister wondering why his mortgage application required no proof of income. A leading banker proclaiming publicly that 'Credit has been democratised, and that is a good thing.' Greek football teams with three stadiums. A dog in Manchester offered a gold credit card. Banks funnelling superabundant credit at poor African-American communities in Baltimore, by paying commission to churches. A G7 leader starting his re-election campaign boasting about one of the world's most expensive hospitals, despite the fact that not even a penny had been paid for it, and it would remain unpaid for into the 2050s.

These are the signs of being close to this invisible line. The flimsy barrier between lender and borrower, between being subject to the kindness of strangers, and actually being the stranger. It's a line that runs through our cities, along our borders, within Europe and through fibre-optic cables responsible for the global $78 trillion trade in debt. And nations, banks, small businesses, politicians, families and people are unexpectedly finding themselves on the wrong side. It's not just about debts and leverage in their financial sense, but morally and diplomatically too. Creditor nations such as China are using their loans as leverage on the world stage. Nations such as India believe the West has stacked up environmental debts that might dwarf even their monetary ones.

This journey across the line, from Europe's gas control room in Moscow to Singapore's parking lot of cargo ships, from New York trading floors to Newport market traders, from booming amateur landlords to impoverished young people, and from rebellious Greek tax inspectors to booming German forklift truck manufacturers, is one I have made in a decade of reporting global economics. Almost all of the story I have witnessed at first hand, a frankly incredible tale of winners and losers, or power changing hands, and a new breed of powerless. It is summed up in the existence of one man: the supervisory chairman of China's national piggy bank, its sovereign wealth fund. He sits on $400 billion of reserves and he knows this weapon is so potent that he denies it is a weapon at all. Instead he happily meets with the Western governments, banks and companies desperate for this source of stable capital. And then he quotes Shakespeare at them.

That piggy bank in China was connected to the 125 per cent mortgage which indebted and nearly upended Esther, a young single mum from Surrey whom I interviewed in late 2008. I remember sitting in her living room with her children's belongings boxed up ready for repossession, as I commentated on various elements of global financial crisis, including the sharpest collapse in world trade in a century. I thought: 'How did we get here? Who let this happen?' The answer was, a chain of disintermediation that started with savings in the East, and in particular in China. This book follows the root canals of Esther's mortgage up through the securitisation department at Northern Rock, the shadow banking system centred on London, bad regulators, conflicted politicians, broken formulaic self-regulation emerging out of Basel, mistakes in the setting of interest rates by central bankers, concurrent problems in Spain, Cyprus, Iceland and Greece, and the prolonging of the crisis in a reluctant Berlin. I will take you around the table at Britain's most expensive dining club, where several bankers were given billions to keep their banks going. There is a tale of the battle between banker and minister over the near nationalisation of one of the world's biggest banks. I'll take you into the cockpit of 'Euro Force One', what passes for a printing press for Eurozone nations without monetary sovereignty. We will go inside the European Central Bank, perhaps the world's most important unelected institution. In Reykjavik you will hear what it was like to be inside a central bank just as it was going bankrupt, something that is normally impossible. On a real fault line in San Francisco you will hear from the hippyish man who wrote the formula which was said to have broken Wall Street, but is still being used to define the safety of the Western banking system, and may well be holding the world economy back. There's the Indian motorbike magnate who thinks climate change is principally a colonial ruse. There are the oil pipelines that threaten the fracture of a fragile nation. There is the constant dance and fight between fiscal criminals and bond vigilantes that has led to curious and patchy austerity. There is the desperate need for central bankers to communicate control in uncertain times. And then there are the migratory journeys within China that were a proximate cause of everything. In Cyprus, all the strands – bad banks, bad politicians and a dysfunctional Eurozone – coalesced into three weeks of high drama in March 2013. Bank bailout turned into human bail-in. All around Europe the real default has been to the continent's social model, rather than its banks or the stability of its currency experiment.

For a decade the economy was rather NICE – Non Inflationary Consistent Expansion on the back of cheap goods from our friends from China. It went bust spectacularly. And now in Britain, Europe and the USA, we are halfway through the CRUDER decade: Consistent Recession, Unemployment, Deleveraging Experiment and Realignment. This is why, as I write this, a new governor of the Bank of England is experimenting with radical alternatives for British economic policy. The old one, the inventor of the NICE concept, developed quantitative easing – opaque, little understood and rather redistributive, and yet in 2009 and 2012 it might have staved off depression. Abroad it was derided as a Weimar republic-style operation to fund a broke government. In Paris and Frankfurt the sense was that Britain and the USA were 'cheating', and would eventually pay for its accommodation of profligacy.

This book is also about financial tectonic plates shifting and impacting on and in Europe. In 2001, I jokingly predicted that by 2030 the headlines in British tabloid newspapers complaining about migration would be about young Brits being locked out of the Bangalore jobs market. I was wrong. It was beginning to happen in 2010.

All these factors are buffeting our lives in increasingly unpredictable ways. I pick out three patterns from this global, continental, economic, political and human journey:

- the mistakes made by incompetent politicians
- the dysfunctional relationship of some nations with property and housing
- the conscious use of complexity by nefarious politicians and financiers to try to blind voters and customers.

All three currents reappear throughout this tale.

To get back to that Surrey sitting room and the imminent repossession. Now, half a decade on, the same mother faces paying a different price, that of squeezed living standards from public-sector austerity. I am not the only economics journalist who wished they could have done a better job in reporting the forces that brought about the world's biggest financial crisis, years before the bust. It was a large-scale journalistic default after having cried wolf on the unsustainable credit boom in Britain in 2003. This story has been seven months in the writing, a decade in the researching, and the result of hundreds of hours of interviews with the key players and their victims. I hope this book redresses some of that balance, and forewarns readers about some of the coming, man-made 'weather' that will nurture, upend and occasionally even bring sunrays to their lives in the coming years. I hope that for viewers, listeners and readers this book does repay part of a debt.

How to read this book

Each chapter of this book is a self-contained story, linked to concurrent goings-on around the world. I have made extensive use of cross-referencing to show the different impacts or perspectives in the same events when viewed from, say, Greece (Chapter 1) and Germany (Chapter 10). I thought that this would be a better use of dead trees and bandwidth than a lengthy unread index.

I describe some complicated things, hopefully in rather human terms. I use the 'ladder of abstraction' – a secret of broadcasting.

I explain high-level stuff, such as negotiations between finance ministers and bankers, and ground-level stuff, the impact on their victims. I've skipped a portion of the detail in the middle. There's the occasional spot of simplification, a sliver of poetic licence. But I have tried to avoid dumbing things down. Indeed, the writing on the formula that is breaking the world economy (Chapter 7), and the global money-printing experiment (Chapter 9) may seem complicated, but such developments are vital cogs in the way that modern Europe's finances have developed, from Northern Rock's mortgage factory to the equations that underpin global banking solvency.

The journey starts with aeroplanes of euros in Greece. Athens then became the alibi for a capitulation to bond vigilantes by Britain in the epic battle that goes on in wild global credit markets. I jump back to Iceland, the first harbinger of the crisis jumping to nations, and the most remarkable and transparent attempts to discover precisely what went wrong. In Chapter 4, in China, you will learn to thank hard-working migrant workers for your high living standards before the crash, and discover why Gangnanomics could save the world. Chapters 5 to 7 are the stories of British financial and credit excess. It starts with the all-encompassing dysfunction of our relationship with property, stretching from celebrity culture, sports-style commentary of house prices, to tacit and occasionally overt political corruption that is shafting young people. Chapter 6 takes you around a Downing Street dinner table with frankly absurd tales of UK banking excess. It sketches out a story of failed former building societies desperate to outcompete one another, as well as the lesser-known story of the darkest penumbra of the unstable shadow banking system that basically collapsed in 2008 – also in London. Chapter 7 takes you to the Yoda of credit, the very origins of derivatives and the shift in risk off loan books and onto trading books.

Chapter 8 is the incredible story of Spain's Gates of Hell, featuring extraordinary house-building, construction corruption and the collapse of the centuries-old caja savings bank system.

The ninth chapter reflects on the Bank of England's record and its experiment in quantitative easing. In Chapter 10 I pick at how Germany got to where it is today, and how that colours its response to the Eurozone crisis. Berlin is the new reluctant and mysterious centre of European power. After that, in Chapter 11, it is natural to turn to Frankfurt, and the home of the powerful European Central Bank, in whose hands the world economy seems disproportionately to rest. Chapter 12 takes us on a global hunt for carbon and the impact on our environment and living standards, from Iraq to Siberia to India and the City. And in Chapter 13 we return to Cyprus, not so far from where Chapter 1 began, with another planeload of euro notes, and a disturbing insight into a future world of 'bail-in'.

My epilogue, 'New Default Lines', is a section that I felt compelled to write because of an overwhelming sense of exasperation at the bad choices made by our political class. The epilogue is largely free of statistics and is a shoot-from-the-hip account of new default lines that I think will define the next decades. I float some vaguely crazy policy ideas from right and left to spark some debate. They are all rooted in something I have learnt or described somewhere in this book. I reserve the right to change my mind utterly about the opinions in this epilogue, as events change. The thirteen chapters that precede it are far sturdier folios of crisis history.

I have begun each chapter with a dramatis personae. This is a human drama as well as an economic crisis. I have personally interviewed or questioned about 80 per cent of the people listed. In certain cases, because some informants are still in their jobs, or have been so illuminating in private, I have felt the need to keep them anonymous. I have changed two names, for obvious reasons. There is much of this tale that is in the public record. There are astonishing stories that can be told from published statistics alone. This subject matter is a moving target, but the cut-off date for news was July 2013. I will keep editions updated, and encourage feedback on Twitter @TheDefaultLine.

CHAPTER 1

HOW THE EURO STOLE THE GREEK SUN

Dramatis personae

Anonymous Troika official
George Provopoulos, governor of the Bank of Greece
George Papandreou, prime minister of Greece (2009–11)
Mrs Antonopoulos, pregnant wife of Athenian tax inspector
Plato, ancient Greek philosopher
Kostas Antonopoulos, Greek tax inspector
Dr Giorgos Vihas, a cardiologist at a Greek health clinic
Mr Karagiannis, an internally devalued businessman having to
live off his mother's pension
Alexis Athanasios and Haris Manolis, striking steel workers
Antonis Stelliatos, Greek yacht-owner
Lee Buchheit, the Red Adair of sovereign debt crises,
and adviser to the Greek government
Jean-Claude Trichet, European Central Bank president (2003–11)
Anonymous Greek solar power magnate
Anonymous senior adviser to Eurozone leader
Nicolas Sarkozy, French president (2007–12)
Kostas Kartalis, PASOK MP
Jan Kees de Jager, Dutch finance minister (2010–12)
Steven Vanackere, Belgian finance minister (2011–13)
Alexis Tsipras, leader of the Syriza Party (2009–)
Manolis Glezos, Greek hero of the Nazi occupation and Syriza MP
Vasili, economics graduate selling fish at Athens fish market

At the time, the Athens Airlifts of 2011 and 2012 were a closely guarded secret. It wasn't a matter of feeding a starving population. No lives were saved, at least not directly. But for the fate of Europe, the Athens Airlifts were no less important than the Berlin Airlift of 1948–9, when for many months the Western allies flew vital supplies into West Berlin in the face of a Soviet blockade. The mission of the Athens Airlifts in the early twenty-first century was not to preserve democratic freedom, but to protect and prolong the economic experiment of a currency without a single home.

It was well known that Greece was running out of cash, in metaphorical terms at least. In June 2011, after months of stalling on its economic reform programme, the foreign Troika that effectively ran the country had run out of patience with the Greek leadership. The Troika – consisting of the European Union, the European Central Bank and the International Monetary Fund – was going to pull the crucial final tranche of funding from Greece's original €110 billion bailout, agreed in May 2010. The final €12 billion slice of foreign funds was required to pay pensions, public servants and interest on Greece's huge debts. It was funding Greece could raise neither in taxes from its own people, nor from the financial markets.

But what most people did *not* know was that Greece was *literally* running out of cash. There were shortages of all denominations apart from the €10 note. Greeks had responded to the uncertainty regarding the Troika's next move by withdrawing euros from their bank accounts at a record rate. Soon there would be not enough euro notes in the country to cope with the number of Greeks trying to get their hands on their money from cash machines and bank branches. A secret plan was activated.

A senior official overseeing Greece's bailout told me that when it became known that the IMF were considering not paying out the final tranche, there was the beginning of a bank run. 'We're talking about June 2011,' he told me, 'when Greeks were taking about one to two billion euros a day from the banking system. And the Greeks had to send military planes to Italy to get banknotes. It got to that point.'

A decade after it gave up the drachma, the world's oldest existing currency, Greece faced the crushing reality that it did not have the sovereign authority to meet the demand for paper currency from its own citizens. It did possess its own state-of-the-art printing facility, at the Bank of Greece's National Mint at Holargos, in northern Athens. All the euro coins could be minted there, and not just for Greece. But coins were not going to sate the desire of the Greek people for cash. At the time, the note-printing presses at Holargos only had the plates for the €10 note. The European Central Bank had dispersed the printing of euro banknotes around member states. Only the German Bundesbank, the National Bank of Austria and the Luxembourgers have ever had the plates for the highly prized €500 note, the highest value paper currency in the world. (This form of manufacturing would appear to have been confined to German-speaking countries.) Intentionally or not, the ability of Greece to meet a huge surge in demand for banknotes had been tightly proscribed. As it happened, in June 2011 demand for paper currency had nearly trebled. To deal with this crisis, the Greek military cargo planes returned from abroad laden with freshly printed euros. The secret mission was intended not only to preserve Greece's fracturing social stability, but also to preserve the single currency itself.

At that time, nervousness had begun to spread to Italy. If the Greek banks had run out of cash and been forced to limit bank withdrawals, the fear would have spread across the Mediterranean. The metaphor used to describe this process relates to the spread of diseases: contagion. The governor of the Bank of Greece, George Provopoulos, subsequently explained that if the demand for notes had not been met, an impression would have been created that the banks were unable to repay depositors. 'It would have caused a collapse of confidence,' he said, 'with dire consequences for financial stability and the general outlook of the country.' A Troika figure later told me, 'There would have been complete and immediate panic. They had no time. A billion, two billion per day in banknotes is a lot of money. This then becomes an industrial problem.'

The airlift was only the first stage of the operation. Dozens, if not hundreds, of journeys by truck and boat spread the new notes across the mainland and the islands, from Rhodes to Corfu, from Crete to Komotini near the Turkish border. Staff worked through the night to ensure that bank branches across Greece had sufficient notes to meet depositor demand, and so contain any incipient physical bank run. Incredibly, this operation proceeded without anyone noticing. The Bank of Greece tracked a demand for paper currency through bank branch orders for currency. Large withdrawals were normally granted with notice of a day or two. The Bank also noticed a spike in purchases of gold sovereigns. It did not have to deploy teams of 'bank-run spotters' as the Bank of England had done in the crisis of 2008. As far as ordinary Greeks were concerned, the cash machines continued to function. However, underneath their very noses a monetary revolution was taking place...

The simple balance sheet of the Bank of Greece showed no disturbance from these tumultuous events on the stock of notes and coins in circulation in the country. The official figures are adjusted accounting numbers, but unpublished numbers can be calculated. The value of notes in circulation in Greece doubled from €19 billion in 2009 to €40 billion in September 2011. By the summer of 2012 the total had reached €48 billion. Typically, developed economies have cash in circulation worth between 4 and 7 per cent of the country's GDP. In 2009 in Greece, the figure was 8.2 per cent. By 2012 it had nearly trebled to 24.8 per cent. On these numbers, in mid-2012, Greece had put a larger value of euro notes in circulation than the Netherlands. The Dutch economy is four times that of Greece.

Actually, there already was a bank run on, but thankfully

for Athens and Europe's central bankers in Frankfurt, not one that could be filmed with television cameras. Officially, some news dribbled out about a slow-motion 'bank jog'. But in 2011 and then again in early summer 2012, the quantities of Greek euro deposits fleeing Greek banks were massive. In the twelve weeks from April 2011, Greek banks were drained of four years of growth in deposits. In May 2011 alone, €12.4 billion of deposits, or 6 per cent of Greece's GDP, was removed from its banking system. These deposits made their way to various 'safe havens', including the London property market, the undersides of Greek bedroom mattresses and the lauded banking system of Cyprus (see pages 403–04). A third of the withdrawn cash was spent, a third was taken abroad, and a third was stored in Greek homes, authorities estimate.

The drama of June 2011 was to abate slightly, and the deposit flows to reverse temporarily, after Prime Minister George Papandreou won a confidence vote in parliament. Amid violent protests and tear gas outside the parliament building, Papandreou's government passed new austerity, reform and privatisation measures by a majority of five. George Provopoulos, the central bank governor, had warned MPs that 'To vote against this package would be a crime – the country would be voting for its suicide.' It was the threat of a return to the drachma that enabled the government to force through politically unpopular decisions – a type of blackmail that I dubbed 'drachmail'. And this blackmail was to continue in some form or another right across Europe, as the continent struggled with the consequences of its experiment in shared economic sovereignty.

The tax inspectors and the Troikan Horse

September 2011. A thousand tax inspectors are packed into a theatre in Athens. There are passionate debates about the latest set of cuts to their pay and pensions. Arguments between the government-affiliated union leader and his members spill out on to the street. The rank-and-file feel betrayed that they have been persuaded to accept a first wave of pay cuts earlier in 2011, only to find that now they are being asked to accept even more cuts. This does not feel like a country being bailed out by its neighbours. As Mrs Antonopoulos, the wife of a tax inspector, puts it, Greece is being 'treated like Hector, being dragged around and around by Achilles' chariot'. Greece's humiliation, she suggests, is being paraded as an example to other nations.

In autumn 2011 this theatre was the front line of the euro crisis. At its heart was Greece's €360 billion debt, a debt it could not repay. These tax inspectors were the very people Greece needed to be out and about gathering up every euro-cent in order to stop the national debt from ballooning completely out of control. For thousands of years the power to tax has defined sovereignty. But here it was not just that the taxmen were spending the morning in angry debate rather than collecting taxes. It was not even that they were soon to go on strike. What was extraordinary was that these tax inspectors were openly advising their fellow Greeks to defy the new 'emergency taxes' on property. One of the taxmen told me that some of Greece's most celebrated politicians had once refused to pay a levy for public service television. 'I think we should do the same now, because we simply can't afford it,' he says. 'We don't have any more money.'

When tax inspectors start to urge non-payment of tax, a country in a fiscal crisis has a serious existential problem. Greece's historic antipathy to taxes stretches back to the days of the republic in ancient Athens. Then, indirect taxes on slaves, houses and wine were more important than direct taxes on incomes. Plato famously suggested: 'When there is an income tax, the just man will pay more and the unjust less on the same amount of income.' That was three millennia ago. Three centuries ago, Athens and most of the rest of Greece was firmly under the rule of the Ottomans. The leading class of Greeks then were the *prokritoi*, the tax collectors and civil servants. In his 2011 book, *Greece's 'Odious' Debt*, Jason Manolopoulos says that at that time the Greeks did not pay taxes 'as a point of pride' against the Ottomans and their imposition of a poll tax on Christians. After the Greek War of Independence in the 1820s, the *prokritoi* took over as the ruling class. According to Manolopoulos, Greeks continued to avoid paying taxes to these politicians, and a culture of tax evasion as an expression of resistance has persisted through the generations. Clearly this theory is impossible to prove. The Greek economic journalist Matina Stevis puts it differently: 'for several categories of [Greek] professionals – especially those who are self-employed – it always made sense to cheat. The probability of getting caught was minimal because of an ineffective and ancient tax-collection infrastructure; tax collectors themselves were at the heart of tax-evasion rings.' The Troika reforms specifically aimed to limit this by curtailing physical meetings between taxpayer and tax collector. The statistics do show that Greece has been somewhat undertaxed compared to its European neighbours. Greece has collected about 33 to 35 per cent of GDP in total annual tax revenues over the past decade, which is some way below the EU average of 40 to 41 per cent. Finland, at 44 per cent, has almost always extracted more tax in cash terms than Greece, from a smaller economy and a population only half the size. Finland has reluctantly found itself using this tax base to help fund Greece's obligations.

I speak to Francesca, an Athenian tax inspector, whose husband has been unemployed for two years and whose son is joining the flood of Greeks leaving their homeland. 'My pay cheque keeps getting smaller,' she says. 'I used to have a salary of €2000 a month, now I barely earn €800. It's not even enough to cover our basic needs.' Government ministers, she says, warned her off investigating the tax affairs of the Greek elite.

This is what a country near default looks and sounds like. There's not just a collapsing economy, there's also a failing tax system, and the social contract between Greece's people and its rulers is broken. Greece has been hit harder than its fellow 'programme nations', as the European Union calls them – or

PIGs (Portugal, Ireland and Greece), as the markets refer to them. From Greece to Germany, government ministers are now liken-ing the euro crisis to a war – and it's not uncommon to hear Winston Churchill quoted during debates about the deficit. The euro crisis is now much more than just a financial crisis. In Athens at the end of 2011 it was reaching a second phase: a remarkable, historic experiment in sovereignty.

A group of uniformed police officers staging a protest is a rare and scarcely believable sight. It was particularly strange to see such a group outside the German embassy in Athens, chanting, 'You're shooting us, you're bleeding us, you're pushing us off the cliff.' It was a measure of how little the Greeks were prepared to thank Berlin for the borrowed euros. The protesting officers waved a banner declaiming, 'Kick out the Troikans.'

That September, what might well be called a Troikan Horse arrived – on 5 million electricity bills. I met 40-year-old Kostas Antonopoulos at the tax collectors' union meeting. He later rang to invite me to his flat, expensively acquired during Greece's euro-fuelled credit boom. He shares the flat with his wife, who is six months pregnant, and his young son. The couple fear for their children's future after watching documentaries about the impact of IMF programmes in Argentina. 'Meet our new tax inspector,' says Kostas, pointing to the electricity meter in his basement. His wages have halved to €900 per month, below the €1000 mortgage payment on the flat he bought during the go-go years. He can scrape the payment together this month, by raiding his savings. But he doubts he'll be able to find the money next month. Even if he did, the electricity meter might prove to be more effective at collecting taxes than he and his colleagues.

The new property tax meant a charge of hundreds of euros for every Greek household, including pensioners and even the recently unemployed. The tax was only invented the month before to meet a €2 billion shortfall in Greece's austerity plan. Originally it was meant to be a small, temporary charge but, as the saying goes, there is nothing more permanent than a temporary tax. So it was to prove: the property tax has doubled and is here to stay until at least the end of 2014. Greeks renamed it *haratsi*, the Turkish word used to describe the centuries-old Ottoman poll tax. Non-payers were to have their electricity cut off. This was 'shock therapy' indeed.

'Wow, we're going to save Greece!'

The shock therapists were the IMF and the EU. Tax rises, spending cuts and so-called structural economic reforms were Greece's side of the bargain for the European and IMF bailout. In Washington the prospect of the IMF grappling with Greece was rather appealing. 'Initially the Greek crisis was received with great excitement,' a senior IMF official told me. 'An advanced country... Wow, we're going to save Greece!' The IMF was far more experienced at dealing with low- and middle-income countries after banking busts. However, it had also learnt that its standard-issue medicine had to be dispensed carefully. The sequencing of policy mattered, as did the timing.

The IMF had been brought in at the insistence of Germany. 'The IMF was the only institution which has the experience with adaptation programmes,' said a senior official in Berlin. 'European institutions have never done it, we were sure that they would be too weak to tell a member country what to do.' It was an early expression of the divide between Angela Merkel's government in Berlin and the European Central Bank in Frankfurt. The ECB thought it could handle Europe's problem nations on its own, a position described as 'complete wishful thinking' at the IMF. The ECB was first and foremost an institution concerned with monetary policy, the setting of a single base interest rate across the Eurozone, as well as the logistics of running a pancontinental currency. The ECB over a series of bailouts was to emerge as bad cop to the IMF's good cop. But there were a good number of splits in the Troika, as well as an Anglo-Saxon/ European split within the IMF itself. The ECB, keen to establish its hardline credentials, was uncompromising on so-called 'front-loaded' tax rises and spending cuts, and, initially, on getting Greece to repay every penny of its debts to nervous markets. 'The ECB has taken a very conservative view on fiscal policy,' the governor of one Eurozone central bank told me. He went on to explain what the ECB view was: 'It's responding to a fiscal problem, and fiscal problems can be solved by cutting back on public expenditure, which no matter how low it is, should be lower.' In contrast, he said, 'The IMF has a longer understanding and perhaps a better understanding of policy and politics.' The IMF was, he said, 'less doctrinaire' than the ECB.

In broad terms, by 2011 Papandreou's Greece had embarked on the fiscal measures: pay cuts, spending cuts and tax rises. However, they had done very little about the rest of the structural economic reforms promised to Greece's new bankers in Brussels, Frankfurt and Washington. To try to get the politicians to act, in the summer of 2011 Governor Provopoulos of the Bank of Greece said the country was voting for its life and to vote down the economic reforms would be 'suicide' and a 'crime'. At this point he had already overseen the Athens Airlift of billions of euros, but could say nothing about it to either the politicians or the citizens of Greece. Provopoulos had a dual role – as representative of the Greek people at the European Central Bank in Frankfurt, and as representative of the ECB to the Greek people. In a dynamic repeated in all the bailed-out countries, the governor's hyperbole in warning of imminent doom was no more nor less than an attempt to oblige domestic politicians to make painful decisions. In Greece, however, this pattern of brinkmanship would repeat itself, on a quarterly basis. The Greeks would struggle with the notion of no longer being sovereign masters of their fate. Each time, the Greek people, the financial markets and the euro itself would be pushed to the brink by the increasingly explicit threats of the drachmailers.

Parliament duly passed the measures demanded by the Troika, and so the latter released the bailout money. However, it was not long before the brinkmanship resumed. When Troika inspectors returned to Greece in September 2011, they found that though the Greeks had passed the measures, they had not actually applied them. Greece's finance minister at the time, Evangelos Venizelos, later told his party that at this point the Troika offered Greece a 'velvet exit' from the euro, smoothed with EU money – another form of drachmail designed to shock Greek politicians into compliance with the loan conditions. The end result was the hated electricity tax, the tax that Venizelos would come to blame for toppling his government later that year.

For the Troika overlords of Greece, the real problem was that the country was not implementing the programme it had agreed – partly because of the actions of aggrieved groups like the striking tax collectors. A former IMF official told me they should have been aware of the 'massive political obstacles' in the way of the required reforms: 'Very, very strong vested interests in Greece blocked most things, and therefore you then get into a downward spiral because you're trying to do things that are not being done. At the same time you have a complete inability to solve problems.'

Greece had a big enough problem even contemplating the size of its debts. But it was not simply a matter of raising taxes and cutting spending in order to fill a fiscal black hole. There was an even more fundamental problem. The standard-issue IMF template for dealing with financial crises among the developing countries, its more usual clients, required two other factors: devaluation and default. In the single-currency Eurozone, however, devaluation was not an option. That meant the internal adjustment, the so-called 'internal devaluation' required of Greece, would be even more brutal.

A nation on the edge

There was a certain irony in the way that, in the run-up to the 2012 Olympic Games in London, the Olympic flame was borne across the mainland of Greece with such grace, calm and efficiency. For, at the very moment that this quadrennial showcase of ancient Greek civilisation was being celebrated around the world, modern Greece was at the point of breaking with the rest of Europe.

The previous two Olympic relays had also marked significant milestones in Greece's decline. Eight years before, the Greek capital itself had hosted the Games amid an orgy of debt-fuelled spending on stadiums and other infrastructure. In 2008, ahead of the Beijing Games, the relay ran through Greece just as fourteen years of growth was coming to a halt. And by the time the flame was heading towards London in 2012, Greece had experienced four years of recession, unemployment, austerity and misery. Greece had become a nation on the edge.

The Helliniko Olympic complex in Athens stands as a monument to this hubris, a decaying white elephant that costs £65 million a year just to maintain. Nearby lies one of a handful of new clinics run to cope with Greece's modern reality: a surge in poverty. Dr Giorgos Vihas, a cardiologist, cannot believe the ailments that he and the other volunteer doctors are treating. 'We never expected to see people looking through the rubbish bins to find something to eat. We never expected that the patients here would bring children as young as five or six months old, who would be underweight because the parents can't afford to provide them with enough milk.'

Dr Vihas blames this unprecedented situation on the 'violent change' in living standards. He also deplores the 'systematic destruction of the health system' after the government signed an austerity deal with the EU. Only the charity of wealthy Greeks, he says, is keeping the clinic going. He also offers a political diagnosis. 'The EU medication is worsening the situation,' he says. 'The medical prescription of the bailout leads to a certain death. The madness is that everyone knows this. The Greek patient has realised what this medicine does, and very soon will follow a different prescription.'

This is what an 'internal devaluation' looks like in practice. In times gone by, Greece would have defaulted on its loans – as it has done quite often – and its currency would have hit the floor, making its exporters more competitive. 'Internal devaluation' is a euphemism for genuinely savage cuts to public spending, higher taxes and collapsing living standards. This type of adjustment is the only route available to a country seeking to stay in the euro. One of the patients at Dr Vihas's clinic, a Mr Karagiannis, appears to have undergone his own personal internal devaluation. 'I am poor now, I was rich before,' he tells me. Three years ago he was a high-flying businessman. Now he stays with his 80-year-old mother and lives off her pension. 'I'm here today simply because I'm very poor and I cannot buy my medicines. There is no future.' He says he feels like 'killing the political architecture', and praises Britain for dodging the single currency. Germany, he says, wants to reduce Greece to Bulgarian levels of poverty.

Mr Karagiannis is one of an army of new voters for Syriza, the radical-left coalition. There are more supporters near another stop on the Olympic torch relay. A steel factory near Piraeus port has been officially occupied by striking workers for six months. They claim they're being asked to accept a pay cut of almost 50 per cent. The factory that a decade ago, during the boom, produced steel for Greece's stadia and bridges, now lies idle in the time of bust. All the pressure applied by the Troika on Greece comes to a concentrated focus on workers such as these. Wage cuts are not an unfortunate by-product of Greece's bailout. These cuts are the key ingredient of the medicine prescribed by Germany for Greece's long-term growth. Leading German economic figures expressed something close to moral outrage at the soaring salaries of Greek workers in the boom time. During the first eight years of the euro, the real cost of employing Greeks surged by 40 per cent – without Greeks working harder or producing more. During the same period, German workers saw their productivity rise while their wages fell.

This tale of two workforces – the 'unit labour costs', to use the cold economic phrase – is as important to the euro debate as the deficit and debt figures. The Greeks point to the scale of the cuts in salary and government budgets. The Germans point to the staggering increases: state spending in Greece soared by a extraordinary 89 per cent over the last decade, almost five times that of Germany, much of it going into salary rises. What Greeks call sado-austerity is seen by their European masters as simply the bursting of a bubble – and a painful return to a reality from which the Germans never really departed. In theory, in order to regain its competitiveness, Greece very much needs what a eurocrat might call 'labour cost realignment'. But actual Greek workers do not respond lightly to suggestions that they need a German-style fall in their wages. 'It upsets me that they believe we get high wages. Our wages are very low,' says Alexis Athanasios, a steel worker. 'We can't even afford to support our families.' Haris Manolis, a 38-year-old technician, blames Germany for wanting 'to come here and have factories with cheap labour'.

The easiest way for Alexis and Haris to regain competitiveness would be for Greece to follow Britain's example and devalue. But that, clearly, is impossible within the Eurozone. So instead Greece has endured three years of internal devaluation. This has only served to deepen and lengthen the recession. Unemployment is at a record 27 per cent; for young people it is at an astonishing 60 per cent; for women it is over 66 per cent.

One extraordinary proposal floated by the Troika in 2012 was the introduction of a six-day week, effectively abolishing the weekend. Pressure was also placed – more fruitfully – on Greece's minimum wage. Germany did not have a minimum wage, so how could Chancellor Merkel sell the bailout to the German people when the Greeks had a minimum wage of nearly €900 per month? Even in Spain it was only worth €750. In Greece the minimum wage had risen by 59 per cent during the first nine years of its membership of the Eurozone. 'We had a huge fight over minimum wages,' says a senior adviser in Berlin. 'The minimum wage was limiting tourism growth, foreign companies weren't expanding because it was too expensive, and there were lower salaries in Turkey, Tunisia, Croatia.' He told me that German companies operating in Greece had to hire people on the black market. The outcome was that, to match the reality of black-market pay rates, the minimum wage in Greece was cut by one-fifth – and by one-third for under-25s. With Greece internally devalued, Berlin argued, northern Europeans could holiday there more cheaply than before, so giving the Greek tourist economy a big boost, and thus helping the country on the road to recovery. In addition, visitor numbers would be boosted by those too frightened to holiday in Tunisia or Egypt during the upheavals of the Arab Spring.

The reality turned out to be rather different. The violent protests, clouds of tear gas and burning banks that marked the Athens Spring were accompanied by a collapse in tourist numbers. By 2012, when I met Antonis Stelliatos, head of the Hellenic Yacht Owners Association, boat rentals were down 35 per cent, conference bookings down 50 per cent, and car rental was down 15 per cent. He was hosting the launch of a large new yacht near Piraeus harbour. He wore a T-shirt sporting the slogan

Greek Sea
Not in Crisis

over a picture of an azure lagoon. The riots and the tear gas were only rare occurrences in Athens, he said, before correcting himself. 'The riots are in fact only in two squares in Athens: Syntagma and Omonia.'

Still, everything was conspiring to push Greece into the doom loop of a collapsing economy: higher unemployment, lower take-home pay, lower spending, lower tax receipts and stubbornly high deficits. On top of that, tourism – representing one-fifth of the Greek economy, and one in five jobs – was being crushed by the images of social unrest beamed into Europe's living rooms.

Year after year, Greece was breaking the record for annual economic contraction, and in three years, one-fifth of the economy had been lost – the equivalent of losing the entire tourism sector. In cash terms, in 2012 Greek GDP had reverted to where it had been in 2005. For context, in 2008 the Greek economy was about half the size of Turkey's. Four years later it was less than one-third the size. The Finns were such critics of what they saw as Greek profligacy, laziness and corruption that, uniquely, they demanded collateral for their rescue loans. In 2008 the Greek economy was 26 per cent larger than that of Finland. By 2012 Finland's GDP exceeded Greece's for the first time in history. Finland's population is less than half that of Greece.

In Washington and in Berlin the answer was the same: if things had got worse in Greece in 2012, it was because the programme had not been implemented. As a leading government adviser in one of the Eurozone creditor nations told me, 'The benefits from these structural reforms take two to three years to see.'

By the summer of 2011 it had already become apparent that Greece had no chance of repaying its debts in full. At this point, at the behest of the IMF, the man known as the Red Adair of sovereign debt crises flew into Athens. Lee Buchheit is an expert in helping nations renegotiate the money they owe their bankers. The theory emerging from Berlin was that the idiots who had lent Greece billions at low interest rates, presuming it was guaranteed by the German taxpayer, should lose at least part of their shirts. Why should German taxpayers bail out the private sector? The European Central Bank took a contrary view, partly because of the impact this would have on a fragile European banking system, and partly because of the risk of contagion to other vulnerable economies. For the ECB, in the form of its then president, Jean-Claude Trichet, this was about honouring the signature on a loan agreement. It also had something to do with the fact that the ECB was increasingly replacing private bankers as lender to the troubled nations. Effectively the ECB was lending to a defaulting debtor, which made a mockery of the core principles upon which the ECB was founded. As at most stages in this crisis, the squabbling Eurozone rescue squad applied the salvational balm of an unintelligible acronym – PSI. Officially, the three letters stood for 'Private Sector Involvement', a phrase that was meant to connote some degree of willingness on the part of creditor banks to lower Greece's debt burden by taking what is known as a 'haircut'. The Frankfurt-based ECB had to tag along. This is where Lee Buchheit came in.

'Buchheit is the kind of guy who will tell me exactly how we should structure this to squeeze the creditors and get the most out of them, how to do it in the most efficient manner,' a senior figure in the IMF told me. Most of the IMF was behind this push because it had worked elsewhere – in Ecuador, Jamaica and Uruguay. The trick was to stretch out the term of the loan, a method called 're-profiling', or 'extend and pretend'. This cut the real value of future debt repayments – a form of default – but everybody could pretend that the cash value of the debts had been honoured. Even though the IMF's favourite weapon of devaluation could not be deployed in the case of Greece, its other favourite weapon, default – rebranded as PSI – was still very much an option.

When the agreement was reached in July 2011, Prime Minister Papandreou, together with José Manuel Barroso, president of the European Commission, and Herman Van Rompuy, president of the European Council, stood confidently in front of a weary press to announce a 'European success' to realise Greece's potential. The terms of Europe's own official bailout were considerably sweetened, with longer-term loans and cheaper interest rates. I asked why they did not simply admit that Greece had defaulted. All three disappeared off-stage rather rapidly, bringing the press conference to an abrupt end. Private creditors had voluntarily agreed to a 21 per cent reduction in the net present value of their bonds, but no haircut to the so-called 'nominal value', the upfront value of the bond. The deal fell apart as Greece's economy and its debts soured, and a new deal, involving a 50 per cent nominal haircut, was agreed in October 2011. This also collapsed. After seven months of hard negotiations on terms, a deal was struck in February 2012, affecting €206 billion of Greek government bonds. The 'bankers' lost 53.5 per cent of the nominal value of their Greek debts. In real terms, over the lifetime of the debt, this amounted to a cut of 74 per cent. The Greek government's debts shrunk by €107 billion, one-third of the total. Most bondholders did agree voluntarily to this offer. It was, after all, an offer that they could not really refuse. But the Greek government also invoked special clauses that forced some otherwise unwilling debtors to take a hit. This triggered credit default swaps (see page 43) – bets or insurance on a country going bust. This had been a 'red line' that Brussels officials vowed not to cross in the first deal. By early 2012 Greece was not just officially in default – it was the world's biggest sovereign defaulter.

Greece's national debt had been heading for a completely unsustainable 160 per cent of its GDP at the end of the decade. After PSI and default that total had come down to a still lofty target for 2020 of 120 per cent. Frankfurt also tried to grapple with the idea that the write-off of Greek debt might prove rather tempting to other countries facing tough programmes – notably Ireland and Portugal. President Trichet commented after the original July 2011 deal that 'Greece is in an absolutely exceptional situation. For that reason it requires exceptional and unique solutions. All other Eurozone countries reaffirm solemnly their inflexible determination to honour fully their own individual sovereign signature.' But the sovereign signatures of other, much larger countries were beginning to be doubted in the global markets. Their ratings were downgraded, the interest rates demanded on their debts shot up. Greece in and of itself should have been an irrelevance. Greece could have been completely bailed out with minimal impact on the rest of Europe. But Greece was a testing ground. And it had the power to infect market perception of other countries, such as Italy and Spain, which really *did* matter.

Lee Buchheit was present at all these negotiations, advising the Greek government. At first he thought that the pre-PSI 2010 Eurozone approach to Greece reflected a view that the crisis was temporary, that it would eventually 'evaporate', and therefore northern Europe's taxpayers could be put at risk lending money to repay their creditors on time and in full. 'Initially Greece [and Portugal and Ireland] all got gross bailouts,' he says. 'They were given the money to pay their creditors in full and on time. If Greece had been restructured in spring 2010 with a haircut, you might have destabilised some fragile northern European financial institutions, forcing a very embarrassing need to recapitalise them directly.' Buchheit suggests that it was 'perhaps more politically palatable' to give Greece the money to repay a French or German bank rather than recapitalising them directly.

In other words, the first bailout of Greece was a backdoor bailout of northern Europe's banks. When the bailout deal had been finalised in Brussels in the early hours of 10 May 2010, German and French banks had promised 'solidarity' with Greece. At the end of 2010 German banks were the largest holders of Greek government debt. But then, at the beginning of 2011, the German banks quietly dumped €10 billion of Greek debts, mostly government debt, leaving the French banks trailing in their wake. German banks were much better prepared for the Greek debt default, pushed for by their own government. President Sarkozy of France was left fumbling around, failing in his argument for limited PSI. French banks were hit by contagion, by funding concerns, and at one point by a complete stop to essential dollar-liquidity funding from Wall Street. 'Greece – exceptional and unique' remained the Eurozone mantra. Buchheit detected at this point the origins of the perception in the Troika that it faced a binary choice when faced with other Eurozone countries that were in danger of defaulting: either repay all debts, or give the bankers a violent haircut. A third option, 're-profiling' or 'extend-and-pretend', had been dabbled with in Greece and had been used in the previous contagious regional financial crisis, the debt crisis in Latin America that began in the 1980s. But now this third option was being ignored. The financial advantage of 're-profiling' is that it enables affected institutions to cushion themselves. The political advantage is that it can appease those in creditor nations who oppose any kind of bailout.

But what of Greece itself? Not only had the Eurozone supplied the funds Greece could not get from international markets, it had also strong-armed the international banking system into writing off a third of Greece's national debt. The shackles of the nation's debt bondage were loosened – a little. But the bankers and politicians negotiating the deal in the Grande Bretagne Hotel in Syntagma Square had a ringside view of the rage and the riots. Protestors actually used marble from the steps of the hotel to hurl at the police.

Nothing to match the anger of the Greek protestors in the squares of Athens was expressed in northern Europe. But the political class – especially in Germany, the Netherlands, Austria and Finland – felt there *was* widespread discontent, and they felt that they had to neutralise it. The process of placating the objectors reached a surreal climax in October 2011, when, after Greece's first bailout had failed, bailout number two was negotiated at a series of crisis summits. The funds would come from a generalised bailout vehicle called the European Financial Stability Facility, rather than the bespoke programme arranged for the original Greek bailout. If the northern countries were to lend yet more 'rescue' funds to Greece through the EFSF, their political leaders needed something to show for it. Some tabloid-friendly German politicians suggested the Greeks put up some of their islands as collateral for the loans, or even the Parthenon itself. The proposal agreed in October 2011 was far more absurd: the surety was to be Greece's sun.

At one of the series of 'summits to save the euro' in autumn 2011, amidst forced smiles and fake bonhomie, the prime ministers of the Eurozone nations signed up to yet another interminable communiqué. Buried in paragraph 13 of this intergovernmental understanding there was something quite unprecedented, something quite extraordinary, relating to a massive solar energy project: 'Greece commits future cash flows from project Helios or other privatisation revenue in excess of those already included in the adjustment programme to further reduce indebtedness of the Hellenic Republic by up to 15 billion euros with the aim of restoring the lending capacity of the EFSF.'

The sun's healing rays were now being focused on Europe's highly problematic experiment with economic union, in which there was a shared currency and a shared monetary policy, but no shared approach to tax, or spending, or borrowing. In the place of a convincing system of European fiscal transfers to compensate for the inability of troubled economies to devalue currency, adjust interest rates or print money, was this deal: a promise to transfer solar radiation.

Project Helios was certainly ambitious. The plan was to carpet 200 square kilometres of Greek land with solar panels, starting in Crete. It had been announced by the Greek energy minister in Hamburg in September 2011. The cost was up to €20 billion, with €3.5 billion probably paid for by German investors. The electricity generated was then to be transmitted through a new €10 billion line to Germany, providing 2 gigawatts of green solar energy by 2020 and 10 gigawatts by 2050. It sounded like a win-win for everyone. As the boss of the private solar park at Athens airport told me, 'Greece can be the Saudi of solar.' At the time, Greece's annual solar output of 0.2 gigawatts was tiny for a country with 300 sunny days a year and which received 50 per cent more solar radiation than

Germany, the world's leader in solar power production. There were also advantages for Germany: the provision of Greek solar power would help to dilute its reliance on Russian gas.

But what paragraph 13 seemed to suggest was that the first chunk of the optimistic estimate of €80 billion of expected revenues would flow directly to Greece's European creditors. Greece was being forced to mortgage its sunshine to pay for the bailout.

The twist emerged later in Athens. George Papandreou told friends that he consented to the deal at the European Council under pressure from northern European countries to come up with some security for the expanded bailout. Mark Rutte, the Dutch prime minister, was one of the loudest voices calling for some kind of guarantee from Greece. At this point, German chancellor Angela Merkel dodged laying down the law directly to Greece. It worked better for all concerned if smaller members of the triple A creditor bloc got their hands dirty rather than Berlin. The putative solar swap was a striking symbol of how Greece was no longer master of its own destiny.

From *demos kratos* to *technos kratos*

Sunshine was not the only asset owned by the Greek government. At the old Athens airport, on the Athens Riviera, the case for the Dutch and German position could be viewed up close. It had remained closed for a decade and largely abandoned since the 2004 Olympic Games. Intact aircraft remain at the side of the runway, used for training emergency services. Part of the old airport hosted a major cluster of Olympic venues. Again, most lie unused, totems of the excess spending during the good times required to host the Games. The original plan had been to create a massive park for Athenians. But hard times meant hard choices, and a more commercial redevelopment plan emerged for a plot of land twice the size of Monaco, with its own marina. There was no shortage of takers to spend billions of euros to develop what would have been the largest redevelopment in Europe, but the Troika representatives faced a reluctance to sell.

'They told us that they had reserved it to build an aquarium. It's a kind of craziness that reflected the real issue: ideologically they were very much against our organisations,' said one Troika official.

Greece though, was a 'complete outlier' with the biggest portfolio of assets to privatise of all the programme countries. Hotels, thermal springs, motorways, airports and lots of land. Land laws dating back to the Ottoman era meant that the Greek state inherited huge expanses of orphaned land and buildings. Not the Acropolis, or the islands, or the national parks, but land. No one knew exactly how much land, because the Greek state did not have a proper functioning land registry. At the IMF they thought the land holdings were worth up to 80 per cent of GDP. A seriously focused sale could have 'dramatically' reduced Greece's national debt within two years, with some quick wins within months.

A figure of €50 billion of land sales and privatisations was agreed with the Troika. By the end of 2012, however, almost nothing had been sold. Understandably, Greek politicians did not want to hold a fire sale at the bottom of the market. Equally, it was a vivid illustration that the Greeks were stalling. For their Troika overlords, it was part of a concerning pattern of behaviour. 'The Greeks are very good at playing brinkmanship, you know,' one former IMF Troika representative told me. 'They say, "This is your problem not ours. You've got to give us the money anyway." For both programmes they got the money at times when they should not.'

This early type of drachmail threatened Europe-wide contagion in November 2011. Papandreou returned to Athens from a Brussels EU summit with a write-off of a third of Greece's debts, in return for more reforms, cuts and taxes. But he felt that the incessant strikes and the strong domestic opposition to the plans were wrecking the Greek economy and making the country politically ungovernable. He called a referendum on the October deal to give some public legitimacy to the controversial austerity plans. Greece, the cradle of democracy, was to exercise people power (*demos kratos* in Greek). But Papandreou had not consulted his own finance minister, Evangelos Venizelos, nor anyone else in his cabinet. Nor had he consulted fellow EU leaders. Venizelos fell ill with appendicitis, and was obliged to telephone the German finance minister from hospital. (There appears to be something of a pattern of Eurozone finance ministers developing illnesses during periods of acute euro stress.) Papandreou's gamble failed dismally. Elected in a landslide just two years previously, in the space of a week Papandreou was to be unceremoniously ejected from office.

In Berlin, officials reflected on Germany's response to these events. 'At the EU Council in October we had the basic decision on PSI, to relieve Greece of €100 billion, very nice. And then Papandreou says that he doesn't know if Greece can accept this, and he's going to have to vote on it. We asked "What happened? Why didn't he say this at the time?"' The Germans believed that any referendum should be on whether Greece would fulfil the requirements of being in monetary union – not on the acceptability or otherwise of a specific bailout programme.

So Chancellor Merkel and President Sarkozy summoned Papandreou and Venizelos to a dinner on the sidelines of the Cannes G20 Summit (Greece is not in the G20) on Wednesday, 2 November. It was, to say the least, an awkward occasion. There was no small talk; Merkel simply dictated terms. She told Papandreou that the referendum would be held quickly, the following month, and that the referendum was to be about Greece's membership of the euro, not the bailout programme. An €8 billion tranche of EU funds to Greece would be postponed until after the referendum. She then announced all this publicly. President Sarkozy was overheard telling President Obama that Papandreou was a 'madman'. But there was, he said, no point 'beating him up' about it. 'He's already on the floor,' Sarkozy said. 'Knockout.'

Incredibly the final blow was applied on the plane back from Cannes to Athens by Papandreou's own finance minister, Venizelos. Upon touchdown at Athens at 4.45 a.m. on Thursday, Venizelos released a statement on his finance ministry's website. Greece's membership of the euro, he said, 'cannot depend on a referendum'. It seemed that he was mounting some kind of bloodless coup. I waited for him outside his ministry. The Greek journalists there did not dare ask him even a single question, confirming my suspicion that as far as the euro is concerned, politicians can get away with limited media accountability. When I suggested that we might soon see the return of the drachma, he gave a nervous smile.

It was democracy – of a sort – in action. A few days before, too much democracy, in the form of the promised referendum, had nearly brought about the collapse of the Greek government and broken the euro. Now there was a remarkable about-turn in the Greek parliament. After abandoning the idea of the referendum, Papandreou hung on to power, surviving a no-confidence motion in parliament by a mere eight votes. 'The last thing I care about is my position,' Papandreou said during the debate. 'I have said it before and I will say it again. I say it to Greece, I say it abroad: I don't care if I am ever elected again.' As Greece's highly unpopular parliamentarians left the parliament building after the midnight vote in their nice new BMWs, guarded by police, they contemplated a new coalition government of national unity, including a far-right party. I asked Kostas Kartalis, an MP in Papandreou's PASOK party, if this was democracy in action. 'The decisions taken today are democratic decisions. . . elections are a different story,' he said. 'Elections will develop political instability in the country at the moment. Because what is needed is to implement agreements with the EU, and we don't have too much time to do it. The parliament is democracy.'

In Italy, at the same moment, leading politicians were piling on the pressure for Prime Minister Berlusconi to resign to prevent a market meltdown on the Monday. At the end of a week of shocks, U-turns, coup fears, rebellions and generalised political bedlam, this is what passed for stability in Athens and Rome, the ancient heart of the Eurozone.

A few days later, Venizelos' efforts succeeded in getting the ruling PASOK party to force Papandreou out of office within days. But he did not win the leadership. In the end, on 11 November, a Greek technocrat named Lucas Papademos, who just a year before had been the vice president of the European Central Bank, was appointed unelected prime minister in an emergency government. A brief gamble with *demos kratos*, in its cradle, ended within days in the establishment of *technos kratos*.

It was not just Greece: Italy saw the defenestration of Silvio Berlusconi and his replacement with the eurocrat Mario Monti. Greece's PSI negotiations continued. These unelected politicians gave some – though not total – confidence to the creditor nations of northern Europe. The German finance minister floated the idea of a new panel of economists with the power to intervene in the profligate borrowing plans of member states. He also advocated that the EU economic commissioner, Olli Rehn, should be able to implement EU regulations over the objections of other commissioners, even over the objections of the EU president himself.

At a highly charged Brussels summit in February 2012 I spoke to the then Dutch finance minister, Jan Kees de Jager, who suggested something similar. 'Each side has to assess whether Greece has done enough,' he told me. 'It was not so last week. It was also not so the week before.' He felt that, given the number of 'derailments' that had already occurred in Greece, it was probably necessary to have 'some kind of permanent presence of the Troika in Athens', rather than a visit every three months. Another journalist, from Spain, asked if Mr de Jager wanted the permanent representatives of the Troika in Athens to be able to veto Greek budgets. His reply gives a crucial insight into what some in the Eurozone elite want of Greece and other programme nations. 'Of course a country remains to some extent always sovereign,' he said. But it is very important, he continued, that when you loan money, 'you are the boss of loaning money,' in other words, it must be the lenders who decide whether or not they will disburse the next tranche. 'That's why I'm in favour of a more permanent mechanism of the Troika,' he declared, adding that he was also in favour of an escrow account, enabling the lenders to decide how the money should be spent, for example prioritising repayments and interest payments on Greece's debt over other government spending. 'So yes,' he concluded, 'I'm in favour of more control, more supervision, a more permanent presence of the Troika, as well as a kind of escrow mechanism, in order to establish more control in Athens of the money itself. Because the money is the thing probably we can control [in] Greece best.' Belgium's finance minister, Steven Vanackere, echoed the point when he told me: 'The whole question of monitoring is a crucial factor in maintaining confidence of euro colleagues.' So, despite the appointment of a technocratic government in Athens, the rich north of the Eurozone still did not trust Greek democracy to carry through the bailout deal.

All of this was to reach a crashing crescendo with the twin elections in May and June 2012. The parties that had enforced the recent Troika reform programmes were obliterated in May. The winners were New Democracy, a centre-right party in office just before the crisis, and partly responsible for it. But ND and PASOK combined, the duopoly of Greek politics that typically accounted for 80 per cent of Greek votes, slumped to below a third of total votes cast. In PASOK's place Syriza, a radical left party headed by the 38-year-old Alexis Tsipras stormed into second place. And the crypto-Nazis of Golden Dawn would also enter parliament, in military formation. None of these parties would cooperate with each other. ND did not have enough to form a government. Always beware of countries where the leading political party polls a lower percentage vote share (18.8 per cent) than the standard rate of VAT (23 per cent).

The election was interpreted as an expression of anger. Greece's patience had snapped. After four years of recession, the Greek public had defiantly rejected the 'internal devaluation' strategy. They did not reject the euro as such. But they did reject the rules that go with being a member of the club. The uncertainty of another election would be required to clarify Greece's fate.

'Achtung Frau Merkel. The Greek people want to live free and they don't want to be again under a new occupation by Germany,' Manolis Glezos told me in his house in Athens. He is one of modern Greece's greatest heroes. As a teenager during the Nazi occupation of Athens in 1941, he climbed the Acropolis to rip down the swastika that flew over the Parthenon. 'Frau Merkel's attitude is the same as was Hitler's during the occupation. The measures taken are not the same of course. But the attitude's the same. Hitler wanted to put the Greek people to submission, to get them to their knees, to extinguish them by starvation and executions. Frau Merkel wants to subjugate the Greeks financially, wants to subjugate us politically, but just as we didn't accept and overthrew all Hitler's plans, in the same way we'll overturn Frau Merkel's plans.'

The German attitude is deeply resented by many in Greece, especially those with long memories. A pensioner at Piraeus port told me that Germany should repay the gold 'they looted from us during the occupation'. Not all Greeks, however, are so angry at Berlin. Some Greeks I've spoken to believe that all these Troika measures are necessary, given what they see as the fiscal misman-agement in Athens. A bus driver in Piraeus described Greece's political elite as the '300 traitors', and told me that Merkel would be 'Willkommen' to sort out Greece's problems. The real anger in Greece seemed more directed at its own domestic political establishment than at Frankfurt, Berlin or Brussels.

But the anti-bailout rhetoric has had an impact. Now 90 years old, Glezos is a member of the Greek parliament and sees himself in the vanguard of a Greek popular revolt. He is the patriarch of Syriza, led by Alexis Tsipras, whose fiery oratory shook Greek politics and the entire European Union. In coalition negotiations Mr Tsipras aggressively played his second-place mandate, refusing to yield to the demands of europolitik. He even wrote to the heads of the European Commission and the ECB to complain about the 'barbaric' austerity plan. Syriza is a coalition of left-wingers, students, ex-communists, ecologists and feminists. Its flag sports the red of the left, the green of environmentalism and the purple of feminism, together with a communistic-looking yellow star: 'the yellow star of hope'. Its surge in support came largely from the young. By the time of the May election, it was already the number-one party in many cities and districts.

When I asked Mr Glezos if Greece was on the verge of a peaceful revolution, he replied, 'Of course. It started already on 6 May [the date of the first election] and the river doesn't run backwards. My country started saving itself when the Greek people chose a new way for themselves and the rest of the world.' Syriza says it wants to keep Greece in the euro, but also says it cannot abide German sado-austerity. In other words, it is calling the Germans' bluff. Either the Germans will have to relent on the cuts programme, or they risk losing a Eurozone member. Glezos reminded me that 'Europe is a Greek word'.

Greece exiting the euro used to be unthinkable. By late spring 2012, however, the possibility was being openly discussed. It had even acquired its own portmanteau word, 'Grexit', a term now heard on the trading floors and in diplomatic meetings around the world. Threatening a Grexit was Syriza's most powerful bargaining chip. A top official told me at Syriza HQ that Greece's mainstream parties had been too scared to refer to this directly in negotiations, knowing the implications. Greece has the ability to infect the Italian and Spanish banking systems with contagion, in the same manner one might be mugged by a heroin addict with a syringe. Syriza's optimistic scenario was that François Hollande, newly elected as French president on an anti-austerity ticket, would come riding to the rescue, accompanied by Merkel's German opponents.

To threaten Grexit involved a heady game of brinkmanship with the EU, the European markets and the banking system, a degree of brinkmanship beyond any ever previously imagined. True drachmail. It risked what US Treasury secretary Timothy Geithner had referred to as 'the threat of cascading default, bank runs, and catastrophic risk'. But Syriza did not have the same fear. Alexis Tsipras's line was that he would do 'as much as I can' to keep Greece in the euro. He also used the analogy of 'mutually assured destruction' (MAD for short), the Cold War theory behind nuclear deterrence, and firmly believed there was no legal basis to throw Greece out. But he clearly implied that there was a price for euro membership that he believed was not worth paying.

Greece's European partners started to make contingencies for what Grexit would mean for their tourists. Plans were made for flying in money to embassies to distribute to holiday islands, and even for the evacuation of tourists from the Greek islands. German tourists pulled their holiday bookings.

In London, the Eurozone Contingency Committee sat at the Treasury, featuring Mervyn King, Adair Turner and cabinet ministers William Hague and Vince Cable, chaired by Chancellor George Osborne. 'Throughout 2011–12 we were very worried about the Eurozone precipitating a UK financial banking crisis again: we created an emergency committee on Eurozone contingency planning, which for a while was meeting every other week, even every week.'

Strikingly, German politicians and leading members of the ECB popped up in the days after the inconclusive May election to say that a Grexit would be 'manageable', as it would 'do more harm to Greeks than the Eurozone'. But the more Greece's hard-left parties were attacked from abroad – and by the discredited mainstream parties in Athens – the more popular they became. In other European capitals officials believed that Syriza's analysis was correct. A Greek exit would lead to uncontrolled contagion, and leave Chancellor Merkel with little option but to move immediately towards sharing Eurozone debts with a eurobond (see page 317). Syriza were open about their plan to play chicken with Greece's euro membership. If they had been miscalculating regarding Germany's patience, Greece would have been de facto out of the euro rather quickly if Syriza had won the election re-run.

And what would exit have meant? All kinds of agony. First, Greece's European bailout money would be cut. The government would be unable to pay pensions and salaries with euros, and would have to print an alternative currency or special IOUs pretty quickly. A government minister, Makis Voridis, pointed out that if the fiscal aid stopped, 'It will almost be a necessity to go back to the drachma in order to be able to pay. So no one will force us out. But probably the Greek government, *if there is one*, will have to go back to the drachma... that is the danger.' But many ordinary Greeks could scarcely believe that the pain could be any worse than being internally devalued. Haris Manolis from the steel factory says many more Greeks are willing to contemplate the return of their own currency: 'Yes, the drachma, or whatever you want to call it. We survived 5,000 years with the drachma but in ten years in the euro we have problems, like we're going to die.' In contrast, his friend says that he wants to stay in the euro to protect stability. But when asked if he'd keep the euro even if there is no change to the EU austerity plan, he changes his mind.

Many in Greece were not prepared to wait for the dénouement of this drama, and began evacuating their euros before they could be converted into devalued drachmas. The Athens Airlifts of large bundles of euros restarted. All the time, a select band of Greek technocrats were well aware of how Greek social stability was dependent on the cash machines continuing to function. While the cash exodus got underway, the European Union and the Greek finance ministry had already started to make contingency plans for a managed euro exit, involving controls of capital and of borders.

The second election in June became a fight between hope and fear: hope that something would change Greece's economic misfortunes, and fear of a return to the drachma. Outside some polling stations waited the curiously well-funded foot soldiers of Golden Dawn. Not all were steroid-enhanced skinheads. The ones I met were slightly avuncular, a bit racist and faintly dim. Others were rather sinister, and openly fascist. A student documentary maker, Konstantinos Georgousis, made a film called *The Cleaners*, following one aspirant Golden Dawn politician around. Migrants were subhuman, the candidate said on camera. 'We are ready to open the ovens,' he went on. 'We will turn them into soap. We will make lamps from their skin.' His party, which has a swastika-like logo, argues he was joking. But anti-immigrant violence has surged since Golden Dawn burst onto the scene.

Greece does have a serious issue with migration. Turkey turns a blind eye to thousands trying to cross into the European Union via its only land border with Asia. Even though most of the migrants have no desire to stay in Greece, Golden Dawn has capitalised on their presence, and this, together with the economic collapse, saw them win eighteen parliamentary seats in June 2012. In the subsequent months, the party regularly polled double digits, equivalent to more than thirty seats. Wherever I saw economic calamity in Greece, there seemed to be a strategically positioned office of Golden Dawn. At the very least, the economic situation seems to have led to an acceptance of openly racist gestures and an escalation of vigilantism – especially in areas where the police decline to act. A leading Greek footballer gave a Nazi salute after scoring a goal. Something extraordinary is happening if Greece, which suffered terribly under Nazi occupation, is seeing its young people increasingly attracted to neo-Nazism.

The rise of political extremism is hardly surprising given the absence of economic hope for Greece's young. Economic calamity has only served to exacerbate the divisions in Greek society. Some left-wing campaigners insist that there is a low-level civil war going on between violent neo-Nazis and sympathisers among the Greek police on the one hand, and left-wingers, anti-fascists and anarchists on the other. A look at economic historian Brad DeLong's seminal history of the economic factors behind the democratic rise of Hitler in Germany (*Slouching Towards Utopia*) shows that Greece now ticks many of the same boxes, including surging unemployment, the politicisation of a formerly apathetic electorate, deflationary budget balancing, acute cuts to welfare, fears about banks and saving, the collapse of an international system of fixed exchange rates, and the obliteration of mainstream parties at the hands of the hard left and the hard right. Of course, right now it seems absurd to think that Golden Dawn could ever top the polling in a Greek election. But in 2011 it was absurd to suggest they could have any MPs at all. In 1928 the Nazis won 2.8 per cent of the vote. By 1933 Hitler was chancellor. What propelled the surge in support for the Nazis? A strong showing by the far left, which drove the centre-right to Hitler. It is not unthinkable that history could repeat itself, in a situation where hundreds of thousands of young men and women have been left desperate and desolate.

Greece is not just about economics. When I visited his local polling booth, Alexis Tsipras was mobbed by supporters and non-supporters alike. He tours the world drumming up support for his anti-austerity message. The public face of Syriza has certainly moved to the centre, in what might be called the 'Syriza shuffle'. After the May election the threat of a disorderly euro exit was Greece's fundamental bargaining chip in a renegotiation of the EU loan agreement. By June, drachmail had been replaced by pragmatism. Syriza said it would stick to some of the headline targets of the Troika deal, but achieve them through tax rises rather than spending cuts. Within a month, all talk of mutually assured destruction had disappeared.

New Democracy knew their trump card. At their final rally in Syntagma Square before the June election, there were flares, dodgy dance music, and an attempt at an impassioned speech from Greece's would-be euro saviour, the ND leader Antonis Samaras. 'The first choice Greece must make,' he declaimed, 'is: euro or drachma?' The mood was not helped when the *Financial Times Deutschland* published an open letter to Greeks, advising them to vote for Samaras, and 'resist the Demagogue Tsipras'. Samaras had greatly angered the Troika by undermining Papandreou, but now he was the devil they knew and therefore preferred. In the Square the expressions on the faces in the crowd were remarkable. Not of hope, but of fear. As one ND candidate told me, 'These are the faces of people wondering whether they'll have to take their life savings out of the bank on Sunday night.' That is, if they had not done so already. Many in the crowd believed in one simple equation: 'Syriza win = bank run on Sunday evening.' Privately, Syriza's top advisers also believe that, in broad terms, Greece's electorate is splitting in two, 'those with bank accounts/savings and those without'.

When push came to shove, Greeks voted to stay in the euro, and Antonis Samaras became prime minister. However unpopular the Troika programme, it was insufficiently unpopular for Grexit. Greece had defaulted on a third of its debt. It voted not to default on the deal to stay in the Eurozone. Instead, like large swathes of the Eurozone periphery, Greece was defaulting on its version of Europe's social contract. But the New Democracy victory rally in Syntagma Square was far from euphoric. Syriza had hugely increased its share of the vote, and party insiders suggested to me they were relieved not to win, as they had not really prepared for government. But the question remains: can a society survive generational splits like this between savers and those with no hope of being able to save?

Greece also left the Troika with a rather inconsistent approach to dealing with sovereign-debt crises in the Eurozone. Everywhere the 'sovereign signature' was to be honoured in full, meaning that banks that had stupidly lent to these nations paid no price – except in Greece, whose foreign bankers were

not so much singed as flamed. Indeed, the Eurozone had quix-
otically placed its own head in the guillotine, in place of private
bankers, for any future repeat Greek debt write-off. The
Eurozone authorities, or 'official sector' in the jargon, are now
Greece's banker. But that is a story for later (see pages 324–54).

The day after the June election I went to Athens fish market
and met Vasili, a 21-year-old worker there. 'Young Greeks have
no dreams any more,' he told me. He does not want to sell fish.
He is an economics graduate from a top university in Greece,
and wants to be a journalist like me. Another fish seller, an
Albanian who had lived in Athens for twenty years, told me he
was planning to return to Tirana, where the economy was
booming and he could earn more. A third man, in his twenties
like Vasili, does not flinch as he calmly explains why he voted
for neo-Nazis. Although they 'occasionally do bad things', he
says, at least they are 'proud Greeks'.

The cash machines *did* work on the Sunday after the election, partly thanks to the second secret Athens Airlift. There
were contingency plans afoot to deal with the consequences
should an enforced euro exit come about. At the Bank of Greece,
there were discussions about whether or not some sort of
controls should be implemented if the outcome of the elections
was 'worrying' and could cause a bank run. The Greek newspaper *To Vima* was told that at one point someone 'stupidly'
tossed the idea of imposing a €20 withdrawal limit from banks,
but that others at the Bank of Greece rejected the idea. However
there was a contingency for the imposition of a specific withdrawal limit, in the event that an Alexis Tsipras election win
had sent Greeks to mount a run on their banks. The night
before the election, an international energy company, fearful of
an immediate return to the drachma, asked for and got payment
of a massive bill in euros. No one could have predicted how a
society as concussed and volatile as Greece might have responded.
A clue was to be provided nine months later, not so far away
– in Cyprus (see pages 385–420).

CHAPTER 2

OF FISCAL CRIMINALS AND
BOND VIGILANTES

Dramatis personae

Nick Clegg, UK Liberal Democrat leader
Sir Mervyn King, governor of the Bank of England (2003–13)
David Cameron, then leader of the UK Opposition
James Carville, adviser to President Clinton
Brian Edmonds, bond trader, Cantor Fitzgerald
Anonymous hedge fund credit default swap trader
George Soros, financier and philanthropist
Jim Rickards, ex-Long-Term Capital Management (LTCM),
lawyer, economist, trader
Gordon Brown, British prime minister (2007–10)
Jesse Norman, Conservative MP, member of the Treasury
Select Committee
Rachel Lomax, deputy governor of the Bank of England
(2003–08)
Dick Moore, mayor of Elkhart, Indiana, USA
Robert Lucas, Nobel Prize in Economics. University of Chicago
George Osborne, UK chancellor of the exchequer (2010–)
Robert Stheeman, chief executive, Debt Management Office
Lord James Sassoon, commercial secretary to the
UK Treasury
John Moody, founder of Moody's rating agency
Corey Lovell, unemployed auto worker, selling his
blood plasma

Perhaps Antonio Clegg had picked up more of what was going on in Greece than his father. Even for a bilingual primary-school pupil, he had an awful lot resting on his judgement.

'My 8-year-old son ought to be able to work this out,' his father Nick had told journalists on 1 May 2010, just five days before the general election that would make him Britain's deputy prime minister. 'You shouldn't start slamming on the brakes when the economy is barely growing... You create more joblessness, and the deficit goes up even further. So it is completely irrational.'

So what turned the 'completely irrational' into a central policy plank of the coalition government in which Clegg played such a key role? A few weeks previously, Clegg had said something even stronger to *Channel 4 News* about the Conservative plan for immediate 'in-year' (i.e. within-the-year) spending cuts as a down payment to the markets on government austerity. 'We think that merrily slashing now is an act of economic masochism,' Clegg said. 'So if anyone had to rely on our support, [if] we were involved in government, of course we would say, "No, do it sensibly."'

Within days of these statements, Mr Clegg had performed an about-face. He now said 'Yes.' The circumstances were somewhat mysterious. Among the points included in the 11 May draft agreement between the Conservatives and the Liberal Democrats was a 'significantly accelerated reduction in the structural deficit', together with 'modest cuts of £6 billion to non front line services within the financial year 2010–11'. Not only had there been the sort of U-turn that happens in coalitions, but a U-turn on an issue of policy that he had specifically said he would not support. To be clear, the amount was modest in comparison to a record deficit, but what triggered the change of view, if not Antonio's abacus?

The 2010 general election and coalition negotiations occurred against the backdrop of the tumult in Athens. Greece's bust would be Britain's fate, said proponents of the new government's deficit reduction strategy, if there was no credible deficit plan. Greece's fiscal woes also provided an alibi for Clegg and the

LibDems. The election had delivered a mandate for some sort of deficit reduction plan. All parties had rhetorically referred to, if not outlined, large-scale cuts to public services during their campaigns. But there were marked differences in the speed and timing of the fiscal consolidation on offer to a crisis-weary electorate. After the hung Parliament, there was in fact a clear majority of popular votes – and not far off a majority of parliamentary seats – for parties that opposed the immediate 'in-year' cuts promised by the Conservatives. So Mr Clegg's change of opinion was the biggest reversal in the coalition negotiations. The LibDem volte-face delivered George Osborne to Number 11 Downing Street and his deficit plan to the nation.

The 'belly-up implosion in Greece' was a factor subsequently mentioned by the LibDem leader. In the weekend between the election and the signing of the draft coalition agreement, Greece's first Troika bailout was signed in Brussels, alongside the setting up of the European Financial Stability Facility (EFSF) and the European Central Bank's agreement to buy Eurozone government bonds. The LibDems made various claims that their change of opinion arose out of a briefing from Mervyn King, the governor of the Bank of England. However, the key phone call between the governor and Deputy Prime Minister Nick Clegg occurred days after the draft agreement was signed. No direct contact was made with the governor by the politicians negotiating the deal. Vince Cable was reassured indirectly by senior civil servants that King favoured the faster-paced and immediate cuts. The strongest direct advice on the feasibility and advisability of following Conservative plans came from the top civil servants advising the coalition negotiators. As Chancellor Osborne puts it: 'That weekend there was the crisis in Greece, and market comment around an inability to form a UK government. The government machine was very concerned. I said to the LibDems that if you have any doubts about this, speak to [Cabinet Secretary] Gus O'Donnell, speak to the permanent secretary at the Treasury, and speak to Mervyn King.'

The morning after the draft plan had been agreed, Mervyn King held a prearranged press conference that endorsed the new government's fiscal plans. He had avoided getting involved in the election campaign or the coalition negotiations. There is, for the historical record, an exchange of letters between Threadneedle Street and Whitehall that confirms this. But the moment the deal was done, King was in crisis-aversion mode, selling the common sense and stability of the infant and novel new British government. 'The Bank has been requested as to the feasibility and advisability of these measures,' King announced. 'The Treasury can advise on the feasibility; our advice on the advisability is that it is sensible to take measures in this fiscal year to demonstrate the genuine commitment and determination of the new government.' The coalition agreement had made the £6 billion in-year cuts contingent on advice to this end from the Bank of England. The Bank of England was being used as an alibi for the LibDem change of policy.

Earlier in 2010 I had interviewed the then Opposition leader David Cameron at the World Economic Forum in Davos. He was selling the early cuts plan. I asked Cameron repeatedly if he would proceed with the cuts even if Britain's economy fell back into 'a severe renewed contraction': 'You must make a start in 2010,' Cameron told me, 'but clearly the scale of what you can do needs to be worked out in conjunction with the Bank of England, because we want to keep those interest rates low.' The next day he softened his line, stressing that the cuts need not be 'particularly extensive' or 'swingeing'. But he set in stone the notion that the public should not worry, the Bank of England would advise. (Mervyn King's response a fortnight later was a blunt 'I don't know what this means.') It was clear that Cameron felt that, in the run-up to an election, the public would be more inclined to respect the judgement of a technocratic central banker than that of a politician when it came to calls for public-sector austerity. Seared into the consciousness of most British politicians was the fact that the only government that had imposed austerity on the British people and then managed to get itself re-elected was the government of Margaret Thatcher.

Back in the coalition negotiations of May 2010, the Labour team were stunned to find in the course of their failed talks with the LibDems that the latter were making in-year cuts part of their negotiating strategy. Both parties had very publicly agreed the opposite during the campaign and in their manifestos. This should have been an area of agreement, but Andrew Adonis, one of the Labour negotiators, revealed that the LibDems were evangelising for the approach they had vociferously opposed just days before. LibDem negotiators Chris Huhne and David Laws both apparently believed that a fall in sterling in the preceding weeks would offer a stimulus to the economy, so in turn creating room for the immediate cuts.

At the Bank of England, Mervyn King had sounded a little cautious on the timing of fiscal consolidation before the election. The day after the formation of the new coalition government, when I asked him why he was now suddenly in favour of imme-diate cuts, he answered, 'I think we've seen several things. We see the recovery beginning to take place, and we expect that the pace of that recovery will pick up. But we've also seen the market response in the past two weeks, where major investors around the world are asking themselves questions about the interest rate at which they are prepared to finance trillions of pounds of money that will need to be raised on financial markets in the next two to three years, to finance government requirements around the world. Markets were not expecting any action before the election. After the election they need and they want a very clear, strong signal, and evidence of the determination to make it work. And I think that it's quite difficult to make credible a commitment to fiscal consolidation if all the measures are somehow in the future. You need to start and get on with it.'

Invisible bond vigilantes had not just influenced the creation of a government in Britain, but were troubling most of the debtor nations of Europe. A tidal wave of economic reform and austerity changes, even the default of Europe's cherished social model, was justified on the basis of the anticipated reaction of these caped crusaders of credit. But who were they? And what did they want?

Bondman begins: how the vigilantes started

At Spink & Son Ltd, the London dealer in old coins and medals, you begin to get the feel for the bond market of the old days, when bonds were actual pieces of printed paper: florid bond certificates from the United States of Brazil, the Lower Saxony Government and the 1911 Hukuang Railways Sinking Fund Gold Loan for the Imperial Chinese Government depicting a glorious steam train. The last certificate had some special historical resonance. It was possibly the last debt issued by the Qing dynasty before its overthrow by revolutionaries in 1911. Historians argue that the granting of this concession to foreign bankers (including J. P. Morgan), secured not just by rail revenues but also by taxes on salt and rice and the tax on the internal transit of goods known as the 'lekin', helped foment revolution and the establishment of the Republic. The Chinese Republic promised to honour the railway debts, and debt interest continued to be paid until the 1938 invasion by Japan. Mao's People's Republic of China then repudiated the debt in 1949, prompting court cases into the 1980s.

The old bond certificates that collectors are able to get their hands on tend to represent defaulted debts, as such certificates no longer have any value as debt instruments – only as collector's items. Bond certificates where the debt had been repaid were usually returned to the borrower, and then destroyed. So the collectors' market is awash with pre-Soviet Russian bonds, while bonds from Britain, which has never formally defaulted, are a rarity.

These days, bond trading is done electronically. And by 2010 Britain was running the second worst deficit in the G20, after the USA. By then, the Chinese were buying the bonds, rather than issuing them. The bond markets determine the solvency of nations and the fate of governments. For Britain, in the months that followed the crisis, a series of auctions was to determine the appetite for British sovereign bonds, known as gilts, like never before outside of a world war.

It was President Clinton's adviser James Carville who mused that in a future life he'd want to return as a trader in government bonds. 'You can intimidate everybody,' he chuckled. The term 'bond vigilante' was coined by the US economist Ed Yardeni in 1983 to describe traders who would sell off the debt and demand higher yields (averaging 11 per cent) to compensate for the perceived risk of higher inflation and higher deficits in President Reagan's America. The bond vigilantes were unleashed again on President Clinton, when in 1993 he introduced his wife's plan for extra health-care spending ('HillaryCare'), and ten-year US Treasury bond yields shot up to 8 per cent. HillaryCare was parked as US politicians baulked at rising mortgage and business lending rates (which tended to go up if government rates went up).

At the midtown New York offices of capital markets investment bank Cantor Fitzgerald, one of America's busiest bond trading floors, Brian Edmonds eyes banks of computer screens. Edmonds is the firm's head of interest rates, and its star bond trader. It's not just the economic data he's interested in, but also the deluge of political dysfunction from Washington DC to Frankfurt and Athens. He deals in dollars, euros, yen – any currency that's doled out by the billion-load to the world's debtor nations, for a price. This and other trading floors like it are where capital markets trump capital cities. The total size of the global bond market is $78 trillion, and half of this comprises government bonds. The USA and Japan alone make up over half of the world's outstanding government bonds. The markets are large and liquid, with thousands of global players constantly trading electronically.

It was August 2011 when I visited Cantor Fitzgerald. It was during a historically turbulent week, when the USA lost its AAA credit rating. Intriguingly, Washington and London were being treated far more kindly than Paris, Athens or Dublin. I asked Brian what the impact had been on US Treasury bonds. 'Positive,' he said. Would a European sovereign get the same treatment? 'I don't think so. In the USA we still have our own currency, and if you look at full faith and credit of the USA, we still have the ability to pay the debt.' By 2011 US bond traders were a little more understanding of the deficits of their government than their predecessors had been in the 1980s and 1990s.

By the time of the crisis, James Carville's reincarnation of choice would have moved from the large investment-bank bond trading floors to the smaller trade in credit default swaps (CDSs) at a small hedge fund. CDSs had become an instrument to take a view in debt markets that previously would have required buying and selling a bond. The prices and market insight from CDSs were very helpful for regulators and central banks as measures of market default risk – and they were more quantitative and timely than the rankings of the credit-rating agencies. At the same time, CDSs were, and are, on the face of it, an insane gambling machine, used for speculative attack on banks and nation-states. They were almost completely unregulated. They had only relatively recently become legal. Before the crisis, the presumption had been that government credit risk in the Eurozone did not exist. But CDSs provided the weapon – and dithering in Europe provided an opening – for US and UK speculators and traders to make a killing.

'I can make profits of five to seven times the cash I put up,' says a hedge fund trader with whom I spent a day. 'It's a much more attractive return than buying an actual bond. CDS is a leveraged product, that's why it grew so much.' While we talk, various titbits of European political news are dripping through on the financial newswires. Of particular interest is the meeting between the Cypriot president and Angela Merkel. The hedge fund's principal is trying to work out how Cyprus will be treated by Germany, and its implications for the debts of the Cypriot government and its banks. It seems impossible to trade this information like one might trade inflation numbers or currencies. We also ponder how the hedge funds based on algorithmic computer-trading cope with having to decode Angela Merkel's glaring smile.

In 2006 'The Big Short' against American subprime mortgages made billions for the hedge-fund traders willing to take a negative view. By 2010–11 it was 'The Epic Short' – against the euro. The victims were not overextended financiers of exotic home loans, but the treasuries of proud Western nation-states. And the bet was again coming from the East Coast of the USA. Some of the same hedge funds that banked hundreds of millions of pounds from subprime were also in on these speculative attacks. But they were joined by more seasoned participants in sovereign-debt markets: the vulture funds that traditionally focused on Third World debt. I suggested to the principal of one vulture fund that the EU authorities were going to ban some forms of the trade. 'Let them. We'll just trade with counterparties in New York or Switzerland instead,' he said.

By 2011, shorting the single currency was proving recurrently profitable. To be clear, traders were not actually shorting the euro. The wisdom in the markets was that shorting the euro in currency markets was far too risky. What if Greece and the other crisis nations were kicked out of the Eurozone, and the euro basically became a twenty-first-century Deutschmark? No, the way to get at this trade most efficiently and with maximum leverage is via the famous credit default swaps market.

The trader explains how the market and the trade works. Traders buy and sell protection against a bond defaulting for an annual fee measured in fractions of a per cent, or 'basis points'. If I am worried about Greece defaulting, I buy protection, pay the fee, post some collateral, and no longer have to worry about a default. If Greece goes bust, the seller of the protection pays out in full the value of the bond, and then has to claim what scraps he can from the recovery process. Simple enough – in essence, it's a form of insurance. If I want to play this as a speculative bet, rather than a service to hedge my default risks, this is also possible. It was being used perfectly legitimately to gain from the demise of the euro periphery. Here's how to make your millions. Step 1: Buy CDS protection for, say, Greece defaulting when the risk was low, at say 300 basis points, or a 3 per cent premium. Step 2: Wait for some riots or an inconclusive election, which skyrockets the risk of Greece going bankrupt. Step 3: Sell the CDS contract back when the risk is high, the spread at 1000 basis points, or 10 per cent premium, at vast profit. Step 4: Repeat with other euro countries.

'Even from a 100 basis points [1 per cent] move,' a trader told me, 'I could make $4 million profit from a trade that required $6 million cash collateral. To make that profit in the bond markets would have required $100 million cash.'

Much hinged on the amount of collateral your counterparty required. For a small hedge fund, the figure would be high, for an investment bank low. For American International Group (AIG) as we shall see in Chapter 6 (see page 180), it was, for a period, zero, which helped fuel the mania that would eventually fell it. Yes, this is the same famous CDS market that – through AIG Financial Products' unbelievable trading activity in London – nearly threatened to bring down half of Europe's banking system in 2008. It's the same CDS market that George Soros had previously told me was 'the sword of Damocles' hanging over the market. 'This is an enormous unregulated market,' Soros told me, '45 trillion dollars, which is equal to the entire household wealth of the United States, five times the national debt, five times the capitalisation of the stock market. It's an enormous amount of liabilities, and you don't know if the counterparty is good for its commitment.' And Soros was speaking some months before AIG collapsed into the hands of the US government in 2008. Still, with returns of 800 to 1000 per cent possible, the gambit proved irresistible.

Some senior bond-market participants believed that the very act of buying the insurance aggressively in markets that are less liquid than that of the underlying bonds actually contributed directly to the rise in interest rates paid on government bonds, and the sense of fear and panic. The market has at least an element of dangerous circularity.

Jim Rickards used to work for Long-Term Capital Management (LTCM), which went belly-up in 1998. He describes the Big Euro Short as a 'piñata party' in which hedge funds were hunting as a feral pack, snapping at the soft underbellies of Greece, Italy and Spain. And then they watched as the money dropped out. He worried that the practice has 'national security implications', in that these three countries are all important Nato allies of the USA. 'They should ban credit default swaps completely,' Rickards says. 'If you want to take a view, take it in the bond market, do it with real money. I don't think this CDS market serves any purpose at all. It's dangerous in ways very few people understand.' Specifically, it is the naked CDS, which are trades made by those with no actual interest in the underlying bonds, that he feels should be banned. He is not alone; so does the German government and the European Parliament. A useful analogy is this: why allow someone with no insurable interest to take out fire insurance on someone else's house? It is an incentive to burn down that house. It does not even require actual pyromania, just an ability to increase the perceived risk of fire. So the CDS traders need not hold the matches – just being able to influence the feeling that firestarters are out there is sufficient. Three French economists, including Anne-Laure Delatte of the Rouen Business School, published a study in 2011 giving some empirical backing to the idea that 'CDS became a bear market instrument to speculate against the deteriorating conditions of the sovereigns'. Traders confirmed that sometimes the conventional bond markets lagged behind the smaller, less liquid CDS market in 'price discovery'. But the reverse was also true on occasion. Delatte's study claimed statistical evidence for CDS setting the price in periods of high distress. The bond market functioned as primary price-setter only in 'core-European countries during calm periods'.

In the USA, 'naked CDS' were illegal under anti-gambling laws until the US Commodity Futures Modernisation Act of 2000, which gave the product specific exemptions. This was one of the last legislative acts of Bill Clinton in the White House. The act also created the 'Enron loophole', which collapsed the energy giant in a mire of corruption. The act was passed after the findings of a taskforce that included Alan Greenspan of the Federal Reserve and Treasury Secretary Larry Summers, whose aim was to block an effort by the commodities regulator to rein in derivatives. Even the intervening LTCM debacle failed to stop the race for derivative deregulation.

The case against CDS and naked CDS is clearly mixed. German regulators did not find they had a key role in Greece's demise. Obviously these bets are only possible because of fiscal excess, because the crisis nations could not print their own money, and because Germany dithered over a longer-term solution. The market clearly gives some price signals. A former Lehman Brothers bond trader called Larry McDonald told me in the middle of the euro crisis that 'It actually costs less to insure Panama than France. Kazakhstan traded inside of Italy. In other words the markets were betting that Kazakhstan was a safer bet than Italy and Spain. It's absolutely insane.' But was France really more of a risk than Panama, as CDS markets declared during the crisis? And Kazakhstan versus Spain? It seemed crazy.

In November 2012, against the advice of the IMF, the City and Wall Street, the EU banned naked CDS trades on European sovereigns. Hedge funds had to be prepared to declare the other trading interest that they were hedging when buying sovereign CDS. If you were shorting Italy by selling its sovereign CDS for example, you would have to be able to show that you owned a connected security, say an Italian corporate bond. Many of the traders simply gave up. The ban happened to coincide with Mario Draghi's 'bazooka' of autumn 2012 (see page 347). Euro sovereign bond markets and their derivatives experienced a prolonged period of calm. However, traders said that if they wanted to 'take a view' they would simply short, say, an Italian bank instead, or some other institution not covered by the ban.

So these were the new bond vigilantes, with a powerful new instrument. The credit default swap reappears in various guises throughout this global tale of excess. On the one hand it was a barometer of credit excess where credit-ratings agencies failed, for example in Iceland. On the other it was part of the machine that fuelled that excess, decapitalised banking systems and helped bring about quite a few of the large financial bankruptcies.

Even George Osborne has taken to quoting various positive CDS numbers for Britain, boasting when it dipped below Germany. In 2008 the Conservatives, then in Opposition, had also pointed out that in 2008 the CDS market rated the UK sovereign as a riskier bet than the burger chain McDonald's. Bond vigilantism in the twenty-first century was a far cry from its roots in the 1980s.

PFI: paying over the odds for schools and hospitals to keep the vigilantes calm

In April 2010 a weary Gordon Brown chose the not-yet-opened Queen Elizabeth Hospital in Birmingham to launch Labour's election manifesto. With its thirty operating theatres, the largest critical care unit in Europe and a helipad for the war-wounded, the new hospital was a tangible reminder of the difference thirteen years of New Labour had made to the country. The Queen Elizabeth was a monument to the power of public-sector investment in healthcare. Except no voter had paid even a penny for this wonderful new facility, which had been financed entirely through the private finance initiative (PFI). But, even though it had cost the voters of Britain nothing, in years to come their grandchildren would still be paying for it.

The Queen Elizabeth Hospital opened its doors to patients some months later, under the coalition government, in the week of George Osborne's emergency Budget, detailing spending cuts and tax rises to rein in a deficit that had reached a peacetime record. Yet the hospital, and hundreds of PFI projects like it, weren't even part of the deficit numbers. PFI means that a hospital that is worth £627 million will cost a stream of payments starting at just under £50 million per year in 2010–11, going up in cash terms every year for thirty-eight years, peaking at £116 million in 2045–46, with the last payment not made until 2048–49. This means that, over the next four decades, taxpayers will have paid a total of £2.725 billion in cash terms, or about £1.221 billion in real terms, for a hospital with a capital value of £627 million.

PFI was conceived on the basis that the private sector could build more cheaply than the public sector, but it could not borrow as cheaply even at the time the scheme was dreamed up. Now, with borrowing costs for the UK at, or sometimes below, 2 per cent, versus PFI costs of 8 per cent, it is scandalously untrue. Originally developed in a limited manner under John Major's government, PFI was propagated as a means of getting round Gordon Brown's tough limits on investment spending in 1998–99. In the manner of Enron, the borrowing would be off-balance sheet. And so PFI was hugely expanded, and the extra cost above what it would cost from conventional exchequer funding was justified on the grounds that the NHS, schools and other public-project PFIs would receive decades of cleaning, upgrades and maintenance. But then various stories emerged of the £963 charged by a PFI contractor for a TV aerial, and the £875 for a £40 Christmas tree at HM Treasury, and the 65p light bulb charged out at £22. The Royal Institute for British Architects and the Audit Commission found no evidence for better design in PFI hospitals and schools.

The total bill for all PFIs signed to date is over £200 billion, 'the greatest ever British public policy experiment' according to the PFI campaigner Jesse Norman MP. The NHS is facing a £70 billion cash bill in the coming decades for PFI hospitals worth £11 billion. Even then, PFI's proponents justified it on the basis of an amorphous 'transfer of risk' to the private sector. Actually, will any government allow a school or a hospital to go bust, and move pupils and patients into an alternative school or hospital? Up to £4 billion in consulting fees have been earned on PFIs, and the cost over and above conventional exchequer funding is in the tens of billions of pounds.

So the Birmingham super-hospital where Gordon Brown chose to launch his election campaign turns out to have been a particularly apt symbol of New Labour's time in power. In 1997 the New Labour health minister and Blairite loyalist Alan Milburn had famously said, 'If it's new hospitals you want, it's PFI or bust.' Alas for the NHS, New Labour's 'Third Way' thinkers seem to have sown the seeds of destruction of their cherished health service. PFI hospitals have been saddled with large non-negotiable mortgages at a time that their other costs are sky-rocketing. The Queen Elizabeth Hospital itself has turned out to be too small for the rising demand from a rapidly ageing population. Wards in the 1930s hospital it replaced had to be reopened in March 2013. Elsewhere, large shiny PFI palaces are draining resources away from tight education and health budgets, simply because there is very little to negotiate. It's turning out to be 'PFI *and* bust'.

The risks and the costs were socialised, the profits privatised and the projects financialised, in what would become the signature of a wide swathe of New Labour economic policy initiatives. It simply made no financial sense to determine that this was the only way to fund such public infrastructure, if the country required it. So why were these projects done in this way? Partly to ward off the bond vigilante bogey men.

Debts private, debts public: the nature of the UK deficit

By October 2005 Gordon Brown was agitating to move from Number 11 to Number 10 Downing Street. That month I found myself in Number 11 at the launch of a campaign imploring a new generation of young entrepreneurs to 'Make Your Mark'. Child stars from the *Batman* movies mingled with the Kaiser Chiefs rock band, Anthea Turner, and hiphop MCs. The then chancellor, riding the crest of a wave after nearly a decade of uninterrupted economic growth, tried to inspire his bewildered young audience with a well-worn joke. 'There are two types of chancellor,' he declared. 'Those who fail, and those who get out in time.' Although the architect of the PFI boom *did* escape from Number 11 'in time' in 2007, the crash that began just weeks later shows that he did also fail.

'You aren't using "in the red" in your headline, are you?' It was November 2002, when I was a journalist on the *Observer*. It was just before the pre-Budget edition of the newspaper went to press, and I was facing one of Brown's faintly menacing lieutenants. He was trying to persuade me that my Budget preview story, that Britain was heading for '£20 billion in the red', was an unfair and pejorative description of the planned deficit, the first under Brown after years of surplus. He wanted me to drop the description 'in the red'. I asked him what colour he preferred. Earlier that year, Brown had taken a big political gamble by raising direct taxes, in the form of one penny extra on National Insurance contributions, to fund a rise in spending on the NHS. A truly reckless fiscal gambler would never have bothered. As it was, borrowing went up, as well as taxes. The bigger picture was that the first decade of New Labour could not be depicted as an uncontrolled spending binge. Taxes, spending and borrowing all went up. But both the deficit (2.4 versus 3.4 per cent of GDP) and the national debt (36.5 versus 42.5 per cent) were lower in 2007 than in 1997. Welfare spending was also just lower in 2007 (11.9 versus 12 per cent). The argument might well be that there was no way Labour should have run any type of deficit given that the economy was booming, and the 'roof should have been fixed while the sun was shining'. Certainly, other advanced nations at the time were running much smaller deficits and even surpluses, and cutting into their national debts. That said, at 36.5 per cent of GDP, the national debt was low by historical standards, and only Canada in the G7 nations had a smaller debt. Even in 2007–08, the deficit on current budget (stripping out infrastructure/investment spending) was just 0.3

per cent. Perhaps a more hawkish Conservative chancellor might have raised more taxes and not spent as much on, for example, tax credits and housing benefit, so delivering a pre-crisis debt/ GDP ratio of 30 per cent, where it had been in 2000–01. We do know that from 2007 George Osborne promised to stick to Labour spending plans, so at that point, by deduction, he could not have been overly worried about a national debt of 35 per cent of GDP. The other consideration is that significantly tighter fiscal policy, right or wrong, would have invited looser monetary policy, or a cut in interest rates in the middle of a credit boom.

Perhaps the real splurge came after the crisis hit in 2007–08. The Conservatives opposed Brown's borrowing-funded VAT tax-cut stimulus, designed to boost the economy after the collapse of the world banking system. Let's look at that record deficit of £156 billion in 2009–10. It was predicted in Alistair Darling's 2008 Budget at £38 billion, so where did the extra £114 billion deficit come from? Actually, the problem was very much more to do with a collapsing tax base and a declining economy. Here's why. The main issue was that GDP ended up far smaller in cash terms versus the 2008 forecast. Spending did end up £23 billion higher than the 2008 forecast, and about half of that was extra benefits, as you would expect in a sharp recession with rising joblessness. But taxes slumped by £91 billion versus the 2008 forecast, so 80 per cent of the epic deficit miss was a collapsing tax take. As Carl Emmerson, deputy director of the Institute for Fiscal Studies, puts it, 'Tax revenue disappeared as the economy disappeared.' Income taxes, corporation taxes and stamp duty all slumped.

Part of the problem was that the government growth forecast was too rosy compared to those of independent forecasters, particularly given the recession. A fiscal conservative would naturally blame the fact that the sustained increase in spending was predicated on a sustained rise in the taxes coming into the exchequer, a predicted rise that was itself based on a hopelessly ambitious growth target. New Labour's run of deficits after 2002 followed a pattern of ambitious boom-time growth projections at the end of the forecast period, which were never met. A fiscal hawk would further suggest that an incorrect guess at ever-increasing taxes coming from an inherently cyclical FIRE (Financial Industry Real Estate) economy is no justification for simply ploughing on with all of those spending rises.

It is important to point out, however, that Britain's record budget deficit was a consequence, not a cause, of this crisis. If New Labour had followed Conservative policy, the record deficit might have been smaller, but it would undoubtedly still have been well above £100 billion, and probably still a peacetime record. The problem was the reliance of the British economy on financial services and property. The golden goose of the City had fundamentally reduced its egg production. Brown's light-touch management of financial services is far more important in explaining Britain's problems, but that is a subject for another chapter (see Chapter 6, page 172). There is little evidence that the Conservative touch would have been any heavier.

This does matter. If the main problem in the build-up to the crisis is wilfully misunderstood, then there may be a problem with the solutions proposed to escape the crisis. Rachel Lomax, the former deputy governor of the Bank of England, put it rather clearly in May 2013, 'We need to get the narrative straight. The fact of the matter is that we have a public-sector debt problem not because Gordon Brown went on a spending spree, but as a consequence of a private-sector credit explosion, much of which was not even in this country. And really the failure to understand the nature of recession that we're in at the moment explains some of the weakness in dealing with it.' Britain clearly had a deficit problem in 2010. It needed to be dealt with credibly. But was public-sector debt the biggest drag on the UK economy? Or was it rather the overhang of debt in the private sector, combined with the fact that large swathes of the City machine involved in the manufacture of toxic derivative waste was gone, along with its taxes, never to return?

How Obama's America chose to ignore the bond sirens

In 2009 all the woes of America's Great Recession seemed to converge on Elkhart, Indiana, the expressway junction to economic hell. The city lived off the manufacture of RVs (recreational vehicles, i.e. motorhomes and trailers), and now it was hit by the crisis in the auto industry, the crisis in the housing market, the credit crisis, and high petrol prices. 'This area has been hit with a perfect storm of economic troubles,' said President Obama on a visit to the county with the second highest rise in unemployment in the whole of the USA. Whenever a crisis in motor manufacturing coincided with a crisis in the housing sector, the trailer industry was always going to get trashed.

RVs are the embodiment of the American dream, the means of driving the open road in luxury. The problem is that they only do eight miles to the gallon. 'When the price of fuel went up to $4–$5 a gallon, and the availability of credit went the other way, our RV industry collapsed and we went from 4.5 per cent unemployment to 20 per cent unemployment in a few months,' Elkhart's mayor, Dick Moore, told me. The day after Obama's inauguration, Mayor Moore went to Washington DC with a list of shovel-ready investment projects: roads, bridges, sewers and an airport runway.

When I visited in July 2009, many of the workers who could not get jobs were losing their eligibility for unemployment benefit. I met a hungry 28-year-old called Corey Lovell, who used to manufacture bathrooms for RVs and lost his job in the crisis. Corey was one of 300 people who applied for a job as a shop assistant at a 7-Eleven in Elkhart. He got a few hours of minimum-wage work at a petrol station, but could only survive by selling the plasma in his blood for $50, twice a week. He pointed to the bruising on his arm. 'I have to, there's no alternative,' he told me. 'I'm not making ends meet. We need assistance now.' I came across Corey at a food bank, where the newly unemployed are given ten minutes to pick up eight free food items, including cereal and bread. They also get a book. Corey is young, healthy, intelligent and articulate – not the type of person you would expect to meet at such a place. The church minister responsible had seen a 40 per cent increase in use of the facility. In the last month alone, in this small town, he had seen 350 new families turn up at the food bank. The demand was so high that they were having to buy food wholesale in addition to donations. The local churches were encouraging people to become more self-sufficient, providing seeds so that they could grow their own food in community gardens in the backyards of houses that had become empty after the banks had foreclosed.

This is not what you expect in America. The fear is that many of the jobs lost in manufacturing will never come back. President Obama wants to replace the eight-mile-a-gallon jobs with green jobs, but I'm sceptical about how many of those there are. The White House poured $40 million into grand infrastructure projects here in Elkhart. At Elkhart Municipal Airport the main asphalt runway had been cracked and was sprouting weeds. Within months of Obama taking office, it was resurfaced with concrete, using a $4 million slice of the $787 billion Obama borrowed for his stimulus plan. The refurbishment created 250 jobs, but these lasted less than two months. The new runway would last thirty years, but is only used by private jets and military planes. There are no commercial passenger flights, although there is a fully functioning airport just fifteen minutes drive away in the neighbouring town of South Bend. The runway was the very essence of the Keynesian response to the financial crisis: borrow money from China to fund an airport runway not viable under commercial market forces. Elkhart is less than a hundred miles away from the nemesis of Keynesianism at the University of Chicago. Milton Friedman would have been turning in his grave, had he not been cremated in 2006.

At the University of Chicago the success drips off the faculty walls. The university boasts nine Nobel prize-winners in economics. They transformed the discipline and then fanned out across the world transforming Western and then developing economies with their commitment to free markets and sound money. Robert Lucas is one of the Chicago Nobel laureates. He told me that the bailouts were wasted, but that the quantitative easing being practised by Ben Bernanke's US Federal Reserve was 'following the Friedman prescription'. He expressed a concern about inflation later down the track, because reversing printing money is 'hard to do politically'.

Lucas said that economists overestimate their abilities: 'You had a bunch of guys who thought they knew a lot. It turns out we didn't know a damn thing about the stability of the banking system, so it's back to the drawing board and we'll see what comes out of it.' But the University of Chicago had nothing to apologise for, he said. 'Milton Friedman was right about some things, wrong about others, but maybe we should all apologise for not grasping the fragile nature of the banking system.'

Would Friedman be turning in his grave? Lucas pointed out that he would have backed a more tightly regulated banking system with '100 per cent reserves'. He defended the 'efficient markets hypothesis', the intellectual basis of pre-crisis financialisation, as 'a law of nature', but conceded his colleague Eugene Fama might have been wrong in naming it 'efficient'. So there was a sliver of self-doubt.

Three years on, and Elkhart was back on its feet. Unemployment had fallen from 20 to 8 per cent. Jewellers who in 2009 had been tempting residents to pawn their gold teeth were now back to selling engagement rings. The RV factories were again churning out their behemoths of the road, and some of them were employing as many workers as they had pre-crisis. True, the runway at the airport was still mired in local political controversy over whether the town should support its losses, but the myriad of bailouts had helped bring about a renaissance in US manufacturing. The industry bailout of GM and Ford had also helped to keep manufacturers of components in business too. At the same time, the credit bailout had helped customers take out loans to buy new motorhomes. Again this government intervention did not seem to be typical of an America that had been so long in awe of the economic thinking of Friedman and friends. Neither Indiana nor Elkhart voted for President Obama in 2012. But elsewhere in the auto industry's Midwestern 'rust belt', particularly in neighbouring Ohio (which was crucial to Mitt Romney's hopes of beating Obama), the message that Obama's 'spine of steel' had saved General Motors and the auto industry won the day, and helped Obama stay put in the White House.

It is important to reflect on this. The company in question, GM, was the pioneer of many shibboleths of US corporate capitalism: consumer marketing and branding; specialised assembly lines; and the idea of shareholder value. But now GM was bankrupt. And the American government, dedicated to the free market, not only bailed out GM and the entire auto industry, it also got the votes for this in Congress. Obama's vice president, Joe Biden, used this fact as the central tagline of his boss's re-election campaign: 'Under Barack Obama, Bin Laden is dead and GM is still alive.' The strategy worked, delivering for the president the wavering rust-belt states, which have since experienced a boom in manufacturing jobs. It is true to say that not all in the USA felt the bailout was in keeping with American notions of freedom. Some conservatives organised a boycott of GM's cars. And while many might disagree with the policy, the hand of the US Federal government in US capitalism had just become rather firm. The combined monetary and fiscal stimulus kept unemployment below 10 per cent (by 2013 it was below the rate in Britain). And by 2012, GM was planning an extensive foreign sales push and sponsorship of the world's biggest football team. In America, the Stimulus Party was winning the austerity war.

The Apprentice Chancellor and the spending cuts

Right from the beginning of his tenure as chancellor, George Osborne was asked why he was pursuing austerity while the US government was not. 'I don't have the world's reserve currency,' was his answer to me in early 2011. The chancellor was referring to what French presidents have called the 'exorbitant privilege' enjoyed by the USA of getting a large flow of global savings, rather cheaply, on the back of the dollar's status as world currency. What worked for Washington would not necessarily work for Britain.

I happened to be standing outside the Treasury when George Osborne returned from Buckingham Palace in May 2010 having received the 'Great Seal of the Exchequer' from the Queen. At 38, Osborne was the youngest chancellor since the nineteenth century. His challenge was enormous. He had to balance the two coalition parties, and the different wings of those two parties. He had to take on Whitehall and the unions. And at the same time he had to contend with a broken banking system and the Eurozone crisis next door. In August 2010, he was at his peak – a colossus confident in his argument, bestriding government with his spending review, and displaying a missionary zeal for his fiscal plans. 'It's an absolute fundamental belief of mine that there is nothing progressive about losing control of the public finances, there's nothing fair about it,' he told me in his office at the Treasury, before listing centre-left and centre-right parties from the USA to Sweden that had cut back large deficits.

The Apprentice Chancellor had some advantages. He had carefully won the argument for some sort of spending cuts in advance of the election, although he had given very little detail of his plans for raising tuition fees, slashing the housing budget, cutting non-pensioner benefits, raising VAT, freezing public pay and hiking train fares. The financial markets clearly felt that a Conservative-led government had more credibility with the markets. Before the election, Osborne even managed to promise a 'cut' to a tax (in reality keeping employers' National Insurance contributions unchanged) that was unfunded save for some amorphous 'efficiency savings'. A Conservative could get away with that. Senior bankers, at that time, were claiming that 'Ed

Balls as chancellor would lead to a sterling crisis.' Such is life.

Part of the early political strategy was to get the pain in early, and to blame it all, including the VAT rise, on Gordon Brown and Labour. That worked too. In fact, Osborne's early 'age of austerity' rhetoric may have been a little too successful. Chris Williamson, the man who compiles the most closely watched measures of UK economic confidence, the Markit Purchasing Managers' Index, told me in the fourth month of the coalition: 'Our business measures have shown that since the June emergency budget, business confidence has collapsed and consumer confidence has collapsed.' The US and Japanese economies were also faltering. Of greater concern, however, for Osborne and his coalition partners, were the verdicts of the respected Institute for Fiscal Studies, who had calculated that the new measures applied by the coalition were 'somewhat regressive'. The new measures hit the poorest more than the richest.

There was a slight change of tack. Britain was in choppy waters, the chancellor said in a speech, but there were spots of good news. Doom was being replaced by 'cautious optimism'. But within weeks, Britain's economy fell sharply back into contraction, and would then cease to grow for over two years. The graph was striking. By March 2013, the economy had only grown 1.2 per cent in total since 2010, versus the 6.5 per cent predicted in the chancellor's original deficit-reduction plan. A recovery from the depths of a terrible recession had been stopped in its tracks in mid-2010, around the time when Osborne took over the Treasury. The first figures revealing the contraction – minus 0.5 per cent in the last quarter of 2010 – were a huge surprise for the chancellor. He initially blamed it on the disruption caused by cold weather and heavy snow in December. But in Germany the weather had been worse and its economy had delivered strong growth. The British press mocked these 'Snowmageddon' excuses mercilessly.

Soon afterwards I spoke to Mr Osborne at the World Economic Forum in Davos. Normally, interviews with politicians at Davos take place outside, with a backdrop of glorious snowy mountains. But this year, British ministers, including the chancellor, were only to be filmed indoors, with not a flake of snow in view. 'The fall in GDP according to the Office for National Statistics was caused by the very bad weather,' Osborne insisted. 'But David Cameron and I would like the GDP figure to be stronger, even without the snow. The truth is that we always said it would be a challenging recovery. We've had the deepest recession of our lifetime, the biggest banking crisis since the 1930s. There is a new government trying to sort out this mess. It was always going to be choppy.' I asked him whether he would alter his plan if the negative trend continued. 'I'm not in the business of speculation,' he replied. 'I look at the central forecast for the British economy, which is for sustained growth and for rising employment. And to make sure we take advantage of that by not going back into the financial danger zone I found when I came to office. Abandoning our deficit-reduction plan would lead to higher interest rates and a threat to our credit rating as a country.' He spread his narrative of blame a little wider, when I gently pointed out to him that Germany seemed to be doing well, despite the snow. 'Where we went wrong in the British economy,' he said, 'was the biggest budget deficit in the Western world. And our model of growth for the last ten years concentrated on one sector, financial services, in one part of the country, the southeast. I already know Germany has a better growth than us so I'm trying to get this country to manufacture, export and invest more so we have more sustainable growth, going forward.'

The last point was presumably intended to appeal to the LibDems in the governing coalition. The government started to make some extraordinary promises. 'We're actually starting to reindustrialise Britain,' the prime minister told me on a successful trade mission to India, three months after taking office. Critics suggested that the government was attempting to make a virtuous strategy out of a brutal necessity to rebalance Britain's economy. It would become a yardstick by which to judge economic progress. Throughout the 2011 Eurozone crisis, rising fuel prices and the impact of the hike in VAT would see a very bumpy recovery. International organisations such as the IMF, European Commission and OECD were revising down their forecasts for British growth – as was the chancellor's own independent Office for Budget Responsibility. The result was that the expected cuts in the deficit were grinding to a halt amid disappointing tax revenues and increasing welfare payments. Borrowing remained stubbornly high.

Nevertheless, the chancellor managed to keep the IMF on side. When asked whether Britain should change its plan, the IMF's handlebar-moustachioed interim managing director John Lipsky emphatically said 'No.' But the VAT rise had added to inflation in Britain, helped reduce real take-home pay, and impacted on consumer confidence. In May 2011, while returning from a Eurozone crisis summit in Brussels on the Eurostar, the chancellor told me: 'The Bank of England argument... is that inflation is set to fall next year and the year after. The VAT rise is an essential part of dealing with the budget deficit.'

The message, even as the economy ground to a halt in July 2011, was that the chancellor was 'absolutely not for turning'. 'If we were to abandon our deficit reduction plan,' Osborne said, 'if we were to borrow more, I think most people in the rest of the world would think we had gone completely mad.' The coalition had created 'a safe haven in the storm'. Yet the public finances were off track, and the prospect of yet more cuts or tax rises loomed. By the end of 2011, there had been a very telling change of course. The chancellor's plans were a little less binding than they had appeared. There was flexibility built into the borrowing targets, in precisely the same way that Gordon Brown had fudged similar targets. Osborne abandoned the plan of having the deficit dealt with by the time of the next general election, postponing further austerity until the next Parliament. There was no 'chasing the targets' with more cuts and tax rises. And at the end of 2012 he pushed the target even further into the future, and for good measure he also parked the requirement for falling debt. These were hugely important moments. Essentially the chancellor accepted a level of borrowing that was much larger than expected, rather than inflicting more immediate pain. But he did not shout about it. The markets were unaffected. He was spending some of the credibility he had earned with the bond vigilantes from his tough austerity rhetoric. Bond yields remained at record lows. Credit-ratings agencies, though, began the process of downgrading Britain. By March 2013, Britain was borrowing £703 billion over six years 2010–2016, instead of the £471 billion forecast in George Osborne's June 2010 Emergency Budget. The political argument in Britain revolved meaninglessly around 'sticking to Plan A' or 'the need for a Plan B' – the Opposition's plan for a Keynesian borrowed stimulus of tens of billions of pounds. It turned out that Plan A was so flexible that it was consistent with hundreds of billions in extra borrowing. In the Venn diagram of fiscal planning, B was a wholly contained subset of A. Still, announcing some £232 billion of extra borrowing over six years generated barely a flicker of interest from the markets. What was this strange hypnotic hold that George Osborne had over the bond vigilantes?

A tale of lost ratings

At the Debt Management Office, a tiny band of salesmen auction off what should be the safest bet in the land – British gilts. British government bonds are known as gilts because of their safety. They have always had an AAA rating because of the UK's standing in the world, and its fiscal stability. I visited the DMO in 2009 just days before the ratings agency Standard & Poor's started the process of downgrading Britain, after the collapse in UK tax revenues under Gordon Brown. The DMO is tucked away in Philpot Lane, a side street in the City close to the Monument. It does not have a grandiose edifice like the Bank of England or the Treasury. It does not even have its own building.

Occupying just two floors are the trading desks where Britain finds the necessary funds when the government spends more in a year than it taxes. This happens more often than not, and has been happening non-stop now for over a decade. The DMO has also subsumed various historical statutory bodies such as the Commissioners for the Reduction of the National Debt (CRND) – whose last minuted meeting was in 1860 – and the Public Works Loan Board. It also operates other government auctions, such as the EU carbon-trading scheme, and the business-loan guarantee scheme. The CRND was established to oversee William Pitt the Younger's dedicated 'Sinking Fund' for paying down the national debt in 1786. It still functions as the vehicle through which 'a few public-spirited people' give or bequeath money or property to the nation, and the proceeds are then used to cancel gilts. It will not be Britain's primary route out of its debt maze. But the activity on the trading screens of the DMO, particularly at 10 a.m. on a Thursday morning, will determine the param eters of politics in Britain for years to come.

On my visit, the traders had just borrowed £700 million from the markets for thirty-eight years, by effectively paying a real yield of 0.78 per cent. The gilt is 'index-linked', meaning that the coupon payment and the principal sum are adjusted in line with movements in the Retail Price Index. This takes away the risk posed to a bond-buyer's returns by future infla-tion. The bond did well. Bids worth two and a half times the required lending were offered to the DMO. In the jargon, it was 'well-covered'. The nightmare is that one day an auction, or series of auctions, will be left 'uncovered'.

In the wake of an inconclusive election, as government borrowing hits unprecedented levels and borrowing targets have been repeatedly missed, a niggling question arises. Can the DMO traders find buyers for all these bonds? Even in 2009 the DMO's head, Robert Stheeman, was attentive to the risks, but at the same time notably relaxed. 'Aren't you getting concerns from potential buyers?' I asked him. 'Not directly,' he replied. 'We are asked questions about the direction and where things are going. But at the same time a lot of the holdings come from highly sophisticated official institutions, and they don't seem to express undue concern.' What about the threat to the AAA rating (which was made the following week). 'A credit rating is ultimately just that. An opinion by the credit-ratings agencies.' If there was an effect, he said, 'it is much more likely to be expressed in price, and it could be imperceptible'.

That was the case in 2009, and it remained the case all the way through to 2013. Record low bond yields in Britain did reflect the fact that the country, despite its large and stubborn deficits, was considered a safe haven, especially during the Eurozone crisis. Certainly the chancellor's tough austerity rhetoric helped. However, the bond vigilantes had largely been disarmed in the USA and the UK. A large chunk of Britain's gilts were being bought a few hundred metres away from the DMO at the Bank of England under its programme of quantitative easing (see Chapter 9, pages 266–97). The market value of Britain's total stock of debt was £617 billion at the end of 2008, and that had more than doubled to £1.35 trillion at the end of 2012 – an increase of £741 billion. More than half of this increase (in fact 56 per cent of it) was explained by the increase in what was owed by the Treasury to the Bank of England, so that by the end of 2012 the Bank owned 29 per cent of the total debt stock of the UK. In effect the Bank of England was funding the equivalent of Britain's entire national debt in mid-2005. The market for gilts has basically been rigged by a monopoly buyer with access to unlimited central-bank funding. The bond vigilantes have not been hypnotised, they had no power in Britain, and so focused on the Eurozone periphery.

Still, the DMO had to find buyers for a hefty £340 billion worth of gilts. As it happens, changes to the regulations governing insurance companies and pension funds obliged these institutions to buy gilts, and their holdings went up by £112 billion over the past four years. Banks, too, upped their purchases of gilts by £70 billion over that period, but other financial institutions (such as hedge funds) sold £77 billion of their holdings. Altogether, of that £741 billion increase in Britain's outstanding debts, only about £200 billion needed to be raised on world markets. As it happened, foreign buyers snapped up £213 billion extra worth of UK gilts over the four-year period. No breakdown has ever been given regarding which countries are bankrolling Britain. The numbers are huge, though. From 1995 to 2005 the UK owed a steady £50 billion to foreign bondholders, around 20 per cent of its debts. By 2008 that proportion spiked to over a third, to 35 per cent. Subsequently, the Bank of England's quantitative easing programme helped reduce that figure to below 30 per cent. (The proportion of foreign purchased gilts issuance rises to 62 per cent if you ignore the bonds purchased by the Bank of England.) Britain's dependence on foreign lenders was still at historic highs. But the proportions remained small in relation to other debtors. Eurozone crisis nations such as Ireland, Spain and Greece owed 70 to 80 per cent of their government debts abroad. The UK government argues, even in a market rigged by the Bank of England, that the very large increase in foreign holdings of UK gilts is a testament to the credibility of its austerity plan.

In September 2010, Lord Sassoon, the commercial secretary to the Treasury, led a sales mission to Saudi Arabia, Kuwait, Abu Dhabi and Dubai. The centrepiece of the roadshow was Robert Stheeman of the Debt Management Office, whose role it was to sell British gilts to the region's oil-fuelled sovereign wealth funds and central banks. Britain, also an oil nation, had mysteriously misplaced its own sovereign wealth fund, squandering its North Sea windfall on current spending and tax cuts. Still, the Gulf nations could be relied on after being reassured about the solidity of gilt investments. A British minister had never gone on a roadshow like it before. The strategy was to see the 'customers' for Britain's gilts, as soon as possible, at the highest possible level. It was a delicate operation, as none of the funds were keen to disclose their holdings. The objective was modest: to offer sufficient re-assurance that the foreign buyers would maintain Britain's weight in their portfolios of assets. George Osborne's team argue that this is where austerity, or at least credible austerity plans, really scored: the chancellor's fiscal credibility has enabled the UK to lower the rates of interest payable on the nation's growing debts. Participants on these roadshows were surprised, however, by the toughness of the questioning and the detailed technical knowledge of Britain's position they encountered. But they were 'pushing at an open door'. The pre-election fears expressed by bond trader PIMCO of gilts 'sitting on a bed of nitroglycerine' had long been forgotten. Investors were generally impressed by the transparency of Britain's deficit reduction plan, versus other problematic European nations. Britain was winning the ugly contest on public finances. There was one concern, though: the interaction of public borrowing and banking stress. These conversations were and increasingly will remain Britain's default line. The country that, a century ago, had been the world's superpower was now dependent on the kindness of friendly strangers and strange friends.

Britain was never heading for actual bankruptcy: such a fate is basically impossible for a nation with its own currency and its own printing press. That was amply illustrated by the Bank of England's massive gilt purchases, though the Bank argues that helping the Treasury was incidental rather than the aim of its policy. Britain, unlike Greece for example, had a credible long-term record of either extracting more tax from its people when required, or carrying out spending cuts. Another reason why Britain has not gone bankrupt is the length or maturity of its debts. The average length of gilts, the time when the principal sum borrowed would need to be repaid, is fourteen years. This is around double the average length of bonds issued by France, Germany or Greece. Ireland and Spain had an average debt maturity of five and six years respectively in 2010.

Britain has much longer to pay back its admittedly large debts. And who should George Osborne be thanking for that? Gordon Brown. Yes, Brown was responsible for a large swathe of debt with his pre-crisis deficits, and with his role in the financial crisis, which indirectly triggered the epic crisis deficits. But Brown secured a good mortgage deal for his mountain of debt. In the late 1990s Britain's debt maturity was already nine years on average. By the start of the financial crisis, Brown's creation, the Debt Management Office, had extended that out to fourteen years on average by issuing thirty- and fifty-year debts. There was less roll-over risk, and less of an immediate financing need of the type that felled Greece and Portugal. In fact, under George Osborne, the DMO extended the average out further, to fifteen years.

Britain's long-term mortgage did not mean that it could skip repayment or tough decisions. But it did offer time, space and options. The credit-ratings agencies repeatedly mentioned the quantitative easing programme and the long debt maturity as reasons why the UK kept its gold standard AAA sovereign rating, even though its debts mounted. The chancellor had invested a huge amount of political capital in the AAA rating. But that would be taken away by Moody's in February 2013, and by Fitch two months later, while the chancellor was at a meeting of finance ministers at the IMF. It was quite some watershed. Moody's had rated the UK AAA since modern sovereign ratings were started in 1978. Way back in the First World War, John Moody himself, founder of the craft, personally researched and signed off a triple A rating to four different types of UK government debt. So February 2013 marked the first time the AAA had been stripped since 1918, almost a century earlier. The fact that the USA and France had already lost at least one of their ratings cushioned the blow. Mr Osborne impishly claimed both that the need to keep the AAA and his eventual historic loss of Britain's ratings were vindications of his fiscal policies. In Opposition he had vocally called for an election when Standard & Poor's merely threatened to take their AAA rating away from Alistair Darling's Treasury.

So Britain lost its prized historical AAA rating, even though it wasn't going bankrupt. George Osborne's austerity programme probably helped reduce the risk of interest rates rising in Britain, albeit at the expense of a severe regime of cuts in some Whitehall departments. But the Bank of England was the overriding reason behind those low rates. Furthermore, senior figures at the Bank were adamant that the alternative plan from Labour – to deal with the deficit over eight years – would have been sufficient to retain market credibility, if fleshed out. In summer 2013 I asked Mr Osborne if he recognised that 'bankruptcy' was impossible. 'No, I don't,' he told me. 'It depends what you mean by bankruptcy: if you mean by bankruptcy a complete loss of international confidence in your ability to fund yourself, and a big spike in market interest rates such that you get into a terrible spiral and end up needing market support, I think that it was an entirely possible situation for the UK.'

As it turned out, the fiscal plans were missed rather spectacularly. Even more borrowing was required. Growth remained stubbornly flat. The recovery inherited from the previous government flattened, partly because of the Eurozone, partly because of oil prices, and partly because of the tax rises, confidence-sapping effects and early spending cuts of the austerity plan. Britain was to lose its AAA rating anyway. The chancellor was to veer off-course from his debt target, and delay the eradication of the British structural deficit by two years. Britain's 'fiscal brutality' was a patchy affair (see Epilogue, page 433), focused on specific areas such as housing, transport, local councils, benefits, business support and spending on infrastructure. Overall spending increased in cash terms. Mr Osborne's *ex post facto* rationalisation for low growth was that the hangover from Labour's credit bubble was always going to be difficult. If that was the case, then he may have chosen the wrong cuts. He was pressured for a change of plan, which we shall return to. But given the relative ease with which his civil servants borrowed money abroad and from the Bank of England, what was all the fuss about austerity?

The answer lay in a PowerPoint scattergram circulated inside the Treasury in the first weeks of the coalition. Britain's government debts and deficits were *a* problem but not *the* problem. *The* problem was the combination of public debt, private debt and bank debt. Britain could not take the risk of immediately losing its AAA rating, resulting in much higher gilt rates, not because of the risk of sovereign bankruptcy, but because of the interaction of sovereign-debt funding with banking funding stress. This was the so-called doom loop. The gilt salesmen were peppered with questions from foreign central banks about Britain's over-large financial system. And in the PowerPoint scattergram ('Risks from financial sector and fiscal position'), which mapped domestic banking assets (UK – 500 per cent) as a percentage of GDP against structural deficits (UK – 8 per cent), it was the UK that was off the scale, a lonely cross in the far northwestern corner of the chart. Britain was worse than every advanced economy on both measures, bar the Greek deficit, and even then only just. It was the combination of public and private debt that created the risks for Britain. The IMF would at first call UK austerity 'an insurance policy' against the collision of these twin deficits. But it was the private debt, the zombie businesses, households and banks that dragged on the economy. The banks that some of the bond vigilantes actually worked for were fairly high-level causes of the fiscal criminality that so irked those very same vigilantes. In some ways it was the mess that Britain's banks had got themselves into that made the austerity programme especially necessary. As Chancellor Osborne describes the situation he was met with in 2010: 'There's an 11.5 per cent deficit: a hung Parliament... and what's toxic is the potential fiscal link to the banking sector.' And given what the banks had been up to, that would have been a difficult argument for a candid politician to explain to the public. Few dared to.

CHAPTER 3

THE REAL NORTHERN ROCK

Dramatis personae

Davíð Oddsson, prime minister of Iceland (1991–2004),
governor, Central Bank of Iceland (2005–09),
editor of the Icelandic newspaper *Morgunblaðið* (2009–)
Bjartur, an indebted peasant character in Icelandic
folk novels
Már Guðmundsson, a rather jovial successor
to Mr Oddsson as governer of the Central Bank
of Iceland
Armann Thorvaldsson, London boss, Kaupthing bank
Sir Mervyn King, governor of the Bank of England
(2003–13)
Alistair Darling, UK chancellor of the exchequer
(2007–10)
Steingrímur Sigfússon, the Left-Green Party leader elected
to government in the aftermath of the crisis, finance minister
of Iceland (2008–13)
Ólafur Hauksson, Icelandic special prosecutor of
financial crimes
Katrín Júlíusdóttir, 38-year-old finance minister of Iceland
(2012–13)
Sigrún Davíðsdóttir, Icelandic broadcaster
and commentator

'You're safe with these banks.' So Davíð Oddsson, governor of the Central Bank of Iceland, told me in February 2008.

It's the sort of quote that in a decade of reporting economics, and in three years of studying it at university, I had never expected to hear. No doubt bankers would think it, and want to hint at it. But to actually say it? In fact, to have the governor of a central bank say it? Absolutely not a chance. Why? Because the moment you have to say that about a bank, or an entire banking sector, then it pretty much becomes instantly untrue. As an attempt to boost confidence, it is inevitably both self-negating and self-defeating.

And yet the governor did indeed utter these words and he spoke them in a hyper-modern fort-like structure, a forbidding black bat-cave of a building overflowing with modernist art, overlooking the Reykjavik fjords and set against a backdrop of the towering snow-capped Mount Esja. The Central Bank of Iceland is possibly the most stunningly situated central bank in the world. And its governor made this statement seven months before it faced a collapse that was every bit as stunning as its setting. In February 2008 the Central Bank of Iceland was on the cusp of bankruptcy. In a room on the ground floor, a ruffled, agitated Davíð Oddsson stood before me. I had no idea why he had agreed to give me an interview in the circumstances. In his shoes, I would never have agreed.

Not much time was to pass before Oddsson's reassurance was to turn out to be demonstrably untrue. He had offered that reassurance because two of Iceland's big three banks had, amazingly, in the face of sceptical world markets, started to fund themselves with billions of pounds from ordinary British and Dutch family savers. So he did have a sliver of a reason for attempting to reassure the rest of the world.

'The banking system has grown very fast,' the governor told me, 'and they have had very sound, handsome profits year by year by year. Last year, the three major banks made £1 billion profits, and the latter part of the year was not the easiest. The risk management has been good too. Now you can say they are northern European banks with headquarters in Iceland, because more than 50 per cent of their revenues are coming from outside Iceland.' I asked him why his banking sector had made the strategic decision to woo foreign depositors. 'I think we should applaud them for that,' Mr Oddsson replied, 'not punish them... I think it was a very good idea, good for both the banks and the people putting deposits into these banks, which are very sound and good banks.'

Before the year was out, all three of those 'Big Three' banks – Glitnir, Kaupthing and Landsbanki – had collapsed, basically bankrupting Mr Oddsson's Central Bank as they did so. Iceland became the harbinger of a new phase in the crisis, a phase in which countries, not just banks and individuals, were going bust, finding themselves left on the wrong side of the default line. In Iceland Mr Oddsson would become a national hate figure, and the bat-cave would find itself besieged by angry protesters.

The roots of Iceland's woes go back a quarter of a century. In 1986 the world's two superpowers met on this chilly rock in the Northern Atlantic. The Reykjavik summit proved to be a historic staging post on the way to the worldwide financial crisis, a staging post at which Ronald Reagan and Mikhail Gorbachev, representing the West and the Soviet Union, met as equals. But they were not equal. Cold War had turned to economic freeze for the Russians and to hot boom for the United States and Europe. The summit witnessed the birth of a hyperpower, yes, but also the beginning of a hyperbubble, as, in a mood of triumphalism, borrowing, debt and deregulation all swelled to unsustainable dimensions – hence the scale of the subsequent financial calamity.

In the official photographs from the Reagan–Gorbachev summit there was a third man. This was the then mayor of Reykjavik, Davíð Oddsson, who was playing host to the two superpowers. A decade later, Oddsson – now prime minister – had followed the Chicago-school formula for growth and had stopped most regulation of Iceland's banks. Two decades on came my uncomfortable interview with a man in denial about the coming financial collapse of his institution, his financial system – and his nation. Meet Davíð Oddsson, the Forrest Gump of the financial crisis.

The extraordinary tale of how Iceland had got to this point, of the global pressure placed on this tiny country immediately after the crash, and of how it subsequently began to extract itself from the mess, is one with lessons well beyond its own shoreline.

Some back-story first. In fact, let's take things back to the early twentieth century, the setting of *Independent People*, a 1930s novel by Halldór Laxness, who was to go on to win the Nobel Prize for Literature (published in Icelandic in two parts, 1934 and 1935; English translation published in 1946). After two decades of humiliating servitude, a peasant called Bjartur attempts to forge a livelihood as a debt-free sheep farmer as part of his 'eternal struggle for independence'. The four parts of the novel are called 'Icelandic Pioneer', 'Free of Debt', 'Hard Times' and 'Years of Prosperity', which could well describe his nation, a century later. Prosperity comes with the First World War, when the price of Icelandic mutton soars. Near the end of the novel, however, following the return of peace and a collapse in demand, Bjartur is facing a return to penury. 'To die of starvation,' Laxness writes, 'such a fate, surely, was infinitely preferable to being ensnared by the banks, as people are nowadays, for at least they had lived like independent men, at least they had died of hunger like free people.' Bjartur is then sent into debt enslavement and rationing to pay the interest on his loan after his bank is recapitalised by the Icelandic state, via a loan from 'a certain bank in London'. His bank? National Bank, now known as Landsbanki, by 2008 one of the disastrous Big Three. In Iceland, financial history seems to move at the speed of its glaciers.

Iceland once took huge pride in the fact that its government used to owe nothing. The phrases 'net debt free' and 'debtless' would pepper the briefings of its senior financial officials – before the crisis. Iceland's national debt in 2006 was no more than a few hundred million pounds, not even 8 per cent of the size of its economy. For two years at the peak of the boom, Iceland's annual haul of fish exports was worth more than its entire historic national debts. But few had accounted for the crazed ingenuity of Iceland's bankers.

At a stretch, the saga begins in 1976, when Iceland won the Cod Wars with the UK after threatening to close an important NATO base. Victory in the Cod Wars was followed by over-fishing, and as a response this nation of fishermen began to dabble in high finance. In 1984 Iceland introduced a quota system for its fishing stocks that limited trawlers to a certain number of tonnes or a certain number of days on the high seas. By 1990 the government had allowed these permits to be freely traded. The winners were the 'Quota Kings', those active in the fishing industry in the early 1980s, who were effectively gifted the mining rights to Iceland's 'silver of the seas'. The losers were those small-scale fishermen who had worked in fishing villages that had lost their quotas. It was a massive legal transfer of wealth of what had previously been public property. The spoils of the Cod War had gone to fishermen-financiers rather than ordinary Icelanders.

But in many ways the quota system was a success. The fish stocks were replenished, giant fishing conglomerates thrived, and a tradable market in fishing quotas began. 'The fishing quotas created a capital base in Iceland where there was none before,' writes former stockbroker Jon Thoroddsen. The quotas, he continues, 'added plenty of fuel for the nascent Icelandic stock market'. Iceland's fish had become the nation's seed capital. As it turned out, however, the future spawn of those fish had merely been mortgaged.

Even in the mid-1990s Iceland's economy was still overwhelm-ingly based on seafaring. As recently as 1993 the Central Bank devalued the króna by 7.5 per cent solely on the back of lower fish quotas. But cod capital had been deployed and by the late 1990s was pushing up the prices of both houses and stocks and shares. More ominously, Iceland's fishing wealth became concentrated in the hands of a few family networks.

The essential philosophy and structure for the later calamity was in place by the early 1990s, when Oddsson's cabinet colleague, future prime minister Halldór Ásgrímsson, was fisheries' minister. At that time, Oddsson himself – as mayor of Reykjavik – was merging and selling off the city's largest fishing firm. Ásgrímsson was to serve on the committee that privatised Iceland's banks under Prime Minister Oddsson, handing the banks to investment bankers. Then, after a job-swap, Prime Minister Ásgrímsson appointed Oddsson as Central Bank governor in 2005.

For a dozen years, from 1995 to 2007, Mr Oddsson's centre-right Independence Party and Mr Ásgrímsson's liberal, agrarian Progressive Party ruled Iceland in coalition. By 1999 *The Economist*, otherwise a fan of the Viking free-marketeers, had noticed one source of rot in '. . . the closed nature of Icelandic society where about 20 prominent families dominate many of the leading businesses as well as the political scene. These coalesce in two groups, known as the Octopus group and the Squid. Inside the Octopus camp are many members of the Independence Party and some of the country's largest privately owned companies. The Squid group embraces the cooperative movement and many members of the Progressive Party.'

Crony capitalism is rather difficult to avoid in a country of 300,000 people, where everybody seems to know everybody else's business. A regular source of dismay for British corporate financiers was how most of Iceland seemed to know which British retailers, banks and football teams were on the target list of the Icelandic billionaires. The secrecy required to close a takeover was often broken by the billionaires themselves. In one case, a takeover of Newcastle United FC was scuppered when the Icelandic billionaire concerned arrived with his aide at Reykjavik airport sporting matching Geordie football shirts (though it's said a customs officer misread the name 'Owen' on the back of the billionaire's shirt for the word 'Owner').

So perhaps the Octopus and the Squid were unavoidable in a tiny country. And it was their interwoven tentacles that were to entrap the entire island in their embrace, contributing hugely to the coming calamity.

In the office of the Central Bank governor

In 2013, half a decade on from the economic collapse of Iceland, I returned to the office of the Central Bank governor, overlooking Mount Esja. I met a rather jovial successor to Mr Oddsson called Már Guðmundsson, who has, with considerable care, been trying to put Iceland back together again. At the time of the disaster, Mr Guðmundsson was working with the Bank for International Settlements, based in Basel, in a team that was noted for the repeated warnings it gave about the credit bubble. In May 2007 he returned to Reykjavik to make a speech in which he gave a clear warning to European bankers. 'Emergency liquidity assistance,' he told his audience, 'will be complicated or even impossible for central banks to deliver when internationally active banks face liquidity problems in currencies other than that of their home country. Iceland is a case in point.'

So back then he had suggested that the Central Bank of Iceland would not be able to offer the traditional central-bank facility of lender of last resort to its overgrown banks. Every bank in the world, ordinarily, has the backstop of a central bank that can give it funding in an emergency, when there is a run on deposits or other forms of financing, in order to repay depositors. But not in this case. At the time that Guðmundsson was giving his speech, the UK regulator was giving Icelandic banks the green light to take billions in deposits from ordinary British savers.

The balance sheets of Iceland's banks grew from under twice GDP in 2003 to ten times GDP by mid-2008. Of course, since banks were invented many have thrown caution to the winds and lent out vast amounts of money. It is rarer, however, for banks to make the bulk of their financing abroad, in a currency that their own central bank cannot print. The majority of Iceland's 'Big Three' banks' lending and funding was from abroad. Two-thirds of their balance sheets were denominated in a foreign currency.

'It wasn't even cross-border banking, it was off-border banking,' Mr Guðmundsson told me. 'Much of it was booked here in Iceland, even though it had nothing to do with Iceland. We had never seen this before. It revealed deep flaws in the whole EU single market. The banks were allowed to operate freely across the area, but the whole safety net was national. Deposit insurance, lender of last resort, and the resolution regime were all national.'

The core of the problem lay in Iceland's semi-detached relationship with the EU. As a member of the European Economic Area, which gives Iceland access to the EU single market, there was little really that the government could do to stop Iceland's banks from marauding through the European Union on a lending and funding binge. Had Iceland been a full member of the Eurozone, its banks could have accessed the liquidity facilities of the European Central Bank in full. But Iceland was stuck in the middle.

So Iceland's bankers and multinationals ran riot in the banking, retail and property markets of northern Europe. On top of that came the trophy assets such as football clubs. Chief executives would discover oddly named companies popping up on their shareholder register. The Vikings would turn up in the offices of their prey to proclaim their new status. Someone had found a pot of gold on this rock in the mid-Atlantic. Private jets and parties with pop stars on the guest list – Reykjavik had become the northern Riviera. Yet, unlike a decade previously, this time the boom was not even secured on fish. This entirely new northern European financial centre had no foundations. 'I hope they have done good shopping,' was Davíð Oddsson's comment when I raised that concern several months before the crisis.

As it turned out, it was the manner of their shopping more than anything they'd put in the basket that had begun to spook the markets in 2006. A bizarre spider's web of cross-shareholdings, intertwined ownership and mutual loans made Icelandic balance sheets rather opaque. Assets were traded between different arms of the same allied companies at aggressive prices, creating illusory accounting profits at every turn of the carousel. Kaupthing, one of the 'Big Three' banks, also liked to lend hundreds of millions of euros to its owners. Its leaked loan book showed its largest loan went to Exista, in turn the biggest shareholder in Kaupthing. Even more curiously, in 2009 a Kaupthing fund manager and stockbroker were jailed for manipulating share prices in order to prop up Exista's value.

That is just one tiny example of the curiosities of capitalism, Reykjavik-style. Investigations continue into a variety of dodgy goings-on: an Icelandic bank tried to manipulate credit-derivatives markets to give a false impression of its own health; the lending of money by banks to clients to buy shares in the same bank; and – my favourite – the use by the client of one Icelandic bank of bank shares, funded by loans from the very same bank, as collateral for further loans from the same bank.

It was Alice-in-Wonderland stratagems such as this that served to mask the true levels of capital in Iceland's banks. Officially the Icelandic banking system was hugely leveraged; unofficially it was leveraged at a quite monstrously high level. As a consequence, a tsunami of credit raced across the North Atlantic and washed ashore in Europe.

In late 2005 and early 2006, Iceland endured the so-called Geyser Crisis, a sudden slump in market confidence. Iceland's banks and currency came under justified speculative attack from the global markets, an early warning of the turbulence to come. But the warning was ignored, and the crisis abated – for a while. The credit-insurance markets, known as credit default swaps (CDS), constituted a key feature of the Geyser Crisis. Essentially they became a measure of the risk of default of a bank or government, but it was expressed as a number, a percentage rather than the alphabetical ratings (AAA, AA, etc.) used by the credit-ratings agencies. When CDS contracts were first written on Kaupthing, its bankers celebrated. They had arrived. But the celebrations didn't last long.

Norway's $455 billion state-backed oil fund had made a commercial decision to bet on the misfortune of Iceland's banking sector. Merrill Lynch, Denmark's Danske Bank and, ironically, RBS joined in with critical reports about Iceland's opaque banking system. Iceland was furious that Norway's sovereign wealth fund had started what seemed to be a speculative market attack on its banks. Norway's giant national piggy bank was filled with the proceeds of oil money, but run on strict market principles. The investment decisions of such state-owned funds were beginning to have a diplomatic impact. The Norwegians retreated.

Yet a small band of Scandinavian economists and bankers, as well as British hedge funds, remained utterly unconvinced by the stability of Iceland's banks. Concerns centred around over-investment in retail, leisure and property in northern Europe and the UK at the peak of a consumer boom. Icelandic tycoons and investment funds went on a spending spree, buying major UK businesses, including Hamleys, House of Fraser, West Ham United and the supermarket chain Iceland, all funded by capital provided by the Icelandic banks.

The sceptics began to circulate emails detailing the spider's web of overlapping ownership between the Big Three – Landsbanki, Kaupthing and Glitnir – their customers and their shareholders. Little wonder, therefore, that funding streams dried up, and the credit markets indicated that Icelandic banks were the riskiest in Europe. 'We realised that we were under attack at the end of March [2006] when Barclays and UBS brought a group of investors to Reykjavik,' wrote Kaupthing's London boss Armann Thorvaldsson. He described a presentation at Kaupthing's HQ that degenerated into a shouting match between fund managers and bosses about the safety of Iceland's financial system.

So Europe stopped funding Icelandic banks in 2006. Or at least sophisticated European money-market investors stopped funding Iceland and its banks. But the banks fought back, raising huge sums at highish interest rates from America by packaging their debt up into the notorious 'collateralised debt obligations' (CDOs), underpinned by the gold-standard AAA credit rating. The global flood of liquidity saved them, temporarily. Incredibly, in October 2007 Kaupthing raised 2.3 billion pesos from bond investors in Mexico, making it the first, and probably last, Nordic bank to raise pesos from Central America. The Geyser Crisis was over – for a few months.

Another wheeze to find alternative funding was to do, three years early, what banks all around the world desperately scrambled to do in 2008–9: raise money from consumer deposits – in other words, good old-fashioned retail banking. One huge problem was that Iceland's own population of potential depositors was simply not big enough. The solution was to adopt, borrow and grab a foreign deposit base instead. Hence Icesave (the internet account from Landsbanki) and Kaupthing Edge (Kaupthing's equivalent) sucked in billions from ordinary retail depositors in the UK and the Netherlands. Public bodies in Britain – such as the police, local councils, the geniuses at Oxford University and even the British government's own internal auditors – also had hoards of spare cash that they willingly deposited with the Icelandic banks.

Mr Oddsson thought this strategy was a win-win. 'I think the Icelandic banks realised from one, two years ago that they should go more in that direction [rather than]... to have to refund themselves in the market on such a large scale,' he told me at that meeting in February 2008. 'It was healthier to do that more by deposits – and they've been doing that. They've been doing that successfully and they've been doing that very honestly with an honest, successful programme. And I think we should applaud them for that, not punish them.'

Around this time, I received a call from a Scandinavian

financial analyst, one of that band of sceptics who could not believe the 'bankrupt Icelandic banks' were being allowed to take deposits from Britain. 'Icelandic banks have been shut out of money markets for two years, but they can ask a British housewife for a deposit?' he asked me incredulously. 'Why are they doing it now? They've been forced into doing this. But you'd never see this on the Icesave adverts.'

A significant proportion of UK savers were simply placing all their money in the savings account with the highest interest rate, as pronounced by internet comparison sites, or the misnamed 'best buy' tables. Icesave played this system brilliantly. It raised billions of pounds of money that it could not raise on the markets from ordinary British families. Kaupthing copied the strategy a few months later. Both banks stressed their participation in the UK's deposit-protection schemes. The Icelandic banks were effectively free-riding on guarantees funded by UK banks and building societies – and ultimately the British taxpayer.

Iceland's lax financial regulators should have stopped this, but the likes of Davíð Oddsson believed that the banks had ceased to be Icelandic banks per se, and were now 'north European banks, headquartered in Reykjavik'. So the strategy of adopting a British deposit base was, as he told me six months before the crisis, 'a very good idea, good for both the banks, and the people putting the deposits into these banks'.

The UK regulator, the Financial Services Authority, should have done more. In its defence, particularly with Icesave, the FSA was not the primary regulator. It had no access to the parent company, Landsbanki, as Icesave was operated as a branch, rather than a UK-incorporated subsidiary. European law, so-called 'passporting rules', obliged the UK to take at face value the Icelandic authorities' assessment of Landsbanki's accounts.

So the FSA can make a reasonable argument that it had no good reason or no legal basis to prevent Landsbanki from opening up Icesave in the UK. However, when it became apparent that the banks had unexpectedly attracted billions of pounds of internet savings, alarm bells should have rung louder. The FSA did retain powers and tools even under the passporting arrangements. The FSA gently suggested to banks in its 2008 Financial Risk Outlook that internet savings were proving more fickle and less 'sticky' than conventional savings. It was talking about Icesave, but could not say so too clearly. When prodded by me, the FSA also advised savers to 'talk to their providers' to check if they were comfortable with different deposit-protection schemes offered by foreign banks. In Icesave's case, the first £18,000 of a depositor's saving was guaranteed by an Icelandic fund. It was never paid, and this is what forms the Icesave debt. It amounted to about 40 per cent of Iceland's entire national income.

However, by the time the FSA issued this warning – in March 2008 – the train crash was unavoidable. A round of increasingly frenzied crisis talks between the Treasury, the Bank of England, the FSA and the Icelandics began, and the details were subsequently divulged by sources in Reykjavik. Icesave began its transition from high finance to high diplomacy.

Yet there is a fundamental unanswered question about this fiasco, a question with important implications for the future. How did Icesave amass so much cash from UK depositors so quickly? As much as £3 billion flowed into Icesave in the first three months following its launch, with total balances peaking above £6 billion. A remarkable proportion of these deposits was transferred directly from the then market-leading internet savings account ING Direct, which had cut the rates it offered just as Icesave launched.

In the UK especially, Icesave's strategy would not have been possible were it not for the evangelical zeal of a populist personal-finance media. The money pundits portrayed Iceland as northern Europe's new piggy bank, a much better prospect than the bad guys at ING Direct or the stingy British high street banks, who had refused to pass on rises in Bank of England interest rates. But the buys in the 'best buy' league tables were by no means the best buys. The offer of a high interest rate was portrayed as an altruistic Viking attempt to shake up the staid British savings market, rather than a reflection of the banks' desperate requirement for funding. Icesave's marketing pitch was unquestioningly and enthusiastically lapped up in the specialist press, which plays such a key role in the savings market. The Icesave public relations team sent an 'Ice Bar' around Fleet Street's personal-finance journalists, offering drinks on the house. Some were flown to Iceland. The high rates were hailed by the media in a series of nonsensical and unquestioning headlines. 'Viking invaders return un- defeated to Britain's financial territory. . . Time for savers to get their skates on. . . The iceman cometh and savers swoon. . . A crystal clear savings account from Iceland. . . Icesave looks a hot deal' – and my favourite, from the *Scotsman*: 'Foreign financial invaders are such progressive geysers.'

Iceland's banks had pulled off a remarkable and perfectly legal heist. At this point it was too late for the UK government or regulators to get the money back.

One issue was that Mr Oddsson of Iceland's Central Bank was in a pickle trying to defend Kaupthing's financial honour. As prime minister a few years earlier, Oddsson had withdrawn all of his £3,000 worth of savings from Kaupthing in protest at their eye-watering bonuses to senior management and their control of important Icelandic media. It was noticeable that he did not do much to defend Kaupthing, when in February 2008 I asked him questions about bank safety. He preferred to talk about Landsbanki. 'Deposits are mainly in Landsbanki,' he told me, reassuring me that they had 'been put in a very safe place'. 'Landsbanki has been around 120 years,' he continued, 'quite respected, doing well, here and elsewhere. I wouldn't say anything else than it was a good decision to utilise possibilities of saving with Landsbanki.'

The end result was that Iceland was sitting on £10 billion of deposits from UK savers. To put this in context, in 2007 the foreign-currency liabilities of foreign branches of Iceland's banks was more than the country's GDP. It was over three times its annual state budget, and four times the government of Iceland's foreign-exchange reserves. Neither the banks, nor the deposit bailout fund, nor the government of Iceland had enough money, and in particular enough pounds or euros, to pay out in the event of a crisis.

I asked Davíð Oddsson how on earth Iceland could stand behind the British depositors' cash. 'The economy of this country is quite extraordinarily good – the country itself, the state, is net debt-free – with good resources and a good situation,' he reassured me. 'The state could relatively easily do it, and afterwards, it would be one of the most debt-free economies in Europe. Afterwards,' he said. 'This would not be too much for the state to swallow, if it would like to swallow it.'

I did not believe him. And it emerged that before my interview Mr Oddsson had already been expressing concerns in Iceland about the health of the same banks I had asked about. Moody's, the international credit-ratings agency, had warned in early February that the Central Bank of Iceland needed access to sterling and euro liquidity, so-called 'swap agreements'. Coincidentally, on the day my interview aired on *Channel 4 News*, Davíð Oddsson was in London, meeting with the Bank of England governor Mervyn King to begin the process of asking for a swap agreement. I did not know this at the time, but it might explain the strange, irate phone call from the Icelandic ambassador demanding a DVD of my report, immediately after the show ended.

That same month, a rather desperate negotiation ensued between the Icelandic and UK central banks over a £1–2 billion currency swap. King was never convinced. The previous year, an IMF board member had remarked at its Article IV economic review that 'Iceland essentially was functioning like a hedge fund, borrowing abroad to acquire foreign assets.' The IMF did not act on these concerns, however, and in fact there was no IMF mission chief for six months as the storm clouds gathered.

The formal request to the Bank of England by Mr Oddsson

began diplomatically enough, but then veered off into warnings about 'unscrupulous forces' that needed to be deterred. And then came the darker negotiation gambit: King should cough up, Oddsson suggested, because an Icelandic crisis would imperil the world financial system through exposures hidden in derivatives. 'Icelandic bank paper is believed to be included in more than half of all CDO structures created in recent years,' Mr Oddsson wrote to Mr King. 'Our international banking contacts have underlined that a credit event stemming from a large-scale liquidation of Icelandic bank obligations would have a serious impact on global asset markets.' It was desperate stuff, from a man who days previously had told me his banks were 'very sound' and that his economy was 'extraordinarily good'.

Mervyn King was unimpressed. He turned down Mr Oddsson's request, saying that Iceland needed to reduce the size of its banking sector by selling off at least one of the major banks. He also said it was 'extremely difficult' for Iceland to provide lender-of-last-resort facilities to its banks, and that the markets knew this. 'The swap might look like a political gesture rather than a credible financial strategy,' he wrote to Mr Oddsson. 'I know you will be disappointed. But among friends it is sometimes necessary to be clear about what we think.' Governor Oddsson replied the same day, simply restating the need for a currency arrangement, and upping the ante on the global damage an Icelandic crisis could inflict. 'The absence of a swap arrangement in the current circumstances could have very severe consequences,' he wrote to King. 'I must emphasise my belief that this is not an isolated Icelandic concern. Difficulties in Iceland could have serious contagious effects in other countries.' He received no reply. The letter almost sounded threatening. Was he talking about the UK depositors' money? The US Federal Reserve also politely declined Iceland's request for a swap.

Extraordinarily enough, despite the UK authorities refusing support facilities and knowing their own government could not support them, Icelandic banks were permitted to continue taking British deposits for six months. And they did. Icelandic bankers in London put King's refusal down to the British banks' jealousy of their cunning in grabbing deposits.

An intriguing army of Icelandic bank loyalists descended upon the British blogosphere and internet personal-finance forums to reassure those savers expressing concerns, and to rubbish my report, and others like it. Some smart Conservative councils reviewed their massive deposits in Icelandic banks. In general, though, there was no way for British savers to get their deposits back quickly.

At this point Iceland's fate was sealed. It was only a matter of time before the collapse. Iceland's banks did try to shrink their balance sheets by selling off loans and businesses. Kaupthing Edge, Kaupthing's version of Icesave, which only opened in the UK in 2008, sucked in the equivalent of a billion euros a month in retail deposits even as the Icelandic authorities knew that the nation could not possibly support its liabilities. British regulators did not step in to stop this. In Britain, 170,000 savers placed £2.7 billion in deposits with Kaupthing Edge. The FSA required that Kaupthing Singer & Friedlander (Kaupthing's UK branch) hold 90–95% of the value of deposits.

In his book *Frozen Assets*, Armand Thorvaldsson, the CEO of Kaupthing's London arm, reveals one remarkable rescue effort. Kaupthing presented the UK FSA with a plan to move its headquarters from Reykjavik to London. Even in the aftermath of the collapse of Lehman Brothers, Kaupthing's deposits increased from £75–100 million per week to £150 million per week. There were more depositors, but volumes were below the £35,000 limit for deposit insurance. It was after the nationalisation of Iceland's troubled third biggest bank Glitnir that the bank run on Iceland started. Thorvaldsson likened it to a 'wildebeest being hunted by hyenas'.

The FSA declared a 'code red' after a net £37 million was withdrawn on 30 September 2008, indicating fears that Kaupthing would not have enough money to last a week. The FSA injected staff on to the office floors of both major Icelandic banks in London for daily monitoring of liquidity. The FSA demanded that over £1 billion in funding be transferred from Kaupthing's head office to its UK subsidiary by the end of the following week. On Friday, 3 October 2008, the European Central Bank issued a margin call for €400 million to Landsbanki. Over the following weekend £318 million had been withdrawn over the internet from Icesave. The FSA demanded £253 million from Landsbanki HQ to cover liquidity shortfalls following the withdrawals. On the Monday, Icesave's website closed down due to 'technical difficulties'. It was the FSA's doing. Landsbanki asked Mr Oddsson's Central Bank, who declined because the bulk of the currency reserves had already been lent to Kaupthing. Amazingly, Barclays, Kaupthing's clearing bank, attempted to stitch together a buyout of Kaupthing's UK corporate loan book at a massive discount, with much of the risk falling upon the UK Treasury. There was no deal. Kaupthing had been trying to meet that demand for £1.6 billion in stages. It did not come. According to a 2009 UK High Court judgement, £150 million of the flow of funding from Reykjavik was blocked by the Central Bank of Iceland. There was however an invisible run, which saw 19 per cent of all Kaupthing Edge's UK internet savings disappear in two days. Easy come, easy go.

Almost instantaneously, Iceland's banks, stock market and currency all collapsed. In London, access to BACS (Bankers' Automated Clearing Services) and CREST (a securities depository and settlement service) was stopped. Kaupthing London tried to sell itself to private equity, but that failed at three minutes past midnight on Wednesday, 8 October. Then at 7.49 a.m., an hour before its final FSA deadline to start increasing its liquidity, Kaupthing tried to participate in the recapitalisation of the UK banking system, announced twenty-seven minutes before, but it was rebuffed. There were actual bank runs – and fights – in Kaupthing branches in Reykjavik. High finance dried up for

Iceland's banks. The British government had used anti-terror legislation to seize assets of Landsbanki and the Icelandic Central Bank. International banking stability was not the intended application of the law, and there was no suggestion of actual links to terrorism, but it was the legal weapon to hand. Special financial powers were used with Kaupthing. Most of the Kaupthing internet deposits that had not disappeared into the mid-Atlantic were – with a certain irony – transferred to ING Direct. The US embassy cables at the time say that 'virtually all international payments to Iceland stopped. Two days later the Icelandic Central Bank established rations of foreign currencies at a fixed price and gave priority to importers of food, fuel and pharmaceuticals.' Solvent Icelandic businesses suffered from the collapse in the króna, and all their transactions had to be pre-paid. Businesses that had taken out loans in Japanese yen (to benefit from zero interest rates) now found that they were 136 per cent more indebted. Similar stories abound about ordinary Icelanders borrowing in euros and Swiss francs to buy cars. Sir Philip Green, the retail mogul, turned up on his private jet in the land of some of his favourite bankers, to see if he could snaffle back chunks of the British high street at a bargain price.

From the likes of Icesave arose a giant IceDebt. Each Briton was owed £40 by someone in Iceland. It was an iniquitous IOU that actually should have been owed by a handful of Icelandic bankers to a relatively small number of British bargain-hunting savers. Icesave had effectively used Iceland's public finances as security. The vagaries of deposit protection and European treaties remade the whole sorry affair into a £2.4 billion intergovernmental spat between two island nations. The UK and Dutch governments had stepped in to ensure that depositors were compensated. In Britain, even the uninsured amount was compensated. Both countries then pursued Iceland for the money. It was entirely reasonable that so many ordinary Icelanders saw this burden as an odious debt.

Iceland at first tried to pay less than the full amount it owed, with no interest. The negotiations became entangled with an IMF financing deal and prospects for accession to the European Union. Treasury officials told US diplomats that the UK would find it 'difficult' to support an IMF review in the absence of an Icesave deal. Icelandic officials told the same people that every Icelandic household would have to have paid a fifth of their annual household income for the next decade just to service the interest on the Icesave debt. 'If the UK had seized France's sovereign gold reserves like they had Iceland's, a war between France and the UK would have broken out by now,' said the Icelandic official. Tens of thousands of Icelanders took pictures of themselves holding 'I am not a terrorist' signs to send to Prime Minister Gordon Brown.

Ultimately, of course, a huge chunk of the blame should have fallen on those 'rate tarts' who decided to chase high interest rates without appreciating the higher risk. Certainly those with savings above £35,000 who were discretionarily bailed out by the chancellor using taxpayer's money can count themselves as incredibly lucky. It is difficult to justify the fact that UK savers lost none of their investments, potentially at the expense of completely innocent Icelandic taxpayers.

Why were they bailed out and not the depositors in BCCI (the Bank of Credit and Commerce International, which went into liquidation in 1991)? As former government pensions adviser Ros Altmann points out, 'If all bank deposits are 100 per cent protected, but pensions and other long-term savings are at best 90 per cent safe up to a £35,000 cap, why bother with pensions?'

The answer is that the Icelandic banks happened to collapse at the same time as half the British banking system. Treasury officials cautioned against a full payout. UK chancellor Alistair Darling calculated that the risk to financial stability of letting any British saver lose their money at that time would be too much. The Treasury only admitted this a year later, when defending a judicial review against its seizure of Kaupthing's UK assets. The UK deposit-protection fund was being bombarded with record numbers of calls from frightened savers. The FSA was concerned about a generalised run on weak banks by British savers. According to court documents, the FSA was worried that 'financial stability would be threatened as more consumers moved deposits to Ireland, where the government had said they would guarantee bank deposits in full'. So the government repaid the savers from taxpayers' money, even above the widely publicised deposit-protection limit. It then tapped Iceland for its share, and hoped to get the rest back from banks and our hard-up building societies, on whom this will fall as an appalling burden. Many UK building societies have had to pay out millions to fund the failure of a bank that used this same guarantee to acquire deposits at their expense. So the pain of the Icesave folly was socialised between Britain's financial institutions, the UK taxpayer and Iceland's taxpayers.

When a deal was done on repayment of the IceDebt, Icelandic MPs backing repayment received hate mail and thinly veiled death threats. Iceland's president called a referendum – only the second in the nation's history – on the repayment deal. On 6 March 2010 the people of Iceland voted '*Nei*' to the repayment plan, after a quarter of the population signed a petition rejecting the 'Icesave Bill'.

In the end Iceland got the IMF loan, but needed bilateral help too. The US strategic position was spelt out in a leaked State Department cable from the ambassador in Reykjavik. Until 2006, the USA had had a base near the airport, which was now used by NATO. The Chinese and the Russians were sniffing around oil reserves and new maritime trade routes opening up in the High North. 'Assistance from the USA at this crucial time would be a prudent investment in our own national security and economic wellbeing,' wrote the ambassador.

In the March 2010 referendum Iceland rejected the terms of the Icesave debt, risking international financial isolation, causing problems with the IMF, and jeopardising its negotiations to join the European Union. In fact Iceland did much more than just reject the pressure over Icesave.

In April 2010 financial calamity was almost matched by natural calamity. The Eyjafjallajökull volcanic eruption caused the largest disruption to air travel since the Second World War, stranding 5 million passengers in Europe and losing airlines £1 billion. Yet little more than 150 kilometres away from the eruption, Reykjavik's International Airport remained open while airports across much of Europe were forced to close for the best part of a week. The volcanic ash dispersed, not over Iceland, but into the jet stream and out over Europe.

Something rather similar had happened with Iceland's financial system a few months before, but that had been no fluke of nature. 'When our banks collapsed, they only partly collapsed on Iceland,' Már Guðmundsson, the new governor of the Icelandic Central Bank told me in January 2013. 'They mostly collapsed onto the rest of the world, into the sea, if you like. A large share of asset losses fell on other countries.'

Iceland took measures to keep the domestic banking system running in an effort to temper an already awful recession. It set up 'new banks' to preserve the access of the common man to the banking system. The Central Bank was recapitalised. Contrary to popular belief, there *was* a bailout of Iceland's banks. As Már Guðmundsson says, 'It is a myth that Iceland allowed its banking system to fail. It allowed the international part of the banking system to fail.' Mr Oddsson's Central Bank lost the funding loans it had provided to the collapsed banks. It was a cost equivalent to 13 per cent of Iceland's economy, a hit that sent the bat-cave into effective bankruptcy. Central banks cannot normally go bankrupt because of their monopoly on the presses that print the currency. Such technology counts for nothing if a crazed banking system is racking up liabilities in currencies it cannot print and for which the host central bank is unwilling to offer swap arrangements. Iceland's government also shelled out to recapitalise the new 'good' banks. Icelandic economic commentators Sigrún Davíðsdóttir and Thórólfur Matthíasson calculate total costs at 20–25 per cent of Iceland's GDP.

Steingrímur Sigfússon, the Left-Green Party leader elected into government in the aftermath of the crisis, put it like this: 'Iceland took an unorthodox approach. We let the banks fail, but it was not a matter of free choice for Iceland. It would not be right to look at this as a calculated decision.'

There were consequences for ordinary Icelanders, however. Although they lived in a country ranked by the UN as the world's wealthiest, they found that their credit cards temporarily stopped working abroad. But approximately 85 per cent of the losses – around €40 billion according to the Icelandic parliamentary investigation – fell on the world's big banks, particularly in Germany and Austria. Unlike the similar situation in Ireland, foreign bondholders were fried, and have not yet recovered their money. Iceland put in controls on the movement of capital. The burden on the Icelandic people would have been intolerable without this.

An emergency law moved deposits and assets to new banks. Landsbanki – the name that featured in a novel by a Nobel prize-winner and which dates back to the nineteenth century – remained. Out of the ashes of Kaupthing came Arion, while Glitnir reverted to its old name, Islandsbanki. The end result is a banking system that now fits the country better. Construction was severely hit too. But other sectors – fishing, tourism, energy, creative industries, the 'real economy of Iceland' – were still there, and benefited from the devaluation. The franchisee running Reykjavik's three branches of McDonald's pulled out on account of being obliged to import now expensive beef patties from Germany. The imports were simply replaced by domestic beef, and the restaurants were renamed 'Metro Burger'. Tourism was growing by 15–20 per cent per year, and more and more airlines were putting Iceland on their route maps. Using its abundant hydrothermal energy, Iceland is setting up new industries such as cheaply cooled data centres and silica purification for solar panels. 'We financed new banks very strongly,' the former finance minister Steingrímur Sigfússon told me. 'The minimum capital ratio was 16 per cent, now they are up at 22 to 23 per cent. They are strongly financed to assist their indebted customers in the real economy of Iceland.'

The end result was a reasonably rapid return to solid growth. Iceland's net government debt shot up to 60 per cent of GDP from below 10 per cent pre-crisis, but this was not a patch on Ireland, which is now 106 per cent. Severe and painful fiscal cuts were required. But Sigfússon says Iceland kept to its Nordic-style social contract. 'We made a very clear promise to preserve a Nordic-style welfare system,' he told me, 'and I believe we have done all we can. We introduced a wealth tax and a three-bracket income tax designed to shelter low-income groups. There was no rise in tax burden for low-income families. What we did is not just socially the right thing to do but also economic-ally successful. We did not cut unemployment benefits. One of the messages from Iceland is don't overlook the importance of keeping up the purchasing power of low-income groups.'

Iceland completed its IMF programme early, repaying all outstanding loans in August 2011. It then dipped its toes in international financial markets to raise government debts. By 2013 the post-crisis double-digit deficits had been stopped.

Ordinary Icelanders tended to take out mortgage loans that were indexed against inflation or in another currency entirely. It was a disaster in the crisis as the value of debts shot up while the króna dived and inflation surged. Property prices typically fell too. The end result was that a 90 per cent loan-to-value loan ended up at 140 or 150 per cent, leaving homeowners stranded in massive negative equity. Some argued for an across-the-board debt write-down of 20 per cent, but that was too unfocused for the new government. Instead, Iceland targeted householder debt relief to write off everything above 110 per cent of the value of the property. The IMF called it the most effective debt-relief programme since US president Roosevelt's plan in 1933 kept

800,000 Americans in their homes at an eventual profit to his government. There were several other schemes to support house-holders. The IMF called a special conference to learn lessons from Iceland's unorthodox policies. 'Iceland set an example by managing to preserve, and even strengthen, its welfare state during the crisis,' concluded the IMF's Nemat Shafik.

So Iceland bailed out its own people rather than the moronic foreign creditors of its insane banks. And the result, to date, is a growing economy. But the bailout has come with a caution. 'I can promise you,' Sigfússon told me, 'we would be watching very carefully to make sure the things that happened in Iceland in 2008 will never repeat themselves. For example, we will put restrictions on foreign-currency loans for a household if its income is solely Icelandic króna.'

Iceland's banking catharsis goes well beyond this. There was retribution as well as recovery.

Mr Hauksson's whiteboard

Sandwiched between India's embassy in Reykjavik and an Indian restaurant is a unique office in world finance. On the one hand it's the typical Nordic, high-design, wood-finished, funky work-space. But there are security keypads and giant steel doors that seem more appropriate to a high-security prison. In the airy loft meeting room, Ólafur Hauksson scribbles onto a whiteboard a complicated spider diagram of cross-ownership and apparent corruption. He is the Icelandic special prosecutor of financial crimes, a genial bear of a man, but a man on a mission. He was elevated from district tax enforcement in the sleepy town of Akranes to become the Judge Dredd of Iceland's financial collapse.

Policing and prosecution occur in the same office. A rogues' gallery of Iceland's financiers have been dragged in for ques-tioning by a staff of 110. 'We have all powers of police: arrest, hearings, searches,' Hauksson tells me. 'And we do not need a court order to enter a financial institution to look for information, because bank secrecy has been lifted towards us, so we do not need a warrant to look at the financial institutions that have been [helped] by the state – which is most of them.'

The cases are complex and detailed – and remarkable. Progress has been slow, but even after his bank investigation winds down, Hauksson expects cases will still be processing through the Icelandic court system for years to come. He has none of the fears expressed in London or New York about damaging the image and stability of a hallowed financial-services sector. 'The "Too-big-to-jail" phrase describes a fear of entering big cases,' he tells me, 'but then you're leaving a part of society without proper policing. You need to have the rule of law, and regulations apply to everyone.'

A large part of the legal difficulty comes in proving individual culpability. It would be simpler to establish corporate negligence, but Hauksson says there's no point in pursuing bankrupt state-owned banks on corporate charges. 'It's very difficult to point to the precise time they stepped over the line. Was it part of a process or a conscious decision?'

Hauksson's biggest scalp was Larus Welding, the ex-chief executive of Glitnir, who, together with one of his colleagues, was sentenced to two months' jail for a fraud involving a loan to a Glitnir shareholder. (Welding is appealing this.) Another case, still to be heard, questions Kaupthing's emergency pre-collapse cash call from the Gulf in September 2008. The money for the purchase by a Qatari sheikh of a large stake in Kaupthing ultimately came from a bank in Iceland called... Kaupthing. The charge is that the bank lent the money to instil confidence in itself just ahead of the massive bank crisis. It is certainly documented that the companies connected to Qatari investors were granted large loans by Kaupthing around the same time as buying a 5 per cent stake in the bank. The defendants in the case deny the charges.

But whatever happens to Hauksson's cases, the process has

been instructive. The excesses of Icelandic financiers are seared onto the national consciousness, and the special prosecution process is now tattooing it on their foreheads. Iceland will not allow such a catastrophic fiasco to happen again.

Part of the process of Iceland's recovery has been the appointment of several high-flying women. In 2013 I was invited to the Althing, Iceland's millennium-old parliament, to meet the new finance minister. Katrín Júlíusdóttir is 38 years old, and has recently returned from maternity leave. She laments the bad decisions of the banks, and the cross-ownership that made the system 'fall like a domino'. 'There was a blind eye from the right-wing government who wanted to be a financial centre of the world,' she tells me. 'It's a crazy idea when you have a 300,000 population and your own currency.'

Norwegian colleagues could not understand why Iceland had not reined in the cronyistic cross-ownership that had felled Norwegian banks in the 1990s. It was not widespread corruption, she said, but 'more the belief in the market and this belief in neoliberalism'. Those who had argued for stronger financial supervision were met with accusations that they were in favour of the 'surveillance industry'.

Ms Júlíusdóttir's government has been fiscally austere, cutting a 14.6 per cent deficit down to 0.2 per cent in four years. But other shibboleths of the market have been dispensed with. As the króna tumbled, capital controls were introduced by the Central Bank as an emergency measure. Iceland has to move delicately in her plan to lift capital controls. About a quarter of the value of the entire economy in Icelandic króna is owned by foreigners, but trapped by capital controls, and waiting for a route off the island. The amount of capital that will potentially leave Iceland will surge once the likes of Kaupthing are unwound. The controls will be slowly lifted for individuals, but Iceland will need tools to control the potential outflow. The ultimate tool for Júlíusdóttir was to join the European Union and the Eurozone, but after losing the April 2013 general election, this seemed off the agenda.

In the absence of the EU option, other economic thinkers on the island think that the way forward for a small open economy like Iceland is to copy the Asian countries. Iceland should have a managed floating exchange rate, and a large build-up of foreign-exchange reserves. 'It has served the Asians well,' says Guðmundsson at the Central Bank. So that's an end to inflation targeting, and for the banks an end to the European single market. A single market without a single safety net in banking was one of the causes of Iceland's excess. 'All of this was nonsense because there's a huge difference between growing tomatoes or making shoes and banking. Banks make money out of maturity mismatches [e.g. between lending long-term and borrowing short-term]. It's risky.'

The ethnic homogeneity of the population of Iceland makes it a much sought-after testing ground for genetic experiments. Iceland's plunge into financial calamity, and its subsequent recovery, have also turned out to be important experiments for the rest of the world – experiments involving burning bond-holders, capital controls, welfare, currency regimes, financial regulation and the criminal prosecution of bankers. The nature of the collapse has also shone a light on some of the most questionable practices in global finance. That could be because Icelandic bankers really were more devious, more cunning and on occasion more fraudulent than their counterparts elsewhere. Or perhaps only in Iceland, on that barren, beautiful island in the middle of the North Atlantic, has a clear picture emerged of what financiers and governments around the world really got up to in the go-go years and the crash that followed.

Nowhere else in the world is such detail available. 'The Althing Special Investigative Committee, and its 3,200-page report, lists loans to certain individuals in addition to close scrutiny of everything the banks did. Icelanders know more – much much more – about the operations of its banks than any other nation,' says the economic commentator Sigrún Davíðsdóttir. In the UK and Germany, for example, I shudder to imagine the equivalent tales, emails and desperation as financiers crossed the line of default. Are we really to believe that none of the cronyism and fraud revealed in Iceland occurred in larger financial centres? The world has been looking at this island through a lens, but I suspect in truth that that lens is really a mirror.

Standing next to Oddsson's bat-cave by night, half a decade on, I can see that Iceland has changed. A spectacular light show sparkles on the side of Reykjavik's new Harpa concert hall, completed since the crisis. The concert hall was meant to be the showpiece gift from Landsbanki's largest shareholder, anchoring a development that would have included hotels, shopping centres and a new headquarters for Landsbanki. The crisis put paid to that, so now Harpa stands majestically alone against a backdrop of Mount Esja, and, on occasion, the northern lights.

Davíð Oddsson was not all wrong. Capital controls remain in place. 'Our' money may not have been safe in 2008. But five years on, 'their money' might just be escaping at last from the danger zone.

CHAPTER 4

12/11: THE CHINESE ROOT CANALS OF CRISIS

Dramatis personae

Deng Zhi, a 24-year-old Chinese, one of 262 million
'migrant workers'
Zhang Youwen, who works in Dong Guan in a
rubber factory
His wife **Li Chun Rong**, an unemployed migrant worker
Yi Bin, a migrant worker from Sichuan province
Emperor Qianlong, fourth Qing emperor of all-China
(1735–96)
Lin Zexu, nineteenth-century Chinese administrator,
scholar, and writer of a letter to Queen Victoria
Jin Liqun, chairman of the supervisory board of the Chinese
sovereign wealth fund; Shakespeare scholar
Lindsey Ashworth, development director at Peel
Holdings in Liverpool
Psy, Korean popstar, singer of 'Gangnam Style'
David Wei, former chief executive, Alibaba.com
Lizzie Lieng, manager of Shanghai Union
lighting factory
Professor Justin Lin, former World Bank
chief economist

12/11 didn't merit much attention. In the closing months of 2001 the world was preoccupied with the immediate aftermath of 9/11. But on 11 December 2001, precisely three months after the attack on the World Trade Center in New York, the World Trade Organisation (WTO) was at the centre of an event that was to cast an even longer shadow over the twenty-first century, changing more people's lives around the world than Osama Bin Laden's attacks on America. Yet few know it even happened, let alone its date.

China's admission to the World Trade Organisation changed the game for America, Europe and most of Asia, and indeed for any country in possession of industrially valuable resources, such as oil and metals. It was a largely unnoticed event of epic geopolitical and economic importance. Up until this point China's global economic role had been principally as one of the world's biggest manufacturers of plastic gubbins and cheap tat. Important, yes, but neither world-beating nor world-changing.

China's accession to the top table of world trade heralded a massive global transformation. A powerful combination of China's willing workforce, its super-high-tech factories, and the special relationship between the Chinese government and Western multinationals has changed the face of the planet. An army of cheap Chinese labour began to produce the goods that underpin Western living standards, as China seamlessly inserted itself into the supply chains of the world's biggest companies.

Economists call it a 'supply shock', and its impact certainly was shocking. Its effects are still reverberating around the world, from China's rural backwaters to the world's most powerful central banks, and to every home in Britain.

It is more than 1,500 kilometres from the lush hills of Zhugao County in Sichuan Province to the factories on China's coast. It's a long journey repeatedly taken by Deng Zhi, a 24-year-old migrant worker. Since the age of 17, he has been regularly making this twenty-six-hour journey from farm to factory. Typically that has meant working twelve-hour days, six days a week, at an electronics factory in Dong Guan, on the Pearl River Delta. Deng Zhi is paid the equivalent of £100 a month.

'How much can you earn from farming?' he asks himself. 'Working in the cities, you make at least 1,000 renminbi [£100] a month. How many kilos of rice can you buy with this money? It just doesn't pay to farm.'

Of his £100 factory wages, Deng Zhi sends back about £30 to his family to pay for health, education and pensions, none of which are adequately provided by the state. That still leaves him with at least four times what he would have earned in the fields. Part of his family's land in Sichuan goes uncultivated. 'I don't even think of farming the land. I don't know how to hold a hoe. As long as you have skills, you'll find work. Even if I can't find any work in the city, I won't come back to farm,' he says.

Deng Zhi is not a slave. But he is paid less than the equivalent of what it cost to hire a slave labourer in the American South in the era of slavery. And, in effect, Deng Zhi works for you. Or at least he did work for you, up until around 2008. Then he started to moonlight for the Chinese government, filling the coffers of its massive sovereign piggy bank. So right now he wants to work mainly for himself. Factory labour whose surplus value has been expropriated by rentier capital, just as Marx and Engels said of Europe's rapid industrialisation. Except in China the ultimate rentier capitalist is the Chinese Communist Party. From farm to factory to sovereign wealth fund and back to free spirit, Deng Zhi's story is also the story of how China kept the West rich, and itself became richer. Now China faces severe growing pains in managing the desire of the mass of its people for a fair share of such riches.

Deng Zhi's life is typical of the 262 million migrant workers who cross the length and breadth of China to work seventy-two-hour weeks, for £100 a month. Together, they form the biggest human migration on the planet, a monumental demographic shift of a quarter of a billion people in search of work, every year, 166 million moving thousands of miles to different provinces. They are the invisible labour force whose efforts have underpinned rising living standards in the West, and the rising influence of China around the globe.

You can trace the roots of this extraordinary phenomenon back to the beginning of this century, when the Great Migration was sparked by the loosening of restrictions on rural migration. The numbers of migrant workers had been static at 60–70 million during the 1990s. But in the first decade of the twenty-first century their number trebled to a size bigger than the workforce of the USA or the European Union. Soon Chinese migrant workers alone will exceed the combined workforce of the USA and Eurozone.

After Chinese New Year, the nation's rural transport hubs swarm with migrant workers returning to the cities. On a packed bus from Zhugao sits Zhang Youwen, who also works in Dong Guan, in a rubber factory. His wife Li Chun Rong has just lost her job in a shoe factory. 'We make money for our two children and our parents,' Li Chun says. 'We need to save for our own old age too. We don't dare to spend money. We have to send our children to school and take care of our parents. Everything costs money.'

That is the double whammy of the Chinese system: enough communism for there to be no pensions, no life insurance, no health insurance, for most workers; and enough capitalism for there to be no unemployment insurance and no welfare state. Between the rock of undeveloped financial services and the hard place of a limited welfare state, Chinese migrant workers are motivated to serve the factory owners.

At the roundabouts that separate the rows of factories in Dong Guan, dozens of migrant workers gather in the New Year chill. With one hand they drag a wheelie suitcase, packed with their belongings. In the other, they hold their *hukou* card, a precious piece of ID to be shown to their prospective employers as they make the rounds of keyboard factory, shoe factory and toy factory, asking for work. In 2006, Communist Party officials from Jintang County in Sichuan set up an office to persuade the factory-owners of Dong Guan to take on their youth. Banners outside some factories invite wandering migrant workers to apply for jobs at under £150 a month, and sometimes specify 18–35-year-old females, who are less trouble.

The *hukou* system is crucial. All workers need this purple, passport-style document (formally known as the 'Household Register'), which is issued at birth by the Ministry of Public Security. The system severely curtails rural workers, or *nongmin*, from access to basic facilities in the city: no housing, no pensions, little health coverage and no educational rights. The children of rural *hukou*-holders are not even allowed to take national college entrance exams in the cities where their parents toil. Instead, they are forced to travel hundreds, even thousands, of kilometres to their rural homes if they want to continue their education after the age of sixteen.

For its critics, the *hukou* system acts as a kind of apartheid that allows discrimination against and abuse of a large chunk of China's population. This is effectively a form of twenty-first century serfdom, for the benefit of factory owners, the Chinese government, and consumers in the West. But its supporters say China needs *hukou* as a tool to control its massive internal flows of human migration. They point out that China's major cities do not have the mass homelessness and sprawling slums found, for example, in India.

There may not be mass homelessness or sprawling slums in China's industrial cities, but for China's migrant workers the outlook is far from rosy. When I visited China in 2009, at the height of the global financial crisis, in the fraught months following the collapse of world trade, the reverberations were visible in the streets of Dong Guan.

I spoke to a young woman sitting outside a factory waiting to hear about her job application. 'I first looked in Shenzhen,' she tells me. 'It's difficult to find work now. It used to be easy to go and work in a factory. Not the same now. We're still waiting to hear from the factory. If we can't find work here, we'll go look in Guangzhou. We won't go home.' An older woman tells me: 'I worked here for three days. They don't want me. I'll go look at the factory down the road. I won't go home. My cousin works in the factory over there. I'll go work there too.' A security guard describes scenes worthy of Dickens at his bleakest: 'Every day, there are workers coming and going from this factory. They hire workers for about a week. If they don't work hard enough, they let them go.'

At a job agency in Dong Guan, desperate migrant workers such as Yi Bin, also from Sichuan, look forlornly for employment. He used to work in factories making toys and electronics, but has had nothing for two weeks. 'I have no social security,' he tells me. 'Some factories provide a little security but not enough. If I don't work, I have no income. I've been spending my savings in the last two weeks. We have lands at home [back in Sichuan]. We don't go hungry. It's just that we have no money to spend.' Yi Bin is fairly philosophical about his circumstances. Again, though, he is working almost entirely to send £1,000 back per year for his children's school and his parent's pension. 'I made about 1,500 RMB [renminbi] a month last year. Before that, when the economy was good, we could make over 2,000 RMB a month. Last year, many factories laid off workers and offered lower wages. We expect even lower wages this year. It's normal. The prices are not lower though. It's a bit of pressure on us,' he says. At this point the boss of the job agency turns up. He looks down at Yi Bin and two of his friends, barking questions about their experience and what wage they would be willing to work for.

Here, in nominally Communist China, this is what an extreme free-market labour force looks like. There are very few social protections, and workers are hired and fired at will. Wages are entirely dictated by supply and demand for workers, and for the products they produce. Europe and North America did not just outsource production, they also outsourced the sharpest edges of the free market. It can be no mystery that workers save as much as they can.

Despite the cut-throat nature of the labour market, people keep flooding from the fields to the factories. As Yi Bin told me, 'It's impossible for me to go home to farm. I haven't farmed for years. It's better to learn a skill and work in the cities. Farming makes no money at all. If we stay on the farm, the whole family would work all our lives just to have enough grain to feed ourselves.'

The appropriate response from us in the West to all the rural Chinese workers who have flocked to the cities should be first and foremost 'Thank You' – although with some caveats. This enormous and industrious workforce underpinned the growth in living standards during the Great Boom in the West. But this ready supply of workers also created a new type of demand.

In 2000, China was the seventh-largest goods exporter in the world, with a modest share of under 4 per cent of the total. It quickly reached the number one spot. China's annual growth rate, already at 8 per cent, went stratospheric, peaking at 14 per cent at the height of the world boom.

Container ships are the juggernauts of global trade. In the five years after China joined the WTO in 2001, the number of containers on ships coming in and out of China doubled from 40 million to over 80 million. By 2011, a decade after China joined the WTO, the number of containers going in and out of China had more than trebled to 129 million. Around half of the containers going into China were empty, whereas nearly all those leaving China were full of exports. Already by 2003 the traders of ship capacity noticed that there was no capacity left.

There were simply not enough ships. And the ships that existed were not big enough. The biggest container ships on the planet at the time of China's WTO accession belonged to the Sovereign class, which each held the equivalent of 8,000 containers. In November 2006, when the 400-metre *Emma Maersk* visited Felixstowe harbour it was laden with 12,500 containers, all of them filled with Christmas gifts made in China. By this point, shipbuilders had given up bothering to ensure that ships could fit through the Panama Canal. All that mattered was the Suez Canal and the vital Asia–Europe shipping route. By 2013, 'Triple-E' class vessels were carrying the equivalent of over 18,000 containers from China to northern Europe.

Not only was there not enough capacity to carry China's exports, there was not enough capacity to make the ships that might in the future carry China's exports. China itself went from building 100 vessels in 2001 to more than 1,000 in 2010, as global banks piled in to fund existing dockyards. China briefly overtook South Korea as the world's number one ship-builder. Speculation ran amok, and there emerged an insane bubble in the price of any greenfield land close to a navigable river that might at some point in the future be used to build ships to carry goods. Prices were being quoted not only for cargo ships that did not exist, but also for the non-existent dockyards that were supposed to build them.

But it is not all smoke and mirrors. In modern mega-ports such as Shanghai, China has given concrete expression to the reality of its export drive – as I found when I drove along Expressway S2. Leaving the neon-lit skyscrapers, the magnetic-ally levitating train and the bright lights of the Shanghai Bund behind me, I followed the six-lane expressway as it snaked 30 kilometres out into the depths of Hangzhou Bay. On a map, it looks like a ridiculous mistake, a bridge to nowhere. But the Donghai Bridge, the world's longest at sea when it was opened in 2005, is an umbilical cord for Chinese intercontinental trade. The great fear for ordinary Chinese truckers is breaking down along the sea bridge. The only licensed tow truck has been known to charge thousands of yuan for a rescue.

The bridge connects Shanghai to China's newest gateway, itself a remarkable symbol of China's economic transformation. In 2000 there was almost nothing here. Yangshan comprised three rocky barren islands, where the only economic activity was fishing. By 2005 the gaps between the islands had been filled in and turned into a giant artificial landmass, hosting one of the world's biggest container ports, reclaimed from the East China Sea. The Yangshan Deep Water Port had to be so far out to sea because Shanghai's river port is shallow and surrounded by mud flats, whereas the biggest modern cargo ships need water at least 15 metres deep. After just half a decade of operation Yangshan now handles more containers than Shanghai's river port did, yet that port has also continued to grow. A terminal for receiving liquefied gas has also been constructed at Yangshan.

Port authorities are reclaiming more land from the deep ocean, helping Yangshan grow exponentially and the Shanghai ports overtake both Hong Kong and Singapore as the world's largest container port. The ambition does not end there. As part of the central government's twelfth five-year plan a new city is to be built on the land side of the bridge, with metro connections, a power station, and an entirely new financial centre for global shipping. Yangshan is just one example of China's investment in freight infrastructure. There has also been a massive expansion of China's highway network, which increased from 4,700 km in 1997 to 25,100 km in 2002 and to 96,000 km in 2012.

In addition to a state-of-the-art freight infrastructure, China also needs materials such as metals, minerals and fossil fuels to support its manufacturing boom. One key material is steel, essential to China's burgeoning automotive and electrical-appliance industries. In 2005 China became, for the first time, a net exporter of steel, and has since become the world's largest exporter. Through the 1990s, China's production of steel had hovered at around 100 million tonnes per year. After WTO membership, it exploded to around 500 million tonnes by 2008. By 2012 it had topped 700 million tonnes. China now accounts for 50 per cent of world production. It now produces more steel on its own than the rest of the globe managed together, just ten years ago. The same goes for ceramic tiles, and plenty of other ingredients of industry.

The cost of shipping dry raw materials, such as iron ore and coal, quadrupled in the two years following China's WTO membership, fell back a little, and then quadrupled again before the peak of the boom.

The Great Migration of rural workers combined with the Great Mobilisation of logistics and infrastructure – these have been the two core Chinese contributors to the mega-boom in the developed world, which has seen the cost of consumer goods tumble. Since 2000, these epic transitions in China's economy have transmitted cheap prices out from mainland China, along the length of the Donghai Bridge, through ports such as Yangshan into the world's container ships and so into the shops, living rooms and ultimately the wallets of the Western world. In electronics, clothing, toys and furniture, China has become the dominant source of supply, forcing down export prices all around the world. Economists noticed a 'once-for-all' shock in global prices following China's WTO entry.

China's clothing exports doubled between 2000 and 2005, and its share of the value of global trade went from one-fifth to one-third. After 2005, production quotas in the textile industry were also lifted, leading to an even bigger production shift to China. In 2000, the Dominican Republic and the Central American Free Trade Area were the biggest exporters to the USA, accounting for 14 per cent of US imports, as compared to China's 13.3 per cent. By 2009, China's clothing exports to the USA had destroyed all-comers, trebling to just under two-fifths of US imports.

What did this massive transition look like on the ground back in China? About four hours' drive around Hangzhou Bay from the Donghai Bridge is Shengzhou, known as 'Tie City'. If you wear a tie, it was probably made here. Two in five of all the ties made in the world come from this town: 350 million fat ties, skinny ties, silk ties, even washable ties. While schools in the USA bulk-order their ties from websites for less than a dollar each, workers in Shengzhou are paid much less than a dollar for an hour of work.

In the mid-1980s, Chinese entrepreneurs travelled to Como

in northern Italy and returned with six high-end tie-looming machines. At the time, Como was famous for its silk ties. Now there are over a thousand tie-makers in Shengzhou, and hundreds of computerised weaving machines. Tie City serves some, though not all, of the top global fashion brands. While US net entrepreneurs sell high-quality silk ties made in Shengzhou for $15 over the internet, tens of thousands of jobs in the silk industry have been lost in Como.

But in Tie City, they point to the fact that Shengzhou has been making silk for centuries. The tie merchants intend to develop in-house design and branding skills to capture even more of the profits from this industry. Five thousand years ago, Confucius wrote legends that told of the start of the silk industry in China. The silkworms have returned to their home mulberry trees, three millennia on from the opening of the Silk Road.

From petrodollar to Sinodollar

China's astonishing manufacturing surge did much more than just cut prices for Western consumers and increase profits for Western multinationals. The dollars, pounds and euros that flowed in to pay Chinese manufacturers had to go somewhere, if not to the workers.

Petrodollars and eurodollars were the names given in the 1970s to US currency earned by oil states but traded, re-used and spent in Europe and not in the USA. In the twenty-first century, a new kid arrived on the block: enter the Sinodollar. China is making so much money from foreign exports that it is throwing up surpluses to match those of the richest oil economies. China's migrant workers have become a tradable commodity.

Take our US tie entrepreneur who sells a dozen Chinese silk ties for $180. Most of that money stays in the USA in the form of higher profits and cheaper goods. Just $12 goes to China to pay the manufacturer in Shengzhou. From that money, the Chinese manufacturer has to pay his workers and suppliers in

Chinese renminbi, as well as taking a profit. So, say he goes to a Shengzhou branch of the Agricultural Bank of China to cash the dollars in. At this point, a bank in the UK or USA would be able to retrade the dollars wherever it thought it could make the most money. Not in China. Here, by law, the surplus dollars have to be passed up to the People's Bank of China, the Chinese equivalent of the Bank of England or the US Federal Reserve. The People's Bank of China then passes them on to the guardian of China's dollars: the State Administration for Foreign Exchange (SAFE). The clue is in the acronym. China's SAFE contained less than $25 billion in 1994, and around $200 billion in 2000. By 2012, its war chest stood at $3.3 trillion.

From ties to T-bonds, the dollars flow in from multinational firms to Chinese manufacturers, and from them, to SAFE, via the People's Bank of China. And SAFE reinvests a hefty $1.2 trillion chunk of this dollar windfall back into US government debt, known as Treasury bonds, effectively creating a cheap loan for the US government, and bailing them out of spiralling debt costs. This colossal intercontinental cashflow makes China the USA's principal lender alongside Japan and the Gulf nations, and increases China's political influence on the global stage.

China's rise as the new banker to the USA was swift and decisive. In 1997 China was the seventh largest lender to the USA. Between 2003 and 2010, a third of all the new debt issued to foreigners by the US government was snapped up by China. An extra trillion dollars helped to pay for President George W. Bush's wars in Afghanistan and Iraq. China officially overtook Japan as the largest lender to the USA in 2008.

Looked at another way, by 2011 SAFE had lent America the equivalent of just under $1,000 from every man, woman and child in China. It would take a single Chinese worker, on average, four months to earn $1,000. It would take Deng Zhi nearly a year. This huge investment in US debt left every single American citizen effectively indebted to Deng Zhi and his colleagues, to the tune of $4,000 per head. The USA is estimated to pay about

$40 billion annually in interest on this debt, or about $30 for every Chinese person – the equivalent of three days' work in a toy factory.

The net result of all of this is that long-term interest rates in the USA and parts of western Europe have plummeted, helping people, companies and governments. China also bought hundreds of billions of dollars of 'agencies', government-guaranteed US mortgage bonds issued by the eccentrically named Fannie Mae and Freddie Mac. So China was essentially lending the cash for the loans that underpin the American housing market. In fact, just before Lehman Brothers' collapse in June 2008, China actually owned more Agency bonds ($544 billion) than US Treasury bonds ($535 billion). China was pouring its Sinodollars into these Agencies at an incredible rate – much faster than into conventional US government debt. In two years, pre-crisis, its Agency holdings doubled. Small wonder that Fannie Mae and Freddie Mac were effectively nationalised in September 2008. China could have faced massive losses. The Chinese government sold off their Agency holdings almost as rapidly as they were built up, halving it within three years, and shifting to US Treasury bonds.

Thus not only were the Chinese peasants migrating en masse, lowering the living costs of the wealthiest people in the world, some of the fruits of their labour were being lent back at low interest to those very same people. Two Thank-Yous are necessary, one for the cheap goods, and another for the cheap loans. It was an insane form of pan-Pacific bonded-labour-vendor-finance. A dim sum, one might say. It surely can't last.

A sign of things that may be to come was glimpsed in September 2012, when a fifty-strong crowd broke away from an anti-Japanese protest in Beijing to surround the car of Gary Locke, the US ambassador to China. 'Pay us back our money!' the crowd chanted. 'Down with US imperialism!' Some of the demonstrators hurled projectiles, damaging the embassy car. Video of this extraordinary protest was captured by dissident artist Ai Weiwei on his iPhone.

The massive stockpile of Sinodollars has begun to enter public consciousness in China and the USA. It is the fundamental axis of global economic geography: a mammoth insurance policy, China's currency con, an economic aneurysm for America – and perhaps even the actual root cause of the financial crisis. There is some truth in all of these explanations. On opposite sides of this dim sum, however, opinions are polarising.

For America, China is manipulating its currency artificially to prolong its export boom. The size of China's foreign currency reserves, at one point half of China's GDP, far outweighs its needs. For China, the reserves are a consequence of the efforts of its people, a sensible insurance policy against the speculative attacks made against the currencies of neighbouring countries during the East Asian financial crisis of 1997. China vowed that the agony, indignity and loss of sovereignty inflicted on its near neighbours then would not occur to it.

China does not have a happy historic memory of how its large trade surpluses have been dealt with by more powerful nations. For centuries, China was not really interested in the goods the West was trying to sell it, as attested by a letter written in the late eighteenth century to George III by the Emperor Qianlong: 'We possess all things and of the highest quality. . . I set no value on the strange and useless objects and have no use of your country's manufactures.' (Chinese officials today are likely to say very much the same thing.) At this time, China was exporting teas, silks and porcelain to Europe, and Britain was obliged to settle three-quarters of its trade deficit by transferring silver to China. Britain – somewhat less than ethically – sought to change the balance in the mid-nineteenth century by growing opium in Bengal for export to addicts in China. British banks such as HSBC (originally the Hong Kong and Shanghai Banking Corporation) have their origins in this trade. Emperor Daoguang objected, and ordered raids on the opium dealers, carried out by the celebrated Chinese adminis-trator and scholar Lin Zexu. In a letter to Queen Victoria in

1839, Lin Zexu wrote: 'The wealth of China is used to profit the barbarians... By what right do they then in return use the poisonous drug to injure the Chinese people?' The British remained deaf to his appeals, and in June 1840 an expeditionary force of barracks ships, gunboats and smaller vessels carrying 4,000 sailors and marines arrived in the Pearl River Delta, so launching the First Opium War. The Chinese have not forgotten this humiliation. The original pits where British opium was seized and burnt are still maintained in Dong Guan, itself now a symbol of Chinese global trade, alongside a statue of Lin Zexu. In 2010, the Chinese government even objected to David Cameron wearing the unrelated Remembrance poppy on his lapel during a trade visit to China.

For opium then, substitute US Treasury bonds today. China's wider surpluses are effectively balanced out by these epic purchases of government debt. Purchases continued through the depths of the financial crisis and past the downgrade of America's AAA credit rating. That seems like an addiction. Arguably it was the USA and parts of western Europe that became addicted to the wave of cheap credit that this trade unleashed. The bond binge was part of the mechanism used by the Chinese government to keep exports booming with a cheap Chinese currency. Buying dollars helps keep the Chinese currency weaker. The exchange rate offered by the bank to the factory and by the central bank to the bank, is also centrally controlled and managed.

What is particularly amazing about this trading relationship, this monetary marriage, this curious economic embrace, is how little either player wanted to talk about it as the imbalance grew. It was not until the debates during the 2008 presidential elections that Senator Obama expressed regret that the USA had borrowed the money. 'Nothing is more important than us no longer borrowing $700 billion or more from China and sending it to Saudi Arabia. It's mortgaging our children's future,' he said.

Fast forward just four months, and President Obama was sending his Secretary of State, Hillary Clinton, to Beijing with the words: 'I appreciate greatly the Chinese government's continuing confidence in United States Treasuries.' Not exactly weaning America off the teat of Chinese credit.

The noises that were previously all about reassurance then began turning rather combative. Again I was dumbfounded in July 2009 by an audience intervention at a speech by White House chief economic adviser Larry Summers. A member of the state-run Chinese press publicly asked Mr Summers if he could guarantee the safety of China's investments in the USA. Mr Summers started talking about healthcare policy. These were the first skirmishes in a new currency war.

The uncertainty over those $544 billion of Agency mortgage bonds, worth 10 per cent of its GDP, must have spooked the Chinese leadership in 2008. Some leading US economists suggested a 'haircut' on the holders of Agency bonds. In the words of US economist Brad Setser, they were 'Too Chinese To Fail'. The then US Treasury secretary put the Agencies into 'conservatorship' – a euphemism for nationalisation. The Chinese, however, started to sell these bonds rapidly. As luck would have it, two months later, in November 2008, the US Federal Reserve announced, under its version of quantitative easing (see pages 280–81), that it would be buying $600 billion of Agency bonds and debts. It was precisely enough to offset the Chinese sell-off.

But when in November 2010 America announced that the Federal Reserve was going to print an additional $600 billion, the quiet reserve of economic diplomacy was jettisoned for the monetary megaphone. Trillions of dollars of extra US government borrowing was seen in Beijing as an attempt at backdoor devaluation of the dollar, to boost US exports and make Chinese goods more expensive for Western consumers. China began to send clear messages, even threats, that it was pondering reining in its purchases of dollar debt. As Premier Wen Jiabao said, 'We've lent a huge amount of capital to the United States, and of course we're concerned about the security of our assets.'

And then, in November 2010, Dagong, China's international

credit-rating agency (a rival to the Western triumvirate of Standard & Poor's, Moody's and Fitch) downgraded US government debt to A+. Naturally it maintained China's rating as AAA. This downgrading was generally dismissed as a joke or propaganda, though S&P followed suit less than a year later. Put simply, though, whose credit rating matters – the lender's or the borrower's? Dagong predicted a world heading for 'utter chaos in the international currency system'.

The statement from Dagong continued, taking no prisoners: 'In essence the depreciation of the US dollar adopted by the US government indicates that its solvency is on the brink of collapse, therefore it wants to cut its debt through the act of devaluation... ; such a move has severely harmed the interests of creditors.'

The joke in Shanghai was that as the Chinese had just paid for their own much-needed £400 billion stimulus entirely from their own pockets, they did not feel the need to pay for America's stimulus too. At the time of the crisis, China stopped treading carefully, and instead decided to show the world it had some muscle – financial muscle.

'Don't take Polonius's words at face value,' I am told by Jin Liqun, the official who supervises China's national piggy bank, the China Investment Corporation. I had suggested to him that the CIC followed the advice offered by Polonius to his son in Shakespeare's *Hamlet*: 'Neither a borrower nor a lender be.' In 2007 the CIC was allocated $200 billion of those massive Chinese foreign-exchange reserves to make strategic investments for China.

Mr Jin, a 63-year-old Shakespeare scholar, does have plenty of advice for the debt-addled, formerly industrialised Western nations. 'You can borrow. We in China borrowed a huge amount of money over the past few decades. Those moneys were invested in basic infrastructure, upgrading our technology. Now we have very strong export performance. So to borrow or to lend is alright,' he advises. 'Don't do it excessively,' he adds.

In its early years, the CIC made some fairly spectacular

mis-steps in financial services. It lost billions on investments on Wall Street. Within China, there was mounting criticism that the nation's carefully accumulated savings were being squandered on saving greedy Western financiers.

A new strategy emerged, and a new type of Chinese investment is on the rise.

The new Chinese empire strikes back

On the other side of the world, on Merseyside, another revolution is brewing. Not amongst the dockers, or within the local Labour Party. This is a new geo-economic revolution, a revolution in which China is starting the next phase of its planned ascent. China is now using its financial muscle to invest in Western infrastructure rather than Western debt.

The willingness of the Chinese state to use its giant national piggy bank to fund Britain's infrastructure is trumpeted as vindication of the UK government's tough fiscal policy. It is quite some coup for Chancellor George Osborne, the result of meticulous attempts to woo great vats of capital from the East. British government ministers actually present investors from China and the Middle East with lists of UK infrastructure projects looking for investment. Even before the election, the men running China's wealth funds were surprised by the inviting offer from Gordon Brown that almost everything in the UK was for sale, bar defence and media. It was some contrast to the attitude they had faced in Paris and Berlin. The approach has paid off. Britain is at the front of the queue, way ahead of the Eurozone banks, which would dearly love a helping Chinese hand.

China's capital is heading to places like the Wirral rather than the financial districts of Paris, Milan or Madrid. The Atlantic Gateway is the name given to an extraordinary project at the mouth of the River Mersey, a project that is regularly mentioned at bilateral ministerial meetings between Britain and China. Developers Peel Holdings have created a Chinese-style vision of extraordinary transformation and development of old dockyards, involving the construction of extensive new office space, skyscrapers housing thousands of apartments, and waterfront leisure facilities. This is the Wirral Waters project, and it is twinned with a similar development on the Liverpool side of the Mersey. This truly is designed to be the Atlantic Gateway to Britain from China in many ways.

'I want Chinese tenants, I've already got a Chinese business partner, and I want a Chinese bank,' says Lindsey Ashworth, Development Director at Peel. 'Money is very tight at the moment. China has trillions of dollars that it's sat on that it wants to invest. We work together with China really well, it's a marriage made in heaven.'

To kick off the Atlantic Gateway development, up to a thousand Chinese manufacturers will share a massive trade centre to showcase their products to the whole of Europe – a bridgehead in the European Union for Chinese exports and investment. It is the first of its kind in western Europe and includes space for Chinese manufacturers to use local labour for final assembly that would officially count as 'made in Britain', and therefore offer free access to the whole European Union.

The Atlantic Gateway is just the start. If this project goes to plan and overcomes local planning concerns in Liverpool, there is a remarkable prize. The developers happen to own the Manchester Ship Canal, and are tilting the marketing of their project to meet the appetite for Chinese-style mega-investments of tens of billions of pounds. Think Chinese funding for a mega-city connecting Liverpool and Manchester, and you might begin to understand the ambition and the spoils that are up for grabs. This is the sort of scale of project that is required by Chinese financiers used to funding ports built on artificial islands, 30-kilometre bridges, and entire new cities.

When I asked Jin Liqun of the China Investment Corporation if China was going to pay for Britain's infrastructure, he giggled like one of the more avuncular Bond villains. 'We would be more than happy to step in and invest in the infrastructure development in the UK. Your country has a very good infrastructure over the years but it needs upgrading, needs renovation or you need new infrastructure facilities. I'm very much encouraged by the vast amount of opportunities we could have in your country. CIC has put a lot of money into your country.'

Mr Jin's attitude to the UK stood in contrast to his colourful scepticism about European labour laws, which he says makes workers 'slothful' and 'indolent' are thus the 'root cause' of the Eurozone crisis. But many in Europe are wary that China is using its financial muscle as a form of diplomacy – to achieve EU 'market economy' status, and freer trade with Europe.

The strategy of investing in Western infrastructure has been sanctioned by the Chinese leadership since 2011. In many ways it is a benign development, one that could help to rebalance the world's lop-sided economy. The result could be a global infrastructure boom modelled on China's own infrastructure boom, a modern equivalent of the post-Second World War Marshall Plan by which the USA sought to rebuilt war-torn Europe and so halt the spread of Communism.

The new Chinese strategy represents a profound and ironic flip – historically, diplomatically and economically. Liverpool was once the most important port of the British Empire, an empire that in the nineteenth century had forced China to accept European control of its most important trading ports – the so-called Treaty Ports, which included Shanghai and Guangzhou. Now Liverpool itself is set to become the bridgehead of China's new ambitions in Europe. And these ambitions go much further than the Atlantic Gateway. Almost all British government departments are suffering from shrunken capital budgets, but ministers are constantly claiming that various foreign sugar daddies, in the form of sovereign wealth funds like the CIC, are queuing up to pay for a whole range of infrastructure projects, from faster broadband and high-speed rail lines to new ports, roads, power lines and nuclear power stations – almost everything.

There is some irony that despite Britain's historically low government borrowing rates, it is effectively the governments of other nations paying for jobs-rich infrastructure. A fiscal stimulus funded by state borrowing. Just not the British state.

Chinese firms face some competition from other state-owned sovereign funds. Britain's attraction is its disintegrating and obsolescent Victorian infrastructure. The London Gateway deep-sea port at Thurrock in Essex is literally a new piece of British land, dredged out of the Thames Estuary, Dubai-style, by Dubai Ports Worldwide. It will allow the new generation of monster cargo ships to offload close to London. As London Gateway's vice-chairman, Jamal bin Thaniah, says, 'In comparison to major developments in the Middle East and China, we noticed that some of the infrastructure in this part of the world, regretfully, is lagging behind in terms of capacity. . . For this reason there is a business opportunity.'

It's not just Britain that China is interested in. The Chinese have offered to share and sell their high-speed rail technology to California. Many of the investments China would like to make in energy, aerospace and manufacturing, are off limits in the USA, which fears that its security would be compromised. No such restrictions hold sway in Britain, however. Almost everything is for sale.

But the question is, what do the Chinese want in return? I asked Mr Jin if his organisation was just a tool of China's global economic and political ambitions. He impressed upon me that China's Sovereign Wealth Fund had the highest levels of modern ethical standards, and would not, for example, invest in tobacco or arms companies. 'Mutual understanding is very important,' he told me. 'So far there was some mistrust from the perspective of the European countries. We are confident that through our behaviour and our actual work, you can enhance your trust in CIC. 'Tis a consummation devoutly to be wished.'

It was not really an answer to the question. Great Britain, the nation that used to fund and build roads, railways and ports around the world, now wants the world to fund and build Britain's own roads, railways and ports. The empire – that is, the new Chinese empire – just struck back. And it did so quoting *Hamlet*.

Gangnanomics

Many believe there are other profound ways in which Chinese influence can rebalance the world economy. According to them, if things go to plan, Gangnam Style will save the world. Specifically, if China goes Gangnam Style, the world economy will rebalance in a benign way, maximising growth and prosperity for West and East alike.

Let me explain. For most of the world, 'Gangnam Style' is an amusing, faintly annoying Korean pop song accompanied by a crazy dance. For anyone looking through an economic lens, however, Gangnam Style was far more interesting, an ironic critique of the absurdities of the crass consumerism that has emerged across South Korea over the past decade.

In the 1980s and 1990s, South Korea had its own export-led manufacturing boom. A key feature of this was the thriftiness of Korean households. For thirteen consecutive years, Korean households were the number one savers in the rich man's club of world nations, the OECD. Koreans saved around 25 per cent of their income. After the Asian financial crisis of the late 1990s, however, household saving collapsed, dropping as low as 0.4 per cent in 2002, and staying below 3 per cent in recent years. It was a spectacular fall to the bottom of that OECD savers' league table.

South Korea's reputation for household thrift evaporated in an orgy of housing speculation, child tuition fees and credit-fuelled purchases of expensive Western brands. If the same happened in China – which could come about if the government allowed the renminbi to increase in value – China's exporters could reorientate towards their massive domestic market. The

USA and Europe could benefit, too, from a more consumerist China. Imbalances would begin to rebalance.

At the Shanghai Union lighting factory, manager Lizzie Lieng is considering whether, or how, to embark on this very shift towards the domestic market. In the early years of the twenty-first century, Shanghai Union boomed by selling chandeliers and metallic green post-boxes around the world. But international custom has been tough after the financial crisis of 2007–8. 'Before, we just ignored the big market in our own country,' she told me. 'Maybe it's more simple to do exports.' The problem is the design of the lamps, aimed at the export market. 'If we can, we hope we can change the demand, but it takes time to get Chinese customers to like these types of lamps,' she said.

In the aftermath of the financial crisis, the Chinese government actually offered subsidies to rural residents to help them buy certain models and makes of refrigerator and air-conditioning units. The aim was to help divert the production of China's factories towards its own 1.3 billion people. But creating a Western-style consumption culture is a challenge in a country where around 40 to 50 per cent of take-home pay is saved, says David Wei, one of China's business elite. Mr Wei, who ran an internet portal for the international showcase of China's factories, explained: 'It's healthy to have a high savings culture, because neither individuals nor countries can live on credit forever. But savings that are too high are also not very healthy. We need a balance, we want Western countries to save a bit more and Chinese people to spend a bit more. And it might be beginning to happen because young people are spending more, but the older people are still saving.'

Despite the trend among the young identified by Mr Wei, it seems that the ethos of saving a high proportion of one's income is far more deeply entrenched in China than in South Korea, say. Speak to the migrant workers, and they are dismissive of the idea of reducing their savings, given the lack of job security.

In the city of Dong Guan, unemployed migrant worker Li Chun Rong gives some idea of the hardship she and her fellow workers have to endure. She had lost her job in a shoe factory. She had hoped to leave her baby with her elderly parents in Sichuan province while she worked in the factory, but her father became ill, so her mother had to plough the fields, meaning her mother had no time to look after her baby grandchild.

'Our family at home cannot afford fridges and washing machines,' she said. 'We migrant workers don't have much money to spend. We don't dare to spend money. We have to send our children to school and take care of our parents. Everything costs money. There's some kind of health insurance at home. It covers very little. It is us who have to take care of our parents.'

Conventional economic models of saving do not appear to work in China. The middle-aged save the least, while the young and the old save the most – a 'U'-shaped graph of savings against age. The theories of famous economists from Franco Modigliani to Milton Friedman suggest the opposite, an 'N'-shape, as people save more in middle age to spend in retirement. Keynes's insights might provide a better explanation of saving in China: the precautionary motive.

At the jobs fair in Dong Guan, around the corner from where I talked to Li Chun Rong, Yi Bin stresses the reason why workers such as himself need to save so much. 'There isn't a sound social-security and healthcare system in China,' he explains. 'We won't know what to do if we're seriously ill. This is what our savings are for.'

Remember, under the *huzou* system, Yi Bin has limited access to healthcare, education, pensions and worker compensation in Dong Guan. Migrant workers fear for their entire future in the all too frequent industrial accidents or even a road accident. But Yi Bin has an idea that could revolutionise the Chinese economy. 'Once we have a good social security system, everybody will spend,' he tells me enthusiastically. 'Who doesn't want to enjoy life? We all only have a few decades to live. Of course we want to live better and not be too frugal.'

The building of social security systems in China and other

emerging economies is one of the great challenges for the world economy. Few leaders in these countries are much impressed by the European welfare system. But they will have to provide. What would a Chinese National Health Service look like? Part of the spike in Chinese savings rates can be dated back to a pension reform that severely limited retirement payouts to state workers. Financial markets will need to develop to help the Chinese masses save and smooth their incomes over time.

In China, however, the experts refute the notion that high savings really are the problem. The flipside of the 'savings glut' in China that America complains about is the 'investment famine' in the rest of the world that China is only too keen to point out. Even the management consultants McKinsey & Co. – those high priests of Western globalisation – calculate that there is a $20 trillion investment shortfall in infrastructure around the world, as Western countries have drastically slashed their investment budgets. Leading Chinese officials such as Justin Lin point the finger of blame for this, and for the imbalances generally, firmly at the USA. There are three reasons, the Chinese argue: lax regulation of Wall Street, super-low interest rates from 2001, and the role of the dollar as the global reserve currency. China, they point out, has trade deficits with other East Asian countries. Over the past twenty-five years, China has simply replaced Japan as the main contributor to the US trade deficit. As much as 60 per cent of China's exports are made by foreign-owned companies, many from the USA. The iPad and iPhone are the most famous US-invented contributors to the USA–China trade deficit.

So exporting China's infrastructure boom around the world is China's preferred route for the much-vaunted 'global rebalancing' agenda. Other post-crisis efforts at rebalancing the global economy have made minimal progress. One leading central banker refers to the discussions at the G20 as a 'depressing waste of time'. The mere absence of a savage trade war in the aftermath of the crisis is the only notable but limited sign of success.

During 2012, Chinese purchases of US Treasury bonds peaked, and then fell substantially. But Japan simply increased its US loans by even more. China slowly began to readjust the value of its currency against the dollar and other currencies. The fundamental imbalance, however, between Western debts and over-consumption, and Eastern surpluses and overproduction, got even worse.

In the USA, the defence secretary and others have played down any potential leverage that China might possess with its still massive stock of US government debt. The situation is broadly described as 'mutually assured destruction'. China would sustain massive collateral damage if, for example, it attempted to dump its bond holdings.

In this situation, the USA does appear to have obliged China to become a forced lender, a type of bonded banker for its ever-growing debts. It is a form of international financial repression. China's currency policy, in effect, holds down the living standards of its people, obliging them, and the nation generally, to lend its hard-earned dollars back to the USA. This arises because the dollar is the world reserve currency, and US Treasury bonds are a trusted form of liquid international mega-cash to be swapped with other nations, banks and pensions funds. For the past decade China has had nowhere else to go to park its massive reserves. The USA enjoys what France has referred to for half a century as the 'exorbitant privilege' of being the world reserve.

The fundamental question is whether the status of the dollar will change. If you look carefully at what China has been doing, you'll see that it has been quietly amassing bilateral deals with key neighbours and oil exporters to swap its currency with other central banks. International trade deals are beginning to be priced in renminbi. The Chinese government have called openly for the replacement of the dollar with an alternative based on a basket of currencies. Slowly, surely, in accordance with Deng Xiaoping's mantra of 'Crossing the river by feeling the stones', the renminbi is being internationalised. In February

2013, the UK became the first Western G7 nation to sign up to a central bank agreement to swap currencies. France followed suit weeks later. Twenty of these swap arrangements are now in place. China will have to fully float its currency, and free up financial flows, before the 'Redback' threatens the 'Greenback'. But the keyboards manufactured (probably in China) for the world might soon require a '¥' key alongside the '$'.

That is for the future. The recent past and present is still a battleground. Was the global financial crisis China's fault or America's? China clearly has some responsibilities, but the overwhelming weight of evidence points towards the USA. Justin Lin goes further, arguing that China does not in fact even manipulate its currency. The evidence for this, he says, is that inflation has not exploded in China despite this suggested manipulation. Indeed, from 1979 to 2002 China's growth averaged 9.6 per cent, and nearly 11 per cent from 2003 to 2010. As Professor Lin points out, 'Prior to 2002, double-digit growth was always accompanied by double-digit inflation. Whereas from 2002 to 2010 the inflation rate was not more than 5 per cent.' That means the inflation-adjusted exchange rate with the dollar, the 'real exchange rate' as it is known, is not actually significantly undervalued. Even if it was undervalued, China's currency has appreciated markedly since 2007, in real terms. Its surplus with the rest of the world is smaller than Germany's. The growing strength of the renminbi has led some global production to relocate to countries such as Bangladesh and Vietnam that have even lower costs than China.

In practice, that means the flows of those Chinese migrant workers from Sichuan and other places to the coastal factories have sustainably increased the capacity of China's economy. It was these migrant workers who were the principal reason for China's giant surpluses. China's increasing wealth really rests on their shoulders, more than on its currency management. But it cannot last: China's single-child policy means that by 2015 the size of its working-age population will peak.

More important than the blame game, perhaps, is what China's growth can teach the rest of the world. As Justin Lin argues, 'If you look at the experiences of all the successful countries in economic development – postwar Japan, Korea and Taiwan, the transition nations of China and Vietnam, or even the early development of the UK, German, US and French economies – all have relied on the market mechanism combined with active interventions of government.'

The future of China, and the pattern of the world economy, depends squarely on China's workers becoming even more productive. Three decades ago, only 1 in 1,000 were graduates. Now the figure is 1 in 40. Almost all are products of the single-child policy. Their challenge is to produce more, raise the value of China's exports, consume more domestically, and also to consume more imports from the West.

Already the transformative geo-economic currents of 2001–2010 seem to be changing direction. China's piggy bank may have to be deployed closer to home, in support of the murky depths of its banking system. The world's central bankers are deeply sceptical about China's conventional and shadow financial system. A glut of cheap credit was deployed in 2009 to keep China growing. Then again, with trillions of dollars saved, the Chinese state has enough cash to keep its banks afloat, without needing to borrow. Chinese factory production is moving inland from the coasts. The great migration appears to be happening closer to the migrant workers' villages. China's army of migrant workers wants a fairer share of the profits made, or at the very least to ensure their wages keep up with rising prices. Wages have gone up in some factories, and some lower-value manufacturing is being outsourced to Vietnam and Bangladesh. Younger generations are becoming more consumerist. In inimitable Chinese style, just an hour's journey from the city centre, the Beijing authorities plan to create a £1 billion 'Music Valley' to house music studios and instrument makers. Whereas much of China's recent growth has depended on *shanzhai* – imitations or pirated copies of Western brands and goods – now the government wants to encourage a more indigenously creative economy. Gangnanomics is half-serious.

When I met Deng Zhi in Dong Guan, he had escaped the production lines, deciding that factory life was not for him. Over the next decade and a half, the wage aspirations, hopes, dreams, eating habits and travel plans of Deng Zhi – and 300 million Chinese like him – will be one of the largest determinants of global prosperity. Just as they have been in the last decade and a half.

As for Deng Zhi himself, he was not left rambling from factory to factory, offering his labour for a pittance. He'd found his calling as a punk hairdresser, catering to his fellow migrant workers. As we spoke, he was dyeing a young man's spiky mullet a shade of neon pink. Perhaps we are now at the point, where he, and others like him, no longer need our thank-yous.

CHAPTER 5

THE HOUSE TRAP

Dramatis personae

Anonymous UK bank chief executive
Esther Spick, thirty-something holder of
Northern Rock Together mortgage
Bertie Ahern, Irish Taoiseach (1997–2008)
Jay Belleti (name changed), Caribbean hotel owner,
former subprime banker
John Muellbauer, Oxford University professor,
expert in housing economics
Adam Applegarth, chief executive of Northern Rock
John Apicella, Mr Vigneswaran, Mr Thorogood,
mortgage brokers
Antony Elliott, former group risk director of
Abbey National
Louise Gowens, struggling with boom-time debts in 2006
Sir John Bond, former chairman of HSBC
Shane O'Riordain, director of HBoS
Brad Rosser, Inside Track property investment club
Andrew Pellegrino, Newcastle buy-to-let property investor
Naomi Jacobs, young first-time buyer in Newcastle,
priced out
The Faircloughs, a couple helped by the UK government's
Help to Buy scheme
Peter Redfern, CEO of housebuilder Taylor Wimpey

'What is the most dangerous toxic financial asset in the world?' This was the question put to me by the chief executive of a leading European bank. Anxious to display my superior knowledge of the darkest corners of the shadow banking system, I replied: 'Credit-default swaps on super-senior tranches of asset-backed, security-collateralised debt obligations.' I thought I had come up with a pretty pithy answer.

'No,' he gently chided me. 'The most dangerous financial product in the world,' he paused a moment for effect, 'is the mortgage.'

The mortgage: from the Old French words *mort* and *gage*. Disputed translation: 'death contract'.

Esther's story

In the middle of the credit-crunch crisis of 2008 I met Esther Spick, then a single 34-year-old mum with two kids living in a maisonette in Surrey. It was the first home she'd owned, bought with an entirely inappropriate mortgage in 2005. She had been living on a council estate in Kingston, Surrey, working day and night to get a deposit to get a mortgage for her £235,000 maisonette. It had been sold – or mis-sold – to her during the boom by Northern Rock, and now the mortgage payments had rocketed by £500 per month. Faced with this, but determined to keep the keys to her home, she had been forced to hand her children over to their grandparents. She'd had to give up her local job and find higher-paid employment further afield. The result? Four hours' commuting per day.

'I don't want to have my home repossessed or for Northern Rock to say I haven't been making my payments,' she told me. 'I will do whatever I have to do, even if it means I have to get out and get a second job. I will definitely make these payments.' At that point, however, she was in negative equity – not surprising, given that she had been lent over 100 per cent of the value of her home. And her new mortgage was eating up two-thirds of her new take-home pay. 'They lent me too much. It was a time when everything was wonderful. There was a great big property boom, the prices went through the roof. You were encouraged to go out and buy.'

Now she had boxed up her children's teddy bears after a charging order arrived in the post. She had fallen behind on just three payments on the unsecured part of the loan. Northern Rock had taken her to court in Newcastle, 500 kilometres from her home. A 'death contract' indeed.

The presumption of ever-rising house prices in the USA was, of course, one of the core reasons behind the failure of banks during the crisis. But it was in the eyes of a young single mother from Surrey that I saw the truth: Britain's housing obsession had become a form of mass psychosis. Housing and property had become hardwired into the sense of national economic well-being. Rising house prices were being reported like football scores. A property portfolio acquired the quality of a household market capitalisation. As house prices surged in Britain, Ireland and Spain, those that pointed out the pitfalls were derided as pessimists, Cassandras and nay-sayers. For example, in Ireland, the then Taoiseach Bertie Ahern said that he could not work out why people 'cribbing and moaning' about the property-fuelled Irish economy 'didn't go and commit suicide'.

Jay's story

The tiny metal skulls were threaded into Jay Belleti's dreadlocked beard by the local Garifuna Afro-Amerindian fishermen. He had every reason to exaggerate his eccentricity to the locals. They were naturally suspicious of this gringo and his partner opening a new bar on the poorer shores of the Caribbean. A taxi driver had recently stumbled into the bar, bleeding from gunshot wounds to his ear. He had been left for dead by a pair of Colombians after his cab radio. It turned out he had only been hit in the fleshy part of his ear.

Eccentricity wasn't always enough. There were plenty of violent chancers in the neighbourhood who saw the forty-something mid-Western couple as easy prey. Belleti needed to make a point. So there, in his yard, the latest pair of would-be thieves dangled upside down. The bandana-sporting Yanqui told them the next time his dog would eat their faces.

This was not the career trajectory Belleti might have envisaged for himself. Before the subprime crisis, he had been a banker in Florida, running a team of loan officers. Some might argue it was a natural progression. This tale is one small vignette of the changes sweeping people's lives in the aftermath of the great crisis of 2008.

'I hired a bunch of really smart girls to work with me,' Belleti told me. 'They had MBAs, masters degrees, they could speak languages. They were really smart. You wanna know why I chose to work with women? Because if a guy makes $12,000 commission, he doesn't come in for the rest of the week 'cause he thinks "Oh yeah, I've earned it." If a woman does that, she comes in real early the next day and works twice as hard. Anyways, these chicks were used to pulling in $200,000 a year and they all bought nice houses and cars. And then all of a sudden things went south, they weren't making shit and they started coming in with black eyes saying they'd walked into a door or something. I knew their husbands, we were all friends, but it was obvious what was happening. It was terrible to watch – broke my heart and sent my blood pressure through the roof. Do you know what they're doing now? Waiting tables in Mexican restaurants because they speak languages. These are real smart, educated people and that's the best they can get. We saw it coming in '07 and knew we had to get out. And do you know what people called me? Chicken Little. Thinking the sky would fall in.'

From democracy to domocracy: Britain's mortgage frenzy

These snapshots of the human cost of the post-crisis bust have their roots in the preceding boom. In Britain and in Ireland it was the biggest credit binge in world history. The apartments sold like hot cakes. The appetite for housing just kept growing. On behalf of property magnates, specialist spin doctors drew on the top end of celebrity culture to fuel the dream, planting fictitious stories such as the rumour that Robert De Niro was buying a penthouse flat in an old warehouse in London. The lies worked.

Britain turned from democracy to domocracy. Every link in the chain – from house-building to mortgage provision to estate agents to the construction of house price indices – became corrupted, common sense sacrificed at the altar of rising house prices. In the decade from 1997 to 2007 house prices trebled. More than that, the home evolved into a multi-faceted financial instrument, on top of its traditional role as an indicator of social prestige.

Every stage of the house chain is still riven with conflicts of interest, poor data, and ultimately a tendency to fuel inflation. Housing is the only basic human need for which rapid price rises are met with celebration rather than protest. The house trap stretches from the estate agents mediating house-selling, to the provision of mortgages to buyers, the supply of mortgage finance to the banks and building societies, the construction of house-price indices, the skewing of finance away from owner-occupiers towards landlords, the supply and construction of new homes, the relationship between elected politicians, property, and the media too. Homes were always castles, not just in England, but also across Europe and the USA. But during the madness they evolved into cash machines, surrogate pensions, principal pensions, and even livelihoods. And in many places, this is still the case.

Let's go back to the foundations of what might be called the bubble machine. Rising house prices, to some degree, reflected underlying supply and demand in a competitive market. Greater increases in demand than in supply, and the prices went up, as in Britain. Large increases in supply over demand, as in the USA, Spain and Ireland after the crisis, and prices go down. Simple enough.

Except, of course, this simple model is entirely misleading. The housing market is not really a market for houses. The housing market is driven principally by the availability of finance, mainly mortgage debt, but sometimes bonuses, inheritances, or hot money from abroad – London in particular has become the preferred residence of the world's wealthiest people, from Russian oligarchs to Arab oil sheikhs.

Let's start with Britain. There are 27 million dwellings in the UK. The short-term supply is basically fixed. The number of new homes built each year has not topped 150,000 since the crisis – that's less than 0.5 per cent of the total stock. The amount of homes traded is around 900,000 per year, about 3 per cent of the total stock. House prices set by the transaction of that 3 per cent of homes determine property values, the solvency of banks, and the statistic that the UK property stock is worth £6 trillion.

The first thing to notice is that this is a highly illiquid market. Only a small proportion of the housing stock is actually being traded, or ever will be traded. In comparison, the stock markets of developed countries trade around 100 per cent per year of the total value of all of the stocks (for Britain the figure is 138 per cent, for the USA 188 per cent, for Japan 109 per cent) These are proper markets, with lots of buyers and sellers – and that, in theory, makes it easier to work out the market price of a share. The British housing market at 3 per cent turnover, on the other hand, is analogous to the stock market in Mongolia, and the American housing market is on a par with the stock market in Peru. In Britain, the market is particularly thin given that transactions have halved since the go-go years. On top of all this, transactions in the housing market are costly. Estate agents' fees in the UK can typically reach 3 per cent, and as high as 6 per cent in the USA, with stamp duty on top of that. These are the crucial features of a housing market: thin trading and high transaction costs. It is a recipe for dysfunction, distortion and inefficiency.

Imagine the entire UK stock of property was called Ladder

Street, with fifty houses on either side of the road. Despite demand for two extra houses every year over the next decade or so, it in fact takes two years to build just one extra house. The result? Some of the extra demand will be met by converting houses into flats. But most of the demand will not be met at all. A house will be sold on Ladder Street only every four months. One house will remain empty. The end result is a long queue of people who will buy anything, old or new, good or bad, for sale on Ladder Street.

Now consider the price. In a market such as this, the buyer with the largest wallet wins the house and sets the price. At one time that would have been the buyer with the highest single salary, and who had saved the largest deposit. House prices would therefore rise roughly in line or slightly ahead of the rise in incomes. But imagine if the entire queue of prospective house purchasers is flooded with mortgage credit. At this point, the house price is set by the greatest optimist. Ladder Street's housing market has become a market, not for homes, but for mortgage credit. It is the availability and terms of credit that have come to determine property prices.

In Ireland's case, the Oxford economist John Muellbauer and his colleagues have calculated that 81 per cent of the rise in house prices was through changes in credit availability. A controlled experiment in this theory occurred in Britain during 2008, when Northern Rock was running down its mortgage book in the first months of its nationalisation so that government money could be repaid. The Rock was charging high mortgage rates to encourage customers to redeem their loans by changing lender. House prices collapsed from an average £196,000 to £160,000 in just a year. The strategy was reversed at the end of the year, and prices stabilised. In Britain, according to Muellbauer's analysis, real house prices may have not increased between 2001 and 2009 – if there had not been a fundamental change to credit conditions. In other words, the boom would have petered out in the early 2000s, instead of prices nearly doubling in the eight years before the crisis of 2008. The Oxford economists infer this result from the relationship between house prices, unemployment, interest rates and credit supply. But it isn't difficult to see how this torrent of extra credit flooded Britain's housing stock. Every sluicegate was unlocked, then left ajar, and eventually flung open to accommodate the tidal surge of credit.

Take, for example, the length of mortgage repayment, beyond a typical twenty-five years. Between 1993 and 2000 the average mortgage period remained exactly twenty-two years. Around 60 per cent of mortgages were for twenty-five years, and, typically, less than 2 per cent of mortgages were for periods longer than twenty-five years. The Survey of Mortgage Lenders then, miraculously, stops for three years. When it restarts in 2006, nearly a quarter of all mortgages are for longer than twenty-five years. Around a fifth are now for thirty years or more, meaning an average first-time buyer will still be repaying home loans into their sixties. The big picture is that the proportion of very long-term mortgages provided by UK banks increased by tenfold during the boom. Mysteriously, the data for this structural change in the mortgage market was not collected during the period of take-off between 2002 and 2005. Two factors were at work here. Firstly, banks began offering mortgages repayable over periods in excess of thirty years. Secondly, there emerged a craze for remortgaging, meaning that individual borrowers effectively lengthened the original term of their mortgage.

This wasn't just in Britain. In Australia, Spain, Greece and Finland (though not in Germany) average mortgage terms also lengthened. In Spain, France and Finland, a fifty-year mortgage is possible. In Japan and Switzerland you can get cross-generational, century-long mortgages. The longer the term, the longer it takes the homeowner to accumulate equity. Initially, the mere rise in house prices makes up for that. But the lifetime cost increases.

If house prices were rocketing, how could conventional calculations of housing affordability keep up? Take the average income of a UK house buyer over time. In the 1990s it floated not far from £20,000. By 2006, it was more than double that, £41,040. In 1995, over half of mortgage loans were to households earning under £20,000. By 2006, it was just one in twelve loans. Even more starkly, a third of all mortgages went to the poorest half of households in 2000. Just six years later, it was only a sixth.

What was happening? Of course average incomes were going up, but how was the median house buyer getting richer much faster? Mortgages were increasingly going to couples, assessed on their joint incomes, and to older remortgagers. So mortgage terms were being lengthened, and they were increasingly based on joint incomes. Lenders began to stretch the so-called 'income multiple' – the number of times a buyer's income they were prepared to lend. Three times became four times – or even as much as seven times, in the case of some new mortgage companies desperate for market share.

By 2003 the dark underbelly of the house-price boom was already claiming victims in the form of first-time buyers, priced off the so-called housing ladder. The amount of deposit required by a first-time buyer in the 1990s had long been around 10 per cent of purchase price – an attainable sum for a saver in a middle-income job. In the first stage of the Labour housing boom, as prices went up, the average deposit required from first-time buyers more than doubled, reaching 23 per cent in 2003. But then the figure fell sharply, down to 16 per cent by 2007. This helped fuel another spurt of first-time buying, just as the housing boom reached its lofty peak. More recently, average deposits for first-time buyers peaked at 27 per cent, then settled at 25 per cent. Such high figures had not been seen since the 1970s, and then only sporadically. In that decade, house prices for first-time buyers were 2.2 times their average income. In contrast, since 2004, that figure has been more like 4.5 times income – well beyond the means of most young people, unless they have help from relatives. We are seeing the bottom rungs of the housing ladder breaking.

'If only we could afford a place of our own,' says one dainty green extraterrestrial to another in the cartoon advertisement as they sit in a pink car parked in Lovers' Lane. 'You can,' exclaims the advert, 'with a Together Mortgage.' The 'Together Mortgage' was launched by Northern Rock in 1999. In effect, it required of borrowers a negative deposit. Customers were able to borrow 125 per cent of the value of a home: 95 per cent as a secured mortgage, and 30 per cent as an unsecured loan. This was the type of loan taken out by Esther Spick. The 'Together Mortgage' was part of what Adam Applegarth, former chief executive of Northern Rock, called his 'virtuous circle strategy'. This essentially turned what had been a solid northern English building society into a giant hedge fund, laser-guiding global flows of hot money into some of the most sensitive suburbs of Britain's property market (see pages 213–23). Although launched in 1999, it really took off as Northern Rock went into overdrive at the peak of the boom, doubling its lending every three years. Single borrowers were also offered multiples of as much as five times their annual salary, to help keep pace with those borrowing off dual incomes. Competitors such as Abbey National and HBoS (Halifax Bank of Scotland) scrambled to get in on the game, also offering 'five times' deals, and zero deposits.

Events have shown that the virtue of this particular circle has been more than somewhat compromised. And it was not just Northern Rock who strayed from the paths of rectitude and probity. At 'Mortgages 4 You' based in Newbury, John Apicella admits he was not entirely exacting in checking the incomes of his clients. Mortgage brokers such as Mr Apicella were the driving force behind the banks' desire to supply credit, and the desperation of ordinary Britons to afford a property. In 2007, two-thirds of mortgages (three-quarters of first-time buyer loans) were sold through brokers in Britain's high streets and on the internet. In the past, prospective home owners had been required to save for months or sometimes years before their local bank manager would even to agree to talk to them about a mortgage. In the boom, that first filter of the credit process was outsourced to a lightly regulated industry with opaque professional standards: the mortgage brokers. The result of this? Self-certification mortgages.

Mr Apicella put it rather clearly in documents published by the regulators, the Financial Services Authority. When he started working in the mortgage industry he was advised to 'just put any income down'. 'I was guilty of all that because that's the way I was trained,' he said. 'That's what the industry did.' The whole of the industry took the same view on self-certification mortgages. He said it was not his responsibility to assess mortgage affordability. 'It's up to the client to see whether they can afford it,' he told me. 'I can't sit in judgement and say you can or can't afford it.'

When regulators eventually began to investigate certain mortgage brokers, they discovered they were using some innovative ways to up the income stated by mortgage applicants. In Colwyn Bay, at Property Park Mortgages, regulators found that an adviser called Darren Button had altered a payslip with Tipp-Ex. Mark Thorogood, also at Property Park, managed to record the income of a family member at £130,000, a convenient extra digit over the actual figure of £30,000.

A special prize must go to Mr Vigneswaran of Cherry Finance, Kingsbury, who was giving mortgage advice as an approved mortgage broker just as the credit crunch hit. The only thing was, he could not speak English. In fact, regulators discovered he knew little about Cherry Finance bar attending an opening ceremony. His son, already removed as an approved broker, had simply got the FSA to set his father up as a so-called 'approved person'.

Spokespersons for the mortgage industry suggest that such practices (and there are hundreds of similar stories) are just the work of a few bad apples. The truth is that we simply do not know. Only a small minority of the deals done by brokers have been checked, even now. The investigations only began in earnest as the bubble was bursting. Up until 2007, there were almost no actual checks on the activities of over 7,000 mortgage brokers, responsible for the majority of new mortgages. This industry grew rapidly during the boom, lured by typical incentives of £500–£1,000 on each mortgage signed. Most brokers were small one-adviser shops advising fewer than a hundred mortgages a year. Of the few hundred that have been investigated, more than a hundred have conducted their mortgage broking in a way that warranted a prohibition, and thirty-five were fined. The time to be cracking down was surely as the bubble was inflating, not after it popped.

If it is regrettable that the regulators have been so slow to act, it is almost incredible that, in the first place, the British banking system handed over the frontline control of mortgage credit to an industry – the mortgage brokers – who had such a buccaneering disregard for the kind of prudence one would expect from a steward of one's money. Not so long ago, a mortgage applicant would have saved for years merely for the opportunity of a meeting with the local branch manager who decided on mortgages. The boom-time bankers must have known this was happening. Their confidence in pushing the boundaries of mortgage provision arose from their computer models, and their ability to offload the risk to other parts of the financial system. The crackdown that followed the bust, however, focused on the foot-soldiers such as Mr Button and Mr Apicella rather than the generals in the smart offices in the skyscrapers.

HBoS was by far the biggest player in the mortgage market, by virtue of its origins in the Halifax Building Society. HBoS also inherited Charles Dunstone as a non-executive director. In testimony to the Parliamentary Committee on Banking Standards in 2012, Mr Dunstone (now Sir Charles) revealed how fevered were the competitive pressures in the mortgage market. 'The difficulty was that the traditional mortgage market had become so unprofitable due to people remortgaging so quickly, which was driven by mortgage brokers. By the time I left, the average mortgage that we signed lasted thirty-six months. You would take a mortgage, get an incentive, have it for three years and then go straight on to the next deal. It was becoming increasingly difficult to write traditional mortgage business.'

The credit feeding frenzy in suburban Britain during this time was feeding off itself. But one innovation casts a particularly long shadow. Increasing multiples, decreasing deposits, allowing self-certification and stretching the term of a mortgage are all rather tame compared to never actually expecting the repayment of mortgage debt. That was the strategy behind 'interest-only' mortgages. In finance, a loan where the entire principal of the loan is due at the end of the term is known as a 'bullet loan', but that name might have conjured the wrong image. Interest-only loans are controversial. Forget trying to get one in Canada. In India, you'll need to hand over a piece of gold. A version of the interest-only mortgage, the endowment mortgage, was popular in the UK in the 1980s and 1990s, but was sold with an investment to repay the loan at the end of the term.

Endowment mortgages were scandalously mis-sold by the banks. This only became apparent in the early 2000s when it became clear that the investments designed to pay off mortgage loans did not have a cat's chance in hell of realising the necessary capital at the end of the mortgage term – let alone the additional bonuses the sellers had suggested were a strong possibility. To compensate for their large-scale mis-selling, the banks were ordered to pay out billions of pounds to disgruntled clients. One might have thought that would have given the banks pause for thought. But no. In place of flawed repayment plans, bankers developed a type of interest-only mortgage that had no requirement for the client to have any kind of verifiable way of repaying the mortgage at the end of the term. Again, competitive pressure amongst banks further eroded standards.

Interest-only deals boomed from 2002 to 2007, providing another fillip to the housing market. In 2007 a third of all mortgage sales were interest only. And for the first months of 2008, the majority of new mortgage lending was interest only. It had briefly become the norm. Interest-only deals were particularly popular with single-earner households. For many it was the only way to compete with dual-income households. Monthly mortgage bills for a £150,000 loan would have been roughly £800 per month at normal interest rates of 4 per cent. An interest-only mortgage would have slashed that to just £500.

Rob McGregor from Reading has spent eight years paying up to £900 per month for his mortgage, except he hasn't paid a penny off his loan. He feels trapped in a dangerous situation: 'In eighteen years' time I've got no chance of paying off the capital amount. If my salary grows in line with inflation I'm never going to have the opportunity to save enough to pay off the debt.' Half of all interest-only mortgage holders have insufficient plans for capital repayment. Ten per cent, that's 300,000, have no plans whatsoever.

The FSA, which waived through what should have remained a niche product into the mass market, warned in late 2012 of a 'ticking timebomb'. By May 2013, the Financial Conduct Authority, which took over the FSA's old premises, restated this 'wake-up call'. Martin Wheatley, the Financial Conduct Authority's chief executive, told me: 'The big concern is the ten percent that as of today could get to the end of their mortgage and simply have nothing to repay the loan.'

Is this mis-selling? 'This is more about credit,' Wheatley told me. 'Mis-selling usually comes about when there is some confusion about what the product is. An interest-only mortgage does what it says on the tin. You're only paying the interest, so I don't think people can really say: "I didn't know what I was getting into." I hope the banks wouldn't have gone on the basis that it didn't matter. I think the expectation, frankly, was that house prices would carry on rising.'

The bulk of bankers and lenders were relying on selling the property, and therefore on property prices continuing to rise. The industry Mortgage Code required lenders to send out a reminder once a year to these borrowers to ensure there was some means to repay the loan. But that was it. When regulators suggested in late 2012 that lenders would be required to verify these repayment plans, most interest-only mortgages were pulled.

Interest-only mortgages were introduced to new markets such as Australia, Denmark, Finland, Greece and Portugal. In Denmark, by 2007, just four years after their introduction, interest-only mortgages represented 43 per cent of outstanding owner-occupier mortgages. The medium-term fallout, is, however, yet to be seen.

All of these innovations had one aim: reduce the early upfront costs of credit, and thus accommodate house prices rising well above traditional levels of affordability. These innovations stretch buying power. Boom-time bankers called it the 'front-end pricing' strategy. But for consumers it's basically an illusion. For nearly a century economists have called this type of delusion 'money illusion'. A government report had shown even in 2004 that most borrowers chose a mortgage solely on its front-end price. While low inflation and low interest rates did bring down the initial mortgage costs, high property prices and low inflation meant a much larger stock of debt. With low inflation, the real value of mortgage debt does not diminish as rapidly as it would if inflation were higher.

Handing out credit like it's crack

This 'front-end pricing' strategy is not dissimilar to that employed by drug dealers. Hook them in cheap, get them addicted, and then fleece them. Indeed, this very analogy was used by an industry insider, Antony Elliott, the former director for group risk of Abbey National. 'Lenders used to be viewed as doctors,' he told me. 'You went to the doctor and he would know what you needed, he would prescribe the appropriate drug. He would also know how it would interact with other drugs. I'm afraid to say now the lenders are more like bartenders serving drinks to people who've already had too much.'

Mr Elliott was particularly concerned with the plethora of

credit cards, store cards and personal loans being thrown at Britain's masses. The story of Britain's mortgage madness is connected to its general consumer credit excess. Both were underpinned by the same wave of easy money coursing from the East, accommodated by low interest rates from the Bank of England and financial deregulation. The bigger picture was the use of credit to artificially boost stagnant and then falling pay packets for middle earners.

The sophisticated abuse of unsecured debt reached its nadir with the habit of lenders actively increasing credit-card limits on customers who 'max out' their plastic each month, only repaying the minimum repayment. Quite quickly, such methods create large debts, subject to massive recurring interest payments. The result? A battery farm of low-income debtors laying a monthly batch of eggs to be gathered in by the banks. As the British economy boomed, Mr Elliott calculated that up to 4 million Britons faced debt problems. At that time the credit industry was spending £1 billion a year marketing and advertising its products on TV and in newspapers, with expensive free press trips, and with 'experiential marketing' strategically placed at the nation's shopping centres. Antony Elliott left his job at the bank to spend a year gathering evidence of the British public's dysfunctional relationship with credit. In one case study, a mature university student from Manchester described to him how he was flirted with by an attractive young woman in the Trafford Centre. 'We're so thick. If you're blonde, gorgeous... bang, you fill out the form, and before you realise it, you've got a credit card in the post.' He then recounted his naive descent into crippling fees, high interest payments and unnecessary consumption – all down to that credit siren at the shopping centre.

Louise Gowens, then 26 years old, accepted responsibility for incurring her £29,000 debts. But she got hold of her first credit card at the age of 16. 'One quickly turned into two,' she remembered, 'and then you're into the trap of moving it round and by the end it was six with consolidation loans on top of that. There should have been an alarm bell ringing somewhere at the banks. But there never was.' Another troubled borrower noted that in the application form for a new credit card there was only space for listing two existing cards, rather than the seven cards he already used. He lent money to his two step-children, even though he was hiding the state of his own debts. His bank gave him a loan that they can never have expected him to repay. 'They sent me a letter, can you call in sometime? I called in and I walked out £20,000 richer. Well, I weren't richer. I'd got £20,000 off them basically in an hour.'

I put some of these concerns to leading British bankers at the point where the boom was turning the Square Mile into a farmyard for record profits: in 2004 they made £30 billion, £1,000 per second. 'People come through our doors and ask for money,' Sir John Bond, then chairman of HSBC, told me in 2005. 'They borrow money. I'm sure when everybody borrows money they believe they can pay it back.' Then he added: 'The second point I would try to make is that successful economies need successful banks.' The then Labour government listened to voices such as Sir John's from within the banks rather than to outsiders like Mr Elliott. Government action focused on the transparency of marketing information, rather than an intervention in the market itself.

'Credit has been democratised in this country,' HBoS director Shane O'Riordain told me in 2005. 'And that is a good thing. When handled wisely, credit is an enabling factor that helps people to lead better lives. . . We're in the business of prudence.' Just three years later a weary Mr O'Riordain would be seen in the headlines of the evening news bulletins, desperately pleading that his bank was stable and safe – at the very same time as an invisible deposit run raged, and the Treasury desperately tried to find a buyer.

A flavour of what was actually going on inside HBoS was revealed by Charles Dunstone's testimony before that parliamentary committee. Despite being a successful mobile phone retailer rather than a banker, he became the chair of the doomed bank's

Retail Risk Committee. HBoS responded to competition from the likes of Northern Rock by moving into riskier types of lending. 'We had an enormous amount of experience in the housing stock: quality of assets, surveying, collections. We proceeded cautiously at first, but then we became increasingly confident about buy-to-let and the self-certified marketplace.'

HBoS and Northern Rock went particularly mad lending through those brokers at the top of the market. Of the £73 billion lent by HBoS in 2006, £60 billion was through intermediaries, according to calculations by Datamonitor. That figure represents 26 per cent of gross new mortgage lending in the UK that year, and 33 per cent of the funds channelled through brokers. Second on the list was Northern Rock. All but £3 billion of its £29 billion lending was channelled through brokers. For the US financial services company GMAC, all £12.1 billion of its mortgages were directed through brokers. For Barclays it was a third, and for HSBC it was zero. The prudent retail bankers planned to keep mortgages on their own balance sheet, and clearly wanted to see the whites of the eyes of their long-term borrowers. It's difficult to escape the conclusion that the other banks, built on the securitisation model, simply did not care about the quality of their borrowers enough to actually meet them. If their mortgages were going to end up in a jokily named Cayman Islands conduit – such as Granite, Grampian or Aire Valley – then why should they have cared?

Computer models might have provided some comfort that loan losses on mortgages were sustainable. The data on arrears, defaults and repossessions were, however, all based on the 1990s UK recession. This posed a problem for banks such as HBoS, Northern Rock and Bradford & Bingley that had pushed into entirely new risky product areas. 'These products – buy-to-let and self-certified products – did not exist in the early 90s,' one HBoS director told Parliament, 'so whatever we were doing in using those data was more judgemental.' For 'more judgemental', read 'more a matter of taking a gamble'.

The helping hand of no house-building

Clearly the fundamental factor underpinning this whole house of cards was rising property prices. Northern Rock's chief executive Adam Applegarth would cite the dearth of housing supply as one of the reasons property prices would stay high and investors could remain confident in the bank's profitability in 2003: 'The economic fundamentals of low interest rates, low inflation, low unemployment and *a very limited supply of new housing stock* will continue to underpin the market... our virtuous-circle strategy is in very good shape.' HBoS's Andy Hornby, in an article for the *Daily Telegraph* in 2007, said pretty much the same thing, at the same time encouraging ordinary Britons to save more (which would have helped the soon-to-fail bank's funding problems). In three successive financial results just prior to the crash, Bradford & Bingley insisted that the UK housing market would continue to be supported by the shortage of housing supply. All of these banking disasters were relying on an inadequate supply of housing as a selling point or even the foundation for their failing financial strategies.

The Labour government certainly delivered on that type of support. Tens of thousands of undesirable flats were built where there were not enough people to live in them, and not enough homes where they were actually needed. In 2001, new flats represented 23 per cent of new homes. By 2006 that figure had jumped to a half. Britain's new homes were also shrinking in size – by floor area, by number of rooms, and by size of rooms. At 76 square metres, the average new British house in 2006 was 10 per cent smaller than the average existing stock. In Ireland new homes were 15 per cent bigger, in land-constrained Holland 53 per cent bigger, and in Denmark new homes were not far off double the size of those in Britain, at 137 square metres. New homes built in Britain during the boom were only 4 square metres larger than the 72 square metres deemed the minimum space fit for human habitation by the Parker Morris

Committee in 1961, and subsequently adopted by the Ministry of Housing. The homes constructed during the British boom were also built to much lower environmental standards (insulation, energy efficiency, etc.) than new homes built elsewhere in western Europe. The credit boom and political inaction had caused breathtaking inflation in house prices, accompanied at the same time by a tangible decrease in the quality of new homes. Lose-lose.

If housing was a free market, then demand would be met by supply. Indeed, not just that, there would be an incentive to innovate, provide extra space, better energy-efficiency standards and hipper designs. But extraordinary limitations on planning in Britain have limited land supply and elevated its price. Land prices in Germany, for example, are much cheaper, and this is reflected in house prices. German planning law offers much more freedom to build.

In a competitive free market, the price of a house would reflect the average declines in quality. But in reality, the UK housing market has an inbuilt mechanism that perpetuates house-price inflation, regardless of quality. This mechanism comes in the shape of the chartered surveyor. Property valuations are governed by the Red Book, the surveyor's bible, published by the Royal Institution of Chartered Surveyors (RICS). In practice, surveyors use the 'comparative' or 'market value' method of valuation. It relies on what other, similar homes in the same area have recently sold for – in other words, the market value – with some uplift to account for rising prices. But the market value is in turn determined by exactly the same process. Supposing a valuer thinks that the market is out of control, and comes up with a lower valuation than the buyer requires to get the mortgage. Well, the deal falls through, and a bank wanting to make a profitable loan will look elsewhere for a more obliging valuation. As Philip Bowcock, a retired surveyor and property academic wrote to the 2004 Government Housing Review as the boom was taking hold, 'It follows from this that valuers, following the

RICS Red Book directions, have been giving added support to the price boom. A number of chartered surveyors who carry out mortgage valuations have said exactly this to me, but for obvious reasons would not wish to state their opinions publicly.'

Buy-to-let and the myth of the property-owning democracy

The Haçienda nightclub in Manchester achieved world fame in the late 1980s and early 1990s as the centre of the house-music boom. Less well known is the fact that, more recently, it became the centre of a house-price bust. The Haçienda closed, mired in financial difficulties, in 1997, but, as the disused mills, lofts and warehouses of Manchester became transformed into flats for a new model of city-living, local developers could not resist the lure of using the Haçienda brand to flog some over-priced property. The building itself was demolished in 2002, and in its place the developers built the 'Haçienda Flats'. The drab reality of mortgages and home ownership was the very antithesis of the pounding euphoria of the Haçienda's dance floor during its heady 'Madchester' heyday.

The flats were very popular with amateur landlords – the so-called 'buy-to-letters'. A notorious property club called Inside Track drove some of the investment. Investors paid a fee of £2,500 per couple to attend special seminars. Then they paid a further fee of £4,000–5,000 for Gold or Platinum membership. In return the investor would get access to Inside Track's special relationships with property developers. The flats, such as the ones in the Haçienda, would be discounted by up to 15 per cent. This would provide 'instant equity' for investors. In 2003 Inside Track's vice chairman, Brad Rosser, banged the drum. 'Property investment,' he said, 'had for far, far too long been a minority sport, enjoyed only by the very wealthy and financially sophis-ticated investor. Plunging stock markets and falling pensions have encouraged many more people to look at property. [Gordon Brown] has woken up to this and is clearly seeking to encourage a much wider audience to invest.' In that same year, Inside Track claimed to have handed £25 million of 'instant equity' to its members. In 2007 the prices of many of the properties, including the Haçienda flats, collapsed. They have never recovered. Buyers certainly got instant equity – of the negative kind. Some properties were never even built. Inside Track seminars went bust. A host of lawsuits followed from aggrieved investors. 'I was sold the unit by Instant Access, sister company of Inside Track,' I was told by one investor. 'It has been a disaster. The rent nowhere near covers the mortgage and it's got worse when the rates are so high now.'

Inside Track was an extreme example of the dark underbelly of the property market. But the rapid growth of the buy-to-let (BTL) market brings together all the elements fuelling house prices. For a start, BTL changed the British housing dream from owning your own property into owning other people's property too. Many expected the credit crunch and recession to put paid to BTL. But the cult of the amateur landlord did not just return in the crisis. It prospered. Property values have held, rents have surged, and there have only been a piddling number of repossessions. After the new coalition government slashed planning red tape, mortgage volumes have ballooned. A year after the crash, the old names in BTL lending were back in the game.

At the National Landlord Show in Kensington in 2010, well-heeled amateur landlords leafed their way through cheap housing for sale in poorer northern English cities. 'Eviction popcorn' was being distributed by a law firm promoting its ability to turf out troublesome tenants. Estate agents explained that few locals could obtain a mortgage to buy a £120,000 house. BTL mortgages, however, were priced on the basis of likely rent received. As interest rates were at rock-bottom, these typically interest-only mortgages were dirt-cheap, and a killing was there to be made for anyone with the 25 per cent deposit required. Even better, the mortgage was entirely tax deductible. Brutally put, local

Mancunians on a typical salary would have zero chance to out-compete the landlords. At the show, some landlords admitted that they were in a 'battle' for property with first-time buyers. 'Yes we take the same property,' said one landlord with ten flats. 'I feel a bit guilty, but they should work harder.'

The highest yields in the country in 2010 were on offer in Newcastle upon Tyne. There a young man called Andrew Pellegrino told me that what drove him was his ambition to become a millionaire before the age of 31. 'I've got about 100 rooms split over 14 properties,' he told me. 'If you've got 50 grand or a 100 grand sitting in a bank account, or your folks have, the probability is sooner or later they're gonna get a bit sick of being short-changed and put it in property. The values are low and if they've got a good-sized deposit they're gonna buy and get a far better return.'

The rebirth of this industry within twelve months of the bank collapse was extraordinary. In fact, buy-to-letters were undoubtedly the unintended champion lucky winners from the emergency slashing of interest rates by the Bank of England, and that has lasted for years now. Whilst they charge their tenants thousands of pounds a month in rent, their interest-only mortgage deals charge just hundreds of pounds – even lower for those who have tracker mortgages.

Good for them, it might be argued. Except BTL was back at the expense of taxpayers and savers, as the ability of banks to service this relatively new market was undoubtedly saved by the British government's bank bailout. BTL only formally started in 1996. Yet, remarkably, in 2010 I established that 56 per cent of BTL mortgages ever lent in Britain were sitting on the books of bailed-out banks.

Roughly half of the outstanding BTL mortgage stock is being nursed by the state in some form. At the time of the bailout, Bradford & Bingley and Northern Rock had, between them, BTL mortgage liabilities worth £30 billion, all of which came into government hands. I subsequently found out – from figures that the mortgage industry did not want released – that about 65 per cent of BTL lending in the year after the banking bust was coming from banks who had been bailed out. In the absence of the bailout, little of this business would have been done, and the existing BTL mortgages would have been dealt with far more harshly. Buy-to-let had become a quasi-nationalised industry.

Bradford & Bingley – which like Northern Rock was an overgrown former building society – lies at the heart of this story. Its roots go back to 1851, when it was established to provide home loans to thrifty workers in Yorkshire's mill towns. In the competitive mortgage market of the early 2000s, B&B converted into a bank and decided to chase the returns available in providing mortgages for prospective landlords. Insanity prevailed. In 2003, a third of B&B's £33 billion balance sheet comprised BTL and/or self-certification mortgages. By 2007 that proportion had grown to three-fifths of the total balance sheet, which was now worth £52 billion. At this stage B&B forlornly attempted to persuade international investors to continue their funding. In 2001 there was just £15 billion in BTL mortgage balances across all UK lenders. Just four years later B&B alone exceeded that figure. By 2007, £121 billion of Britain's outstanding mortgage stock, a tenth of the total, was buy-to-let. By 2008, as funding markets closed, B&B effectively went bust and was more or less taken into state ownership, as agents from the Bank of England furtively waited on street corners to see if another bank run would materialise. In its last crazed attempts to persuade the markets for funds, B&B's chief executive Steve Crawshaw presented some figures to the markets, in the form of a table, depicting a typical B&B customer. Average loan size was £121,000, and the average loan-to-value ratio (LTV) was 76 per cent. This compared with the average loan needed by first-time buyers: £131,000, which represented a 90 per cent LTV. Even better, Crawshaw maintained, was the fact that the average B&B buy-to-let customer was a 44-year-old on £80,000 a year, compared to the average first-time buyer, who was a 29-year-old on £35,000. The last column said it all:

Number of mortgages
BTL: 1.8
FTB: n/a

In Bradford & Bingley's last death throes, its chief executive was trying to persuade funders that his bank was more prudent than many others. *His* bank had concentrated on buy-to-let customers, rich people in their mid-forties with £80,000 salaries, who already had two mortgages. *His* bank had not taken a risk with poorer, asset-less young people. It deserved saving.

The question is: why did the state step in to back what was not core housing finance, but high speculation?

None of this would matter if buy-to-let was unequivocally good for everybody. But it is not. It is clearly redistributive in the negative sense, a means of concentrating wealth where it already lies. It therefore has questionable impacts on social mobility. Peter Williams, New Labour's housing-affordability tsar, told me that buy-to-let investors had been directly outcompeting first-time buyers for the same housing stock. Two-thirds of private landlords source their properties from the existing housing stock. It is common knowledge at the top of the mortgage industry that between 2005 and 2008, BTL replaced first-time buyers as the 'marginal buyer' in the housing market. In other words, BTL pushed up house prices ever more, at a time when they appeared to be falling. Good for some, but not for all.

I saw for myself how, even in 2010, estate agents would market £100,000 houses in Greater Manchester to well-heeled investors at the National Landlord Show in Kensington on the basis of rental yield. In BTL, multiples of rental yield replace multiples of salary as the pricing mechanism for our homes.

Young first-time buyers such as Naomi Jacobs in Newcastle finds herself more in a property nightmare than a property dream.

'I'd love to buy a little house now,' she told me. She wants to have a family, and as the family gets bigger so she'd want a bigger house. That is the dream. Naomi is a science graduate, a science graduate with a job. But she can't get a mortgage. She blames the buy-to-letters. 'The smaller flats that first-time buyers would want are ideal for them to rent out,' she sighs. 'But that's the way it is these days. It's slightly cruel when you think about it.'

The double whammy for the young is described to me by the economist David Stevens: 'I think the government has a responsibility to look at whether the market is actually func-tioning in the long-term interests of the country. And it certainly pushed house prices higher in the latter stages of the boom when speculators piled into the market. In the aftermath of the boom it seems to be pushing rental prices up, when we need them to be lower.'

Here's how the insane British economy works. We bailed out the banks, and slashed interest rates to 0.5 per cent, meaning savers can't get a return. So retirees pour their capital into the housing market, and the demand is met by banks diverting mortgage funding to buy-to-let. Young people can't afford to compete with investors with larger deposits, mortgage firepower, and tax breaks (partly paid for by the first-time buyers themselves). Because young people can't afford to buy houses there is an increase in rental demand, which in turn pushes rents sky high. This attracts even more mortgage funding and retiree capital from no-return savings, exacerbating the problem. Because it is so expensive to rent, the young have no chance of saving a deposit to compete with the buy-to-letters – so completing a self-perpetuating vicious circle.

And yet the same buy-to-let investors then complain their children or grandchildren can't buy or even rent houses. Meanwhile politicians pretend they care by having 'first-time buyer summits'. But in reality they make sure they do nothing to offend those voters who own multiple properties, and see increases in house prices almost as a totem of their success. What is more, the government actually makes a number of active interventions in order to sustain this vicious circle.

The government's last survey of private landlords in 2010 revealed that over half of new landlords (those who'd owned their rental property for less than three years) bought solely in the expectation of cashing in on a house-price rise. A quarter of new landlords and a fifth of all landlords reported zero income from their buy-to-let property. Three-quarters of private landlords were buying properties as an investment pension, and about the same proportion were financed by mortgages. Nearly two-thirds of landlords have no relevant experience or qualifications.

Amazingly, one in five private lets are at least partly funded by the government through housing benefit. Half of these landlords get the housing benefit due to their tenants paid directly to them. Taxpayers underpin rents, help to bail out banks that lend buy-to-let mortgages, subsidise interest payments, and effectively hold massive mortgage books. As if that was not enough, low interest rates from the Bank of England disproportionately aid buy-to-let landlords. And to top it off, when in 2012 the Bank of England announced special funding subsidies to back mortgage and small-business lending, this 'Funding for Lending Scheme' was used directly to underpin more buy-to-let lending from bailed-out banks. It could hardly be described as a free market. Some councils are refusing planning permission for rental properties. Yet most attempts at any sort of regulation of buy-to-let are stymied by squeals that the free market is being distorted. So buy-to-let has a dark side. It has undoubtedly pushed house prices up, and reduced the stock of owner-occupier housing. That said, for those suffering from non-existent returns on savings, it is easy to see why they are attracted to the returns from landlordism.

Now that the government owns the majority of this industry, the fact that it creates winners among the rich and wealthy, and losers amongst the poor and young, is a matter of profound public concern. Indeed, in a Treasury Select Committee investigation into the financial crisis, one of the ignored recommendations was for the government to come up with a strategy for what to do with 'its' buy-to-let book.

It could – perfectly reasonably – be pointed out that this is part of a healthier long-term trend away from Britain's obsession with home ownership towards more renting. Instead of the historic UK aspiration of 80 or 85 per cent of households being owner-occupiers, we are heading back down towards the EU average. 'We're settling at a new norm, which is probably closer to 65 per cent. Big difference,' says Peter Williams, the ex-housing affordability tsar. 'I think [the government's] not being clear about the debate. Lord Turner [chief of the FSA], in suggestions about the Mortgage Market Review, has said there should be a political debate about this. Well, there hasn't been one and there should be one.'

Buy-to-let is just the natural endpoint of Britain's current political, financial and cultural approach to property. The 'property-owning democracy', as Mrs Thatcher defined it, is over. She inherited home ownership levels of 57 per cent, which rose to 65 per cent as the first of 2 million council homes were sold under her 'Right To Buy' policy. Home ownership reached 71 per cent, at which point Gordon Brown voiced the aspiration that it rise to 80 per cent. It is now back down to 65 per cent. It might be reasonable to suggest Right to Buy was a generational giveaway to Britons born in the 1950s and 1960s. It seems difficult to imagine how it could be repeated. If you strip out the 'one-off' of Right To Buy sales, the like-for-like percentage is now already below Mrs Thatcher's 57 per cent. Lastly, if – as some bond traders believe – the 1.3 million Britons with an interest-only mortgage and an inadequate repayment vehicle are enduring 'glorified renting', then you can take the home ownership figure down to around 50 per cent, or where we were in 1971 – or roughly German levels. In other words, the Thatcher 'property-owning democracy' was really only a property-owning generation given a one-off gift of their council houses. It undoubtedly felt very real to those who benefited, but it is not proving to be a genuinely transformational and enduring force. At the very least, very high house prices are undoing the political promise of the property-owning democracy. Arguably, though, the property-owning democracy is a myth.

The underside of the boom in property prices is beginning to be seen not just in the broken, or perhaps missing, lower rungs of the housing ladder, but also in the state of the finances of those who took out mortgages at the top of the boom. The FSA calculates that just under half (45 per cent) of all people who took out mortgages since 2005 are 'mortgage prisoners', unable to remortgage or move house. The majority of first-time buyers since 2005 are also mortgage prisoners, says the FSA. There can be no surprise that housing transactions are still around half normal levels. Even before the bottom rungs of the ladder broke, it appeared that the housing ladder had turned into a one-step house trap.

Rise of the *domocracy*

At the heart of all of this is the unwillingness of anybody in finance or politics to say that ever-rising house prices have been a disaster. In reality, ever-rising house prices constitute what is more or less a zero-sum game, a mechanism that redistributes from the poor and the young to the rich and the old. The test case for this is, of course, Germany. Since 1980 real house prices in the UK nearly trebled, and are still well over double their level in 1995. In Germany, real house prices have fallen 17 per cent since 1995. Which nation is better off? Will there ever be a day when a British chancellor of the exchequer welcomes stable, or even mildly falling, house prices?

The political economy of housing policy is dominated by the connection between rising house prices and the political feel-good factor. Throughout the boom, the Labour government emphasised the low interest rates that benefited owner-occupiers, while the value of their investments soared. British politicians them-selves were immune from the downside of the property boom. Their mortgages were and are still paid for. During the biggest housing boom in Britain's history (and some economists argue in world history), many of the politicians who had the power to rein it in were in a position to benefit handsomely from that boom, at taxpayers' expense. It's what might be called culturally corrupt rather than actually corrupt. MPs are able to claim mortgage interest on a second home as an expense, and they can also claim for other costs involved in running this second home – an asset that soared in value during the boom. The huge increase in house prices did not benefit all in Britain. It was a massive redistribution to home-owners from home-seekers. It was a redistribution that led senior Bank of England figures to question privately why younger people weren't kicking up more of a fuss. MPs' expenses may anger the public for many reasons. But the question arises: did they indirectly contribute to the severity of this recession?

Our MPs were at the very best immune from the downside of the property boom thanks to their parliamentary perks. At worst some MPs appear to have built small buy-to-let empires on the back of the taxpayer. Politicians talked a good game about 'affordable housing', but fundamentally their own personal financial interests – in pure economic terms – could have been to make housing less affordable.

Let's put it like this: if MPs were as nakedly exposed to the dark underbelly of Britain's house-price surge as mortgage pris-oners or first-time buyers, without the featherbedding of their taxpayer-funded expenses, would there have been more political pressure to rein in the boom?

In March 2013, the many strands of Britain's dysfunctional relationship with property entwined themselves in a government scheme called 'Help to Buy'. There's no getting away from the delight of the Faircloughs, only the second couple in Britain to complete through the scheme on a new-build project on the site of the old St Helens rugby league ground. 'We've got our own home now and we've got big ideas,' said Mark. They got married last year, and now a home and a conservatory is a possibility. 'Knowing what the mortgages are like now you need a 10 to 15 per cent deposit. We were renting as well as saving up for deposit: it was hard,' Lindsey told me.

Many couples like the Faircloughs have been hit by what the chancellor calls a failure in the mortgage market since the crisis. Banks that made huge losses have been unwilling to lend to people with small deposits. Help to Buy gets around that by the government providing a loan to top up deposit which should increase housing market transactions from current low levels.

Housebuilders also build to order, they are delivered 'just in time' to demand, rather than en masse. If more people move into new homes, construction – a weak part of the economy – will start growing again. Peter Redfern, the CEO of Taylor Wimpey, told me definitely hundreds, maybe thousands of extra houses would be built because of the scheme, creating knock-on growth. 'It enables us to pick things up to build more homes on the sites we've already got open, and also gives us more confidence about investing in future sites and the infrastructure and land to grow the business,' he said. 'We're certainly talking hundreds... probably talking thousands – that's creating more jobs, and more economic activity locally.'

The mechanics of the scheme are rather intriguing. From mid-2013 the Treasury has been paying between £20,000 and £120,000 in cash per home directly to housebuilders. It adds to the national debt for five years, but not the annual deficit, because the Treasury takes a 20 per cent stake in the house. Although it is borrowed money, it doesn't count as public-sector borrowing but as a 'financial transaction' instead. The banks fund 75 per cent, a less risky and therefore cheaper mortgage, and the buyer pays a 5 per cent deposit. It basically opens up affordable mortgages to buyers with small deposits.

Was there not a simpler solution to jump-start the market?

Why not let the market clear, and prices fall to reflect falling real incomes, weak economic growth? Indeed, why doesn't Taylor Wimpey just cut the prices of its homes? 'Life's not that simple,' Redfern tells me. He mentions the impact on local existing homes if new home prices were cut. 'I don't think it's very desirable for people who have already bought from us, and people in the surrounding village. Everybody wants a certain stability in housing.'

Yet there was no loosening of planning law. So the combination of taxpayer-funded and guaranteed mortgages, central bank-subsidised banks and limited housing supply, led to the inevitable: an artificial rise in house prices. The policy of deploying housing spend on benefit rather than houses continued. Since 2000 the UK has spent £140 billion on housing, and double that, £280 billion, on housing benefit. One form of spending supports jobs, construction, and living standards. The other supports landlords, house prices, and rent inflation.

Are we going to load the burden of adjustment from a decade-long bubble onto people who happen to have been born in the 1980s and 1990s? Progressive voices keen to redistribute through benefits have said very little about the overarching negative redistribution caused by the trebling of house prices. All political parties claim to want to foster 'social mobility', yet it seems that where you live will be determined more now by where your parents lived.

The recent history of property in Britain is wrapped up in notions of freedom and the social mobility of owner-occupation and right-to-buy. Yet right now, Britain faces a return to a more traditional relationship with the land, in which property is the principal agent for holding back opportunity-for-all. The property ladder was a one-off opportunity for a lucky generation-and-a-half. Now we are back to a kind of neo-feudalism, in which your quality of life depends on who your parents are, and what they owned.

CHAPTER 6

THREE FUNERALS, TWO BANKING SYSTEMS AND A WEDDING

Dramatis personae

Bob Diamond, Barclays, various (1996–2012),
chief executive (2010–12)
Cristiano Ronaldo, Portuguese footballer
Alistair Darling, UK chancellor of the exchequer (2007–10)
John Varley, Barclays chief executive (2004–11)
Eric Daniels, Lloyds chief executive (2003–11)
Peter Sands, Standard Chartered chief executive (2006–)
Fred Goodwin, Royal Bank of Scotland chief executive (2001–08)
Monty Slater, prospective RBS customer, Stockport
James Crosby, HBoS chief executive (2001–06);
non-executive, then deputy chairman of the FSA (2004–09)
Andy Hornby, HBoS chief executive (2006–08)
Christine Lagarde, French finance minister (2007–11)
Beth Jacobson, former loan officer, Wells Fargo
Sheila Dixon, mayor of Baltimore
Brad Setser, economist, subsequently US Treasury
Joe Cassano, AIG Financial Products, Mayfair, London
Lord Turner, chairman of the FSA (2008–13)
Lord Myners, Treasury minister
Mervyn King, governor of the Bank of England (2003–13)
Shriti Vadera, adviser to Gordon Brown, Business
Department minister
Hector Sants, FSA chief executive (2007–12)
Marcus Agius, chairman of Barclays (2007–12)

On 13 May 2007 Bob Diamond had only one aim: to give a wide berth to Cristiano Ronaldo. Europe's best-paid banker was no fan of Europe's soon-to-be best-paid footballer. It was bad enough for Diamond – a Chelsea season-ticket holder – that he had to hand that year's Premier League trophy to Manchester United's Ryan Giggs and Gary Neville on the Old Trafford pitch. Diamond had become used to presenting it to Chelsea captain John Terry. Now he was faced with handing a winner's medal over to Ronaldo, for whom he had developed a Chelsea fan's dislike, on account of what he felt was the young Portuguese forward's arrogance.

Diamond even precision-timed with fellow Barclays executive Gary Hoffman, the other dignitary handing out the prizes, to avoid having to hand Ronaldo his winner's medal. So, having gained Hoffman's agreement, Diamond counted down the line of multimillionaire footballers and timed it so that he would give Wayne Rooney his medal, not Ronaldo. It almost worked – until Ronaldo, wearing a shirt with the letters 'AIG' across his chest, swapped places in the line and gave Diamond a humble thank you for his first Premier League champions' medal. Diamond gave him an awkward couple of pats on the shoulder. A brief encounter between the King of British Football and the King of British Banking.

May 2007 was pretty much the end of the long peacetime for British banking. Events had been set in train that would lead to the collapse of hedge funds, the collapse of investment banks, the collapse of lending to banks, the collapse of Northern Rock, and eventually the collapse of half the UK banking system. The conventional high-street banking crises, epitomised by the bank run on Northern Rock, was the most visible manifestation of failure in UK banking. But there were twin crises in Britain, centred on the City of London. The one most commonly read about in the news, and another, just as important, in the invisible banking system. So May 2007 was also the high watermark of what would become known as the 'shadow banking' system – a parallel international system of loans, lending, creditors and debtors that operated on low levels of capital, and had few of the safety systems of the conventional banking system. This shadow system was global, and spewed out credit, profits and bonuses and became intertwined with the raciest elements of the conventional system in Britain – until its collapse.

Bob Diamond found himself at Old Trafford because Barclays Bank sponsored the English Premier League. Diamond was then chief executive of Barclays Corporate and Investment Banking and Wealth Management. But the Premier League sponsorship was not about Barclays' high-rolling casino arm. The bank had inherited the sponsorship from Barclaycard, the bank's pioneering but separately run credit-card unit. In 2001 football was part of a conscious effort to get the Barclays credit card away from its up-market image and into the hands of every Briton, even those classified as 'near-prime'. It was an effort to increase the use of credit cards in the UK from one in twenty-five transactions closer to the one in four seen in the USA. Less than half of Britons had credit cards, versus 70 per cent in the USA. The answer was 'risk-based pricing': Barclays dropped its credit standards and offered cards to some of the 700,000 applicants turned down every year, in return, eventually, for higher interest rates. It did not end well.

Arrears surged. Bad debts mounted. Punters lured by a combination of football and fleetingly free credit could not afford to repay Barclaycard's famously high rates of interest. Yet Barclay's then chief executive was also admitting that he would not advise his own children to pay the high rate of interest on his bank's own cards.

Barclaycard's 'near-prime' strategy went into rapid retreat. Insiders say this was part of the reason that Barclays decided to take on football sponsorship at corporate level. And that's why, a few years later, Bob Diamond found himself scheming to avoid the world's best football player. But Diamond's presence also marked something much more important. He was at Old Trafford because Barclays got burnt by consumer credit very early in the consumer-credit binge. In those early days, it also got burnt by its mortgage lending. In 1990–91 Barclays needed to tap shareholders twice for new capital, after the crash in property values. Prior to the crash, it had been all too eager to offer mortgages to all and sundry, in an effort to win market share from NatWest (itself later bought by Royal Bank of Scotland).

'The 1990s were regarded as seminal in a bad way,' one senior insider told me. 'Barclays got it so long on property and so wrong in property that it was seared into the consciousness of the corporation never to let that happen again.' In the subsequent boom of the 2000s, the property exposure of its global bank-loan portfolio was below 8 per cent. On this score at least, Barclays had become extremely cautious, although, as we shall see, this is not the full story – particularly in relation to Mr Diamond. But in the great British credit bubble, in most areas of mortgage finance, consumer credit and property-development funding, Barclays let other British banks make the running. For almost all of the competitors who chose to take up the slack, it proved fatal. For Barclays, it was the first of many dodged bullets. And this dodged bullet would in the end have a very important role to play as large swathes of the British banking system collapsed into the hands of the state.

The Bankers' Last Supper that changed little

Through the early autumn of 2008, Britain's most exclusive dining club would convene in an upstairs room at Number 11 Downing Street. Here they were confronted with the mortality of the banks they represented. However, many seemed more concerned with the preservation of the status quo and their own pay packets than the imminent collapse of the UK's cash-machine network. With the benefit of hindsight, one could pinpoint these dinners as missed opportunities, when the relationship between Britain and its banks could have been fundamentally reshaped.

At one such dinner Chancellor of the Exchequer Alistair Darling told his guests that the entire British banking system was going the way of Northern Rock a year before, and Bradford & Bingley a few weeks previously. If necessary, he said, he would nationalise the major banks.

Fred Goodwin of the Royal Bank of Scotland sat underneath a painting entitled *Death's Head*. Next to him sat Barclays' John Varley, the tall patrician chief executive who, according to the City folklore, reined in Bob Diamond's aggressive investment-banking style. António Horta Osório represented Santander, the Spanish bank that had swallowed struggling areas of British high-street banking, including Abbey, Alliance & Leicester and, days before, the remains of Bradford & Bingley. All were overstretched demutualised building societies. Alistair Darling wrote that Horta Osório 'took care to sit well away from the centre of the table'. Graham Beale represented Nationwide, a rare success, the big beast of the surviving building societies. Peter Sands or Richard Meddings came on behalf of Standard Chartered, which had helped shape the UK recapitalisation at its offices in the City. Dyfrig John or Douglas Flint attended for HSBC; like Sands, they ran an Asia-focused bank headquartered in the UK and did not require any government capital. Lastly, representing Lloyds TSB, there was Eric Daniels, who, according to the chancellor's book on the crisis, 'had presumably by now had the opportunity to open the books to the horrors of what he had bought' after a government-aided merger with HBoS. HBoS chief executive Andy Hornby was at some of the meetings, and the ghost of ex-chief executive James Crosby lurked somewhere close to Mr Daniels, in hellish chains of property debt. The banks had been given secret Treasury codenames since the beginning of the crisis, either an animal or a planet or on one occassion a dead rockstar. The Badger had already been trapped. Elvis lived, but only in state ownership. The Phoenix was not going to rise again. And the Tiger had been tamed with some help from Spain.

The RBS chief executive led the delegation from the first

dinner. Uniquely, Sir Fred, as he then was, actually signed off the bulk of Scotland's banknotes. RBS, alongside Bank of Scotland and Clydesdale Bank, continued to issue bespoke Scottish notes backed by deposits at the Bank of England. If they were really lucky, Sir Fred's sporting heroes, sponsored by RBS, got to feature on a commemorative note. Lord Myners, a Treasury minister at the table, would later tell Parliament that at RBS's futuristic Gogarburn HQ a man was employed to ensure that only notes with Sir Fred's signature should be stocked in the cash machines (RBS denies this). Here was a man who not only ran the world's sixth largest bank, but who could also delude himself that he ran his own currency. Indeed, his bank had assets of £2.2 trillion, one and half times the size of the UK's annual GDP. The UK's assets were still far bigger, but if any bank was too big to fail, it was RBS. Perhaps that is why Sir Fred remained defiant to the end, despite admitting that his bank was entirely reliant on the day-to-day life support of overnight borrowing from the Bank of England. Delusion and denial were combined with a knowledge that an uncontrolled collapse of RBS would wreak havoc across the nation.

The chancellor had been concerned about RBS, codenamed Phoenix, ever since Sir Fred, like a particularly depressed carol singer, had appeared uninvited at the door of Darling's Edinburgh house the previous Christmas, carrying a wrapped panettone as a present. At this point Sir Fred had probably begun to digest the sheer insanity of RBS's cash purchase of ABN Amro, which had gone through after the credit crisis began – and without RBS seeing the Dutch bank's books. Sir Fred had arranged a consortium of international banks to mount a hostile takeover that snatched the bank from an approved deal with Barclays. The Scottish bank was hailed by the press and by the Scottish first minister, Alex Salmond, for its daring deal-making. But rival chief executives were troubled. 'If you look at the RBS accounts in '08 and '09,' one chief executive told me, 'there's this big lump in it, which is basically an unexplained set of things which is ABN. How anybody had any idea of what was going on. . . We couldn't work it out.' The original motive for the purchase of ABN was to get hold of the bank's successful US unit, La Salle. Strangely, even after La Salle was sold to Bank of America, RBS was still just as keen to buy. RBS also left the booming and very profitable South American parts of ABN Amro to Santander. The remaining core of the company was chock-full of toxic derivative waste. As the takeover was hostile, Sir Fred would not even have had the chance to find out if the deal was good or bad. As it turned out, it was fatal. Barclays' guardian angel, meanwhile, had saved it from buying ABN.

Back around the table at Number 11, on Monday, 7 October 2008, RBS was just hours from running out of money to put in its cash machines. An anonymous press briefing – blamed by ministers on bankers – suggested that all the banks around the table were in trouble and had asked for capital, not just RBS and HBoS. A similarly false rumour had emerged earlier in the year about recapitalisations. On the morning of 8 October there was blind panic in trading of shares of UK banks, and RBS in particular. There were also large corporate withdrawals from RBS bank accounts. An executive recalls that even sophisticated investors made errors. One man withdrew £50,000 from the Bishopsgate branch in the City of London, but then redeposited it in a NatWest around the corner – essentially the same bank. Alistair Darling broke off from a Luxembourg finance ministers' meeting and flew home on an RAF plane to deal with the crisis. The government's recapitalisation plan had to be brought forward. RBS took a somewhat aggressive stance, even with the Bank of England, which was trying to help it. The central bank's Special Liquidity Scheme was meant to trade cheap funding strictly for then illiquid and untradeable bundles of British homeowner mortgages. RBS attempted to cash in a bundle of debts which on close inspection included a Spanish car park. The bank had built up a property portfolio that extended as far as the USA, where its assets embraced a cemetery in the

Deep South and a golf course dozens of miles from the nearest road. It is a grand fallacy that RBS tripped over simply because of the calamitous takeover of ABN Amro. RBS was hugely outcompeting other banks on commercial deals, and on property. 'We were losing a lot of business to RBS and HBoS,' another UK bank chief executive told me. 'I certainly remember saying to my guys "When are we going to see RBS and HBoS trip up, because trip up they must?"' RBS's global exposure to property at the peak of the crisis was 33 per cent of its total loan book. A reconstruction using the latest capital standards of RBS's balance sheet at the time it bought ABN Amro, by regulators, revealed a capital ratio of just 2 per cent. Competitors were flabbergasted that the FSA waved through the ABN Amro purchase. But RBS might have failed in any event.

Perhaps the regulators should have paid more attention in 2003 when RBS offered a gold credit card with a £10,000 credit limit to Monty Slater from Stockport, Cheshire. It wasn't just that Monty could not afford to repay, nor even that he had not asked for the card. Monty was a dog, targeted by a consumer database. The story was treated as an amusing boom-time banking distraction. Actually it was a vivid example of how the essential bond between bank and borrower was breaking. The banks did not know what they were lending, nor to whom. Indeed, by 2008 a Shih Tzu might have ranked as one of RBS's more solvent debtors.

HBoS: bailing out a basket case

For an artificial hill, the Mound in Edinburgh, dominated by the Assembly Hall of the Church of Scotland, has seen its fair share of history. The 'Sermon on the Mound', in which Margaret Thatcher addressed the Kirk's 1988 General Assembly, is widely believed to be the moment that the prime minister proclaimed, 'There is no such thing as society.' That quote actually came from an earlier interview with a women's magazine. But in her speech to the General Assembly she presented a philosophical and theological justification for her ideas on free markets and capitalism. Perhaps she would have received a less frosty reception at the neighbouring Mound headquarters of another venerable Scottish institution – the Bank of Scotland. Certainly it was during the Thatcher era that BoS embarked on a lending boom that over the following two decades grew at 20 per cent per year. But it lacked a commensurate growth in its deposit base. The problem was temporarily solved by access to high finance, the so-called wholesale markets, but those did not even cover half of its lending. To fill the strategic gap, in 1999 BoS tried to buy NatWest, a bank double its own size, but lost out to RBS. A deal with Abbey seemed on the cards, but fell through. In 2001, on the rebound, BoS hosted talks that would lead to the creation of Halifax Bank of Scotland (HBoS), and the end of three centuries of independence. Halifax's 11 million savers would fill some of the deposit gap, and BoS's then conservative commercial lending teams would find the companies to fund. What could go wrong?

The official corporate HQ was located in Scotland, but four top executives, including James Crosby and Andy Hornby, all came from the Halifax, and another was recruited from a top insurer. None of the five had banking qualifications. All the executives gave themselves massive pay rises of over 55 per cent for the success of completing the merger. Just a decade earlier, calculates Ray Perman, author of *Hubris* (2012), the salary of the highest-paid BoS director was sixteen times that of the average BoS salary. Now, including bonuses, James Crosby was earning forty-three times the average HBoS salary. Perhaps he would have deserved his pay if the new company had lived up to its billing as 'the new force in banking', illustrated with a closely shot handshake on the front of the Annual Report.

While the mighty Bank of Scotland had lasted 306 years as an independent entity, HBoS only lasted seven. Even once it was taken over by Lloyds, HBoS still needed to be bailed out. In fact, so rotten was HBoS that Lloyds itself had to be bailed out by the taxpayer. A bank run by overpaid amateur bankers that had a lifespan less than the average dog, and was so bankrupt it required taxpayer bailouts for two banks, HBoS might more accurately be described as a 'new *farce* in banking'.

Before relaxing competition rules to allow Lloyds to pursue the takeover, the FSA had hawked HBoS around to other banking groups, but it turned out that only a purchase by Standard Chartered would have been legal under UK competition law. Tellingly, HBoS was not offered to Barclays. One chief executive who looked at the books could not believe what he saw. 'We just thought this thing was deeply scary,' he told me. 'The wholesale [corporate] bank was asking for trouble.' He went on to tell me that HBoS's funding model for its mortgage book was 'incredibly vulnerable' to stress. 'And this mattered obviously a lot more than, say, Northern Rock, which was bad enough. This was huge, a massive great institution.'

The consensus in the boardrooms asked to step in to buy HBoS was that it was a basket case. A key indicator of trouble was the high number of football clubs in its portfolio. The books of HBoS Australia, which had been auctioned in a last-ditch attempt to save the bank in the summer of 2008, were an eye-opener. One top banker who looked at the figures concluded that HBoS Australia was sitting on a 'high-risk book of leveraged lending and commercial property, but entirely wholesale funded on a cross-currency basis. They didn't really have any local funds. We were just stunned.' At £3.6 billion, HBoS Australia's cumulative loan impairments from 2008 to 2011 were worth 28 per cent of its entire 2008 loan book. As the Parliamentary Commission on Banking Standards (PCBS) concluded, this dire state of affairs was all the more remarkable given that at that time the Australian economy was growing robustly, and its banking system remained profitable and free of bailouts. In contrast, HBoS's travails in Ireland could be partially excused by the generalised economic collapse there. Nevertheless, HBoS Ireland still managed to become the second worst bank in Ireland, with 2008–11 impairments at 36 per cent of its 2008 loan book. Of £11 billion in Irish losses (worth 6 per cent of Ireland's entire GDP), £6.5 billion related to commercial real estate. So large were these losses that Alistair Darling, at one point, argued that the Irish government should take the rotting assets of HBoS Ireland and the problem loans of the RBS-owned Ulster Bank into NAMA (National Asset Management Agency), its state-backed 'bad bank'. Eventually, the UK Treasury settled on being a 'good neighbour' and took the pressure off.

HBoS's disasters abroad were all brought about by three factors: an aggressive pursuit of rapid market growth, limited deposit funding, and concentration on property. It was a toxic recipe, originally concocted in Britain itself. It is best illustrated by the table published by the Tyrie Commission report into the failure of HBoS. There is an anonymised version of its last book of large loan facilities presented by its infamous head of Corporate Lending, Peter Cummings, to the board. In 2008, of its forty-four largest corporate loans (worth between £85 million and £2.9 billion), twenty-nine were property companies. Most of the others were either related to property (hotels) – or to credit (debt collection). For context, there was one accountancy firm, one oil-infrastructure designer, one health-club company and one presumably Irish 'whiskey distiller'. The bank did not even have the money to lend to these companies. HBoS's 'funding gap' – the difference between loans and deposits – was £213 billion in 2008. It needed to find this money from market investors – but they had all disappeared. HBoS had turned into a machine for channelling hot money at property. Its bankers would agitate housebuilders and retailers for mergers, takeovers and restructurings, predicated on rising property prices, cheap debt and easy funding. HBoS would then lend the money, invest risky equity in a share of the business, and take advisory fees. Competing banks could not get a look-in. HBoS had become, in the words of one of these competitors, 'a giant UK property hedge fund'.

One FTSE-100 chief executive, not a banker, told me that

in January 2007 he had asked an HBoS director why his board was not more concerned about the bank's overall exposure to the UK housing market, mortgage lending and the construction industry. It was a question few dared ask. The reply was flippant, but no joke, and it exposed the recklessness of the people at the top of the bank. 'We're so exposed to the UK housing market anyway,' the HBoS board member told him, 'that if it goes tits up, we're screwed anyway. So in for a penny, in for a pound.' It was an open secret. Even after the collapse of Northern Rock, the HBoS board rebuffed enquiries from the regulators, who had begun to wake up to what was going on. 'Our management has done enough,' HBoS chairman Lord Stevenson, wrote to FSA chief Lord Turner in November 2007. 'There could be some release of the FSA paranoia button!'

A few days before the inevitable catastrophe, HBoS tried one last brazen deal-making gambit. It offered to buy Bradford & Bingley. It would have been a desperate union of two shoddily run, bankrupt banks that had overstretched themselves fuelling an insane property boom. But it would have given HBoS access to a much-needed funding stream – the depositors of Bradford & Bingley. Both the Halifax and Bradford & Bingley building societies had been built on the common sense saving habits of ordinary Yorkshire folk, but now they were being destroyed in an orgy of executive incompetence. As banks, neither lasted longer than a decade. If the takeover had gone ahead, it would have culminated in the supernova of all bank busts. Fortunately, the proposal was quietly and quickly turned down.

Under pressure from the regulators, some of the bankers around Darling's table had pondered taking parts of HBoS from the FSA's fire sale. One offered to take the retail bank for free, but only if there was temporary government liquidity support to fund mortgages, and the taxpayer took on the rotten corporate bank. It didn't sound a bargain for the Treasury. That said, the bank's models calculated that HBoS's fair value was strongly negative. 'We were stunned when Lloyds were prepared to pay a positive price,' reflected one leading British banker. 'Indeed, I asked our guys who'd done the analysis to have another look at it because I thought we must have got it wildly wrong.' In fact they were wildly right. Little wonder that a few days after Lloyds bought the bank, Alistair Darling noticed that the Lloyds chief Eric Daniels, sitting around the bailout table, had a rather shocked look on his face. The high-street banks were, however, only half the story.

New Labour, light touch

Under Gordon Brown's chancellorship, the same Number 11 conference table had seen happier times. Brown had set up a 'High Level City Group' on financial services. All the names gathered in ignominy around his successor's table in October 2008 were there in glory in October 2006 for the first meeting, hosted by Brown and his then City minister Ed Balls. The emphasis was on the high finance of the City of London, rather than plain-vanilla retail banking. Conventional banks had been largely left to their own devices. New Labour, always trying to triangulate rather than lead, convinced itself that competition and consumer protection were sufficient guarantors of the public interest.

On the odd occasion when the supine regulator got a little worried, bankers would complain to politicians. Tony Blair and Gordon Brown would send a letter or write a speech on the need for a 'light touch'. This was not an accident. It was a choice. Other countries, even anglophone nations such as Canada and Australia, operated prudential limits on credit, with no suggestion of a lack of commitment to a market economy. 'A combination of good supervision and good macro-prudential policy could have stopped all that happening,' one UK bank chief executive told me. 'For example, for the HBoS corporate lending practices, it didn't take a rocket scientist to work out they were pretty adventurous.' Another senior UK banker admits that such a 'macro-prudential policy' – involving the reining in of loan-to-value ratios on mortgages – would have been 'a complete pain', and that he and other bankers would have undoubtedly campaigned against it. 'But is it what a central bank should be prepared to do?' he asked, and then supplied his own answer: 'For sure.' As we shall see, banks rarely seem to know what is good even for themselves.

For its part, New Labour, in its desperate efforts to prove that the party did not secretly harbour Trotskyite instincts, settled on an approach to the UK's tax-abundant, credit-spewing retail banking system that was somewhere between 'light touch' and 'no touch'. For investment banking – the so-called 'casino' – the touch was heavier, but it was not a regulatory hand on the shoulder, but rather a crazed embrace. What passed for industrial policy in Blair's Britain was to entrench London as a lucrative loophole in global finance.

All roads lead to London

'In the computer industry, when there are security intrusions, the best experts today are those who are former hackers,' said a smiling Christine Lagarde. 'There's something to be said about someone who knows the system from inside, who can actually suggest how to fix it, and I really welcome the complete change of view from UK authorities.' Lagarde was in one of her more mischievous moods. This was in 2009, and Lagarde was then the French minister of finance. She was chatting with a senior British cabinet minister about the role of the City of London in the crisis, and the UK government's sudden conversion to regulating the world financial system. In her analogy, the hackers in question were the ministers of Britain's Labour government, former proponents of regulation-lite. But re-regulation of the world financial system was never going to start here in London: home to the most bankrupt floor of office space in the world that nearly bankrupted the whole European banking system; home of the worst bank takeover and the worst bank merger in world history; the manufacturer of toxic mortgage bonds for

Lehman Brothers; home of the traders who nearly felled UBS; and base of the sober Treasury operation that cost J. P. Morgan billions. And then there was the systematic rigging of Libor, London's inter-bank interest rate, the scandal that came to symbolise everything that was wrong with global finance. Why did all roads lead to London?

London was, and still is, the global clearing house for socially useless financial innovation. In France and in Germany this has long been the accusation. But even in the USA, accusatory fingers began to be pointed at London. The ever-lengthening shadows in the world financial system were being cast by the ever-rising skyline of the City.

Mis-selling mortgages to poor African Americans

Cut to Baltimore, the setting for the greatest TV drama series of all time: *The Wire*. Through five seasons, *The Wire* shone its spotlight on the frailties of human nature by exposing the rotten core of five strands of life in the Maryland capital: its drug gangs, its police service, its declining dockyards, its schools and its local newspapers. But they missed the banks. The non-existent sixth season should have been about rich bankers selling mortgages to poor African Americans.

Beth Jacobson glances along her mantelpiece. A number of trophies tell of the old times when she was the top-rated mortgage loan officer at leading US bank Wells Fargo. In some years she earned commissions of $700,000. She was rewarded with a swim with dolphins, an Aerosmith concert, crystal vases, and six iPods. 'They treated you as royalty – making money on the back of people who couldn't afford the loans,' she says. 'It seemed the good times were going to continue forever.' Between 2004 and 2007 loan officers such as Jacobson earned commission of up to 1.8 per cent of the total value of the loan, if it was a high-interest subprime loan. An ordinary loan to a 'prime' customer – a loan that could be underwritten by the US government mortgage guarantee scheme (via Fannie Mae, Freddie Mac, etc.) – earned a commission of 0.5 per cent. In addition, subprime loans required less paperwork than the guaranteed prime loans, and could be signed off in days rather than weeks – all the more crucial in the crazy Maryland housing boom of the mid-2000s. Clearly there was an incentive for loan officers and external mortgage brokers to sign up as many borrowers to subprime loans as possible, even if some borrowers qualified for the cheaper prime loans. It was worth up to $1,500 extra for a typical loan. And according to the US Department of Justice, that is exactly what happened. In 2009 Beth Jacobson turned whistleblower on her former employer and her whole industry. She and her fellow employees had targeted poor African American communities in Baltimore. 'These people did not stand a chance of paying the loans back. And you do have a certain amount of guilt thinking you're putting people in that and you try to justify saying, "Well, they really wanted that house." But they were looking to us as experts to guide them on their finances.' She told of $300 donations made to churches to host mortgage seminars, with an additional $300 paid for every mortgage signed off.

In 2009 the mis-selling of mortgages to poor African Americans was taken up by Sheila Dixon, the entrepreneurial mayor of Baltimore, and the real-life inspiration for *The Wire*'s Nerese Campbell. When I met her she was indignant. 'What they are doing to average citizens who want to meet the American dream. . .' She left that thought hanging. 'In this day and time you would not think a company like Wells Fargo would use subprime mortgages to target a certain population.' The Department of Justice and the Office of the Comptroller of the Currency both published reports showing such a pattern. Wells Fargo always denied that African Americans had been targeted for what became known as 'reverse redlining' (targeting bad credit at poor neighbourhoods, as opposed to 'redlining' which was withholding it entirely). But the bank did in July 2012 settle a legal case brought by the

Department of Justice, which cited 34,000 people from minority groups across the USA who had been sold mortgages on worse terms than white Americans of the equivalent credit standing. No guilt was admitted, but Wells Fargo paid out $175 million, including $50 million to initiatives in Baltimore.

These tales from the Default Line would appear to be firmly rooted in bubble-era America. But much of the ultimate source of this credit was to be found in Europe and – especially – in London.

London: capital of the shadow banking world

Shadow banks were structures that walked, talked and acted like banks, doing many of the same things as banks, but which were not regulated as banks. In 2009 I spoke to Brad Setser, now a US Treasury official, just before he joined the Obama administration as a White House economic adviser. He told me about the shadow banks. 'They were buying lots of securities, and issuing lots of short-term liabilities. They were taking on a lot of liquidity risk, and running a mismatch between the maturity of their assets and liabilities.' In other words, they were lending, aggressively, taking in a type of sophisticated deposit, and performing the roles of conventional banks. 'Yet they didn't understand the risks they were taking, and a lot of these institutions were undercapitalised for what they were doing.' The shadow banks were not single institutions but byzantine microstructures of hedge funds, insurers, investment-bank trading desks, credit-raters, off-balance-sheet conduits, special investment vehicles, master trusts, and parts of the normal banking system. The shadow banking system was self-unaware – each cog operated independently – but the end result was the bubble machine that fed Northern Rock, HBoS, Caja Madrid, US subprime providers, Anglo Irish Bank, and all their indebted customers. The billions whose life it affected didn't even know the shadow banking system existed, but it was worth ten trillion dollars. In 2008 it collapsed, and we are beginning to notice now that it's gone. Its impact was felt everywhere, from the letters landing on your doormat offering unsolicited credit and 125 per cent mortgages to private equity buyouts of the world's biggest companies. The shadow banking system turned risky on-balance-sheet loans into supposedly indestructible financial instruments deemed as safe as a government bond by ratings agencies, and insured by the world's biggest insurance scheme to stay that safe. The system worked well in an era of flexible credit ratings and even more flexible regulators. But it lacked the insurance against bank runs present in the conventional banking system. There was no backstop for liquidity in the event of a run on the shadow banks. London was its capital – and in 2008, we got the run.

Like the dark matter that makes up much of the mass of the universe, the shadow banking system is detectable only by deduction, rather than by direct observation. The US Treasury International Capital (TIC) reporting system offered some light into the financial shade. It was set up in 1934 to track international investment and capital flows, and requires most US financial entities to track foreign purchases of bonds and shares. All purchases are anonymised and given a numerical code corresponding to a nation, with the information returned to the New York Federal Reserve. The TIC is most famous for detailing the amassing of US Treasury bonds by China since 2000. This was a cause of great international angst and financial-market commentary. Some argue that it was the root cause of the build-up of global economic imbalances and thus of the financial crisis. By 2002, according to the TIC data, mainland China (country code 41408) had acquired long- and short-term US government debt totalling $93 billion. By 2007 this had ballooned to $476 billion. A flood of Chinese-earned dollars returned to the USA, so helping to keep Chinese exports cheap, and US lending rates low (see Chapter 4, page 111). Meanwhile, elsewhere on the TIC spreadsheet, another foreign nation, code number 13005, was seemingly hoovering up a broadly similar proportion of another type of US debt. In 2002 its holdings of long- and short-term 'US corporate debt' was $101 billion. By 2007 it was $423 billion. That country, the largest holder of US private debt, was the United Kingdom. In the run-up to the crisis, Britain had been buying up as much US debt as the much-feared China, albeit 'corporate' rather than government debt. How on earth was the UK managing to ingest American private debt worth one-seventh of the entire British economy?

In the US classification system, 'corporate debt' included, yes, an IBM or General Motors bond, as one might expect. But it also included non-Agency mortgage bonds. Traditional parcels of mortgage debt that conformed to Agency standards (and were therefore underwritten by the US state through the agencies Fannie Mae and Freddie Mac, etc.) were thirty-year loans given at a fixed rate. The market for non-conforming loans included subprime, interest-only mortgages, and as we know, this sector was booming at the time. The non-Agency mortgage-backed securities market showed up in the US TIC data as 'purchases of corporate debt'. For Setser this points to purchases by securitisation vehicles, key parts of the shadow banking system, based in the UK, in the City of London.

'A lot of the shadow banking system was operating through London,' Setser told me. 'You see it in the capital-flows data. You see it in 2005–6–7 when every risk, every mortgage was being repackaged and spliced and diced, and AIG Financial Products [based in London] was selling [credit default swap] insurance to banks. During this period there was a huge boom in US TIC data of US corporate debt sales to London. Then, in 2007, that stopped. These institutions were operating through London – both sides of their balance sheet were actively operating through London. European banks were borrowing a lot of dollars and using the funds to buy a lot of repackaged but still risky mortgages. London was a critical part of the US financial system for regulatory and tax reasons.'

No other G7 nation had acquired anything like the amount of US corporate debt as the UK. Japan, and China of course, amassed US government bonds. But the only other jurisdictions that saw such a rapid boom-time increase in purchases of US corporate bonds were the Cayman Islands ($80 billion in 2002, rising to $375 billion in 2007), Luxembourg ($78 billion to $370bn), Belgium ($92 billion to $323 billion) and Ireland ($43 billion to $216 billion).

The TIC data only gives a glimmer of the bigger picture. The UK figure does reflect the way that Wall Street washed its dirtiest laundry in the City of London. It also reflects the fact that big European banks operated their dollar trading through the City. The full reality would only be revealed if the UK published its own version of the TIC data. Although the chancellor has often told us that Britain owes a portion of its debts to China, a figure has never been published. Why?

In the realms of international financial diplomacy, fingers point towards the UK's 'appallingly bad' data on financial flows, more suited to a secretive offshore financial centre than the world's capital of finance. London's wish to protect its role as manager of Gulf oil money and as a conduit for China's surplus dollars might explain why. A portion of China's purchases of US government bonds were originally scored as 'UK' purchases. 'More attention is needed in the USA to flows through UK banks,' Setser told me. 'There are important lessons to be learned, and the UK needs transparent flow of money in and out. These would be important crisis warning signs.' UK TIC-style data would be revelatory for global finance. But perhaps the City fears that would be a step too far out of the shadows.

The most tangible manifestation of the shadow banking system was, as Setser pointed out to me, an office in London's smart Mayfair district. The people who worked there were told it was the most profitable office per capita in the world. This was the office of AIG Financial Products (AIG FP), run by Joe Cassano. The philosophical core of this triumph of high capitalism was, as Cassano triumphantly told AIG investors, 'the bifurcation of credit from the host contract'. (This splitting of the credit atom is described in detail in the next chapter.) Such was the confidence that prevailed in Mayfair barely ten months before AIG's collapse. The business written in London was primarily for 'regulatory capital management' by its banking clients.

AIG had begun selling so-called credit default swaps (CDSs) in 1998. J. P. Morgan were first in line to take advantage, having developed the underlying derivative technology. In the eyes of J. P. Morgan's bankers in London, they had 'stuffed our leftover positions into AIG, getting rid of risks'. The theory was that AIG, with its giant insurance-company balance sheet, could offer to protect the owners of parcels of loans – everything from subprime mortgages to corporate bonds to car loans – from the risk of default. AIG would charge a fee worth a fraction of a percentage of the security, and in return AIG would make good the loss in any default. J. P. Morgan began to arrange more and more such trades with AIG for its clients, beginning with an Italian bank. At first, these trades principally involved corporate debt, about which there was a wealth of historical default data, and well-tested modelling of losses (see Chapter 7, page 205).

In essence AIG's clients paid a small amount to make their trading risks disappear. AIG itself collected the fees, but did not then further hedge these risks, and did not at first put aside any collateral. The financial system had, in theory, found a way to make credit risk pass along a chain of buyers, and then at the end, at AIG's Mayfair office, it simply *disappeared*. It was magic. How so? AIG's AAA credit rating was the bedrock, as it meant there was little or no need to post collateral, as was normally the case with these CDS trades. AIG also employed the services of Ivy League quantitative analysts, who used a broad number of models filled with data from banks, central banks and international think tanks, detailing losses in past recessions. They had special models for Dutch real estate, for example, and a different model for German small- and medium-scale enterprises. Mortgage securities would model the likelihood of default of each of the 80,000 individual mortgages. Even before the modelling stage, AIG staff would visit the banks writing the original loans, check their internal models, visit the repossession department, and identify lax credit standards. AIG would 'positively select' loan portfolios so they were neither too concentrated on a single industry nor too risky in general. They were replicating the credit-risk function of a bank. Except they were covering several banks at once, using the same model. There were two results.

Firstly, the trades were fabulously profitable. AIG had assumed away the loss statistically, so they had no need to post collateral or hold buffer funds for the contingency of a default, because the model said that default was impossible. The annual fees paid on credit default swaps could be booked as almost pure profit. Then, if modelled in the right way, a future stream of these fees over a period of years could be booked upfront as day-one profit. This is how you get fabulous profits: (1) offer an insurance policy against a risk that you prove will never happen; (2) assume it will never happen; (3) take all the fees as profit; (4) take all the future fees as upfront profit. This is how AIG FP ended up with what its employees were told was the most profitable office space in the world. In 2006 Joe Cassano received $44 million in salary and bonuses. Even in 2007, as things began to unravel, he got $24 million.

AIG's major customers were the European banks. So the second result was that AIG was at the core of a machine that was decapitalising the basis of the European banking system. Andrew Forster of AIG explained how it worked on that fateful December 2007 conference call: 'The majority of our trades are regulatory capital-motivated rather than for economic risk transfer purposes. . . And buying the Super Senior protection from us, they're able to reduce their capital charges down from 8 per cent to just 1.6 per cent.' In essence, European banks could trade away their credit risk with AIG, and hold dangerously low levels of capital, safe in the knowledge that AIG would cover their backs in a disaster. Prior to its takeover by RBS, the Dutch bank ABN Amro had $56 billion of these trades, which accounted for $3.5 billion of questionable 'capital', intended to satisfy the regulators. Danish, German and French banks were all involved in a quarter of a trillion dollars worth of these so-called 'regulatory capital swaps'. It turned out that it was only a short step from decapitalisation to decapitation. Not surprisingly, Christine Lagarde, then French finance minister, was at the forefront of efforts to persuade US authorities to bail out AIG in the immediate aftermath of Lehman Brothers collapse. The net result was that European banks held much less capital than they had done, and could deliver even higher returns to shareholders and bankers.

AIG fell over in 2008. But it received the largest-ever injection of US government cash into a private entity – not because of defaults, but because the models underestimated the impact of collateral calls. Reductions in the value of the underlying loans, and reductions in AIG's own credit rating, would result in AIG having to post collateral to its trading partners. At first, its AAA rating protected it, but that was lost, and AIG suffered a series of downgrades, ultimately requiring $50 billion of collateral. This spiral of doom accelerated because AIG also had to account for the fall in value of the CDS contracts on its accounts. It protested vehemently that the contracts were at no risk of actual default, and that its rude financial health meant that it could ride out any dip in the value of the contracts. Ultimately, though, both risks combined, and AIG's trading partners demanded collateral it did not have, until it ran out of funds. It had suffered an invisible but epic cross-continental modern-day bank run. And it wasn't even a bank.

What was allowed to happen at AIG said an awful lot about regulatory standards. No one in London really seemed to know what was going on. An insider told me that officially AIG FP was regulated by the French central bank, the Banque de France, even though trillions were traded from London. 'Inspector

Clouseau turned up twice a year and pretended to understand our accounts,' he told me. Another former insider, Shirley Beglinger, told me: 'The FSA should have noticed that AIG's name popped up all over the place, and should, as a result, have started to take a more piercing look at AIG Financial Products. As long as it was going right, heaven help the regulator who tried to stop it, and they just weren't willing to pick that fight, I suspect.'

The FSA chairman Lord Turner told me: 'I don't think we did fail as regards AIG, because although some of the execution was done through the London office, the legal entity... which really should have been regulated more effectively, was the American legal entity. I think the Americans all understand that what happened with AIG was probably the worst case across the world of something literally falling between the stools of the regulatory process.' AIG's US government bailout would eventually turn in a profit. But in October 2008 it was far from certain that Treasury Secretary Paulson would do it. Only the sheer panic that followed the Lehman collapse changed his mind. At Barclays, which was minutes away from saving Lehman, there was a big 'What if?' If Barclays had bought Lehman Brothers and prevented its bankruptcy, then the US Treasury probably would have allowed AIG to fail. If AIG had failed, many more banks, particularly in Europe, would have failed too. AIG was an earth-shattering one-way bet on the global credit boom, yet at the same time it was an essential cog in producing that boom. And its credit sorcery occurred in London.

London was the capital of the shadow banking world. The City hosted AIG FP, the creation of the CDS market, as well as much of the Lehman Brothers mortgage business and the hedge funds that traded the mortgage bonds. But there was no clear divide between these high-risk operations and the conventional banks. The 'universal' banks that bestrode this divide were increasing risky exposures to, say, property on their trading books, while reining in property exposure on their conventional loan books. It made little sense.

It goes back to the deregulatory Big Bang of 1986, and even before that. One British financial CEO filled me in. 'What is the City since Big Bang? Mostly American-owned or American-influenced,' he told me. 'You should stop thinking of the City of London during the boom time as anything other than an extension of Wall Street.' The City grew fat on offshore dollars traded internationally (nicknamed 'eurodollars'). From the 1960s a US tax change called 'Subpart F' offered huge tax breaks to US multinationals on dollars earned abroad, as long as they stayed abroad. Again this boosted the City. Eurobonds were created after another change to the US tax code. 'It was American corporate interests creating American pools of money,' another senior financier told me. 'American investment banks then snapped up all the British banks that then directed those American pools of money that were outside of America in London.'

London was clearly far more than the financial equivalent of George Orwell's 'Airstrip One'. But seeing the City as essentially a part of Wall Street is a useful way of looking at the boom and the bust. It did seem as if London was where Wall Street did its dry-cleaning. There can be no doubt that the UK FSA started the race to the bottom on lenient treatment of derivative exposures. It boasted about the business won through this approach. Wall Street regulators tried hard to keep up. David Cameron himself, in a speech to the City after the crisis began in March 2008, fully endorsed the strategy of outcompeting Wall Street on deregulation. 'The UK has a long history of benefiting from over-regulation elsewhere,' he told his audience. 'The worst response to the current crisis would be a knee-jerk response and proscriptive over-regulation.' A crisis bank chief executive concurs: 'There's some truth in the Americanisation story. The City moved to take advantage of the Sarbox Act, and Gordon [Brown] was not interested in taxing "nondoms". The Nondom rules were designed specifically to attract American bankers.'

The Americans brought meritocracy, technology and a can-do attitude to the cosy gentlemen's club of the pre-Big Bang City.

Many City figures bitterly resisted the Big Bang reforms forced upon them by Mrs Thatcher. It was another example of the City not even knowing what was good for itself – at the time, at least. But Big Bang was clearly a necessary, though not sufficient, condition for what followed two decades later.

The two biggest casualties of the credit crisis, AIG and Lehman Brothers, ran their riskiest operations through their London offices. US investigators found Lehmans operating an extraordinary trade through London called Repo 105, which saved on Lehman's capital requirements. The entire deal required the sign-off by City lawyers for something that would never have been allowed in the USA. Even more shockingly, both Lehman and AIG had senior London-based executives who were loudly warning of the consequences of the credit cataclysm. At AIG it was Bernard Connolly. At Lehman Brothers it was John Llewellyn. Both were seasoned watchers of global finance and of economic history. They were the same age, and of a similar background – former international government economists, from the European Commission and the OECD, who had ended up in the City. It is frankly incredible to read back the apocalyptic forecasts of Connolly, AIG FP's chief strategist, and realise that at the same time, at the trading desk just outside his office, they bet the farm on a never-ending credit boom and nearly brought down the entire European banking system.

John Llewellyn was a little more reserved. But in many ways his intervention was even more subversive, as Lehman Brothers unknowingly hurtled towards oblivion. He had developed a magic formula that was proving rather effective at predicting which economics were about to succumb to their economic imbalances. It was called 'Damocles'. And in 2003 he applied it to the USA, partly as a spot of pre-Christmas amusement. The USA came out as flashing red on the Damocles analysis. It turned out that America was the nation with the riskiest finances in the world. Llewelyn briefed Dick Fuld, Lehman's combustible chief executive. Fuld told him to stop publishing the Damocles assessment of the US economy. Llewellyn chaired Lehman Brothers' risk committee during the height of the boom. He was the elder statesman who was supposed to try to take away the punch bowl from the likes of Mr Fuld. In practice that proved rather difficult.

Back at the Number 11 table, it is possible to see why the likes of Peter Sands of Standard Chartered and Douglas Flint of HSBC were a little detached from their fellow bankers. Sands had helped shape the recapitalisation that was about to be announced. As for Flint, during the boom HSBC had been under repeated attack from a Chicago-based hedge fund, which called for the lumbering giant to be broken up and handed over to 'proper' capitalists. HSBC did not really participate in the boom. It maintained a capital ratio of 8 per cent, double that of its soon-to-be defunct competitors sitting around the table at Number 11. Even though HSBC was the most directly exposed to subprime, after a disastrous purchase of US consumer-finance company Household International, it sailed through tests of its solvency. HSBC's equity was higher while its returns were lower, as, unlike the other banks, it had eschewed chasing the yields of risky loans. HSBC had not joined in the party. It was only at the funeral out of politeness. Flint determinedly told the table that the government should be extremely careful that actions taken to protect weak banks would not lead to questions about strong banks.

John Varley, CEO of Barclays, cut an owlish figure at this supposed 'last supper'. He did not say very much at all. Most of the talking was being done by the Scots, Douglas Flint and Sir Fred Goodwin. But in many ways it was Varley who found himself under the most pressure. The Scottish banks and Lloyds had no actual choice other than to cleanse themselves of their delusions. They would all be taking the government capital on offer and going into varying degrees of state ownership. Barclays, however, had a way out. As Varley would tell me a few days later, he had to 'protect Barclays' self-determination' from the dead hand of even partial ownership by the British government.

Lest anyone confuse John Varley with Woodrow Wilson after the First World War, the banker defined self-determination as the 'freedom to compete aggressively'. To some of those around the table, it seemed that the freedom that Barclays wanted to hold on to was the freedom of its top bankers to go on receiving large pay packets.

A chairman of one of the banks being bailed out was to telephone Treasury minister Paul Myners hours before the final agreement, at 2 a.m. in the morning, to say that his chief executive was insistent on keeping his bonus. Another chairman told the Treasury that he would resign if there was 'any hint' of direction or interference in their failed corporate strategies, now that the government was on the shareholder register. 'Can I stop you there?' Myners broke in. 'It is a condition of this recapitalisation that you resign anyway.' The bankers gathered at Number 11 were not a particularly self-aware bunch.

Barclays felt it could escape Gordon Brown's embrace. The foundations of the recapitalisation plan were laid months before. Gordon Brown and the FSA had prodded the banks to raise their own capital in January 2008. Brown wrote articles in the *Financial Times* urging transparency on balance sheets, and called in accountants and the accounting regulator to explain what was going on in dark corners of the balance sheets of the UK banks. In March 2008 Mervyn King, the governor of the Bank of England, had outlined to the US ambassador in London and the visiting US Treasury deputy secretary, Robert Kimmitt, a plan for global recapitalisation of the over-leveraged banking sector by a small group of countries. The account of that meeting, in secret US embassy cables published by Wikileaks, indirectly quotes the governor as telling his American guests: 'It is hard to look at the big four UK banks [i.e. RBS, Barclays, HSBC and Lloyds TSB] and not think they need more capital.' The big banks and also the smaller ones all attempted to raise more capital from shareholders in the following months, with varying degrees of desperation, failure and the odd success. By summer it had dawned on officials and ministers that a 'showstopper', if necessary a forced recapitalisation with taxpayers' money, was on the cards. There were all sorts of different views within the tripartite committee representing the Treasury, the Bank of England and the FSA. Britain going it alone on recapitalisation had risks, and so the various UK authorities were keen on a concerted international plan. However, just after the collapse of Lehman Brothers, the US Treasury secretary, Hank Paulson, announced TARP (Troubled Asset Relief Program) – an entirely different type of rescue plan involving the purchase of toxic assets, rather than bolstering up the banks with new capital. Britain paused its bank recapitalisation plans.

In August 2008 two senior government figures communicated to the bosses of Lloyds TSB and HBoS that 'If you want to ask us a question then you should ask.' HBoS was causing the government more sleepless nights than RBS. An HBoS rights issue had failed weeks before. In addition it was hugely dependent on the Bank of England's Special Liquidity Scheme, a £185 billion pawnshop for toxic mortgage assets. And HBoS was coming to be seen, quite rightly, as fair game by aggressive speculators. The fear was that an HBoS collapse would have hit RBS, then Barclays, then the domino effect would have been impossible to stop. The question HBoS and Lloyds did ask was whether competition law could be waived to enable a merger. The Treasury was split, as was most of the tripartite committee, and there was a dither. It took the collapse of Lehman Brothers to convince the doubters. At this point, many in government were convinced that having seen HBoS's rotten books, Lloyds would drop its bid. It did not. 'Taxpayers got a great deal. It would have cost a lot more to separately bail out HBoS,' reflects a former minister. Nonetheless, separate plans to do just that were prepared in case Lloyds pulled out of the HBoS deal. Eric Daniels of Lloyds reached a point where he felt it necessary to take lengthy long-hand notes of everything being said at these meetings.

How Barclays scraped through the stress test
and escaped state ownership

On 26 September 2008 Gordon Brown met President George W.
Bush. It was during the latter's frenetic last months at the White
House. Markets were still reeling from Lehman's collapse ten
days previously. British officials were still trying to come up with
the show-stopping number for a bank recapitalisation. While
Gordon Brown was in the Oval Office, a fax arrived from the
Bank of England. Mervyn King was suggesting that £100 billion
of government capital be forced on the banks, including the
relatively healthy HSBC and Barclays, even if they had access to
the private capital markets. The governor feared the impact of
market stigma on bailed-out banks if the recapitalisation was
optional. But he was also taken with the aggressive stance of the
Swedish government in 1991–92, when it had pushed through a
recapitalisation by threatening nationalisation. In the end, profits
from sell-offs refunded almost all the cost of the Swedish bailout.
Governor King even suggested employing some of the Swedish
pioneers to run the UK bailout. The USA too, by October 2008,
would be forcing government money on its banks, even on the
likes of Goldman Sachs. A hundred billion was the number they
worked with, but it ended up being half that. On the flight home
from DC, Brown and his team began to work on the numbers.
Peter Sands of Standard Chartered also began developing the
recapitalisation plan from his office in the City. The Treasury
joked wryly that if Mervyn wanted £100 billion for the banks,
then he had better start printing money quickly ('printing' began
five months later).

A significant problem arose. There was no legal means to
oblige a bank to take the capital. 'We were beyond the point
of legal precision,' said one minister. 'If they had declined, we
might have had to say it was not in the national interest for
the Bank of England to provide central-bank funding.' Sir Fred
Goodwin, for one, resented this combination of implied threat,

bluff and incentive. He said his only difficulty was liquidity, not capital. The only problem in terms of capital was that RBS had 'the wrong sort', and that could be solved by a liability-management exercise. Until the markets stabilised, RBS told Paul Myners at the Treasury that all the bank required was continued covert funding. By the early hours of the next morning Sir Fred had spoken to his board, and also to Treasury officials and business minister Baroness Vadera, and decided RBS only needed a smallish pot of government capital, around £5 billion. Vadera was shocked that the number was so low. It ended up being four times that amount. The Treasury tactics were working. It made access to cheap, guaranteed, medium-term funding conditional on some form of recapitalisation. Crucially, though, this recapitalisation could be privately funded, where possible.

Banks were told that they had to be in a position to hold a board meeting at a moment's notice. Chairmen, CEOs and chief financial officers were told to stay in London so that they could attend meetings at an hour's notice. For HBoS and RBS, the senior independent directors were also required to await the summons. The fate of the existing bosses at the two Scottish banks was already sealed.

The detail of recapitalisation deals for each bank were thrashed out individually over the weekend. RBS was first through the door at the Treasury on the Saturday afternoon. Then HBoS, and then Lloyds. Shriti Vadera picked up the phone to John Varley at Barclays: 'We need you to know that everybody else is here,' she told him. 'If you wish to come in we will talk to you.' Varley was holed up at his Canary Wharf office, refusing repeated requests from Vadera and Myners to come to the Treasury. Instead, Varley and his team waited for notification of the amount of capital required, and handled all meetings by conference call. Varley's team sensed 'menace' from the Bank of England and its desire to avoid 'moral hazard'. In his office a board member challenged Varley to convince him that refusing government capital was not simply about keeping his job. He conceded that a failure to raise private capital would see him in a difficult position. By March he had agreed to raise £7 billion, a figure he told friends was 'seared onto his heart'.

By the end of October, Barclays had indeed paid £300 million in fees in order to acquire £7 billion of expensive capital – principally from two private investors, connected to royal families in Abu Dhabi and Qatar. So Barclays paid a huge price to avoid UK nationalisation but instead became partly owned by Gulf governments. (In 2013 the UK financial authorities were scrutinising the deal with Qatar, and it emerged that Barclays had made large loans to Qatari entities at the same time.)

The government feared that Barclays was exhibiting an 'emotional reaction' against government capital that might prove to be a risk to financial stability. Around the same time the Bank of England deputy governor, Paul Tucker, emailed Varley and Bob Diamond to express concern about Barclays' high costs of funding. At some point this message was misinterpreted, down the Barclays chain of command, and the bank began to 'lowball' – to report artificially low funding costs for the Libor benchmark. The entire process had an air of superficiality at the time. At the Bank of England they had already nicknamed Libor 'the rate of interest at which banks don't lend to each other'. Other banks such as RBS were arguably more active in Libor manipulation and received a larger fine. Barclays insiders say that the main manipulation was in fact the then secret massive loans from the Bank of England providing £36.6 billion of funding to RBS and £25.4 billion to HBoS. 'Only the government knew about that,' said a top Barclays insider at the time. When authorities raised concern about Barclays' Libor manipulation, the banker commented that it was mainly done 'by you, dude'. But despite the fighting talk there was considerable concern about Barclays' accounting for the complex derivatives and trades. A combination of this concern and public pronouncements about possible nationalisation drove Barclays' share price down to just 47 pence. On two days between January and

March 2009, Barclays' total market capitalisation was less than £5 billion.

Myners and Vadera spent two hours questioning Bob Diamond and a colleague at the Department of Business about the accounting practices in his part of the business, the so-called trading book, which was full of derivatives and opaque securities. Many felt that Barclays had not marked various toxic assets appropriately. By 2008, Barclays balance sheet was over £2 trillion, and £1.6 trillion of that was Mr Diamond's Barclays Capital. Barcap alone had assets worth more than the UK's national economic output. The crucial leverage ratio was forty-three times, more than RBS (thirty times). The models used by Barclays would later be described by the FSA as 'clearly at the aggressive end of the acceptable spectrum'. Diamond parried the inquisition.

The attention heightened anxiety at Canary Wharf. 'I think Gordon fancied the idea of nationalising the entire banking system,' said one Barclays board member. In turn, the government suspected that paranoid members of the board were 'obsessed with the idea of a Labour plot to nationalise Barclays'. Even as Barclays had evaded government capital the previous October, a new danger lurked in a scheme to remove rotting assets from the banks' balance sheets. This was the Asset Protection Scheme (APS). For a fee, paid in shares of the bank, the government would insure losses in a giant 'bad bank'. It was designed to get banks lending into the real economy. The original deal, with RBS and HBoS, was announced in January. It was the largest financial contract signed by the British government since the Lend Lease agreement with the US government during the Second World War. Few noticed its significance at the time because, to divert attention, Number 10 leaked details of Fred Goodwin's pension on the same day.

The question was: would Barclays sign up to the APS, and on what terms? At a likely fee of £4–5 billion, and a market capitalisation not much higher, Barclays again faced the spectre of de facto nationalisation. The key was a series of secret 'stress tests' of its solvency conducted by the FSA. The tests subjected the bank's books to the impact of a severe downturn, involving 12 per cent unemployment, a 50 per cent fall in house prices, and a 60 per cent fall in commercial property prices, but this was not revealed in advance. 'None of us was expecting them to pass,' says one former government minister. At Barclays the view was that this was their 'High Noon'. They had heard directly from the lips of one government minister that they were not going to pass the test. The bank was only hours from part-nationalisation, from losing its previous self-determination.

In the early hours of 27 March the first edition of the *Financial Times* appeared with the headline: 'Fears rise Barclays will need injection'. And then, a few hours later, that had been updated to 'Barclays' stress test signals no new funds' – pretty much the exact opposite. The test had not been published, indeed it never was to be published, unlike similar stress tests in the USA. But there was some truth in both headlines. In May the FSA released a statement saying that the threshold was a Core Tier 1 ratio of 4 per cent. Lloyds and RBS were to say later, however, that they were being judged at a ratio of 5 per cent. Officials suggest that banks that had already claimed government capital would require a larger buffer. The end result was that Lloyds could have achieved a greater solvency score than Barclays, despite the fact that Lloyds was for the rest of 2009 effectively owned to an even greater extent by the UK government, and yet Barclays escaped completely. Government insiders believe Barclays scraped through the stress test on close to 4 per cent. Barclays' insiders emphasise that this was a matter of pass or fail and they were told that they had passed. In any event, news had got out early. In government, it was suspected that Barclays had bounced the FSA into announcing a better result by leaking an early arithmetic result to the press. By this point, the Tripartite Authorities had not issued an official verdict. There were large elements of discretion in an exercise that the FSA had not formally carried out before. Stress tests would differ from bank to bank. By the time the papers were carrying stories about Barclays passing, financial stability demanded sticking to the public story, said one sceptical member of the government at the time.

At the top of the Barclays tower they believed that Brown had taken fright and retreated from Mervyn King's plan for blanket state ownership. The key trigger was the concurrent G20 meeting and the revelation of the impact of the RBS and Lloyds part-nationalisations on Britain's parlous public finances. It suited everybody to leave Barclays free. Other leading Barclays figures are adamant that the bank was never in any actual financial difficulty, and was always going to sail through any fair and independent stress test. The real fear, for Barclays, was that it had been decided in government that, by hook or by crook, Barclays would fail the test. Why? Because the government had earlier promised the other banks, particularly Lloyds, that this would be an across-the-board UK bank recapitalisation, and that had cemented Lloyds' purchase of the HBoS disaster at a point of near collapse. In a subsequent interview with the *Telegraph*, the then Lloyds chief executive Eric Daniels confirmed that Lloyds had expected other banks, presumably Barclays, to be taking government cash. 'We entered it [the recapitalisation scheme] on the understanding that there would be multibanks involved. The same assertion was made at the time of GAPS [Government Asset Protection Scheme]. Things didn't turn out as they were presented.'

The fear about the first-edition headline of the *FT*, was that it was murky government figures forcing Barclays' hand. A furious effort involving warning journalists off the first-edition splash was galvanised. Framed copies of both editions of the newspaper were displayed in one director's office.

The crucial stress test was not fully discussed by all regulatory authorities before the results were made public to the papers. Indeed, Barclays' official announcement three days later was curiously worded: 'On 27 March 2009, Barclays confirmed that its capital position and resources were expected to meet the capital requirements of the UK FSA.' The independent review into Barclays, chaired by Anthony Salz, described the result as 'a close call involving extensive debate with FSA officials and a significant milestone in avoiding government ownership'. The FSA itself refused to supply details of the tests, even under freedom-of-information requests. The whole exercise was slightly arbitrary, in any event. Barclays could pass or fail depending on how stringent the FSA decided to make the test. 'We did not have a problem passing the stress test. We had a political problem,' said a Barclays official. The parameters were not decided in advance or confirmed for weeks afterwards. At a subsequent 2011 stress test the FSA chairman Lord Turner did critique the presentation as 'confusing and potentially misleading', and left his staff with the impression that its capital was above the then intended threshold of 10 per cent, when it was 9.8 per cent. The 'pass mark', though, was changed to 9 per cent. Back in 2009, the most the FSA would do was to release a general statement about its methodology two months later. No details were given about the marks used on the Barclays' trading book that had been the subject of that two-hour meeting with ministers. In 2013 the FSA's most senior executive, Hector Sants, who signed off the stress-testing exercise, joined Barclays. History might have turned out differently if the current structure, with the Bank of England as lead regulator, had been in place in 2009, leaving the stress-test judgements in the hands of Sir Mervyn King.

The big picture, however, was that Barclays scraped through the stress test and escaped part-nationalisation because of the conservative nature of its exposure to property in its conventional bank loan book – despite its very large exposure to property derivatives in its trading book. Barclays represented the bipolar nature of Britain's banks in a nutshell. There was a conventional high-street bank trusted by depositors; and, inextricably entwined with it, there was a high-bonus, high-adrenaline, high-risk international investment bank. The same heady combination that had seen Bob Diamond on the pitch at Old Trafford had saved Barclays at its 'High Noon'. Through 2008 Barclays did quietly reduce its exposures to notorious opaque property derivatives. 'Looking back on it, we weren't anything like aggressive enough in just shipping out inventory. Quite a lot of the trading book that was sickly over that period from mid-2008 had a property flavour to it,' says one insider. Barclays had learnt the lessons of its history on one side of its bank; less so – perhaps not at all – on the other side of the bank.

The answer for some would be a legal split of some sort. The coalition government that came to power in 2010 opted for a ring fence to remove the implicit multibillion subsidy to the borrowing costs of investment banks. The so-called 'too-big-to-fail' subsidy arose from the presumption that a troubled investment bank connected to a high street bank would always get bailed out by a government. Darling and others pointed out that the most high-profile failures in the banking crisis – Lehman, Northern Rock and HBoS – would fall and fail on either side of a ring fence. But it is also true that Northern Rock and HBoS were not pure retail banks: their massive securitisation requirements were an intrinsic part of the shadow banking system. It did seem at one point that the government's bank-reform proposals would most greatly impinge upon HSBC and Standard Chartered, the two banks that did the least to cause the problem. It should also be pointed out that high-street banking arms were less pure than bosses at Barclays suggested. A number of scandals concerning the gouging of fees, loan-insurance payments and mis-sold interest swaps to small businesses showed the impact of the sales culture on the high-street arm of the bank. The fact was that the retail arms had to compete for capital, and at least try to match the return on equity in the casino arms of the banks.

It appears that a careful assessment of the failure of the Scottish banks and the demutualised building societies was not at the heart of bank-reform proposals. Bankers and politicians tacitly colluded in failing to learn the actual lessons of the crisis. Britain never had its catharsis, and the delusion that British banking could go on as before remained. There were two separate problems: loss-making property-centric ex-building societies (a failure of Mrs Thatcher's 1986 Building Societies Act); and the loss in confidence in the regulation of investment banking, credit derivatives and the shadow banking system in London, which occasionally lived off high-street depositors. The former is often overlooked in a haze of anger at the pay packets of the latter. Internationally, London's reputation was tarnished. Alistair Darling could smell the *Schadenfreude* at meetings with other finance ministers. Trade missions trying to push British banking abroad met with somewhat frosty receptions.

On a trip to Mumbai, Lord Turner of the FSA found himself excitedly explaining to the chief of India's central bank how Britain was reining in the excesses of its banking system. His hosts were rather sceptical. No Indian bank had fallen during the great financial crisis of 2008. Half the British banking system had. But this did not stop Britain's banks from pressing their government to help prise open the doors to India's middle classes and their growing desire for financial services. Lord Turner explained to his hosts how in the future UK banks indulging in risky property lending would be forced to set more buffer funds aside. He was somewhat taken aback when his hosts told him, 'Oh, we do that already.' A somewhat incredulous Lord Turner asked when the Indians had discovered this radical new form of financial regulation. 'Oh, we never stopped doing it since you the British told us to,' his Indian host replied, pointing out that India, unlike Britain, had simply not stopped features of bank regulation that had been standard issue for decades. Britain's chief bank regulator had been taken back in a time machine to the 1970s.

The story of Barclays' escape from state ownership does shine a new light on Bob Diamond's eventual fate in the 2012 Libor scandal. From the moment Diamond became chief executive, the

British economic establishment had been extremely concerned that the boss of the worrying side of the bank's business had been promoted. There were a number of skirmishes over such things as Barclays' aggressive tax schemes and its accounting wizardry. When details of the Libor scandal broke, the Barclays boss was still standing, despite Andrew Bailey at the FSA warning of a 'fundamental breakdown of trust'. The Barclays chairman, Marcus Agius, tendered his resignation, but the regulators thought the wrong man had resigned. Diamond was fighting for his job. He even phoned Ed Miliband to gauge support, but Miliband publicly called for him to resign. Agius' resignation simply set the hares running. Two days later, Barclays released damaging email notes for a parliamentary committee, seemingly ascribing a role in the Libor affair to the deputy governor of the Bank of England, Paul Tucker. Diamond appeared to be taking on his own central bank. Threadneedle Street was apoplectic. But it had no formal legal regulatory power over Barclays at the time. Mervyn King believed enough was enough. He contacted Adair Turner and George Osborne, before calling Agius and Sir Michael Rake, who was still on the Barclays board, to see him at the Bank of England. He had no power, he said, he was not the regulator. But the Bank of England was to become Barclays' chief regulator within a year. 'Bob Diamond no longer enjoyed the support of his regulators,' he told Agius and Rake. The two board members went straight from the Bank of England to Diamond's house. 'He [King] does not have the authority to do that!' was Diamond's response to the news about the governor, he told the *New York Times* a year later. He resigned the next morning. I spoke to Marcus Agius, who had by this time 'unresigned', and he did not deny the pressure from King and Turner: 'Last night Bob Diamond made a personal decision which we discussed.' He told me, 'We have let the public down, we have let our shareholders down... I am truly sorry.'

At a packed parliamentary committee, Diamond's testimony was no longer about saving his job. Diamond was never actually shown to have acted improperly in the Libor-rigging scandal he is most associated with, and he would later say that the truth was that he did not even know how Libor was set, let alone how to manipulate it. But his enemies had taken their opportunity. A series of leaks from highly confidential internal FSA assessments revealed a litany of more general concerns about Mr Diamond's style. The committee chairman Andrew Tyrie caught Diamond unaware. He ended up confirming the idea that the Barclays board thought the Brown government was trying to nationalise it. The comments were lost amid the drip-drip of documents about the conduct of the bank under his leadership and Diamond's saccharine comments about 'loving Barclays'. Diamond protested that his bank had remained profitable throughout the crisis. His trading book turned out to be profitable too. The 'stress test' pass was vindicated, but the politics had become even more toxic. It was all too late. His defenestration from the highest floor of British banking was complete. More importantly, after a relentless globalising process since the Big Bang, Britain had reasserted some national sovereignty over its errant banking system. The war over the shadow banking system, though, was far from over.

CHAPTER 7

THE FORMULA THAT CREATED THE SHADOW BANKING SYSTEM

Dramatis personae

Motorcycle courier, transporting mortgage documents
Anonymous UK mortgage securitiser
Oldrich Alfons Vasicek, the 'V' in KMV Corporation, who split the atom of credit risk
Donald MacKenzie, Nicholas Dunbar, Felix Salmon, writers on derivatives
Jon Taylor (name changed), part of the Northern Rock securitisation team
Adam Applegarth, chief executive of Northern Rock
Nassim Taleb, trader-turned-probability philosopher and anti-economics campaigner
Andy Haldane, Bank of England executive director for banking
Anand Sinha, deputy governor of the Reserve Bank of India
Hyun-Song Shin, banking expert, Princeton University
The chief executive of one of the world's biggest banks

The courier had been knocked off his motorbike and lay dead on the side of the road. For the man himself, and for his family, it was a human tragedy. But for the mortgage securitisation team at one British bank, it was a waking nightmare. They had to get his package to London before the close of business. This was how banking from the shadows actually worked on the ground.

The business of this particular banking team was built on transferring mortgages that they had written off their balance sheet into offshore trusts based in tax havens. But the transfer of the mortgage, and the cash, had to be made the same day, in one go. Ordinarily this could be done electronically. The 'pain in the arse', as far as the team was concerned, was the insistence in Scottish law on 'declaration of trust'. In essence this meant that physical signatures were required on the first and last pages of a printout that included all the names and addresses of those whose mortgages were to be transferred. So the bankers had to hire a courier to transfer a large parcel of papers to get the mortgages signed off in London. But then he crashed.

'We had to get his package down to London though,' a former member of the team told me. 'So some other courier came, took the package from the back of his bike. Because if you don't get that package, the deal won't happen.' After this tragic fiasco, they stopped using motorbike couriers. Instead they sent an office junior on the train.

The indecent haste of this British bank to shift a pool of mortgages off its balance sheet is just one of the inside stories of an industry that created a quarter of a trillion pounds' worth of mortgages in Britain alone. In Britain this industry involved only about thirty people, called 'originators'. Credit that used to flow regionally and locally from savers to borrowers through building societies had through securitisation become a matter of massive flows of hot international money. It was part of the 'shadow banking system' of flows of credit that seemed to bypass the banks. These mortgage transfers seem complex, and yet they are one of the more straightforward aspects of this murky world.

The formulae that made complex credit derivatives possible

After the great San Francisco earthquake of 1906, only one building remained standing in the red-light area known as the Barbary Coast, just north of Telegraph Hill. It was a mill built in 1884 by Del Monte, the food-processing company based in the city. A photograph was recently discovered of 1620 Montgomery Street on fire, as the rest of the area lay in rubble. Around that time, the streets surrounding the mill were notorious for opium dens, whorehouses and 'shanghaiing' – the trickery used to get sailors tempted by California's gold fields back onto merchant ships.

San Francisco lies on the most active geological fault lines on earth. But nine decades on, within the steel-reinforced walls of the old Del Monte building, something far more shaky was going on. The former mill had now become the global epicentre of market credit-risk analysis. The San Andreas Fault of finance ran through this building, and through the office of one brilliant mathematician. Three formulae that shook the foundations of finance were written not on Wall Street, nor in the City, nor at Chicago, MIT or Cambridge, Mass., but here at the understated warehouse offices of the KMV Corporation.

The chances are you've never heard of KMV, nor of the man behind the 'V' in KMV, a Czech-born mathematician called Oldrich Alfons Vasicek. Vasicek's formulae made complex credit derivatives possible. They also form the basis of credit ratings, and became the regulatory core of how most banks calculate the capital they keep aside to stop them going bankrupt. And yet the formulae were basically beautiful abstract mathematical theories proven only under such restrictive conditions that they were of limited practical relevance.

I met Mr Vasicek in California's January sunshine. The Master Yoda of credit appeared opposite me wearing a Californian peace insignia pin badge. The peace is a little upset when I explain how the final Vasicek formula has become central to the Basel rules on bank safety. No one is more surprised by how his formula has been applied to the core of the banking system than Mr Vasicek himself.

'It's completely nonsensical. Completely silly. These are completely independent parameters,' he tells me forcibly. 'How can you hardwire them together? Who came up with that? People at Basel? It blows my mind. If this is right, they should go into revolution with barricades and send Basel to hell.' Bankers, traders and regulators used derivations of Vasicek's work to create the so-called 'Gaussian copula' (named after the brilliant German mathematician Carl Friedrich Gauss, 1777–1855) that would come to be known as the 'formula that killed Wall Street'. The arc of credit complexity that led to the crisis began more benignly here, at 1620 Montgomery Street, San Francisco.

Vasicek's first innovation was to assess the probability of individual corporate loans defaulting. He used information from share prices to calculate 'asset values', also known as 'enterprise values'. It drew on the theories of two of his friends, the Nobel prize-winners Robert Merton and Myron Scholes (later to come to grief at Long Term Capital Management). Vasicek's formula estimated a probability of default based on the movement and volatility of the share price. It was a more timely and useful measure than, say, a credit rating. KMV was surprisingly successful at selling these default predictions for vast sums to financiers sceptical about the assessments of the Big Three credit-ratings agencies.

'We saved a lot of clients a lot of money on assorted Enrons,' Vasicek told me. 'That was an accounting fraud not really revealed until late November 2001. But there were very strong signals in the equity market that something strange was going on. I don't know what generated these signals, but I guess some strange news must have found its way to equity investors. The way it manifested itself was a drop in share prices maybe six months before.' But even more significant, Vasicek opined, was an unusual increase in the volatility of the share price.

Traditionally credit had been a staid, inert and boring corner of finance. Banks held loans for the long term, earning a modest amount of interest, and hoping there would be no default. Vasicek had connected that staid world of credit with the daily trading frenzy of the stock markets.

Vasicek's first formula opened up the revolutionary notion that credit risk, instead of marinating for years on a bank's balance sheet, could begin to be traded like a share on a stock market. Vasicek took his analysis a stage further, by coming up with an equation to model the losses on a portfolio of loans. Under a certain set of simplifying assumptions, he could solve the maths with a pencil and paper. The credit revolution began here. 'Our model could find an implied correlation between 5,000 listed US businesses in 1989,' Vasicek pointed out. 'By the mid-90s we had extended 25,000 time series of the enterprise values for every listed company in the world.'

Vasicek had introduced the idea of a daily valuation of default probabilities and loan losses. Prior to this innovation, corporate loans would be measured by credit rating and the associated historic default record. KMV were directly competing with the credit ratings agencies. The agencies were worried about this revolution from San Francisco and talked down KMV's approach to clients. With Vasicek's new method, data on past losses, arrears and defaults were not required. His work had split the atom, making credit risk tradable. From the mid-1990s J. P. Morgan would then industrialise these insights to develop credit derivatives – which are at the same time both the atomic power stations and the weaponised nuclear warheads of credit risk. The rest of Wall Street and the City would then start dropping these weapons from the so-called shadow banking system in the easy money years before the crash.

But it was Vasicek who found the mother lode that sparked the credit gold rush. Through the mid-1990s, risk officers from thousands of the world's banks made pilgrimages to KMV in San Francisco. Three-quarters of all the globe's major banks were

KMV's customers. Many of the visitors would get lost, not realising that this part of the street was not part of the skyscraper-laden Lower Montgomery ('the Wall Street of the West') containing the headquarters of Wells Fargo and Bank of America. A large hill bisected Montgomery, and north of that lay the offices of KMV in the historic docklands area. It didn't feel like the epicentre of the credit revolution. At first the purpose of these visits was to access KMV's database of default probabilities and correlations for alternative measures of bank credit risk. This was a relatively straightforward task, and KMV would send monthly CDs full of data to their clients. 'KMV was the most advanced of the credit modellers quantitatively, so it was a very useful input and really helped our portfolio-management techniques in the late 1990s,' says one of J. P. Morgan's pioneering credit-risk team. A British bank chief executive adds: 'We were certainly quite early in reaching for KMV. The idea was to have a common language across your risks. KMV created a common language across our trading and loan book. It created comparability and it was rigorous and innovative, an important part of how risk was analysed in any sophisticated bank.'

So in due course Vasicek's formulae were to spawn the industry of quantitative credit-risk modelling, taken up with gusto and commercialised by J. P. Morgan and described in the book *Fool's Gold* by Gillian Tett. At its core the Vasicek model required two inputs or parameters: a probability of default for the individual corporate loans, and a measure of the 'correlation' or connectedness between seemingly unrelated loans in the portfolio. The first part, the 'PD', could come from the bank's internal rating, or from credit ratings, or from KMV. The second parameter, the correlation, came from KMV's database.

For a large number of loans, Vasicek's equation could approximate the probability of certain levels of loan losses. The shape of the answer hinged crucially on the correlations. It is worth understanding a little about correlation. Imagine a competition for ten gardeners in a local village. The chances of Barry winning the marrow contest is 10 per cent, the chances of his marrows being eaten by slugs is 10 per cent, the chances of a drought are 10 per cent and the chances of him forgetting to use fertiliser is also 10 per cent. A trader would price these risks the same, given the probabilities.

But if his next-door neighbour Colin was also growing marrows, what are the chances of both gardeners ending up in the above predicaments? Even if Colin and Barry have the same-sized garden, soil quality, equipment and skills, the so-called conditional probabilities are much more difficult to calculate. Barry and Colin both forgetting to use fertiliser is unconnected. Colin's forgetfulness is not dependent on Barry's, so the correlation is zero. On the other hand, if Barry's garden suffers a drought, it's almost certain that his neighbour's garden will as well, so the correlation is 1. If Barry's marrows get eaten by slugs, then it is not certain, but the chances are Colin's marrow's will also get slimed. Call that correlation 0.4. And then if Barry wins the gardening competition, Colin cannot and the correlation is negative – in fact it is –1.

'If investors were trading securities based on the chances of these things happening to both [Barry and Colin in my example], the prices would be all over the place, because the correlations vary so much,' explained Felix Salmon, the writer who first brought Gaussian copulas to the attention of the non-financial world.

Back to Vasicek. If the recipients of the loans are all truly unconnected, for example a food-processing company in Canada and a software developer in Cambridge, then the likely losses cluster pretty closely to the probability of default, the other parameter. The higher the correlation, say a food company and a farmer in the same state, the wider the spread of likely losses. It is no longer wise simply to expect the average outcome: losses much lower and much higher are plausible. At very high levels of correlation the Vasicek equation showed that the bundle of loans behave like a single loan, and the probability of likely losses became, in the jargon, 'bimodal': losing everything is on the cards. The equation illustrated how a diverse uncorrelated loan book could help to neuter credit risk – in theory. It was an essential insight into how the world financial system developed over the next two decades. 'Correlation' became the core of credit-risk trading. It became a shorthand for assessing the risk locked up in a portfolio. But then what began as an observation of patterns in data, itself became the object of trading.

For many years, Vasicek's formula was something of a secret, the proprietary knowledge underpinning KMV's sales. A Scottish academic called Donald MacKenzie, based at the University of Edinburgh, conducted interviews with many of the quants ('quantitative analysts') who created the financial models that underpinned the great expansion of credit. David X. Li, one of the most famous quants, recalled how he had seen a photocopy of a handwritten version of the Vasicek equation, probably written by the man himself. 'That was one of the most beautiful pieces of math I had ever seen in practice,' Li wrote to Mackenzie. 'But it was a one period model.' Vasicek had assumed all loans were paid off at the end of the time period. Others would introduce time into the equation.

David Li built on Vasicek's work by introducing a concept from the insurance industry to 'couple' together different probabilities in a loan portfolio. 'Broken heart syndrome' is the name given to the actuarial phenomenon of a surviving spouse dying shortly after the death of a husband or wife. Johnny Cash and June Carter are the most famous example, the latter dying just four months after the former in 2003. In insurance, the maths behind this phenomenon reduced the value of joint annuities by up to 5 per cent. Li thought that the survival time of a company after the default of another company could be modelled like a bereaved Johnny Cash, through a piece of maths that enabled a joint probability of corporate survival to be calculated from individual probabilities. This was the Gaussian copula.

Specifically, Li's formula based these correlations on trading movements for the two corporations in the growing credit default swap (CDS) market. KMV's historic data points on corporate asset prices weren't required. An appreciation of historic defaults was not required. And even if this measure of default risk was not deeply flawed, the data underpinning it stretched back for, at most, only a few years. Did the equations include data, patterns and correlations during periods of time when there were actually lots of defaults? For corporate debt, not really. When it was to come to mortgages, the answer was 'not at all'. A fanatical supporter of the model might suggest that all of that information was contained within the wisdom of the crowd – the efficient market price – of the credit default swap. Obviously that was nonsense.

Never mind, the fully fledged Gaussian copula helped the market for corporate Collateralised Debt Obligations (CDOs) explode. These were pools of corporate debt that were then sliced up to offer bespoke returns for investors, depending on the risk they were willing to take. If you were confident that the pool of debt would repay, you could opt for a higher annual return, in exchange for being far back in the queue for repayments if defaults actually occurred.

The game for the credit engineers was to put together packages of debts, or even synthetic debts, with low correlations so that as many tranches as possible would qualify for high credit ratings, preferably the much-coveted AAA rating. The formulas were put to work within banks and credit-ratings agencies to evaluate these new products.

The modellers were still having difficulty finding values for the correlations in products that simply had not existed for that long. By 2003 a new, quite crazy, innovation had appeared: back-solving the formulae to extract 'implied correlations' from the market prices for the CDO tranches. There was one problem, though: J. P. Morgan discovered that at some prices back-solving the models failed to work, or when it did, it gave two wildly different answers for 'implied correlation'. J. P. Morgan stepped up with 'base correlation' – a final tweak creating what became the standard way of modelling CDOs: the Gaussian copula base correlation model. It is still in use today.

It is a thicket of complex maths and finance, and it's designed to confuse and obfuscate. Only the help of Edinburgh's Donald MacKenzie and longstanding derivatives writer Nick Dunbar helped me clear some of the branches away. But it is hugely important to at least try to see what was going on.

The remarkable series of interviews with dozens of quants, conducted by Donald MacKenzie and his colleague Taylor Spears, led them to conclude that there was a singular motivation for the use of these deeply flawed extensions of Vasicek's model: bonuses – specifically the ability to mark an uncertain pile of byzantine debt slices as being worth a certain value at a certain time. As one quant told the academics, even more accurate models were sacrificed at the altar of a model that could fatten up bonuses by claiming a future stream of profits in advance. 'That effectively allows me to do a ten-year trade and book P&L [Profit & Loss] today... without that people would be in serious trouble, all their traders would leave and go to competitors,' was how one quant explained it anonymously to the researchers. Flawed models were fine, as long as everyone used the same flawed model, because at least they could come up with a price for these exotic and toxifying debts, upon which to base their remuneration. The key here is that the model was 'tractable', and could be used as a common market standard.

According to the Edinburgh study, 'Interviewees reported a universal desire amongst traders for the profits on a credit derivatives deal (most of which lasted for between five and ten years) to be recognised in their entirety as soon as the deal was done – as "day-one P&L [profit and loss]"– and so to boost that year's bonus as much as possible.' Such an arrangement would not necessarily be malign. There are simple trades where it might be justified to book profits on a stream of future certain payments. But in combination with faulty pricing models, up-front bonuses were inflated, while at the same time shunting the risk of losses to a future date after profits had been booked and bonuses paid.

The net result of this was that a transformation began in the balance sheets of the banks. The formulae had liberated credit risk from the banker's loan book. Traditional bank lending saw the loan and therefore the credit risk stay on the bank's balance sheet, subject to fairly straightforward capital requirements. Capital ratios were like dams on fast-flowing rivers. Derivatives enabled the water flow to be rerouted through a different valley, via the largely undammed trading book. Governments and regulators could marvel that the dam was still holding at one point in the topography of world finance. But downstream, the inundation was overwhelming. In the much less constrained world of their trading books, banks could now take huge credit risks in the markets, using the methods described. So where were the regulators? On the sidelines, cheering on 'innovation', and participating in a beauty contest, led by London. From 2000 the UK Financial Services Authority (FSA) began handing out approvals for credit-risk models that allowed the massive expansion of credit-derivatives business with only tiny amounts of capital set aside for the bad times.

In his book *The Devil's Derivatives*, Nick Dunbar recounts how New York firms found it difficult to trade derivatives under the rules of the US Security and Exchange Commission (SEC) – rules that had not been updated since the 1970s. For them, 'the new opportunities in Europe were hard to resist, so they set up London-based companies'. According to Dunbar, the FSA boasted that 'international firms that have established their operations here welcome the flexibility of the UK regulatory regime'. New York regulators began to fret about London's light touch, so the Wall Street firms extracted from the SEC 'broker dealer lite' rules that meant the rubberstamping of internal risk models. Regulatory arbitrage meant one thing: massive transfers of credit risk from a bank's loan book to its trading book.

Still, at least models of copula base correlation made some

sense in relation to the corporate debts. The slicing and repackaging of these debts passed risks from one side of a bank's balance sheet where they used up part of the bank's precious capital to another part where it did not. But it was the move into mortgages that was to stretch the models designed to shift corporate risk to breaking point. In particular, it was the misuse of the Gaussian copula in relation to mortgages by ratings agencies that was to prove disastrous.

'Empirically estimating the correlation between asset-backed securities is an even harder econometric problem than estimating corporate correlations,' write MacKenzie and Spears. They go on to say that with little data to draw upon, the CDO groups at ratings agencies 'employed largely judgement-based correlation estimates'. Standard & Poor's CDO group, for example, simply used the same correlation (0.3) for mortgage securities as for companies in that industry. Remember that the formulae were developed with corporate debt in mind. Even so, the assumption of low correlation for mortgages was a wild stab in the dark made by ratings agencies, with catastrophic consequences. The end result? More of the tranches or slices of the pools of mortgage loans could be given the feted gold-standard AAA rating, despite low underlying mortgage quality. This is the alchemy behind changing subprime mortgages into riskless debts.

A board member responsible for the retail side of one of Britain's largest banks recalls the realisation that his investment-banking colleagues were effectively bypassing him and lending direct to clients. 'We spend ages controlling our exposures to consumer debt and limiting ratios on mortgage lending,' he tells me, 'only to see the investment bank writing billions of mortgages to people they've never met in a country where we have no branches.'

Attempts to model the risk in these loans centred on a history of defaults during a time of almost no recession, when national house prices had only risen. 'HPA' was the acronym of the type of modelling done by the Wall Street banks on the income flowing from the complex packages of mortgage debt. It stood for 'house price appreciation' of various levels. At least one British analyst, Toby Nangle, asked the American bankers about HPD – house price depreciation. 'Everyone thought it was an absolutely terrific joke,' he told me. 'We were being quite serious though.' One model was based solely on defaults in Louisiana after the collapse in the oil price. A more widespread form of modelling involved gaming the system and working out the worst mortgage quality possible to secure the AAA rating. One quant in the Edinburgh study 'reported that there were companies that discreetly sold software packages designed to perform this fatal optimisation'. As MacKenzie and Spears conclude, 'The use by rating agencies of Gaussian copula models with low default probabilities for mortgage-backed securities and only modest correlations among those securities helped create (via the "gaming" of those models) an outcome that involved huge levels of highly correlated default.'

In other words, even given the flaws in the use of these models and formulae, when applied en masse, they can change the characteristics of the financial patterns originally observed. The models stop being merely useless and become dangerous. This is known, somewhat awkwardly, as counterperformativity. It was seen with other formulae in the LTCM hedge-fund crisis of the late 1990s, and also in the 1987 stock market crash.

Part of this process was the emergence of a conveyor belt, a sausage factory of credit risks repackaged via 'conduits' in tax havens, an opaque route by which money from conservative banking institutions in places like Germany ended up being lent to financially insecure subprime mortgage borrowers in some of the poorest neighbourhoods of the USA. The AAA ratings, the pattern of rising house prices and the light-touch bank regulations all supercharged the industry before the debacle. These factors were underpinned by the models and assumptions of low correlations in mortgage defaults. All these factors helped cause the disaster.

In Europe there has been a certain amount of *Schadenfreude*

at the fate of US hyper-capitalism. Yet Europeans were disproportionately the end-purchasers of these steaming vats of unintelligible garbage. German banks that would never have dreamt of
attempting to lend aggressively to actual Germans found themselves inadvertently losing vast sums exporting their capital to
bankrupt Americans. And, of course, the City of London
performed the role of 'reg haven', approving the use of aggressive
capital-free credit engineering. I will show in the chapter on Spain
(see pages 235–65) that the idea that there was 'no subprime in
Europe' is a canard. It walked like a duck, it quacked like a duck
– it was just a different species of duck. Even in very basic forms
of credit engineering, Europe stood out as one of the leaders in
the field. In Britain, the subprime duck found its true home on
the waters of the River Tyne.

The Tyne: rolling river of mortgage credit

If you went out on any Friday night during the go-go years to
the classier pubs and clubs of Newcastle, you'd find them heaving
with American investment bankers. Now Newcastle has many
charms, but it was not the pleasures of the Bigg Market entertainment quarter nor the games at St James' Park that had
attracted the sharp-suited moneymen to the foggy northern
corner of England. They'd come here for Northern Rock.

Seven years on, it was all to end in ignominy and bank runs.
Northern Rock had the dubious honour of being discussed for
some time at the September 2007 meeting of the mighty US
Federal Reserve. This prompted Fed board member Richard
Fisher to suggest that Newcastle might be better known as
Sandcastle. Alistair Darling, the former UK chancellor who
himself had a Northern Rock mortgage, recalls the smug hand-
rubbing amongst European finance ministers as they witnessed
what they thought was the downfall of Anglo-Saxon capitalism.
Plenty has been written about the collapse, the runs and the
nationalisation of Northern Rock. But even a sandcastle needs

to be built by somebody. This is how you grow and then harvest a 125 per cent mortgage.

For Northern Rock, an ex-building society with a low credit rating, the key question was how they could borrow significant amounts of money in order to lend it on. At its peak, Northern Rock had no more than seventy-five branches, over a quarter of them in the northeast. So it was never going to get enough retail deposits in, even if noughties Britons had wanted to save. So how to fund the desired growth? 'You can't do it in the capital markets,' I was told by one member of the Northern Rock securitisation team, whom I shall call Jon Taylor (he wishes to remain anonymous). 'You're Northern Rock, you don't have a great rating. Until secure technology. Whatever you say, it gave Northern Rock a level playing field.'

Adam Applegarth, Northern Rock's cricket-playing chief executive, was a marketeer rather than banker. He looked after his staff very well, and he came up with the 'virtuous circle strategy' that sought to gobble up market share with cheap innovative mortgage products (see page 137). 'He just wanted a headline-grabbing punchy product in the market,' Taylor told me. 'And naturally, we [in the securitisation department] were the gap. We came up and said "We can do this, this and this." And of course he was always going to bite our arms off.' Before 2007, Northern Rock securitisation meant both a source of mortgage funding and off-balance sheet treatment. 'So by securitising,' Taylor continued, 'not only did I get in funds to lend again, but I also freed up capital to hold against that lending. It was the perfect, perfect tool. I needed nothing else to fuel my mortgage business.'

Specifically, this 'perfect tool' was called 'the master trust'. It was designed by First National Bank of Chicago in 1988 for use in credit-card lending, and became the means by which banks could offer a flexible combination of interest rates, credit limits and rewards or cashback from their cards. Citigroup brought it over to Britain. In mortgages it enabled the continuous recycling of that small amount of capital that had been earmarked to support securitised lending. The basics of it was that a multibillion pool of mortgage loans would be transferred to a Jersey-based trust called Granite. Half of Northern Rock's funding came through Granite, but more than half of its mortgages would cycle through Jersey as they churned off Northern Rock's balance sheet.

'Securitisation was a tiny quirky tool early in the 90s,' Taylor told me. 'But it really kicked off in 1999 and 2000. And in 2001 they came up with the master trust, which we came to revere.' That revolutionised securitisation in the UK, he said. The master trust 'just made it incredibly friendly for investors, so it just took off'.

The mechanics of its operation are extraordinary.

Customers have no clue that they have been transferred. The day a mortgage is securitised, anything to do with that mortgage is no longer the business of Northern Rock. 'It's very important,' Taylor emphasised. 'Your systems have to be actually rock solid, to make sure that any penny of payment, any pound, any arrears don't go to Northern Rock. It just had a flag against it on Northern Rock's internal systems, which means that any cash that comes in, any payment that comes in, because this mortgage was flagged, will get hived off to this bank account, instead of that bank account. So you tracked it and you knew it. The man who looks at the screen who you phone up, he can't tell if you're securitised. There were only three or four people who had access to tell if you were securitised or not.'

To the outside world Northern Rock dealt with every customer in exactly the same way. It didn't influence how a customer was dealt with if they had a query about a new product, or if they were asking for a product switch, or, most importantly, if they found themselves in arrears.

The Granite prospectus meanwhile contained all the details of the individual mortgages it was absorbing: account number, postcode, salary of the borrower, age of the borrower, internal credit score, everything but the name and address – but they were just an internet search away. It was not just new mortgages that were securitised. Most banks in the UK securitised mortgages back to 1994, because of a change in the terms and conditions of mortgage transfer in the UK.

'That was the beauty of it,' Taylor told me. 'I couldn't go securitising a 1992 mortgage at Northern Rock, because I'd have to write a letter to you, saying "Hey, I've sold your mortgage to Granite." If it's a 1995 mortgage, I can go and sell it to Granite, and not tell you. Because Granite has sourced back the administration of that mortgage to Northern Rock, so you're still going to get Northern Rock setting interest rates, Northern Rock headed paper, everything.'

All of this was done with most of the British population completely unaware. Esther Spick's mortgage (see page 129) is probably in Granite. Alistair Darling's mortgage certainly was, and might still be. The treatment of arrears was vital, because the whole system depended on making sure that the risk, and the loss, went to Granite. The regulator feared that in order to access cheap funding, Northern Rock would put the best assets into Granite with minimal losses. Mortgages were randomly assigned for the journey to Jersey.

Where Northern Rock differed from other banks using master trusts was in the speed with which it transferred mortgages off its balance sheet. This was the key feature in the Rock's eventually failing business model. Traditionally a bank would look at assets and liabilities and work out the pricing of their loans. At Northern Rock what mattered was that products such as a three-year fixed mortgage 'washed its face' in terms of the cost of funding from Granite. The mortgage portfolio was the funding stream, so the securitisation could stand by itself. So how did they raise the money?

This is where the marketeers came in. Northern Rock dispatched roadshows around Asia, looking to drum up investment. They played on the prestige of Newcastle United, dressing their salespeople in the club's strip, occasionally gleaning approving shouts of 'Shearer!' The Toon strip played less well in the USA, where the black and white stripes resembles a referee's jersey – but all the same, 65 per cent of the Rock's funds came from the States. Insurance companies, bond investors, even charities like the Bill Gates Foundation poured money into Adam Applegarth's Newcastle bank, which in turn focused this money like a laser beam on British property. The Rock was offering returns above Libor (the inter-bank lending rate), at a time when the interest rate on US credit cards was below Libor. Amazingly, in November 2006, on behalf of the mortgage-seekers of Britain, the Northern Rock roadshow reached Africa. Scarce African liquidity, which could have funded local infrastructure, was instead diverted into Northern Rock to fund instant negative-equity mortgages at the very top of the UK housing bubble. For half a century the 'efficient markets hypothesis' conquered all in financial thinking. Of the many refutations of the hypothesis since the crisis, this African investment in Northern Rock stands out as one of the most egregious examples.

Northern Rock did not itself slice up all the risk into CDOs. The Rock's methods were relatively simple. It did, however, pioneer relentless attempts to reduce the capital set aside to underpin their offshored mortgages. Typically, banks would need to set aside 4 per cent capital to cover losses on a mortgage book. Securitisation got that number down to below 2 per cent. Northern Rock always retained some 'skin in the game': unlike some subprime US mortgage companies, some degree of risk was always retained on its balance sheet. In the master trust structure this was called the 'reserve fund'. But the Rock found a way to limit even that.

In 2005 Lehman Brothers' London office helped design Whinstone, named after the rock that is often found below a layer of granite (the teams thought carefully about these names). Whinstone was the £423 million securitisation of the Granite

Reserve Fund. It was a further securitisation of 80 per cent of the Northern Rock's remaining risk in the Granite securitisation, using those credit default swaps. It was the largest international transaction of this type ever tried, sold to the world in pounds, dollars and euros. The Lehman Brothers' bankers earned fat fees. Standard & Poor's upgraded the outlook for Northern Rock's credit rating on the mere announcement of this deal. Applegarth had been seeking this for many years. Insiders suggest that Whinstone had been designed specifically for the credit rating. After a second Whinstone deal in 2006, S&P upgraded Northern Rock's rating to A+. In 2007, just forty days before the run on Northern Rock, and the ensuing collapse and bailout, the Whinstone transaction was cited in the Rock's financial results as the key factor behind 'an anticipated regulatory capital surplus over the next three to four years'. Whinstone was behind a planned rise in dividends for shareholders and a plan for massive share buybacks. Yet, just three months before, Northern Rock had breached its regulatory capital ratios, and days earlier had completed the forced sale of £833 million of commercial loans to Lehman Brothers to rectify that.

Amazingly, at one point Whinstone was rated higher credit-wise (BBB) than the Granite portfolio it supported (BB). This made absolutely no sense. The risk was all in the reserve fund, also known as the 'first loss piece', because if mortgages soured, it would take the first loss. But the end result was that, even in a hyper-competitive market, Northern Rock's lending took off like a rocket. The conventional Granite securitisation had more than halved the capital that Northern Rock put aside to cover the mortgages, from 4 per cent down to 1.6 per cent. There was a competition on with other mortgage securitisers such as Halifax, Bradford & Bingley, Bank of Scotland, and a host of smaller building societies. Alliance & Leicester had managed to beat the Rock, however, getting the figure down to 1.4 per cent. But then Whinstone regained Northern Rock's bragging rights in the crazy world of British mortgage securitisation: the capital set aside on these mortgages dropped down to just 1 per cent.

With this measure, the team at Northern Rock was again top dog among the feral pack of soon-to-be-bust securitisers.

At its peak in 2007, this sausage factory of mortgage credit on the Tyne was funding a quarter of Britain's house loans. Perhaps the most incredible thing about this whole machine, though, was the fact that there was no profit in it. Funding through these vehicles channelled a mass of credit through Northern Rock at very cheap rates, sometimes just 0.1 per cent above the London interbank market. But Northern Rock then lent this borrowed money out at a rate only a tiny fraction above that figure – as did many other mortgage lenders. Northern Rock also pioneered computer analysis, and internet rather than branch-based mortgage-writing. Costs were driven down. The end result was the allegedly 'virtuous circle' of cheap costs, cheap funding, cheap mortgages, growing market share, cheaper costs, and so on. It was a result of competition in the market. Executives at HBoS, for example, were to admit that from 2005–7 there was very little profit to be made in UK mortgages. In the first instance, new custom was essential, because new custom paid up-front one-off arrangement fees that kept a mortgage just about above water in profit terms for the first few months.

That is why Northern Rock had to grow: it had to write more mortgages in order to continue its business. It wasn't hubris when in early 2007 Adam Applegarth announced Northern Rock's ambition to become the third biggest mortgage lender in Britain. It was a matter of survival. The Rock was a Ponziistic monster that had to consume Britain's mortgage market in order to sustain itself. At the peak of the bubble, Northern Rock's profit target was the same as its growth target, because they had to grow to be able to book a profit. But the orgy of mortgage giving, the drive to flog even more new mortgage products than one's competitors, whatever the cost, was to get even crazier.

Taylor ruefully remembers sitting in marketing meetings and realising that his colleagues assumed that the only way cheap two-year fixed-rate mortgages were going to make a profit was if the clients stayed with the product for six months after the two-year term, and went on to standard variable rate (SVR). 'That's where they'd claw some back. The insanity, though, is that they fucking wrote to them after eighteen months and said you can get a new product at this lower level. So I was sitting there going "I know this will make a loss."'

So cheap money channelled into the UK mortgage market for profitless mortgages. The winners were the investment bankers who designed the deals. Northern Rock could book up-front profits on essentially loss-making mortgages because of the arrangement fees. In the familiar pattern of the age, bonuses would be paid on day one to all the bankers, even on business that was clearly going to become unprofitable, even within three years. At the Bank of England, many viewed Northern Rock as a glorified hedge fund. Property owners gained. Politicians who care principally about the illusory wealth accruing to the property-owning class gained. Newspapers gained from adverts placed in their personal finance pages. But taxpayers were to lose. And younger people were to lose out big time, becoming the sucker last buyers at the top of the market.

Could it have been stopped? In theory, it might have gone on forever. Or at least until Northern Rock was funding all the mortgages in Britain. The beauty of securitisation was that the funding was trapped for decades. Once an American or Asian or African investor had bought into Granite, the Rock's customer was funded for ever. The problem in 2007 was that Northern Rock had the largest ever pipeline of mortgages to fund. Net residential lending had been 42 per cent higher in the first quarter of 2007 than the year before. And the Rock was between securitisations, with the biggest gap of funding to find. It had a monumental short-term funding gap. Additionally, neither the Rock nor its competitors playing a similar game had worked out that the end-investor in these securitisations was the money market. In August 2007 the medium-term money market basically stopped. No roadshow to the far corners of the planet would have made a difference. Even so, if the Rock had set aside a few billion pounds reserve (a so-called 'warehousing facility') as insurance it could have ridden out the credit crunch, at the expense of higher costs. Adam Applegarth told MPs later that Northern Rock's wide funding base meant he thought such a reserve would not be necessary.

Northern Rock spread the cushion against unexpected losses thinner and thinner. At the end, the ratio of its assets to its equity base was 58:1, the highest in Europe. But the Rock was compliant with all laws and financial regulations at the time.

The UK regulator, the Financial Services Authority, signed off Northern Rock as one of only four lower-risk banks that only needed a full risk assessment every three years. Northern Rock was deemed so safe that it was singled out for special treatment amongst the thirty-eight major UK banks: Northern Rock did not have to be subject to the FSA's 'Risk Management Programme'. As a result, the FSA stopped even bothering with Northern Rock. The top five banks were inspected just under once a week between 2005 and 2007 under the 'close and continuous' regulatory framework. Slightly smaller banks were inspected once a fortnight. Northern Rock was not inspected at all in the whole of 2005, once in the whole of 2006, and on only three separate days in 2007. So the regulation of the small bank growing into Britain's biggest mortgage provider – inspected only four times in the three years leading up to its collapse – was neither close nor continuous.

It was problems with liquidity that ultimately felled Northern Rock. But at the main regulatory meetings in 2006 the regulators were largely uninterested. There *was* a meeting between the FSA and Northern Rock on liquidity in April 2007. The FSA signed off the Rock as having passed its stress test on securitisation. This assumed that the funding market never shuts. Indeed, according to a Rock insider, 'There was no concept of the market shutting.'

The FSA itself says in its internal report into the collapse of Northern Rock that its assumption was slightly different. The FSA's 'approach reflected a presumption that, in the event of a crisis like that experienced in August 2007, general market liquidity provided by the Bank of England would be increased and in extremis, liquidity would be provided for systemically important institutions'. This presumption was included in Rule 11.1.19G of the FSA's handbook (in 2009 it was deleted).

Was Northern Rock systemically important? Did the then governor of the Bank of England consider Northern Rock systemically important? It is clear that Northern Rock and the FSA initially believed that funding markets would never close; even if they did, the Bank of England would be there as the UK's lender of last resort. Northern Rock's mortgages, profits and bonuses were all built on the backstop of the Bank of England. With my own eyes, on the first day of the Northern Rock run, I saw one of Britain's top regulators struggling with the reality that the glory days of light-touch regulation were over. 'We've got to allow innovation,' he repeatedly insisted, his face contorted with fear. It was as if he could not quite bring himself to utter the unspoken question: 'Don't we?'

Those that work inside Northern Rock point out that holders of Granite bonds have not lost even a penny (although any investors who sold at the bottom of the market did lose their shirts). Credit quality held up sufficiently, even on the high-risk 'Together' mortgages. The technology worked, and then it worked for the taxpayer when Northern Rock was eventually nationalised. Indeed, one insider points to the fact that securitisation has helped the entire banking system survive after the crash by enabling banks to cash in assets at central banks. 'It's how I sleep at night,' said one Rock insider. Others might argue that it made the British state a one-way all-in bet on sustaining high property prices. A great crash has failed to materialise so far, but only at the cost of the destruction of savings and a stagnant zombie economy. House prices remain high, and repossessions remain low. Some of the same people who created Granite now look after it for the taxpayer at UK Asset Resolution. The end result of this process was that many first-time house-buyers have ended up with a huge burden of debt, funded profitlessly in the medium term, but upon which bankers in Wall Street, London and Newcastle extracted huge day-one profits, and a taxpayer bailout that is set to cost £2 billion in losses.

All that from a bank that only existed independently for a decade, a bank that thought it had found the elixir of modern banking – funding tens of billions of pounds of mortgages without the need for real capital, because its credit risks had been engineered away. The FSA was so convinced of the efficacy of this elixir that it barely regulated the bank at all. It was a mistake, admitted the now defunct regulator, but the FSA insisted that it was a one-off error. Yet the credit fault line seen so clearly in Newcastle extended in one form or another across the entire global banking system.

Earthquakes real and earthquakes economic

California is used to tremors. The 1906 earthquake in San Francisco is the most famous of many. Oldrich Vaoicek remembers the 1989 quake, when buildings started to make faces and whole panes of glass crashed down onto the street. 'You can see the temperament of different people,' he says. 'Some rushed out of the buildings crazily, some hid under the table. I myself am a complete fatalist.' He recalls a meeting of the loan committee at Wells Fargo HQ on Montgomery Street in the mid-1970s, just a few years after he was forced out of Czechoslovakia following the 1968 Soviet invasion. At Wells Fargo they were trying to push through a hike of 3 per cent in interest rates on car loans. A big quake came, the room on the sixteenth floor of the skyscraper swayed, floating on a bed of sand. And when the aftershocks stopped, the committee reconvened. Perhaps disturbed by the interjection of plate tectonics, the hawks on the committee backed down, and the car loan rates were frozen at 13 per cent.

But in the engineering of a Montgomery Street skyscraper, or even in the construction of the Del Monte mill that survived the 1906 quake, there are lessons to be learnt about probability and risk. Earthquake losses have fat tails – one might say obese tails. This refers to the curve of probabilities of various losses from an earthquake.

The most famous version of such a chart is the bell curve, which represents the so-called normal distribution (also known as the Gaussian distribution). Such a curve, in the shape of a bell, is the core of modern statistics. The bell-shaped curve illustrates how certain kinds of variables (such as human height, weight and arm length) are predictably and evenly dispersed around an average. Variance around this average is called the standard deviation or sigma. The further one gets away from this average, up or down, taller or shorter, heavier or lighter, longer or smaller, the less likely is that outcome, until it basically becomes impossible. In a normal distribution, the thin tail tapers away exponentially to zero as the event rapidly becomes more improbable. Earthquakes, it turns out, are far from normally distributed. The upper tail is fat.

If earthquakes *were* normally distributed, it would be possible to calculate definitively the probability of significantly larger-than-average tremors. The probability of a so-called four-sigma catastrophe (which means four standard statistical deviations away from the average) would be just 0.003 or 1 in 33,000. If that were the case, the people of San Francisco could rest a little easier and might even risk working or living in a warehouse without a steel-reinforced roof. In reality, the fat tail means that the four-sigma catastrophe is fifty-one times more likely than a normal distribution suggests. A 2008 Harvard University study used US Geological Survey data to show that deaths from earthquakes have fat tails. The highest number of deaths, around 283,100, was from a 9.0 magnitude earthquake off the west coast of Sumatra in 2004. This was 3.5 times the death toll of the next worst earthquake, in Pakistan in 2005. 'This is the characteristic of a distribution with fat tails; events in the far-right of the distribution can be really large,' says the Harvard study.

What things are actually normally distributed? Economics and finance? It turns out, they are more like earthquakes than physics. Andrew Haldane of the Bank of England has calculated that, assuming normality, an economic catastrophe, such as a three-sigma fall in the stock market, would occur once every sixty-four years, while a three-sigma fall in GDP would only come about every 800 years. (It should be noted that the GDP measure was only invented in the 1930s.) But in reality, such falls occur every eight years in the markets and only about once a century for the economy. Normal distributions occur only in spheres such as the dynamics of gas molecules, the physical characteristics of large populations, and long runs of coin-tossing or dice-throwing.

'Where there is interaction,' Haldane argues, 'there is non-normality. But risks in real-world systems are no game. They can wreak havoc, from earthquakes and power outages, to depressions and financial crises. Failing to recognise those tail events – being fooled by randomness – risks catastrophic policy error.'

But – no surprise – normal distributions are hard-wired into economics and quantitative financial modelling. The towering example of this is value-at-risk (VaR), the measure used by banks and regulators to assess risk on their trading books, and to set limits on traders. VaR is supposed to tell a bank and its regulators how much a trading portfolio will make on 99 per cent or sometimes 95 per cent of trading days. Remember that at the time Northern Rock and its competitors were going crazy, credit risk was migrating off balance sheets and out of the regulated loan book and into the trading book. The regulatory dam was a flawed set of equations rooted in normal distributions, and the notion that a limited history of past pricing patterns could be extrapolated into the future. This method of assessing risk was developed by J. P. Morgan. Quantitative risk managers would be the first to admit the flaws in the measure, or indeed the flaws of boiling risk down to one number. But global regulators demanded banks calculate, and sure enough the familiar pattern of misinterpreting, gaming and reverse engineering formulae was quickly applied to VaR.

The *Financial Times* quoted Goldman Sachs' chief financial officer during the 2007 credit crunch as saying that twenty-five standard deviation moves were happening several days in a row. To put that in context, he was suggesting that occurrences that his financial model suggested would only happen once in a period of many trillions of lifetimes of the universe, were actually happening every day.

The 'fatal flaw' of VaR, as Haldane argues, is that it is silent about the tail risk. A trader could be given a so-called 99 per cent VaR limit of $10 million, but VaR would be blind to the trader's construction of a portfolio that gave a 1 per cent chance of a $1 billion loss. J. P. Morgan itself discovered in May 2012 that the 'London Whale' corporate credit portfolio that was assessed with a 95 per cent VaR of $67 million in early 2012 had lost them $2 billion within weeks. In its February 2008 annual results, RBS calculated a 95 per cent VaR on its trading book at £45.7 million. The disastrous purchase of the toxic asset-laden ABN Amro had increased that measure by just £6 million. A footnote did warn: 'VaR using a 95 per cent confidence level does not reflect the extent of potential losses beyond that percentile.' And sure enough, just a few months later, the losses on the trading book in 2008 topped £12 billion. A basic problem is that past trading performance is no guide to the future. VaR models were routinely specified to assume that the very recent past is the best guide to the future. Before long VaR came to be seen, quite incorrectly, as an upper-end assessment of likely losses. In fact, the VaR measure essentially slices off the tails full of catastrophic risk. So it is useless as a means of managing catastrophe risk. It is a little like having an emergency parachute that opens swiftly – except when you jump out of a plane. VaR was never designed for this.

In the wake of the crisis, central bankers around the world have responded to a campaign against Gaussian thin tails by the former-trader-turned-probability-philosopher Nassim Taleb. Taleb noted wryly that Friedrich Gauss and the bell curve itself were the images printed on the last German 10-mark note before it was replaced by the non-existent bridges of the inane 5-euro note in 2002. Taleb makes the point that the exchange rate on the 10-mark note fluctuated between 4 per dollar to 4 trillion per dollar in the hyperinflation of the early 1920s, and so was the very illustration 'that the bell curve is meaningless as a description of the randomness in currency fluctuations'. (Intriguingly, though, the postwar Deutschmark went from 4 per dollar to 2 per dollar in the five decades of its existence – a rather more stable career. For the thirteen-year period that the occasionally maligned Gauss was actually on the DM10 note, the Deutschmark went from 1.8 per dollar to 2 per dollar. Gauss's image turns out to have been a stabilising influence on that note – or perhaps Taleb himself was fooled by the random data point.) Taleb told me during the crisis that he had been trying to persuade the King of Sweden to rescind the Nobel Prize for Economics, on account of the damage done by its winners to mankind.

To the extent that the world's central bankers can understand what Taleb is saying, they are listening. Anand Sinha, the deputy governor of the Reserve Bank of India, puts it best when he says that economists have 'physics envy'. 'The mistake has been in elevating quantitative finance to the status of physics,' Sinha mused in Mumbai, in a speech that drew on the work of Taleb's collaborator Pablo Triana. 'Physics deals with the laws of nature governing the universe. The objects have unique physical attributes (i.e. position, velocity, temperature, etc.) and the universe evolves according to the immutable laws of nature. Any observation or measurement of physical attributes does not change them, or even if it does, it does so in a predictable way. During measurement interactions the results are not deterministic but follow a probability distribution which, however, is stable. On the other hand, in finance, there is no such law of financial markets.'

Where there is interaction, there is non-normality, argues Haldane – as LTCM spectacularly found out in 1998 when its Nobel laureate-inspired quantitative strategies blew a $4 billion hole in its finances. The model could not account for the influence of the model itself in altering the market. Formulae forged in observation, when deployed as a trading strategy, immediately changed the basis of those formulae. It was a VaR model.

As Sinha argues, 'The "values" of assets are not inherent attributes of the financial instruments and the economic agents are not outside observers of the financial system. In fact, it is the human mind, its ambitions, drive, competitiveness, caprice and greed which drive the actions of the economic agents, and it is these actions which determine the value of the financial instruments. Thus, unlike in physics, in finance it is the observers who provide value to the financial instruments. There is no unique value: it is determined by the collective psychology of economic agents.'

So the normal distributions were wrong, ignoring the fat tails was wrong. Even if they had been right, there was insufficient historic data upon which to base price patterns. And measures like VaR in any case ignore systemic risk. But it doesn't end there. In fact, away from the flaky trading books, back on the bank loan books, things are getting rather strange indeed. Abnormal, even.

The pseudo-science that led to default

There is a point to this whistlestop tour through correlation trading, Gaussian copulas, credit derivatives, earthquakes, dodgy trading books, probability philosophers and bell curves. This is a world of risk and uncertainty begging for quantification and false comfort. As Friedrich Hayek said in his Nobel Prize lecture of 1974, entitled *The Pretence of Knowledge*, 'While in the physical sciences the investigator will be able to measure what, on the basis of a prima facie theory, he thinks important, in the social sciences [such as economics] often that is treated as important which happens to be accessible to measurement.'

None of which is to say that attempts to model and measure risk should be condemned. Some banks launched simple models, and then made them better. They skewed their normal distributions. They used a variety of models. They based their risk judgements on data that stretched back before the boom. Unfortunately, many banks saw these flawed models as a target to hit rather than as a guide to their safety.

So how did this soup of mismeasurement and misspecification come to be hardwired into the rules that seek to ensure the solvency of every major bank in the world? New rules for bank capital requirements, Basel II and Basel III, have emerged over the past decade. At their heart they make use of Vasicek's work. For the trading book, it is the VaR method, as discussed already. For calculating possible losses on their traditional loan book, banks can volunteer to use the 'advanced internal ratings basis' (AIRB) for calculating capital, which was identified in 2005 as a modified version of the Vasicek model. I showed this to the man himself.

Oldrich Vasicek is flabbergasted on a number of levels. 'This loan loss distribution [the 'Vasicek distribution'] was developed strictly for corporate loans under some restrictive assumptions,' he says. 'It was not intended to address mortgages (which are quite different in structure), credit card loans, or any other types of loans to which Basel II applies it.' Remember the important role of both the probability of default and the correlation? The Basel formulae blend these two factors. 'The distribution has two principal parameters [the probability of default and the asset correlation] that are completely independent. An attempt to derive one from the other, as Basel II and III do in their formulae, is completely unjustified and, frankly, outright silly. I am appalled by that arbitrary decree.' A meaningful estimate of these two parameters for each loan portfolio is necessary, Vasicek says, 'in order that the portfolio loss distribution has any applicability. It is a lot of calculation, but computer time is cheap. Without it, it is GIGO [garbage in, garbage out].'

He acknowledges that questions remain about the applicability of the shape of the distribution. Andrew Haldane, for example, has written that 'Standard applications of the Vasicek model assume that underlying risk models, and hence portfolio losses, are normally distributed.' Crunching an erroneous normal distribution of GDP through the model would lead to the need to hold a 3 per cent capital buffer on a typical loan portfolio. If you use the actual fat-tailed distribution of GDP in the same equation, then the required capital buffer shoots up to 12 per cent.

This creates something of a mystery. It is true that the asset values, the enterprise value of a firm, used in the Vasicek formulae are distributed normally (actually log-normally). But the output of this formula is 'very very non-normal', says Vasicek, and always has been from the beginning. The precise shape of the curve was also corroborated by one of the world's most important regulators, using masses of data in a chart that has never been published. 'The portfolio loss, derived from this assumption, is actually extremely non-normal,' says Vasicek. 'To cover, say, one in a thousand possible cases, the bank needs to hold an amount of capital equal not to the expected loss plus about three times the standard deviation, but to the expected loss plus some ten or twelve times standard deviations.' Basically, using the original formula would have required banks to hold massively more capital. Somewhere in the process of applying it to the capital requirements of banks, the formula became 'normalised'.

'No one in the Basel task force ever consulted me on the applicability and proper use of my formulas,' Vasicek concludes. 'In fact, I learned only much later that these equations were incorporated in the regulations. Moreover, Basel makes changes to my formulas that I very much disagree with.'

So the original author of the models that currently determine the safety of the world's biggest banks says that those models are wrong. This is exacerbated by how banks in practice have responded to Basel II.

One small piece of proof for this comes from the minutes of the HBoS board on 24 June 2003. '"Advanced" status was the only credible status for HBoS. "Advanced" banks would have the capacity to undercut competition on chosen tranches of business, with cost of capital being a key strategic weapon,' said the minutes. In other words, gaining AIRB status, using some version of the Vasicek formula, would enable HBoS to hold much less capital than its competitors. In evidence to the Tyrie Commission, the HBoS leadership team admitted that 'tens of thousands of hours' were spent by HBoS staff trying to secure the Basel II waiver. Ex-chief executive Andy Hornby said it was a 'huge distraction'. HBoS was not granted the waiver in June 2007, but Northern Rock, its key mortgage competitor, did get it, just months before its collapse. HBoS eventually got the waiver in December 2007.

Basel II's formulae should give the answer to the question: 'When I have lent this much, how much capital do I need?' The input should be the portfolio of loans, and the output should be the size of the capital buffer required to keep that bank safe. When I discussed this with Professor Hyun-Song Shin of Princeton University, he made the following point: 'In practice, the banks ask "If I have this much capital, how much can I lend?" The same Vasicek formula gives the answer to both questions, but the second question is a recipe for a credit boom when the financial market becomes more tranquil. What's worse, the greater lending by the banks leads to further compression of spreads and other measures of risk, which induces the banks to lend even more. So, Basel II made banks and the financial system much more procyclical and prone to booms and crashes.'

In other words, this mis-specified simplification of a formula was reverse-engineered by regulators and bankers, and used inevitably as a target, rather than as one of a series of constraints to ensure bank safety.

Many questions remain – above all, why?

The chief executive of one of the world's biggest banks took me through how his team calculates its capital under the formula, by sketching out various expected loss, curves on a piece of paper. 'Conventional risk modelling is very bad at calculating the risk on mortgages,' he says. 'The reason it's so dangerous is that if you have a very low expected loss, the models generate a very low-risk weighted asset. You're sitting there with the thing that is fine most of the time, but when it blows up there's no way you'll have enough capital for it.'

Vasicek himself confirmed that this reading of his actual formula was correct – unlike the Basel derivation. 'A portfolio with low probabilities of default and high correlations may need as much or more capital to support it as a portfolio with high individual probabilities and low correlations,' he told me. 'That is what my formulas are supposed to quantify.'

It is clear there was repeated interference with the Basel formula from bankers and governments to help channel lending into mortgages. A study by Manchester Business School showed that the advanced internal ratings basis (AIRB) formula ultimately results in banks putting insufficient capital aside to cover a systemic mortgage and property crisis, while at the same time putting too much aside to cover the risks in lending to businesses. American researchers have blamed German lobbying. Europeans have blamed the US Federal Reserve. George Christodoulakis, author of the Manchester study, says, 'The Vasicek model was adopted because of analytical tractability – [it is the] only structural model that produces a formula. Vasicek's work is great – [it] contributed very important knowledge, but it was the starting point. But Basel adopted it, made very strong assumptions, misused it and misunderstood it.'

One of the world's most lauded and respected investment bankers and the inventor of many derivative technologies says that governments skewed finance towards mortgages on purpose to keep house prices high and voters happy. 'That's always been the case,' he told me. 'I'd go as far to say it was an objective of all regimes. Because governments like people to own houses. That's why most credit crises comes out of the mortgage market.'

In effect the formulae, as applied by banks, bias lending towards mortgages and away from business. To some degree this would always be the case. The original 1988 Basel formula, Basel I, attached an arbitrarily low-risk value to mortgages and sovereign debt, but a high risk to business lending. Bankers either want exhaustive amounts of information about your ability to repay a loan, or they want collateral. Property is the strongest form of collateral. Yet what countless studies of the Basel model show is that its formulae go further than this. Property has low specific or idiosyncratic risk, but very high systemic risk. Mortgages rarely go wrong, except when they really go wrong, which can cause an epic existential disaster for entire banking systems.

The way these formulae have been applied, therefore, amounts to a form of interference in the banking system, helping divert lending from productive to unproductive purposes. They show that at the very heart of the banking system there is a continuing problem: bankers deliberately deploy complexity to confound and bedazzle, with the aim of extracting hefty bonuses from profits that turn out to be illusory. This involves the concentration and multiplication of credit risk, rather than the more sensible strategy of spreading risk around the banking system. Most people know that already. But there is also a high-level political interference in the banking system, dressed up as science. In fact it is no more than a dangerous extrapolation of past losses using faulty models. If interference like this has to exist, why not tweak the core of the banking system towards useful production rather than useless credit bubbles?

Mis-specified credit derivative models have been a significant factor in the default of households, banks and whole nations. Even assuming the bankers *had* got everything right, the crisis would still have occurred – for the simple reason that regulators miscalculated risks. At the same time they created regulations that motivated risk-taking by banks. But it was the pseudo-science behind credit derivatives that created the shadow banking system.

'It's hard for me to believe that a formula or a bunch of quantitative methods would cause the crisis,' Vasicek says. 'Greedy investment banks who took too many risks because they are gambling with other people's money. The collusion of regulators and politicians and government agencies not exercising even most rudimentary oversight, letting them do whatever they want. A naivety on the part of the public, homeowners and mortgage borrowers who would accept mortgages forced upon them while any reasonable person must see that they could not handle them.'

But in splitting credit risk from a bank loan book, Vasicek's formulae *were* ultimately responsible for creating the shadow banking system. The story of these formulae illustrates the role of complexity as a conscious tool of bonus-seeking bankers. It also reveals the subtle hand of political interference. And it is the engine of the dysfunctional relationship between finance, politics, people and property that lies at the heart of the crisis.

CHAPTER 8

THE GATES OF HELL

Dramatis personae

Nelson Hernandez, a waiter from Ecuador
His wife, **Kelly**
Samuel, from Ghana
Paco 'el Pocero', Spanish construction magnate
José Luis Ruiz Bartolomé, Spanish property expert and
author of *Bye Bye Brick*
José Manuel Campa, Spanish secretary of state for
economic affairs (2009–11)
Rodrigo Rato, ex-managing director of the
International Monetary Fund (IMF)
Cándido Méndez, leader of the UGT, one of
Spain's biggest trade unions
Luis Garicano, professor of economics and strategy at the
London School of Economics

They are called the Puerta de Europa – the Gateway to Europe: two 115-metre, 26-storey towers at the end of Madrid's main thoroughfare, leaning into each other like crooked fangs. They are the tallest leaning skyscrapers in the world. Impressive, yes, but they are far from practical. To get to the highest floor you need to take two lifts, one to floor 13 and another to the top floor, floor 26. And to clean them is a hugely expensive business, requiring a specialised €1 million gondola to glide underneath the 15-degree slant of the towers.

They may be the Gateway to Europe, but to many Spaniards they have become the Gateway to Hell. There was an uncanny premonition of this in Álex de la Iglesia's 1995 cult comic horror movie, *El día de la Bestia* (*The Day of the Beast*), in which the towers become the birthplace of the Antichrist, a terrifying portal to the infernal regions that lie beneath.

Unfortunately for Spain, the reality turned out to be worse than the film's worst nightmares. The east tower was to become the headquarters of Caja Madrid, and then of its wretched spawn, Bankia. The west tower housed a real-estate company half-owned by Caja Madrid. The denizens of the east tower helped to bankrupt tens of thousands of ordinary Spaniards, inflated Spain's calamitous property bubble, and funded reckless spending by a number of Spain's regional governments.

In May 2012 the people of Spain lost trust in the bankers in their leaning towers and began withdrawing their money by the tens of millions. Caja Madrid (by this time wrapped into the new institution called Bankia) itself went bankrupt. So bankrupt was Bankia that the proud Kingdom of Spain required a €100 billion external bailout of its entire financial system. Spain could not raise the money itself, and was forced to accept the supervision of foreign monitors.

Caja Madrid was not really a bank. In the UK, a *caja* would be called a building society. In the USA, it would have been called a savings and loans association (although many of these disappeared in the notorious 1980s S&L debacle). The primary business of cajas is savings and loans – or rather, it *was* savings and loans. By 2012 the entire caja system, bar two tiny institutions, had been dismantled by the centre-right government under the watchful eye of the Troika – a tripartite committee of the European Commission, the European Central Bank and the International Monetary Fund. Just three years previously, the demise of the cajas would have been unthinkable: local and regional cajas had been a vital feature of Spanish society and finance since the 1830s. The impact of their disappearance was to be felt well beyond Spain's finance system. The back-story of the cajas is also the central story of Spain's incredible boom and its spectacular bust. Financial excess, incompetence and corruption all infected the heart of simple, social institutions long trusted by ordinary people with their money.

'*Si se puede, si se puede*,' chant the throng of Spaniards angry at house evictions, banking excess and corrupt politicians. It is the Spanish translation of President Obama's slogan 'Yes we can', and it is the creed of an unlikely coalition of citizens and residents who are beginning to alter some of the easy certainties of Spain's austerity plan. In February 2013 thousands of Spain's dispossessed gathered at the Plaza de Colón (Columbus Square), 5 kilometres due south of the leaning towers, along the same road. Among the crowd were immigrant workers in Ecuador football tops who'd lost their jobs in construction, pensioners in pointy green hats whose savings in preference shares in Caja Madrid were being wiped out, and young Spanish families facing eviction. Their placards bore angry slogans: 'Danger: thieving banker', 'Where is our money?' and 'People without a home, homes without people'. It was a march of the Platform of Mortgage Victims, a powerful grassroots organisation that had successfully resisted and challenged evictions in cities throughout Spain, using the law, direct action and social-media campaigning.

A few months before, I had attended one of the weekly Tuesday night meetings of the Platform in Madrid. Rhythmic '*Si se puede*' chants rang out as mortgage victims told me their shocking tales of financial mistreatment. I was in the midst of a sea of poor families mired in hundreds of thousands of euros of negative equity, their misery made worse by unemployment. But they were not going to accept their fate meekly. One mulleted Spanish father recounted how he had used legal mistakes made by a mortgage broker to prevent his eviction. A mother implored the crowd: 'The bankers are pulling your leg. Don't let them get away with it.' One group of borrowers was particularly hard done by: these were the South American and African immigrants who had come to Spain to work during the property and construction boom. Renting a flat was difficult in Spain, particularly given the fairly common demand for a year's rent up-front as a deposit. But although many could not rent, they found instead that they could buy – by taking out massive mortgages. As soon as they arrived at Madrid-Barajas airport, they were bombarded with advertisements from lenders eager to do business.

And so these immigrants ended up buying Spanish property at vastly inflated prices, at the very top of the market, just prior to the crash. Nelson Hernandez, a waiter from Ecuador, and his wife Kelly were attracted into buying by a raft of local high-street 'worker groups' that turned out to be fronts for estate agents and mortgage brokers. In many cases, mortgages were, without the borrower's knowledge, fraudulently cross-guaranteed with another immigrant family. The result? Despite not being behind on their own payments, Nelson and Kelly faced repossession because they were unknowingly the guarantors of another Ecuadorean family's mortgage. 'We tried to rent a flat around here, but they would not let us, because they could see our financial situation in the bank,' Kelly told me as the couple showed me round the modest flat from which they expected to be evicted. 'We have a mortgage problem – we already have a debt of €222,000, and that puts you on a blacklist.'

At the Platform event, another 'victim', Samuel from Ghana, explained to me how the Spanish justice system had repeatedly left him disenfranchised after his eviction in similar circumstances.

His entire family of four had to live in a single rented room as he serviced the debt from the overpriced repossessed flat.

There were endless stories like this. But the victims resisted. Evictions were prevented by concerted action from campaigners. Spain's courts became clogged up with repossession cases. It is difficult to assess the scale of the problem, as statistics on repossessions are not even collected in a detailed manner. The 400,000 repossessions since 2008 also include a huge number of properties seized by banks from real-estate developers. Banks have put the number at 172,000. Only in December 2012 did the Spanish government order the production of detailed repossession statistics. Whatever the truth of the figures, the suicides are real. Every month there are stories of Spanish homeowners taking their own lives, sometimes during the actual course of an eviction.

Homes without people, towns without communities

It is April 2012. A giant white banner is flapping in the wind, draped down the side of a new block of flats in Seseña, a town south of Madrid. It reads: '2, 3 and 4 bedroom flats from €65,000'. The price is a third of the original selling price. Only a few months previously, the same flats had been the headline offer at a property show, starting at €89,000. The current price is below the building cost, and so assumes a zero or negative cost for the land. It's a bargain that few want to take up just yet, and certainly not here. As in many other boom-time developments, entire blocks in Seseña remain empty. The original plan was to house 40,000 new residents in a town of just 10,000, half an hour south of Spain's capital. The main attraction was price, compared with booming, unaffordable Madrid. The apartments were just beyond Madrid's official border in Castilla-La Mancha, sandwiched between two motorways with limited access roads, and next to an 11-hectare dump of used tyres. By 2012 Seseña, along with other such schemes, was being called a 'ghost town'. But this suggests a place once inhabited by a mass of living people who have passed into the afterlife. Not so in Seseña and thousands of developments like it. There aren't even any ghosts.

Elsewhere in La Mancha, 150 kilometres south of Seseña, is the city of Ciudad Real. For some reason, the city permitted the construction of a new, private airport with a runway long enough to host the world's biggest aeroplane, the Airbus 380 superjumbo. The attempt to brand it 'Madrid South' was a quixotic stretch too far, even for Ryanair, though there was a plan to connect it to a high-speed rail link to the capital. The station was never completed. For a time it was actually called Don Quixote Airport, and was to be accompanied by a theme park celebrating the man and his horse. It closed completely to air traffic within four years of opening, after hopelessly overestimating demand. Astonishingly, there are another three completed airports in Spain that currently do not host (and two of them have never hosted) a plane – in Castellón, Huesca and Corvera.

Homes without people. Towns without communities. Airports without planes. And most of this empty real estate is heading into the reluctant arms of the Spanish state. Welcome to the eighteenth region of Spain: Sarebria.

Since the death of Franco, Spain has been divided into seventeen regional communities, from Andalusia and Murcia in the south to Cantabria, Galicia and Catalunya in the north. These regions have varying degrees of political autonomy. Since the financial crisis, an eighteenth region has emerged, a region that stretches from the Mediterranean to the Atlantic, from the Bay of Biscay to the Strait of Gibraltar, taking in the plains and hills and valleys that lie in between. It exists on the outskirts of almost all of Spain's towns and cities, takes form in a myriad, identikit redbrick apartment blocks, a plethora of lurid architectural experiments, a whole herd of extravagant white-elephant projects. Call it Sarebria, the land of Sareb. Sareb stands for Sociedad de Gestión de Activos procedentes de la Reestructuración Bancaria ('society for the management of assets proceeding from the reconstruction of the banking system'). It is the state-backed 'bad bank' set up to become the buyer of last resort for tens of billions of euros' worth of empty new homes and unfinished property developments. It has been given a decade and a half to carry out this task. It is far from autonomous. Its establishment was a condition of the European loans to bail out Spain's financial sector.

At Sareb's offices opposite Real Madrid's Bernabéu stadium the mother of all clean-ups is underway. They are trying to find a hangover cure after the world's longest fiesta. Sharp-suited financiers from American hedge funds and European pensions companies file through the glass-walled offices in an attempt to grab a property bargain. Sareb might be regarded as Europe's biggest property company, but its staff reject the label. That would only be true, they say, if they foreclosed on the loans they have been passed.

Señor Hernando and the giant mortgage

Señor Hernando looked up proudly at the bronze sculpture of his parents. They are holding hands, his father looking down fondly on his mother. The large bronze statue stands on a plinth in the middle of the roundabout at the entrance to the complex in Seseña that he named after himself: 'Residencial Francisco Hernando' 'This is my city, everything you see here is mine,' he told a British journalist from the *Daily Telegraph* in 2009. 'I've built eight cities, and I have six more in mind. I'm like a painter, I love creating things.'

Señor Hernando goes by the nickname 'Paco el Pocero', alluding to his first job, drilling sewers in Madrid. He did not go to school. As a youngster in Franco's Spain he says he lived in a shack in a working-class quarter of Madrid, rummaging for food in the rubbish dumps, and 'eating banana skins and cheese crusts from the bins outside the houses of the rich'. By 2009 he had ridden Spain's construction boom to its very peak, becoming a billionaire with a frigate-sized yacht, a private jet and a helipad. His dream for Seseña was that it should be a haven for working-class Madrileño couples who could not afford their first home. The quality of the flats was, and still is, rather good. There are wooden floors, extra bathrooms. Other phantom developments such as Aranjuez in the south, or the area of El Escorial in the north of Madrid, fared as badly. Valdeluz, next to the town of Guadalajara (also in Castilla-La Mancha but further away than Seseña) was another 30,000-capacity town built by a different developer, Reyal Urbis – now Spain's second biggest bankruptcy. In February 2013 it owed its creditors €3.6 billion, including €700 million to the Sareb 'bad bank', and €400 million to the Spanish tax office. Seseña's particular notoriety came as a result of its positioning on the main motorway south out of Madrid, and the reputation of el Pocero. After the crash, Seseña's external infrastructure was left incomplete. Prices plummeted.

The unlucky few were the ones who in 2007, before the crash, shelled out (according to local estate agents) something like €185,000 euros for an apartment. Only 5,000 of the planned 13,000 properties were ever completed. Of those, many of the flats were left without the required certificates for water and other utilities. Between the empty blocks, the eerily desolate streets take their names – with a certain hollow irony – from the Old Masters who hang in the Prado, not forty-five minutes' drive away: Velázquez, Goya, El Greco, Titian, Rubens. The street called Calle Rafael has a gaping hole where a residential block should have been. Public transport is inadequate, and there aren't enough schools, roads or hospitals, despite a long-running argument with the local authorities. But there is a swimming pool in each block, an athletics stadium, and a park named after el Pocero's mother.

Part of the problem was the quarrel between el Pocero and the local mayor, who was reluctant to grant the development a full licence even after work had started. The mayor, noting that el Pocero had acquired the land just days before the previous mayor had changed its zoning classification from farmland to greenfield development site, called for an inquiry. Why, people wondered, had the old mayor suddenly come into the money? But no charges arose, the old mayor explaining his apparent windfall as a win on the lottery. The developer was defiant. 'When I arrived here nine years ago,' he told *El Pais* newspaper, 'all Seseña had was a man with a cart and donkey. The land was here for anyone who wanted it.' A war of attrition arose between el Pocero and the new mayor. The local newspaper, owned by the developer, attacked the mayor, while el Pocero's workers demonstrated outside the municipal office, demanding the mayor issue the necessary licences.

In other places, there was clear corruption. A 1997 law had loosened most constraints on development, opening the flood-gates to corruption. 'Where there's construction, there's crime,' admitted the urban planning coordinator in Prime Minister Zapatero's Socialist government, which was in office through the boom and the subsequent bust. On the coast, from Marbella to Valencia, tens of thousands of homes were completed without planning permission after bribes were paid to local officials. Only the construction companies benefited. Where it was not explicit, there was a tacit form of corruption. Town halls relied on building permits for up to a half of their revenues. Regional governments were funded by property taxes. Spanish regional and local governments had every incentive to join in the party.

'Land planning in Spain is designed by local municipalities,' explains José Luis Ruiz Bartolomé, a Spanish property expert and author of *Bye Bye Brick*. 'There isn't a big strategy made by the province or the region – even though it is the region which, in the end, allows the local plan. So, town mayors have the magic wand to decide what is buildable and what is not. That's the origin of corruption: the monopoly of the land that every town hall exerts in its municipality.'

So what were the banks, the cajas, doing? Well, they too were being sucked into the web of political patronage, investing in property and development themselves, and even setting up as estate agents, while maintaining their more traditional role as mortgage lenders. In UK terms, the whole of the Spanish savings-bank system seemed to turn into one giant HBoS, with a Northern Rock to fund the mortgages. The cajas became an all-in, one-way bet on property prices never falling. Yet they also funded the very over-developments that ensured that the bet would fail and prices would fall. This was tacit corruption, combined with what appears to be monstrous stupidity.

The politicians who tried to burst the bubble

What is particularly remarkable is the fact that the government in charge during the boom, Zapatero's Socialists (the PSOE), was well aware of the dark underside of ever-rising house prices. They did not buy into New Labour's tacit encouragement of rising house prices in the UK. In their 2004 election manifesto, the PSOE promised to end the housing bubble. The manifesto expressed concern about company and household debt, and promised to change the Spanish economy, 'which is highly indebted and geared towards bricks and mortar'.

José Manuel Campa, who was deputy finance minister in Zapatero's second government, puts it like this: 'Back in 2004, the main economic agenda of the Zapatero government at that time was to change the growth model away from real estate. The manifesto said to stop the bubble in real-estate prices, so there was some recognition. The diagnosis was there,' he told me. In 2004 the Bank of Spain even started an annual assessment of the overvaluation of Spanish property, calculated at 30 per cent even then, a time when there were already over 100,000 unsold Spanish homes.

Here's what actually happened in Prime Minister Zapatero's bubble-bursting first four years at the Palace of Moncloa. House prices surged, up by 36 per cent in cash terms, and 23 per cent after accounting for inflation. The longer-term international comparisons are telling. Overall property prices rose 115 per cent in real terms in the decade before the boom. Although the bubbles in Ireland (160 per cent) and the UK (140 per cent) were bigger, Spain was well out of kilter with the rest of the Eurozone (40 per cent).

Zapatero's big play was that mass house-building would temper prices. Between 2004 and 2007, credit to the construction sector grew at an annual rate of 24.6 per cent. For the real-estate sector it was 43.1 per cent per year. By 2007 property development loans were 30 per cent of Spain's GDP, and construction loans were 14.5 per cent. Credit to both sectors was worth nearly half of Spain's entire economy, when the two sectors only represented a fifth of the economy. Between 2001 and 2008, Spain increased its overall stock of housing by over a fifth to 25 million, an extra 4.3 million homes. If there had been no domestic population growth, Spain could have re-housed every household in Portugal, and still be left with some empty properties. In the entire decade before the crisis, Spain built a total of 5.3 million extra homes, which could have accommodated the population not only of Portugal, but that of Ireland as well (although it would have been a bit cramped). As it happened, there was a large influx of 5 million migrants into Spain in the decade before the crash, with 3 million arriving between 2003 and 2009. This soaked up some, though not all, of the excess house-building. Perhaps the best measure is that by 2011 the number of dwellings in Spain, which has a population of 45 million, nearly overtook the number of dwellings in the UK, with its population of 63 million.

The cajas boomed. Even the most casual amble down a Spanish high street would have revealed the curious excess of bank branches in amongst the tapas bars. Every municipality with at least 5,000 residents had a caja branch, and there were over a thousand villages where cajas were the only bank branches. In bigger cities, sometimes entire high streets were filled with competing cajas and banks. In fact Spain's total branch network (including conventional banks) peaked in 2008 at 46,221 branches – half the number of branches in the whole of the USA. In a decade and a half the caja branch network doubled in size – at a time when the number of normal bank branches was being cut. At the peak of the bubble, Spain had one bank branch for every 952 Spaniards. In America, that number is one for every 2,857, while in Britain it is one for every 3,846.

'The cajas had three inherent disadvantages,' says José Manuel Campa, now a professor of financial management at the IESE Business School. 'They were purely domestic institutions channelling their growth domestically, unlike Spain's multinational banks. Institutionally they were structured as foundations and did not have the ability to raise equity. And their governance was complex and likely to have problems with conflicts of interest.'

The last of these points was reflected in the way politically appointed representatives conspired to direct caja funding towards their own pet infrastructure projects. It might have started with 'Guggenheim envy', the urge by other cities to imitate Bilbao's iconic regeneration, epitomised by the opening of the striking new Guggenheim Museum in 1997 in the city's derelict dock area. It may even stretch back to 1992, when Barcelona played host to the summer Olympics and found itself in the world's spotlight. Such developments prompted copycat schemes in regions across Spain that needed debt-funding. Another pattern involved banks granting loans for megaprojects such as airports or theme parks – but the loans only covered the construction and not the long-term viability of the projects. The result? A series of white elephants. Again, only the construction companies seemed to benefit. One caja appointed a ballet dancer to its board.

Political dominance of the banking system was nothing new. In the Franco era, the dictatorship practised a form of credit intervention that directed savings to investments declared as 'qualifying' by the Junta de Inversiones. This essentially forced Spanish caja savers to lend money to Franco's government and preferred companies at below market rates. It was a type of tax, a form of financial repression that helped Franco's treasury to avoid having to fund its deficits on the markets. The system only ended in 1977, two years after Franco's death. At this point, Spain's cajas began funding small business and housing loans. Although founded back in the 1830s, in proper credit-market terms Spain's cajas were born at the same time as those young Spaniards whom they would plunge the deepest into debt.

The transformation of private-sector indebtedness was astounding. In the pre-crisis decade mortgage loans as a percentage of Spain's economy ballooned from 28 per cent to 103 per cent. The average Spanish household's stock of private debt rose from 53 per cent of disposable income in 1997 to a peak of 132 per cent in 2007.

Given their lack of capital, and the broadly fixed amount of savings from the pueblos of Spain, how did the cajas provide this tsunami of funding? Meet the *cédula* (pronounced thed-u-la) – also known as a covered bond. This amazing piece of financial engineering, known in German as the *Pfandbrief*, was invented in 1769 by Frederick the Great of Prussia as a way to fund rebuilding after the Seven Years War. In its long history, this type of bond has not seen a single default. The key innovation was that the loan was secured or 'covered' by assets, normally property, and so offered cheap wholesale funding to financial institutions. The bonds quickly spread throughout Europe. Spanish covered bonds or *cédulas* were around in the nineteenth century, but only really took off in 2000 as an alternative to raising deposits from ordinary Spaniards. In particular it was the jumbo *cédula hipotecaria*, or billion-euro-plus mortgage covered bond, which grew from a market of just €7 billion in 2000 to €57 billion by 2003. And by 2007 Spain had overtaken Germany with €267 billion of outstanding *cédulas*. The public sector also joined in, issuing *cédulas* for large projects, leaving the total outstanding in 2011 at €402 billion, of which €369 billion was covered by mortgages. Cajas alone were responsible for €250 billion of that. Even smaller cajas could get in on the act by clubbing together to form a 'multicedula'.

That €369 billion is a massive sum. In total it represented

55 per cent of the value of the outstanding mortgage stock of Spain. To put it another way, outstanding residential mortgage balances in Spain increased between 2003 and 2011 by €354 billion. Outstanding *cédula hipotecarias* increased by €312 billion in the same period. As much as 80 per cent of the growth of Spanish household mortgage debts in the go-go years of the boom were funded in this way. Over the same period in Germany, the biggest issuer of covered bonds until 2004, mortgage *Pfandbriefs* outstanding fell by over €50 billion. Meanwhile, the boom raged in Denmark, France, Sweden, the UK and Spain. Especially in Spain.

It all sounds a little like the Northern Rock model. But there were some crucial differences.

Covered bonds of this type were kept on the balance sheets of the banks and the cajas. The security for the lender was the portfolio of mortgages on the balance sheet. No funny business with offshore, off-balance-sheet financing, no hiking up the loan-to-value ratios. Eligible mortgages could not be worth more than 80 per cent of the value of the property. For this reason, Spanish mortgage lending tended to require at least a 20 per cent deposit. Even during the boom, average Spanish mortgage loan-to-value ratios never went above 65 per cent. For this reason, the funding costs were low, even for a small caja with nothing in the way of genuine capital. So the *cédulas* naturally got high credit ratings. The model was markedly superior to the opaque, complex off-balance-sheet mortgage securities favoured in the USA and UK. Indeed, after the crisis the former US Treasury secretary Hank Paulson implored American banks to copy this German-Spanish model. Spanish bankers even flew to Hong Kong to present the idea to China's booming banking sector.

Northern Europe fans the flames

So what was the ultimate source of this river of credit? Not much of it came from Spain itself. One Spanish bank said two-thirds of *cédulas* were sold abroad. The biggest buyers were banks in Eurozone nations with healthy surpluses, such as the Netherlands and especially Germany, looking to make a return. At this time the German economy was depressed, mortgage demand was weak, and German banks were racing to lend somewhere to take advantage of expiring government guarantees. Where better than in the covered-bond market, itself the invention of one of the greatest Germans in history? An investment yielding a return, with no currency risk – and as safe as Spanish houses. 'Fundamentally,' says José Manuel Campa, 'in aggregate it was institutional savings from Germany and the Netherlands, which, even now, still have large surpluses, channelled in two different ways: the banking sector and the financial markets.'

Effectively Germany and other creditor nations were the source of the euros that ultimately added a third to Spanish household debt. Germany had, through intermediaries, lent people like Kelly and Nelson the boom-time cash. But they had left the credit risk with the Spanish banks. This method of lending turned out to be a very important factor during the bust. *Cédulas* were not a form of credit alchemy that had disappeared default risk, despite the German engineering. This was a zero-sum game. All the covered bonds did was to shift risks around. The additional security offered to the *cédula*-holders was at the expense of other unsecured lenders to the cajas. As Spanish credit quality declined, more high quality assets were sucked in to secure the interests of the holders of covered bonds. Ultimately the sheer size of the market, over a third of Spanish GDP, must have hastened the demise of the cajas. The ultimate sources of the credit, in northern Europe, got away scot-free. Eventually, as it was clear that the cajas were heading for bankruptcy, the risk was transferred to the Spanish taxpayer. It was for this reason that the Dutch Central Bank, among others, limited the issuance of covered bonds for Dutch mortgages in the Netherlands.

Some of Spain's most senior officials are frustrated and irritated by the attitude subsequently shown by Germany and the Troika.

'One of the problems we have,' one official told me, 'is the long, long list of moral judgements. The problem was economic not moral. Germans are depicted as sensible savers, hardworking people. We "pigs" don't work, we spent much too much, and enjoy our fiestas and siestas lying on the beach, with a German and a Dutch guy giving us free beers. But this really is all about monetary policy and incentives.'

He traces the root cause of the problem to German reunification in 1990, when a 1:1 exchange rate was agreed for the West German and East German mark. This generated a very deep real-estate recession in Germany that lasted a decade. And then the euro arrived with super-low interest rates and a relaxed monetary policy, matching those of the USA. Eurozone interest rates were naturally focused on helping the depressed German economy, by far the biggest economy in the zone, without much heed being paid to the consequences elsewhere within the monetary union. The end result for countries such as Spain was very low interest rates for a very long time – so low, that taking the still-elevated level of inflation into account, such peripheral countries in fact experienced an extended period of negative interest rates.

'With negative interest rates the rational thing is to grow debts,' the Spanish official told me. 'It's not lazy. It's the direct outcome of negative interest rates, year after year after year. The whole time we were saying we have a huge problem. In the meantime German banks were desperate to escape very low interest rates in low-yield Germany, so they looked outside to the USA and Spain. German banks were buying the high yield that they could not provide domestically.'

After this conversation, the official said he would deny ever having met me if the quotes were attributed. Such are the sensitivities in a nation-state where sovereignty is not absolute, but shared with its partners. The former minister Campa puts it like this: 'The side effect of real negative rates is that people and companies want to leverage. A single monetary policy for the whole euro area has these side effects. At the time monetary policy was focused on German weak growth. Is there a domestic financial policy that could have dented that boom? There's no real effective policy. It's very difficult in general to stop a build-up of a bubble of this kind, when everybody is benefiting.'

Actually, Spain did have a go at halting the growth of its bubbles, using bank buffer funds and government deficits, and did better than most. It managed to rein in the very worst excesses of the credit cycle through a Bank of Spain tool known as 'dynamic provisioning'. From 2000, banks and cajas were obliged to put 20 per cent of their income aside as a buffer in the good times. At the time it was bitterly opposed by Spain's big banks, international accounting regulators and foreign regulators. The profits of Spain's big banks were certainly hurt by the policy. 'You're crazy,' a Bank of Spain official recalls a caja lobbyist telling him in 2000. 'You're conservative, you're harming us internationally, you are mad.' Half a decade on, as the cajas found themselves using these provisions at the onset of the crisis, the same lobbyist said they were not so bad. A full decade on, the lobbyist told him that the Bank of Spain should have been even tougher. In the same way, the major international Spanish banks, such as Santander and BBVA, complained about dynamic provisioning during the boom, but by the time the crisis hit they were boasting about it. All of which goes to confirm that over the medium term a banker cannot be relied on to know what is good, even for themselves.

Obviously a crucial flaw of such a plan is that in a severe double-dip recession, the buffer is depleted without being replenished. That is precisely what happened in 2011/12. A more subtle flaw was that it created opaqueness around the true state of the caja balance sheets. More fundamentally, it allowed the regulator to take its eyes off the ball with the cajas. But Santander and BBVA did remain in strong health relative to other European competitors, particularly considering the ill-health of their domestic market. The more bullish proponents of the policy say that €30 billion of taxpayers' money was saved. There was no bailout of the private banks. Dynamic provisioning helped smooth the wave, but did not prevent it from breaking.

Spain is also justified in feeling a little hard done by, given that, like Ireland, it kept to the rules of the game on deficits. Berlin and Brussels designed the so-called 'Stability and Growth Pact' to limit government deficits within the Eurozone. Unlike Germany and France, Spain stuck to the strictures of the pact until the crisis. The best performers were Finland and Luxembourg, followed by Spain and Ireland. The worst performers were Italy and Greece, then Germany and France. Whether you were a fiscal fiend or a fiscal saint turned out to have very little bearing on whether or not you needed a bailout. Spain and Ireland showed the best predictor of euro-crisis pain was a country's net financial position – basically those huge international inflows of hot money into domestic credit markets.

The entire economy of Spain turned out to be a giant mortgage: an epic one-way bet on property, estate agents and construction. When the Lehman Brothers crisis of 2008 put a stop to those international inflows of cash, the Spanish property market collapsed, homes were left unsold, construction companies went bankrupt, millions of workers were laid off, property taxes collapsed, and regional-government deficits spiralled as welfare payments to people and banks surged, as more and more cajas needed to be bailed out. 'Throughout the period,' says Campa, the former minister, 'we were always under pressure, but never at the front line of the threat. Another country was always seen as more vulnerable, and we had the ability to react with significant policies sufficient to restore confidence – but at a very high political cost.'

Zapatero's government saw the Greek sovereign-debt crisis emerging in 2010. In May of that year it responded with an austerity package, reversing social policies and freezing pensions. It prompted massive protests and was seen as political suicide. Zapatero left office without contesting the election in 2011, and the centre-right Partido Popular won a landslide. The new prime minister, Mariano Rajoy, doubled up on the austerity, with brutal cuts to government spending. Spain always benefited from the fact that Italy looked much worse. After the technocrat Mario Monti was appointed Italian prime minister, the bond markets switched their attentions from Rome to Madrid. Rajoy's efforts were made more difficult because some of the toughest cuts he wanted were actually not his to make, but in the hands of Spain's strong regional governments. The protests were huge. Rajoy was anxious to avoid the humiliation of a Greek-style bailout. But the 'doom loop' – in which rotten banks created market fears about governments, which in turn worsened funding for banks – was in full flow. The problems in Spain's cajas proved overwhelming. The final trigger was the slow-motion run on Bankia.

The palatial offices of the Bank of Spain in Madrid have a regal air: there are Royal Steps, there are vaults full of gold (though nearly three-quarters of the original gold reserves were shipped to Moscow in 1936, after the outbreak of the Spanish Civil War), and there are rooms hung with priceless Goya paintings. Goya was paid in share certificates for these portraits of senior Bank officials, and so became a shareholder in the original Bank of Spain. By 2011 there were various other curious additions to the Bank's asset base. The Bank of Spain was increasingly finding the country's debts ending up on its own balance sheet – and, as the Bank of Spain is part of the eurosystem, these debts ultimately ended up on the balance sheet of the European Central Bank. In fact, Spanish banks were creating packages of mortgage loans and corporate loans specifically to use as collateral for ECB cash. The bulk of those mortgage-covered bonds were now effectively funded by the ECB, after the funding from German and other foreign institutions dried up. *Cédula* issuance for mortgages reached record levels in 2010 and 2011, after the collapses of the cajas and the property market, and in the wake of fears about the future of the euro itself.

In the summer of 2011 Bankia cashed in a €773 million portfolio of loans called Madrid Active Corporations 5 (MAC

5). This portfolio included tram lines, the metro station at Barcelona Airport, some wind farms – and the world's most expensive footballer, Cristiano Ronaldo. Caja Madrid had lent Real Madrid €76.5 million to buy Ronaldo from Manchester United. It was the second largest single loan in MAC 5. Unusually, the transfer fee was paid up-front and in full. Originally the loan for Ronaldo had garnered an AAA rating. But by 2012 that had been cut, just after the team and the footballer had become Spanish champions. Still, Real Madrid were good for their money.

At the same time, a large quantity of Spanish property junk was being parked on the ECB's balance sheet, for a time the only form of funding available to weak Spanish banks. During March 2012, Spanish transactions of this type doubled in a month to €315 billion, which in practice meant large chunks of the Iberian Peninsula's decaying property assets were being cashed in at the Frankfurt pawnshop (alongside some government debts). At the height of Spain's banking crisis the rate of issuance of mortgage *cédulas* actually accelerated, reaching record levels – but this was essentially funded by the ECB, rather than by north European banks.

The Spanish banks were running out of assets to underpin the existing *cédulas* for mortgages and public-project borrowing. So they scoured their balance sheets for other assets that could be transformed into a *cédula* and therefore traded in for ECB cash. Spain even issued a Royal Decree Law in July 2012 to create an entirely new type of *cédula*, backed by loans for exports. The Madrid office of the credit agency Moody's said that it showed the banks were running out of conventional mortgage assets to parcel up.

By August 2012 more than a third of all the ECB's emergency funding was in Spain. It had increased by eightfold over a year. The assets were being quality-controlled at the Bank of Spain. The more toxic ones were given a 'haircut', their value slashed to protect the central bank. In Germany, newspapers conducted investigations into the quality of Spanish quality control.

Developments echoed what had happened in Ireland in autumn 2010. Spanish government borrowing costs shot up at the same time, making it impossible for the government to inject the funds necessary to stabilise the Spanish banks. With deposits fleeing, Prime Minister Mariano Rajoy had to do what he had promised he would not: ask Europe for the funds.

The blister and the bailout balm

I sit in the large office of one of the Spanish financial officials who deals with the Troika. Spain avoids using the word 'bailout' to describe the programme. Officially the IMF is merely an adviser, rather than a lender. Spain is not Greece, after all. But sovereignty has sapped away from this nation. The official describes the first meeting with the Troika: 'Do you have a plan?' they asked in relation to Spain's cajas. 'OK, this is your plan,' they said, presenting a paper. My official offers a personal opinion. 'The external presence is extremely helpful,' he says. 'I never imagined we would have done what we have done in financial reform in the past few months without their presence. We have done in six months what would have taken a decade.'

A Spanish minister does not like to have bureaucrats from Frankfurt, Brussels and Washington sitting on his office sofa, telling him what to do. But ultimately he accepts the predicament. 'There is useful pressure,' my official says. 'Sometimes you have to do things that it's better to blame on other forces. It's tough, there is some loss of sovereignty, but we negotiate with partners what to do.' I ask him if he is enjoying his job. 'No,' he replies.

The precise course followed by the torrent of credit from northern Europe en route to Spain weighs on minds in Madrid. In their search for yield, German banks (memorably described as 'stupid Germans in Düsseldorf' by the writer Michael Lewis in *The Big Short*) had also been investing in toxic US subprime mortgage debts at the very top of the market. When German loans to Americans went sour in 2007–08, the German banks lost, and required massive bailouts from the German taxpayer. When German loans to Spaniards soured in 2010–11, the Spanish lost out, assuming the credit risk, and the German banks got paid off in full. The mechanics of the covered-bond market and the insistence from the ECB that Spain bail out its banks meant, in the first instance, that Spanish taxpayers were left with the bill.

At the heart of Spain's bailout is the FROB – the Fondo de Reestructuración Ordenada Bancaria ('fund for orderly bank restructuring'). The FROB was set up by the Zapatero government to deal with the rotting cajas. By June 2012, under Rajoy's government, it was the receptacle for a financial bailout of €100 billion. The FROB can be seen as an undertaker preparing an entire part of Spain's financial system for burial. Or perhaps it is more like a matador planning one clean, forensic blow to finish off the weakened, bleeding bull of the banking industry. The day I dropped in, the FROB's staff were moving to offices near Real Madrid's Bernabéu stadium, not far from the HQ of Sareb. 'The new government couldn't trust the cajas,' a senior official told me, 'because behind the cajas with some exceptions were politicians. Perhaps not in the retail business, but in the case of corporate business there was a lot of mistakes.' He pointed the finger at regional, rather than national, politicians.

FROB's initial attempts to sort out the cajas failed horrifically in the case of Bankia, which it created out of the merger of seven cajas – three of which, including Caja Madrid, were in a bad state. It turned out to be a monster worthy of Dr Frankenstein, a monster that increased, concentrated and made systemic the financial problem, rather than reducing or even solving it. In Bankia, Spain had created a too-big-to-fail institution, two years after the 2008 crisis had shown the dangers presented by such vast financial organisations. In December 2010 Rodrigo Rato, ex-managing director of the IMF, was brought in on a multi-million-pound salary to run Bankia – seemingly at a profit. But weeks after he resigned in May 2012 it became apparent that

Bankia was making multibillion-pound losses. A few months later the leaning tower of Bankia lodged the largest loss in Spanish corporate history, principally caused by the rotten legacy of Caja Madrid and Bancaja, a similar institution from Valencia. The controversy was politically charged because Caja Madrid had been officially owned by the local Madrid government run by the Partido Popular (PP), the centre-right party that came to power nationally in 2011 under Mariano Rajoy. Bancaja's board in Valencia had been similarly close to the PP.

Regarding the mess left by Bancaja, a senior Bankia board member told *El Pais* about the reality of the assets on its balance sheet. 'We were told about land on the beach front; when we went to look at the land we found it was 500 metres from the beach behind the A7 highway. Another caja had invested in a gated community of 1,000 houses in a village of 800 people.' In Madrid a billion-euro loan for land purchases by a property company that went bust within a year was bad enough. Buying skyscrapers as the credit crunch hit the world economy was worse still. Before joining the IMF in 2004, at the beginning of the property bubble, Rato had been minister of the economy in the Partido Popular national government. So the central government was bailing out a financial institution with close links to its own party. In fact, the mess was so colossal that the Spanish nation needed help from the rest of Europe to foot the Bankia bill. Extraordinarily enough, when he was MD of the IMF, Rato failed to persuade Argentina to take the IMF textbook bailout medicine. Yet in his home country, the failure of his bank had brought IMF advisers in rather rapidly. In fact, one of the factors that understandably sparked deposit flight was an IMF statement demanding the strengthening of Spanish bank balance sheets, 'especially the largest one' – that of Bankia, run by the IMF's former boss.

But the mess runs even deeper. Bankia was desperate to raise capital. The international markets said a swift '*No, gracias*.' When still prime minister, Zapatero forced some domestic banks to lend a helping hand. New shares were marketed and sold to ordinary Spanish investors for €3.50 each. In addition, some hard-up savers took up so-called preference shares offering 7 per cent annual returns – a higher rate than they could get elsewhere.

During my visit to FROB, it became pretty clear that these ordinary investors were going to lose the shirts off their backs. From €3.50 to €0.01 was the rumour. Officials were considering sparing them a few extra cents. Amazingly, these investments had been made on the basis of an unaudited set of accounts. Ordinary Spanish savers were left holding the baby after a decade of excess, incompetence and cronyism. Many even joined the protests against evictions, even though those evictions were ostensibly being carried out to recoup some money for the savers. Bankia had sparked a humiliating national bailout and the largest loss, at the time of writing, in Spanish corporate history. And what happened to the executives responsible for creating this beast that was too big to fail? While others lost their homes, they kept their high salaries.

At FROB, forensic accountants were searching through the balance sheets of all the cajas for evidence of wrongdoing. A week later they sent five cases to court. Most of these related to massive managerial pay packets, sometimes not even revealed to the board of the bank in question.

What a way to go. Cajas had been founded by churches on the Benthamite principle of achieving the greatest happiness for the greatest number, and set out to help farmers and ordinary Spaniards in the tough years following the Peninsular War with Napoleonic France. The profits from cajas were used to fund regional social projects, such as schools, hospitals and libraries. Caja Madrid, even after its own tragic accident, still funds many of Madrid's ambulances. I had imagined that Spain might feel nostalgic for its all-encompassing savings banks. But no. One Spanish official told me that after all the scandals relating to managers' pay, 'the romantic notion of the cajas has disappeared'.

There is an interesting exception to the general rule. Catalunya's savings bank, La Caixa, had a much more successful entry into the world of 'real' banking. As a caja it had always been run more commercially than most, with fewer of the political pressures that felled Caja Madrid and Bankia. When the cajas needed capital that they could not raise as mutual organisations, CaixaBank was created. CaixaBank helped with the rescue of other banks, bought back billions of euros of its mortgage covered bonds, and even continued to be the largest funder of social projects in Spain. The cajas were not born to fail, even if they have all now disappeared. The logic suggests that the problem was regional political interference – as seen at its most acute in Madrid and Valencia.

'There was a moment in time when the caja model made sense in Spain,' a Spanish treasury official told me. 'They provided credit and let capital flow to the regions. It was a special model, but weak regional governance was the main weakness.' The view from Spanish officialdom is that this was a standard-issue albeit gargantuan property boom-and-bust, exacerbated by a layer of incompetence due to the cajas indulging in a frenzy of politically motivated lending.

The image of the bubble suggests a benign and even playful process. Both the inflating and the bursting can be fun. But what happened in Spain might be more accurately described as a blister. When a blister bursts, the rawness of the underlying wound is revealed. An influential German official who knows Spain intimately says that he watched in 2005 as Spain's property boom hollowed out its export base, affecting expansion plans for German-owned car factories in Pamplona and Zaragoza. Workers were being sucked into the construction industry, lured by the inflated wages on offer. Car production fell sharply as Spain's economy oriented itself to serve the blister of credit, rather than manufacturing and export. Industry could not compete. This colossal misallocation of investment had a real impact.

A lost generation of *milleuristas*

The people left to pick up the pieces are the *milleurista* generation. In 2005 a 27-year-old graduate called Carolina Alguacil
wrote to *El Pais* to point out that large swathes of Spain's
best-ever educated youth were struggling on insecure jobs paying
a thousand euros (*mille euros*) a month. 'You had better not
complain. You can't save, you don't have a home, or a car, or
any children. You live for the day,' she wrote. By 2012, things
had got unimaginably worse as youth unemployment soared to
unprecedented levels. Now an income of a thousand euros a
month represented an unachievably lofty aspiration for Spain's
lost generation.

In April 2012, in Madrid's Puerta del Sol Square, Europe's
youth seemed to be stirring again. A large crowd of young
people – the *indignados* – systematically shut down the square's
shops, chanting, 'Don't shop while we can't work.' It was the
build-up to a massive march through Madrid and all of Spain's
major cities as part of an all-encompassing general strike. Before
the Bankia collapse it was the most severe test for Spain's
conservative government. In 2011 they were *indignado* – merely
indignant. By 2012, as Europe's fourth largest economy became
an economic laboratory for Berlin–Brussels sado-austerity, they
were *enfadado* – angry.

Spain simply had to grow in order to get its young people
back to work. Not just for their sake, but also for the sake of
the national finances, which were reeling with an annual unemployment benefits bill of €40 billion – 4 per cent of the country's
GDP. At this moment the Partido Popular government introduced a brutally austere budget, which helped crush growth in
2012, and brought in a double-dip recession.

It is impossible to overstate the desperation of the youth of
Spain. They are the best-educated Spanish generation ever, and
for the most part they are jobless. Generation zero they're called,
or 'ninis' – neither in work nor further education. I talked to

three typical twenty-somethings with no prospects: Alex had qualified as a teacher, Diana had a degree in human resources, and Ana has studied psychology. When they look for part-time work at low-paid fast-food joints they are told they are over-qualified. These three represent the norm, not the exception, in Spain. Two of them had never worked at all, despite applying for some 200 jobs. 'My experience is I have never had a job, I've always had temporary jobs. That's for eight years,' said Diana. Another had lost her job. All lived with their parents and expected to do so until their forties. They see these problems lasting until the 2020s. 'We have to leave Spain, to go to England or Germany,' said Ana. The teacher, Alex, said that he would go to Brazil.

Spain's youth are leaving. During a trade mission, Spanish industrialists went as far as lobbying Brazil's president for more visas for Spanish graduates. Spain's massive immigration between 1995 and 2005 now seems to be a decade-long aberration in a continuous exodus of Spaniards out of their country. The worrying thing for Spain is that before 1995 this emigration was mainly of the least-qualified workers. Now Spain's highest skilled sons and daughters are leaving, seeing no future in their domestic economy.

The millions of jobs created in the boom proved to be fleeting. From January 2003 to January 2008, Spain added 3.3 million jobs. By January 2013 it had lost those 3.3 million jobs, returning almost exactly to where it was a decade before. A former minister puts it slightly differently: 'In Spain we are very good at hiring and firing. We created more jobs than anywhere else in the EU between 2000 and 2007. And then we fired them all.' The 3.3 million jobs lost over the past half decade also mask a remark-able generational inequity. Almost all the jobs were lost by those aged 34 and under: 8 million of these young people had jobs in 2008, but by 2013 this figure had fallen to 5.1 million, a loss of 2.9 million. Those in the age range 35–50 were much more likely to keep their jobs: less than half a million were shed at this age range, with the workforce remaining around 8 million. Incredibly, in the over-50 age range, there was a net gain over this period of more than 300,000 jobs. The conservative government that came to power in Spain in December 2011 wanted to improve the lot of the jobless youth by making it easier and cheaper to fire highly protected older workers. Spain's 'two-tier' labour market meant it was much easier to lay off younger workers, while older workers stayed in their jobs. The new government's reforms should in theory help the younger workers, but when I put this to a group of them, they didn't buy it.

Neither did Cándido Méndez, the leader of the UGT, one of Spain's biggest unions. 'If you add together the labour reforms and the cuts to public spending,' he told me, 'we'll be caught in a vicious circle. The economic crisis will get even bigger, there will be more job cuts, youth unemployment will grow, Spain will get poorer and we will endanger the whole European Union.' He drew an imaginary vicious circle in the air to ram home the point. Méndez has been calling for a general strike. (It's worth pointing out, however, that the UGT effectively had a representative on Bankia's board, paid a salary of €181,000. As a further illustration of Spain's Byzantine power structures, it should also be mentioned that two decades ago the UGT set up a housing project that was partly funded by Caja Madrid. The scheme, which featured a folly in the form of a 100-metre sphere, went bust.)

The protests spread. And they intensified when the general stench of low-level local corruption started to percolate up to the very top of the Spanish government. At the heart of two cases were brown envelopes, secret payments, plush suburbs, construction companies and regional-government contract awards. Again, Partido Popular politicians in Madrid and Valencia were implicated, and in 2013 PP treasurer Luis Bárcenas was detained in jail ahead of a corruption trial over the origins of a multimillion-pound fortune and allegations of secret payments. He maintained his innocence. The timing could not have been worse. Grudging acceptance of austerity was always likely in a country as pro-euro as Spain. But austerity imposed by a political party implicated in bubble-era patronage, payoffs and corruption? Luis Garicano, a professor at LSE, believes that enough is enough. 'During the bubble years, our society accepted a dangerous barter, in exchange for huge apparent prosperity,' he told me. 'We Spanish closed our eyes to corruption.' Not only did the Spanish government have a credibility problem; people were also questioning its goodwill. Reforms meant to save Spain were being delegitimised. 'In a life or death situation this weakness is dangerous,' Professor Garicano argued. The recapitalisation of Spain's banks could have been achieved with little fuss in 2008, 2009, 2010 or even early 2011, when financial markets were relaxed about Spain's low national debts. The cost would have been cheaper than Britain's bank bailout in 2008. But strong regional political interests attempting to protect the doomed cajas stood in the way.

The collapse of the cajas is leading to a considerable power shift within Spain. Power is being centralised, undermining the post-Franco settlement of autonomous regions. The cajas were tools of regional influence, tools that are now gone forever. Regional government was largely funded by property taxes – and these are not going to return to former levels any time soon.

On the way into this crisis Garicano describes how a tsunami of credit from northern Europe (caused by the euro's structural flaws) disappeared into a Bermuda Triangle made up of the regional governments, the cajas and the real-estate developers. On the route out of this crisis another triangle is apparent, consisting of a distrusting Eurozone, divisive politicians, and a demoralised people. Spanish kids are returning home from primary schools singing playground songs with new rhymes, such as 'I'm on the dole', to their shocked parents. On the outskirts of Madrid stands one of the grand plans to revive the post-blister economy: this is EuroVegas, a giant complex of supercasinos. Madrileño parents wonder if their children's ambitions may be limited to becoming a croupier in a brash Las Vegas-style monstrosity.

Much of the burden of adjustment has fallen upon Spain's

strong family networks. The massive increase in household debts is strongly concentrated on a smallish slice of Spanish society. Even after the crisis, nearly half (47.5 per cent) of all houses in Spain are owned mortgage-free. In Germany and the UK that number is around a quarter. So as Spanish society defaults on parts of its social contract, families have stepped up to fill in the gap, helping indebted young relations, and housing jobless workers. Foreign workers too are helping each other in the battles with the banks. This is why Spanish officials insist that the *cédula* system remains a top-quality credit, with zero defaults. They say that if a mortgage has been repaid for more than four years, then it is likely to go on being repaid. But at some point, even the support cushion supplied by families will wear out.

Bye Bye Brick, the book by the real-estate expert Señor Bartolomé, is dedicated to 'the tens of thousands of families who bought a house at the top of the market'. But, Bartolomé tells me, 'finally, the victims are the whole country. I am a victim. My children are victims. Governments (especially the Zapatero one, but the current as well) have mistaken priorities, leading the country to a Japanisation of the economy in the best scenario, or to the default if Germans get fed up of us.'

Yet beneath it all, Spain has pulled off something that Britain, for one, has not. The houses, airports, theme parks, high-speed trains and villas may lie empty and unused. But they are still there. Spain has been left with an amazing infrastructure, and lots of cheap housing. Exports are beginning to recover, and indeed the export boost has already exceeded that enjoyed after Spain's last economic crisis, in 1992–3 when the peseta was devalued.

At Sareb they are attempting to fend off international sharks looking to buy up large tracts of Spanish property for a pittance. Massive rental programmes and some demolitions will occur in the ghost estates that litter the plains and the coast. But there are some innovative plans for Spain's boomtime unused property assets. One idea is to turn Spain into 'The Florida of Europe'. The surplus housing, sun, excellent medical facilities and availability of young workers might be the raw materials for a health tourism and retirement industry. Through it's probably not the future the educated *milleuristas* had in mind.

I missed something when I first saw the flapping banner at Seseña, offering flats for sale at the knock-down price of €65,000. Behind this sale was the bank Santander, who were trying to liquidise their stock. It turned out that in 2009 Paco el Pocero had sold half his development – 2,000 flats – back to his bankers, including Santander, to pay off his construction debts before trying his luck in Equatorial Guinea. The banks had paid a high price, thought to be around €150,000 each. But by 2012 the hitherto empty flats that had become a symbol of the failure of Spanish economics were beginning to shift. 'They sold more than 300 houses in two weekends,' Señor Bartolomé tells me. 'Now many people are living there, and you can see children, guys walking with dogs, and shops opening. When the price adjusts, everything fits.'

That banner at Seseña, offering homes at knock-down prices, was a rare sight across the world in the years after the bubble burst. It was the policy of 'extend and pretend' coming to an end, a sign that losses were being taken on the chin, as a healthy bank dusted itself down. And the end result is that a decade of pain after Zapatero promised that mass house-building would keep prices under control – a family finally gets a home it can afford to buy.

CHAPTER 9

MERVYN'S MAGIC MONEY MACHINE

Dramatis personae

Sir Mervyn King, governor of the Bank of England (2003–13)
Alistair Darling, UK chancellor of the exchequer (2007–10)
David Cameron, UK prime minister (2010–)
Robert Stheeman, head of the Debt Management Office (DMO)
Simon Ward, chief economist at Henderson
Danny Gabay, Fathom Consulting; former
Bank of England economist
Christian Noyer, governor of the Banque de France (2003–);
sits on the governing council of the European Central Bank
Markus Kerber, German economist who has led the
constitutional charge against the ECB's existing Italian
and Spanish bond purchases
Richard Werner, now of Southampton University,
an expert on Japan, and the man who coined the term
'quantitative easing' in 1994
David Bone, a pensioner who lives in the Hampshire countryside
Ros Altmann, pensions expert and director-general of
Saga Group
Charlie Bean, the Bank of England's deputy governor (2000–)
Toby Nangle, a clever City analyst
Robert Lucas, University of Chicago, Nobel prize-
winning economist
Richard Koo, the foremost expert on the post-bubble economic
policy failures in Japan

Doormen with black top hats and pink tailcoats – like eunuchs in a Turkish sultan's harem – guard access to that most virtuous of women, the Old Lady of Threadneedle Street. It was James Gillray, in 1797, who first personified the Bank of England as an old lady with a dress made of paper money, sitting on a pile of gold. In his cartoon, entitled *Political Ravishment: or the Old Lady of Threadneedle Street in Danger*, Gillray shows the Old Lady resisting the advances of Prime Minister William Pitt, who had demanded that the Bank redeem its notes not in gold, but should print £1 notes instead.

Top hats and pink tailcoats might not be the way a modern brand agency would seek to project the image of the guardian of national monetary policy. But the 'Pinks', as they are known, are part of the fabric of the Bank of England: inexplicable, quirky and unyielding, like the institution itself. Marble-lined halls, mosaics depicting the founding of sterling, ancient weather vanes – all add to the aura around Britain's central bank, founded over three centuries ago, in 1694. This long history, even more than the £150 billion of gold stored in an underground vault that once served as a wartime canteen, underpin the institution's hardy credibility. And in central banking, credibility takes centuries to acquire, and just a few moments to lose. In the current crisis, stability, independence and credibility are all being tested.

As the euro threatened to collapse in 2011, I found myself ushered by one of the Pinks into the office of the governor, Sir Mervyn King. 'None of us, neither you nor me nor any of the savers in this country have a crystal ball that will tell us where the world economy is going,' he told me. 'This is undoubtedly the biggest financial crisis the world economy has ever faced, and it's continued now for four years. I do not know when it will come to an end.'

As the crisis raged through the American, British and European financial systems, the Bank of England was pushing the boundaries of monetary policy further than any other central bank. Behind the imposing façade that glowers over Threadneedle

Street, the Bank was preparing an experiment in 'financial repression', an experiment that was to test the balance between credibility and calamity. It was called quantitative easing.

Every schoolchild is familiar with 'The Magic Penny', the morning assembly song:

> *It's just like a magic penny,*
> *Hold it tight and you won't have any.*
> *Lend it, spend it, and you'll have so many,*
> *They'll all roll over the floor.*

Only in Britain could there be a ubiquitous children's song that invokes the concept of the velocity of circulation of money. After all, it was in Britain that David Hume and John Stuart Mill developed the quantity theory of money, the classical basis for modern monetarism. So it is entirely appropriate that Britain is currently conducting the world's biggest experiment in the creation of magic money. Quantitative easing (QE), as it is officially known – or 'printing money' as it has been more colloquially described – has seen a flood of magic pennies wash through Britain.

By 2013, an additional £375 billion had been conjured into existence at the stroke of a computer keyboard in the Bank of England. But almost all the major economies have also dabbled in the monetary dark arts in the aftermath of the financial crisis. Although the European Central Bank has only reluctantly stuck its toe in the water, the USA, Japan and Britain have dived right in. It was widely assumed that QE programmes had run their course in the spring of 2010, but policymakers in the big Western economies had not done with printing new money, and further rounds of quantitative easing, known as QE2 and QE3, followed.

Yet even as the world's central bankers cranked the handles of their magic cash machines, odd and unintended consequences – with social, political and even diplomatic implications – have arisen. It is far from clear that the experiment has worked.

'No, it isn't working.' 'It definitely has worked.' 'Not yet.'

'Yes, but not in the way I expected.' These are among the answers from leading economists to the rather simple question, 'Has QE worked?' The IMF's initial verdict was that QE is 'not a panacea'. But, they said, it 'does not have to be a curse', adding that QE is 'not a non-event'. Did anyone, anywhere, really know what was going on?

'It was one of the many measures to get confidence back in the system,' Alistair Darling, the former chancellor, told me. But as the man who had to sign off on the Bank of England experiment when it started in March 2009, his candour about our ignorance is almost shocking. 'Nobody really knows what impact it's having,' he says.

Monetary policy is conventionally about raising or lowering interest rates. The target rates are the short-term interest rates used by the central bank to lend to commercial banks. When this 'official' base rate is lowered, typically this reduction is passed on in the form of lower mortgage and corporate borrowing costs for the medium and longer term. Think of the Bank of England lowering its base rate as monetary *price* easing. When that *price* – i.e. the interest rate – reaches close to zero, that might seem to be the end of the matter. The Bank can then switch its attentions to the *quantity* of money, shovelling more and more of it into the economy – hence the term '*quantitative easing*'. This more unconventional policy is meant to bring down all sorts of other, longer-term interest rates across the economy, such as government, corporate and household debt.

Imagine that Britain is suffering from economic scurvy. Our benign economic dictator, 'King Mervyn', knows that vitamin C is the answer, so he uses his monopoly control of the supply of oranges to bring down the price, and so encourages an increase in the consumption of oranges. Eventually oranges are as good as free, but still the scurvy scourge endures. What does he do then? He uses his magic skills to create even more oranges out of thin air, rents out a fleet of trucks and delivers thousands more oranges to every greengrocer and supermarket in Britain.

Quantity still has an impact, even when the price remains zero. Such is the flood of fruit that it brings down the price of derivative products such as orange juice, marmalade and vitamin C tablets. King Mervyn cures scurvy.

In practice, money has been injected by offering to buy assets – almost exclusively government debt, in the form of bonds – off any holder of that debt, with the Bank's invented cash. Pension funds and insurance companies in particular faced plummeting returns from their holdings of government debts as interest rates fell, giving them a strong incentive to do something more risky with their money – thus stimulating borrowing and investment.

That is the basic mechanism of QE. But to understand fully where the monetary mountain went, one needs to understand its origins.

Britain: world champion of QE

Quantitative easing was an initiative of central bankers. In the weeks after the collapse of Lehman Brothers in September 2008, it was clear that British base rates, then at 5 per cent, were going to be cut quickly towards zero. World trade collapsed in a manner not seen since the 1920s. Once again, around the globe, ports were full of ships with no cargo.

The central bankers' arsenal of stimulatory weapons had to be widened. Mervyn King later recalled the stark warnings made by Japanese officials at IMF meetings in the autumn of 2008. They told their international colleagues that they must at all costs avoid the mistakes made by Japan a decade before.

So, in principle, the Bank began to map out how it would use its unique power to create money, in order to buy up various assets. But, in Britain at least, there was a problem. The institutional structures of the economy had not been shaped with quantitative easing in mind. QE required a closer relationship between government and central bank than had been envisaged when the Bank of England was handed independence to set interest rates in 1997. The Bank needed the Treasury to indemnify any losses that might arise out of the asset purchases. That made it a little less independent, and in theory that could in turn have damaged its inflation-busting credentials.

At the time, however, inflation was a distant concern compared with the reality of a collapsing economy. Prime Minister Gordon Brown was now taking a keen interest, alongside Chancellor Alistair Darling, and between these two big political players, the Treasury and the Bank, a compromise was beaten out that would preserve Bank independence but allow QE to go ahead. This compromise took the form of something called the 'asset purchase facility'.

In January 2009, as these institutional discussions were taking place, there was much grumbling from Opposition politicians. The office of George Osborne, then shadow chancellor, issued a press release saying that speculation about printing money showed that Gordon Brown had 'led Britain to the brink of bankruptcy' and that 'printing money is the last resort of desperate governments. . . In the end printing money risks losing control of inflation.' Vince Cable, the Liberal Democrat Treasury spokesman, referred to 'the road to Harare' and the 'Robert Mugabe school of economics' in relation to the risks he saw inherent in QE.

The then leader of the Opposition, David Cameron, was more measured at the time. He appeared to have taken some intensive tutorials in advanced monetary economics in early 2009. In January of that year, he regaled me with the finer details of Dutch economist Willem Buiter's blog, and with his own appreciation of the difference between quantitative easing and qualitative easing. The former referred to the sheer amount of buying the central bank could do, the latter concerned an attempt to lower interest rates in specific markets, such as mortgage debt and corporate credit.

So this was a policy initiated and decided upon by the Bank, but with considerable input from the government. At the top of the Treasury the assumption was that the structure created would be used, as was the case in the USA, to buy a wide range of commercial, government and mortgage debt, but that operational decisions regarding such purchases would be left to the Bank.

And so, on 5 March 2009, quantitative easing was launched in Britain, accompanied by a cut in the base rate from 1 per cent to an unprecedented 0.5 per cent. Mervyn King announced £75 billion of asset purchases, with Alistair Darling authorising the same amount again, if required. (A year later, the full £150 billion had been used, plus another £50 billion authorised that year, with a further round launched in 2011.) The Treasury encouraged a break with convention and pressed King to appear in front of the television cameras. At lunchtime, with about an hour's notice, the major broadcasters, including myself for *Channel 4 News*, were invited to the Bank to interview the governor. This was somewhat unexpected, given the fact that King – unlike his counterparts at the US Federal Reserve and the European Central Bank – had declined all TV interviews for the entire duration of the financial crisis. But, once in front of the cameras, Mervyn King proved the epitome of calm authority. The essential message: keep calm and carry on, while we try this new thing out, which should work – eventually.

Senior Bank officials did their best to explain the new world to journalists used to a world in which interest rates changed only 0.25 per cent at a time. One official said there was no theoretical limit to how far the policy could be pushed, other than wryly pointing out that it would have to end if the Bank 'bought every asset in Britain'. The bank fended off a series of questions about whether this was a backdoor way of Britain funding its deficit, not through raising taxes or cutting spending but through printing money, the so-called 'monetisation of debt,' with all the inflationary dangers that that entails. King tried to reassure his audience that the actions were 'a standard central bank procedure'.

But what counts as 'success'? I suggested to King that he could not know that this policy was going to work. 'I believe these measures will work,' he tried to reassure me, 'though I cannot tell you exactly when or indeed the scale of purchases we may need to carry out in order to reach our objective. But our objective is clear: to see an increase in the supply of money in the economy, so we can see a level of spending return and a beginning to economic recovery.' I pressed the governor on the idea that the financial system would simply hoard the cash on their own balance sheets. He replied: 'We are putting money directly into the wider economy. It doesn't have to go through the banks.' My question was more important than I realised at the time.

By the beginning of 2010 (relative to the size of Britain's economy), this policy had been pushed further and faster than ever before, and further and faster than in any other major economy. That world record still stands. Britain is, for now, the undisputed QE world champion. So 'Is QE working?' has become the £375 billion question.

Passing judgement on QE is a bit like divining the impact of water fluoridation on the state of Britain's dental health. The sparklier teeth in Britain's credit markets are evident, but is that attributable to the Bank's experiment? And what about the wider stimulation of the economy that was intended?

Between April and June 2010, about a year after QE was launched, the economy raced out of slump to post an incredible growth rate of 1 per cent, the fastest growth in nearly a decade. Unemployment and repossessions were far lower than in previous, milder recessions. But the direct effect of QE appears to have been negligible. The broad money supply was not going up, and that had been one of the main aims outlined by King. The bank's magic money was finding its way into corporate credit markets, but it wasn't being passed on by commercial banks. After four years, the growth impact had faded, as Britain bounced between contraction and sluggish growth.

One effect of QE is not controversial. At a time of record issuance of British public debt (mainly in the form of government bonds or gilts, with a fixed annual interest payment attached), the interest paid on that debt was driven down thanks to the Bank becoming a large new customer.

The mechanism by which the Bank bought government debt was convoluted, for operational and legal reasons. On any given morning the Debt Management Office (DMO), an arm of the Treasury, sold billions of pounds of British gilts to the world. Then in the afternoon, barely 400 metres away, the Bank of England held a reverse auction in which it effectively bought up billions of almost identical government debts. Under the terms of the Maastricht Treaty it would have been illegal for the DMO and Bank to trade with one another. So instead the City stepped in, making profits on trading both sides of this slightly bizarre monetary merry-go-round as it has played out for four years.

'I fully admit it does look strange,' Robert Stheeman, head of the DMO, told me. 'On the other hand, we must make the distinction – we are raising money by selling new gilts but the Bank is buying old gilts in the secondary market.'

The end result: that the Bank bought about the same amount of government debt as was issued in a record year. Now the Bank of England owns 30 per cent of Britain's outstanding gilt stock, worth just under £400 billion, and points to falls in the interest rate on gilts of about 1 percentage point as evidence of QE's impact.

Some of the commercial banks saw it another way. Stephen Hester, chief executive of Royal Bank of Scotland, appearing before the Treasury Select Committee, was asked how RBS had been boosted by QE. He replied: 'Quantitative easing so far has taken the form of the government effectively funding its deficit by printing money...'

Hester's view is one that is commonly held in the City. Former Treasury aides say that is 'nonsense'. To the contrary, they say they have been frustrated by how the Bank has chosen to buy government debt rather than corporate debt. Moreover, the Bank has barely used a Treasury-backed option for 'qualitative easing', a purchase up to £50 billion of private debts. One aide even described feeling 'a little tricked' by the Bank. The coalition government faced the same tension in 2011 when it attempted to coax the Bank of England to lend money to credit-starved businesses in the private sector. George Osborne came up with a Treasury-backed 'credit easing' scheme called the National Loan Guarantee Scheme (NLGS). This put some pressure on the Bank of England. To everyone's relief, the Bank of England essentially launched its own version in summer 2012, called the Funding for Lending Scheme, or FLS, and the NLGS was parked in a corner.

To understand the sensitivities here, consider the 1797 Gillray cartoon – which is pointedly on display outside the room in the Bank of England where the votes on interest rates and QE are held. As Prime Minister William Pitt prints paper money to fund the war with France, the Bank of England, in the form of the Old Lady of Threadneedle Street, cries, 'O you villain! What, have I kept my honour so long to have it broken by you at last?' The Bank must guard itself against political meddling at all costs, and almost as important, it must be seen to do so. If not, thus begins the self-fulfilling cycle of elevated expectations of inflation and rapid growth in prices.

The Bank maintained its credibility, Sir Mervyn argues, by keeping its commitment to hit its inflation target, and promising to sell back the mountain of government debts it had amassed at some point in the future. The resale is much more than a simple financial transaction; the result would be to contract the money supply and raise longer-term interest rates for mortgages and businesses. So QE might look like monetisation of Britain's debts, but as long as you confidently believe the debt will be resold into the market, it would not actually be 'printing money'. But if it had been done at the behest of government, and the inflation target was being ignored, and you were more sceptical about a resale, then it is monetisation of debt – a modern version of letting the printing presses roll. For the Bank of England, what mattered was its intentions rather than its actions.

In effect, though, QE is a mild form of 'financial repression'. The UK deficit is funded at negative real interest rates, effectively channelling funding to the government.

Once they were in government, Mr Osborne and Mr Cable quickly warmed to the very policy that they had derided in Opposition. Now they said that, theoretically, QE provided an option for boosting the economy at a time when the government's austerity policies had weakened it. By 2011 three coalition cabinet ministers, including the prime minister and the chancellor, began to bang the drum for more QE, referring to themselves as 'monetary activists'. And they were calling for more QE at a time when inflation was persistently more than double the Bank's target. Indeed, the Bank had just released its own study showing that QE pushed up inflation, by up to 1.5 percentage points. The Bank pressed the button on more asset purchases, so-called 'QE2'. As soon as this was announced, I rushed to Threadneedle Street. I asked the governor if the fact that inflation had been above target in sixty of the previous seventy-two months amounted to a backdoor abandonment of the targets he had so long cherished. 'There's absolutely no question of our commitment,' he told me, referring to the inflation target. 'We will not take risks with inflation, but if we had raised interest rates in the last two or three years significantly in order to bring inflation down closer to our target, we could have done that only by generating a really deep recession... That's not part of our remit. And it would have been a disaster for the UK economy.'

Yet it is undoubtedly true that having an independent Bank of England gobbling up 30 per cent of the issuance of government debt has been useful for the Treasury during the crisis – and essential for George Osborne as his deficit numbers got worse rather than better during his austerity programme. Somewhat remarkably, the credit-ratings agencies repeatedly pointed out that a vital reason for Britain keeping its AAA rating until 2013 was the fact that the Bank of England was buying so much government debt. The prime minister, the chancellor and – most clearly – the business secretary, Vince Cable, had all been openly calling for more QE in the preceding weeks, so did the Bank of England succumb to political pressure?

'Certainly not,' said Sir Mervyn. 'The Bank of England is independent. Not one of our nine members [of the Monetary Policy Committee] would dream of staying on that committee for a day longer if people thought they were trying to put pressure on us. And I can say this, that neither this government nor the previous one have ever since 1997 tried to influence a decision on interest rates or asset purchases by the MPC.'

That was 2011. Just a year later something rather odd happened. The Bank had been purchasing government bonds on an epic scale. And then, after a final purchase on 1 November 2012 of £3.2 billion (taking the total up to £375 billion), it paused. Even at low interest rates this loan from the Bank of England to the Treasury had earned a hefty amount of interest (known as coupon payments). About £37 billion of QE 'profits' were sitting in a Bank of England bank account. The Treasury had initiated talks with the Bank about what it called 'cash management operations'. Around the time of those talks the interviews for a new governor of the Bank of England were taking place, and there had been some loose talk from some candidates about so-called 'helicopter money', which essentially would involve cancelling the debt owed to the Bank in order to fund a boost to Britain's flagging economy.

On 23 October 2012, Sir Mervyn King made the following comments in a speech in Wales, thought at the time to be referring to these radical suggestions about monetary policy. 'When the bank rate eventually starts to return to a more normal level, as one day it will, the Bank would then have no income, in the form of coupon payments on gilts, to cover the payments of interest on reserves at the Bank of England that we had created. The Bank would become insolvent unless it created even more money to finance those interest payments, and that would lead ultimately to uncontrolled inflation. That is a road down which the Bank will not go, and does not need to go.'

On 9 November the Treasury announced that the coupon payments were to be transferred to the Treasury. Except, it was not really a profit, as the funds were required as a buffer against future losses for the Bank of England from the sales of that portfolio of government debt. Sir Mervyn secured a guarantee that the cash would return by the tens of billions to cover a future shortfall. This was an up-front exchequer windfall caused not by raising taxes, nor by flogging state assets, nor by cutting spending. The Bank's independence and credibility rest on the notion that this promise of repayment, made binding on any future UK government, is fulfilled.

In effect, the government itself had announced, opaquely, a further round of quantitative easing. The Treasury called the grab a 'cash management operation', to convey the idea that it was a run-of-the-mill accounting reshuffle. The manoeuvre did flatter the public finances at a time of stress. But it was likely to cost taxpayers more money in higher interest payments on the debt in future. It was basically a backdoor form of borrowing. And it did not stop there, as further QE profits would be banked by the Treasury too.

Effectively the British government was to stop paying interest on the third of the national debt owed to the Bank of England. Whilst this was not the actual monetisation of Britain's national debt, it had come perilously close. Officials pointed to the fact that this was standard procedure for other major central banks, such as those in the USA and Japan. But the timing was unfortunate in Britain. It helped improve the state of Britain's public finances at a time when the government's austerity plans appeared off target. It seemed to set Britain on the path towards so-called 'fiscal dominance' – a situation in which the Treasury gains the upper hand over the central bank, and Gillray's cartoon becomes reality.

At the very least it was a sign that the QE experiment was never intended to last three years. At most, it was a sign that the Bank of England's independence was becoming far less sacrosanct. In half a decade's time, we might discover whether it actually was the start of a monetisation.

QE: a bandage for a burst credit bubble?

So, apart from reducing the government interest bill, what else has QE achieved so far? There had been a flurry of activity by big companies bypassing the banks and raising money direct from capital markets, typically in the form of issuing corporate bonds to pension funds and insurance companies. But the big companies use this borrowing to pay back bank debt, then it acts as a drag on bank lending and impedes the desired growth in the broad money supply. Despite the injection of £375 billion, annual growth in the wider measure of the money supply, including notes, coins and bank deposits, has been a paltry 1 to 2 per cent for most of the first two phases of QE, creeping up to 4 per cent at the time of QE3, still under half its decade-long pre-crisis average. So where are the missing pounds?

'QE didn't go into broad money,' says Simon Ward, chief economist at Henderson, 'because a lot of it was used to repay lending from the banks. That negated the boost to M4.' (M4 is a measure of the broad money supply.) A wounded banking system also meant that money was not circulating through the economy as it should. But the velocity of circulation of those pounds that *are* washing through the economy did creep up.

Proponents of QE say that it prevented deflation and a global depression by providing a bandage for the US and UK economies after the bursting of their credit bubbles. Other economists are unconvinced. 'The bank has chopped and changed its metrics of what QE is meant to do,' says a former Bank of England economist, Danny Gabay, of Fathom Consulting. 'Even though M4 growth is close to zero, they now say look at how much worse it would have been, the counterfactual.' Such speculative counterfactuals are, of course, unprovable. Gabay even questions the claim that QE has lowered the interest rates paid on government debts. He points out that these gilt yields have fallen even more, during some of the periods when QE was put on hold.

Political and diplomatic impacts of QE

One thing is certain about QE. The policy has had political and diplomatic impacts. There have been two types of response. The emerging countries saw QE as a backdoor devaluation of currency, which would damage their exports. The Eurozone, for its part, was trying to avoid the Anglo-Saxon injunctions to forget twentieth-century German history and print money.

The 'foreign-exchange channel' is an important additional way for QE to boost an economy. As the New York Federal Reserve puts it in its guide to QE: 'As normally happens when the Fed lowers interest rates, [QE] may lead to a moderate change in the foreign exchange value of the dollar that supports demand for US-produced goods.' The USA has come a long way since the 'strong dollar policy' that existed until 2002, and was still officially articulated under Treasury secretary Hank Paulson as late as 2008 as the dollar tumbled.

In Britain too, anticipation of QE partly coincided with and partly helped cause a sharp fall in sterling. Over four years it was the sharpest fall in sterling since Britain exited the gold standard in 1931. 'The best thing the Labour government did [to boost the economy] was to engineer a sterling devaluation without anyone really noticing,' said one UK bank chief executive. The Bank of England's economists calculated that the first £200 billion of QE alone saw a depreciation in sterling against other major currencies of 4 per cent.

China and Brazil were concerned about the impact of this money creation on their economies, through competitive depreciations, rising commodity prices and unsustainable flows of hot money. The Brazilian finance minister talked about a new era of 'currency wars'. At the central bankers' central bank, the Bank for International Settlements in Basel, Switzerland, arguments raged between the emerging and the developed world.

'QE is like doping in the Tour de France,' one well-connected Eurozone financier told me. 'And America is like Lance Armstrong.'

The concerns expressed in Europe were different from those of China and Brazil. Europe felt the need to push back against strong pressure from the USA and the UK to stop dragging its feet on QE, and to 'fire the bazooka' – basically by copying London and Washington by buying the bonds of its member governments. European central bankers began openly to criticise QE in the UK and USA as a form of cheating market discipline.

The governor of the Banque de France, Christian Noyer, who sits on the governing council of the European Central Bank (ECB), pulled no punches. 'We are paying the price for our virtue and our refusal to liquify our debt through massive monetisation of our fiscal deficits,' he said, in a clear reference to Britain, and to a lesser extent the USA.

It was a rather telling quote. Viewed from Paris, Berlin or Frankfurt, Anglo-American quantitative easing lacked 'virtue'. The 'massive monetisation' Noyer was talking about in 2011 specifically referred to the Bank of England's then £275 billion purchase of UK government bonds – which contributed to the UK's record lows for funding costs, and would help Britain keep its AAA rating for a time. He compared Britain's record unfavourably with that of the ECB. 'Those purchases amount to 51 per cent of the total debt issued since 2009 in the UK, 21 per cent in the USA and 7.6 per cent in the euro area,' he said.

Again, the Bank of England denies this is a 'massive monetisation' of Britain's debt pile, specifically because it has promised to resell this debt back into the market at some point in the future. But many in the markets share Governor Noyer's doubts that this will actually ever happen. When I mentioned to Mr Noyer that it was great to interview a central bank governor, because in the UK we only seem to get an interview when the Bank of England is printing money, he warily burst out laughing. Nothing beats a good joke about quantitative easing.

Other senior European monetary officials, speaking privately, struggled to hide their irritation with Britain. The balance sheets of both the Bank of England and the Federal Reserve had more than doubled during the crisis. The ECB's purchase of sovereign debt amounted to 1.6 per cent of its GDP. For Britain it is 16 per cent. The general view of these officials was that, when the financial markets had come to their senses, Europe's 'virtue' would count.

Markus Kerber, the German economist who has led the constitutional charge against the ECB's existing Italian and Spanish bond purchases, put it clearly. 'German sovereignty is not compatible with any piece of advice by the US president or the British PM, who have already printed a lot of money,' he told me. 'They should know that Germany will resist this piece of advice, [because] mega-inflation is the nightmare consequence, the unavoidable consequence of printing money.'

British inflation has been by far the highest of the major European economies, and the Bank of England acknowledges that its quantitative easing policy has contributed. Europe had begun to notice Britain's quantitative easing – but as an example to avoid, rather than to follow.

Professor Werner's view

With no consensus among British economists about QE, who better to consult than the person who coined the term in the first place? Richard Werner, an expert on Japan, now of Southampton University, came up with the name in 1994. He has an unexpected perspective. He believes the whole QE exercise in Britain, as it was in Japan, is a 'sham', and isn't really QE at all. 'The Bank has dug a PR hole for itself with quantitative easing. I don't know why they are using my expression,' he tells me.

His 'expression' arises from a translation of a specific Japanese term, *ryoteki kanwa*, which he devised a couple of decades ago to shine a light on the inadequacies of the sluggish policies of the Bank of Japan. He says his idea involved efforts to increase credit, because the money transmission system, the banking system, was broken. He derides monetarists and their obsession with obscure measures of money, and suggests, instead, a laser-like focus on creating credit. When the Bank of Japan belatedly adopted QE in 2001, he argues it was not QE at all, but rather completely bog-standard monetary policy that the Bank of Japan wanted to dress up as something new, for reasons of political spin. It was a type of economic placebo. Now he argues something similar was happening in Britain.

'It's not to say that what the Bank is doing is useless,' he says. 'It has helped the banks but it doesn't inject new money. That is only injected when the money leaves the banking sector and goes into the economy. So far the money has just been passed from central banks to commercial banks.' And while healthier bank and corporate balance sheets are clearly positive, until the money flows across the economy, Britain's recovery, like Japan's a decade ago, is fated to be choppy.

Werner is particularly withering about a new generation of economic computer models that are being widely used in the world's central banks to model economic behaviour. They are known as Dynamic Stochastic General Equilibrium models. 'These DSGE models are nonsense,' he says. 'Until the crisis these models didn't even include the banking sector. They are abstract mathematical dream worlds, and they are wholly irrelevant for the situation we find ourselves in.'

The Bank of England had a suite of such econometric models, called BEQM (pronounced Beckham), described as 'state-of-the-art' upon their introduction. The Bank used BEQM to calculate the impact of their decisions on interest rates and QE. Except QE does not work in conventional 'New Keynesian' models, such as this. The Bank's forecast is compiled by about eighty of Britain's and the world's finest economics brains, in six divisions – covering monetary analysis, financial markets, medium-term demand, the economic model, the world economy, and writing the Bank's inflation report.

The forecast is a continuous process that layers all new economic data onto the previous forecast. Vitally though, the forecast is not a product of pure dispassionate economics, but rather represents the 'best collective view' of the nine members of the Bank's Monetary Policy Committee. How do all these economists agree on a forecast at times when there can be a four-way split on the decision on monetary policy? Only once, in spring 2002, was there sufficiently different views on the economic outlook for a 'minority report' with an alternative forecast. That beggars belief, given the five years of economic torpor in Britain. Part of the answer lies in the fact that the forecast has a dual purpose: prognosis and propaganda. The forecast is tweaked and changed to make sense of the decisions of the Monetary Policy Committee, and is a crucial form of communication to markets and the public. It is not the work of pure independent economics such as the 'staff projection' that is presented at the US Federal Reserve.

So how did it do? For the five years before the crisis, the forecasters rarely got economic growth wrong. Alas, since the crisis, they have rarely got it right. Forecast performance was noticeably worse than pre-crisis, and also worse than outside forecasters predicted. As an independent review of its forecasts concluded: 'The forecast errors of the MPC have been characterised by persistent over-prediction of output growth and persistent under-prediction of CPI [consumer price index] inflation.' All central banks struggled to predict the 'Great Recession' of 2007–09, but the Bank of England's errors were larger than the ECB's or the Fed's. And, unlike the others, since the crisis the Bank of England's errors have always been biased in the direction of over-predicting UK growth.

The Bank's defence rested on the notion that it did not factor in the rise in energy prices, and its subsequent impact on British consumers. The forecast simply assumed that oil prices would move in line with prices in futures markets. But they stayed much higher for much longer.

Perhaps alarmed by the irrelevance of their 'state-of-the-art' suite of models, the Bank of England introduced a new model in 2012 called Compass (Central Organising Model for Projections and Stochastic Simulations, if you were wondering), holding out the hope that they at least vaguely knew which direction to head in.

Compass had a simpler core than BEQM – sixteen economic variables, from GDP to prices and the jobs market, supported by a range of other models. Staggeringly, as an independent review calmly concluded, the 'Bank's current forecast model – Compass – has very limited financial detail'. So, after a financial crisis had devastated the world economy, bankrupted half of the British banking sector and seen the nation's annual finances descend to their peacetime nadir, *after that*, the Bank's principal method of divining the future had 'very limited financial detail'. It gets worse. Compass was still, at core, a New Keynesian DSGE model. As some of the Bank's own economists admitted, 'QE is irrelevant [in these models] unless it signals something about future policy that gets incorporated into expectations of future interest rates or inflation.'

So in the Bank of England's current model, there is little or no financial sector, and little relevance for QE, currently the principal lever of UK macroeconomic policy. I'm surprised they have not yet reverted to the weather vane on the roof of the Bank, which long ago gave its clerks at least some sense of when ships might be arriving in the London docks, and with them a demand for credit. The Bank of England is and has been flying as blind as it has ever done.

A monetary policy for the wealthy

Why does this econometric dream world matter? We are all being invited to view QE decisions as if they are analogous to a decision to shift interest rates by 0.25 or 0.5 per cent, the subject of an involved science. Yet it seems apparent that it is more of an art. One technique employed is to pretend that £200 billion of QE is in fact a negative interest rate, of say −2 per cent.

A negative interest rate is an intriguing concept. In the case of King Mervyn and his scurvy, it would mean not just flooding the market with oranges, but effectively paying people to eat them. In credit terms it would mean paying borrowers and charging savers. It is a vivid illustration that QE has had a significant – and, for some, an unfair – distributional impact. Nowhere is that more clearly seen than in the paltry incomes of recently retired pensioners, unlucky enough to have swapped their pension pots for annuities since QE began.

David Bone lives in the Hampshire countryside. His healthy £1100 monthly pension reset in February 2012 to take account of the record low interest rates on UK government borrowing. His pension was cut by £500 per month. This extreme case was as a result of a combination of factors, but there were many millions with some version of this story. 'It's dropped off the face of a cliff, it's halved. It's driven by low interest rates, QE and government policy,' he told me in his kitchen on the day another £50 billion of QE was announced. I put to him the Bank of England argument that he had benefited from the fact that QE had kept the economy out of depression. 'I don't need low interest rates, because I don't borrow any money. They're good for some people, but they're absolutely no good to me,' said Mr Bone. His predicament was making this once staunch Conservative question his support for the government.

As the pensions expert and director general of Saga, Ros Altmann, says, 'QE is the worst thing that could happen to pensions, it's devaluing and destroying pensioners' income, and all for a short-term sugar rush for the economy.'

This is the dilemma for central bankers. Their monetary interventions have created large bands of winners and losers. In the late 1990s, the governor of the Bank of Japan gave speeches saying he would refrain from cutting interest rates too far, in order to protect the interests of Japan's army of elderly savers. I had the opportunity to put such points directly to the Bank of England's deputy governor, Charlie Bean, in 2010. He admitted that if you'd taken out an annuity recently it would have been 'impacted by our QE', because QE drives down longer-term rates. 'On the other hand,' he said, 'if you were somebody who already held some government or corporate bonds, then actually you would have benefited from QE because the underlying price of those has been driven up by our actions.'

The Bank's view was that the long period in which the base rate had remained at 0.5 per cent had had a bigger impact on savers than QE. Between March 2009, when the base rate was cut from 1 to 0.5 per cent, and 2012, borrowers, particularly mortgage holders, had gained £104 billion (and £89 billion of that has gone just to the holders of variable-rate mortgages). Savers had lost £70 billion in interest payments since the attempt to boost the economy in 2008. Many people save and borrow at the same time, so some of these numbers cancel out. But it's not difficult to see why many believed that the feckless were being bailed out at the expense of the prudent. It seems to be a massive transfer of wealth. But there was a context. Almost the reverse had occurred, generationally, during the property bubble (see pages 128–59).

'It's like the opening scene out of *Harry Potter*,' said one Bank policymaker of the deluge of letters received when the Bank used to cut interest rates. (They haven't been cut since 2009, when they were cut to rock-bottom.) Savers complain more in writing to the Bank of England governor when it puts interest rates down than do borrowers when rates go up, so the Bank claims to be 'very aware of the different interests of different sectors of the economy'. But the deputy governor, Charlie Bean, explained to me rather directly in that 2010 interview that despite sympathy for savers, there had been 'swings and roundabouts', and that it was wrong to condemn borrowers as feckless. 'Most borrowing is carried out by younger households. The bulk of it has been to buy houses, which of course have risen in price, and very often the older households have actually benefited from the fact that they've seen capital gains on their houses,' he told me in his office. It was not a popular argument in a Britain that had come to view house price appreciation as a type of human right.

'I think also it needs to be said,' Mr Bean continued, 'that savers shouldn't necessarily expect to be able to live just off their income in times when interest rates are low. It may make sense for them to eat into their capital a bit. Conversely of course when interest rates are high they might want to build their capital back up again. Now, there's no doubt that at the current juncture we're in a situation which is not particularly good for those savers, but it's not good for people who've lost their jobs.' Neither was it good for those people in work who had only received minimal pay increases, in the private sector at least. 'Because prices have been rising,' Mr Bean went on, 'that means they've been suffering real income losses, so a lot of people have been suffering pain in this recession, not just savers.'

Although Charlie Bean is one of Britain's most respected economists, his delicately balanced argument was met with derision in the mid-market pensioner-friendly press. The Bank was in difficult territory trying to explain that its policies were favouring some groups and costing others. Detractors such as Ros Altmann believe even the core thinking here is wrong, given Britain is suffering something of an economic hangover. 'As borrowers are already heavily in debt,' she told me, 'they are not spending more if borrowing costs fall. They accelerate debt repayments, rather than boosting growth. As interest rates fall, academic models say QE should lead households to bring forward spending at the expense of saving, which should boost growth. But in an ageing population, older households are not substituting spending for saving, they are actually cutting their spending as they fear for their financial future when their current income and prospective pension incomes have fallen.'

Ultra-low interest rates and, in particular, QE were leading Britain's central bank into the uncomfortable realm of politics. A central bank likes to project itself as a trusted high temple of dispassionate wisdom and prudent beneficence. No more. The Bank of England's decisions have been impacting the living standards of some groups more than any cabinet minister would care to imagine. But Charlie Bean's delicately balanced argument was also a statement of the obvious. The UK press, politicians and public were not ready for such a flash of lucidity, but it represents what they think at Threadneedle Street. At a dinner in spring 2007, just as the boom was fading, a very senior Bank of England figure told economic journalists that issues of tax/spend and Bank of England independence were overshadowed by a far larger economic shift. 'By far the most profound change in Britain's economy in the past decade,' he told the assembled company, 'has been intergenerational redistribution caused by rampant house price growth.' He went on to mention his 'surprise' that younger people hadn't kicked up more of a fuss (see page 157).

The Bank's concern was the paradox of thrift, also known as the paradox of policy. In the longer term, Britain needed more savings and investment. Right now, to get savers to spend, what was needed was a near-zero interest rate (negative in real terms), plus quantitative easing. Mr Bean was again amazingly clear: 'What we're trying to do by our policy is encourage more spending. Ideally we'd like to see that in the form of more business spending, but part of the mechanism that might encourage that is having more household spending. So in the short term we want to see households not saving more, but spending more,' he told me. 'I would fully recognise that in the longer term we would expect to see a higher savings rate than we saw in the decade or so before the crisis.' It was one of those truths that normally goes unsaid.

Two years on, after prodding from the Treasury Select Committee, the Bank did produce a fuller analysis of the distributional consequences of its actions. The results completely contradicted the popular wisdom, but fleshed out the thinking outlined to me by Charlie Bean. Firstly, it was not pensioners who suffer the most from QE, but in fact the young, or indeed anyone without assets who needs to build them up. And secondly, QE makes the wealthy even wealthier. Astonishingly, the Bank calculated that the increase in household wealth from the bank's £325 billion QE programme was £600 billion. That includes pension wealth. If you exclude pension wealth, then I calculated that of the £300 billion remaining in non-pension wealth, 40 per cent of assets are held by the wealthiest 5 per cent of the population. That is a remarkable £120 billion, or £96,000 for every one of the 1.25 million of Britain's wealthiest. Including pensions and making different assumptions, the wealth increase for the top 5 per cent could be anywhere from £50,000 per wealthy household to over £200,000 (statistics on wealth are derived from data on estates, and are notoriously uncertain).

For comparison, the half of the British population that is most asset-poor (excluding pensions) did not benefit at all from this principal channel of the impact of QE on the economy. However, it should also be pointed out that the wealthiest households have not definitely become wealthier. The asset-rich took a big hit from falls in share and house prices at the start of the crisis. The big picture, though, is pretty stark. QE is monetary policy for the wealthy. QE disproportionately benefits the already wealthy, even if people like Mr Bone, the pensioner in Hampshire, are unlikely ever to notice the fact that their house price, for example, did not collapse. One Bank of England official told me privately that QE works through increasing the prices of assets, significantly property. 'If you don't hold assets you don't directly benefit, he said. 'The most affected are those short of assets but who need to acquire them.'

The Bank argues that others will also benefit from QE, for example, by not losing their job. The clearest message from the Bank, though, is that many of us are not taking into consideration an estimated 28 per cent boost to the price of all assets from its programme of quantitative easing. That includes the pension pots of those who have suffered the most from being locked into scandalously low annuity rates. Yes, the flow of income is small. But the size of the pot is greater than it would otherwise be. And these two factors cancel each other out.

But even that was far from the end of the story. The Bank does admit that pension funds that were in deficit by (for example) 30 per cent, would be a further 10 per cent in deficit as a direct result of QE. A critic might argue that this has hastened the end of some defined benefit schemes. It might also have cost the exchequer tens of billions of pounds in taxes as profits were squeezed to fill pension accounting holes. Still worse, one institutional quirk of the UK could mean, argued Toby Nangle, a clever City analyst, that QE was largely counterproductive. The lower long-term borrowing rates in the economy depressed the value of company pension pots, so the companies were obliged to pour billions into those pots to cover annual accounting deficits. So rather than increase the tendency of a company to invest and create jobs, QE in combination with accounting rules was acting like a mega-tax on Britain's largest corporates. As Mr Nangle put it, 'Bank of England purchases of long-dated bonds that depress their yields might serve to tighten rather than loosen monetary conditions.' It took nearly four years of QE for anyone to spot this. The Treasury announced plans to change the accounting rules. The risk on the other side is that pension funds will blow up, at huge expense to the taxpayer in the years to come.

There were other winners and losers. QE had its fans on the City trading desks, as they saw the value of their bond portfolios soar. Other beneficiaries include the sovereign bond dealers who passed bonds from the DMO to the Bank at zero risk, making margins and fees on both sides of the deal. The commercial banks also benefited, gaining a supportive source of basically free funding.

The Treasury under Labour was convinced that much of the City was making riskless windfall profits from QE. In the mid-2009 private talks between leading City bankers and senior Treasury aides, the issue of QE profiteering cropped up. The Treasury told the banks that these unearned windfalls were part of the justification for their planned multibillion-pound tax on bank bonus pools.

Another injustice of QE has been the differential access to credit for small companies and large companies. For those large corporates that can tap capital markets directly, QE has opened up cheaper finance, seen a return to merger-and-acquisitions activity, and helped to bypass the banking system in favour of direct funding from pensions and insurance companies. QE is changing the nature of corporate finance. For the small- and medium-sized enterprises dependent on the banking system for credit, there is no such luck. Unfortunately, such firms happen to employ 60 per cent of the private-sector workforce.

It is for these and other reasons that Britain's former chancellor, Alistair Darling, told me he thought that Britain should 'take stock,' and that he has concerns about QE profiteering. So much so that he would not have automatically granted the Bank an extension to the QE programme, had he remained chancellor instead of George Osborne. 'Were I still chancellor and the Bank came to see me again, then I would want to see some assessment of what has happened,' says Darling. 'In the current climate I can't see any problem with it being a public report. Where is this money? We need a Treasury/Bank of England evaluation as to where it is. Is it in circulation, or is it sitting in bank vaults?' he asks. But if Darling had blocked another round of QE, it could have created a huge stink, and raised those institutional questions about the extent of Bank independence.

And what would such a report actually reveal? The impetus towards QE2 and QE3 had been pretty strong. The Conservative establishment, including the Institute of Directors and the think tank Policy Exchange, repeatedly called for more QE. Since the election, George Osborne has been rather candidly describing his budget austerity policy as a way in which the Bank can keep interest rates lower for longer. Monetary and fiscal policy are no longer clearly separable. From 2010 David Cameron's view was that the failure in Japan related to its three-year delay in moving from zero interest rates to QE. This view has shaped the coalition's macroeconomic strategy. The Treasury's job is to get the public finances in order. Economic fine-tuning can then be left to the Bank of England. Both George Osborne and David Cameron have repeatedly made very supportive suggestions about new rounds of QE. The prime minister describes himself as 'a fiscal conservative but a monetary activist'.

At the University of Chicago, Nobel prize-winner Robert Lucas sees it the same way for the USA. 'It's explicit in Milton Friedman's work on the 1930s that policies like QE should have been done,' he says. 'Instead the Federal Reserve sat around and watched the economy sink deeper into the depression, and did nothing about it. This time round we are doing something. Most of the work is being done by monetary policy, not the stimulus package, but the line isn't that sharp.'

But Richard Koo, the foremost expert on the post-bubble economic policy failures in Japan, told me at the beginning of the QE programme in 2009 that this is wrong: 'There are some statements from the Bank that suggest that with QE they can solve all the problems. Well, we thought that in Japan, and when we put it in, absolutely nothing happened. Asset prices kept on falling, and the economy kept on weakening. When we removed it, still nothing happened. Even if there is a lot of liquidity injected into the system through QE, that liquidity will sit in the banking system, won't be able to come out because these [over-indebted] people won't borrow, and that's basically what happened in Japan. And what is key is whether deleveraging is still happening,' he says. By 2012 Mr Koo was being proven right on this. 'In spite of the largest quantitative easing programme in the history of the world,' he wrote, 'the UK money supply did not increase and the BoE was unable to prevent the UK economy from contracting again.'

A furious debate also raged in the USA about a huge new trillion-dollar bout of QE, of the kind tried in Britain – buying US Treasury bonds. In turn that raised questions about the real motive behind such a move, with an assertive China suspecting that this was a backdoor dollar devaluation. In the primaries for the US presidential election of 2012, one Republican candidate even suggested that QE was a form of treason, and presidential nominee Mitt Romney promised to fire the Fed chief Ben Bernanke.

There is some irony in Washington looking to a London-style QE when there was so little evidence that it had been a success. And, yes, at the same time, influential voices in Britain were pushing for the adoption of a more US-style variety of QE aimed at stimulating a broader range of activity. Back in 2009, people in the Treasury wanted the magic money to be used to stir the mortgage bond market into life, or for more direct lending to companies. This is the difference between qualitative and quantitative easing about which David Cameron had mused. But the Bank at first said 'no'.

Independent Bank of England policymakers such as Adam Posen suggested that such a policy would make a useful contribution as a Plan B. Giles Wilkes, the author of a LibDem pamphlet that advocated using magic Bank cash to direct funding to small businesses through a Treasury fund, is now an adviser to Vince Cable. Richard Werner thinks that 'Green QE' could be directed at boosting investment in environmentally friendly infrastructure. Danny Gabay has the most innovative of plans. He contends that the failure to cleanse Japan's bank balance sheets of 'zombie' property companies was what caused its lost decade. 'Zombie' households with large debts and overvalued property is the British equivalent. QE could be used to buy up houses, setting a discounted floor price for property.

'I'm a supporter of QE, but it needs to be more imaginative,' says Danny Gabay. 'The UK has been doing it in a very unimaginative way. We need a sniper rifle rather than a scatter gun. So far we are filling a big manual on what doesn't work.'

Monetarists could not disagree more. The velocity of broad money had ticked up, and economists such as Simon Ward believed more QE risked the rise of the inflationary dragon: 'The strength of commodity prices is related to QE2 speculation.'

George Osborne's Treasury tried the NLGS, his own version of 'credit easing', in late 2011 after limp efforts to get banks lending to businesses. Insiders admit that this should have been done a year earlier. With Britain's economy still mired in contraction, the Bank of England finally did act on lending, launching a huge funding-for-lending scheme, which subsidised banks for maintaining lending into the real economy. Except this too had adverse impacts on rates paid to savers.

Almost all economists believe that too much QE will eventually lead to raging inflation. It is only the limp economic recovery that is keeping that in check. But is there an exit strategy? Just as the Bank of England bought the debt, so it will soon have to sell it. But when should QE shift to QT – quantitative tightening? As this has not been done before, the Bank needs to think carefully about this question. Rates could go up first, with room to fall back if necessary. This would be followed by pre-announced sales of the Bank's gilts, coordinated with the Treasury, and spread over a series of months. That seems to be the plan.

Or not. Some economists are assuming that this pile of government debt will never be sold. The reversal of QE sounds like a doomsday machine designed to snuffle out any nascent recovery. Long-term interest rates would rise aggressively, and the Bank of England would be sitting on losses on its portfolios of gilts. Monetary tightening, and a requirement for fiscal injection from the Treasury. Is this really going to happen? Or will the gilts be left to expire? There are suspicions about how seriously the Bank of England is taking its 2 per cent inflation target. Inflation has been above this number in sixty out of the past sixty-five months, since 2008 averaging 3.3 per cent.

For Richard Werner, it is time for the Bank to quietly park that target and instead publicly embrace its quest for moderate inflation in a manner that Japan was very shy about. 'The Bank needs to set a nominal GDP growth target,' he says. A nominal GDP target incorporates a bit of inflation and a bit of growth in one target. In September 2012 the US Federal Reserve considered such a target, alongside a 'price level' target, that would basically allow for higher inflation in current circumstances. Vince Cable's adviser Giles Wilkes suggested, before joining government, that for five years the Bank of England replaces its totemic 2 per cent inflation target with a 'nominal GDP' growth target of 6 per cent. The new governor of the Bank of

England, Mark Carney, dabbled in versions of policies such as this in his previous job in Canada. 'Open-mouth operations' involve using communications to guide down expectations of future interest rises. 'Forward guidance' is the innovation of the moment, involving the managing-down of expectation using speeches and press statements. The hope would be that a company would be more likely to take out a loan for more equipment, or a homebuyer a mortgage, if there exists confidence on low rates over a period of years. Both Mr Carney and the ECB president Draghi deployed forms of 'forward guidance' in July 2013. The end result is lower interest rates for longer. The guidance can be supplemented with a conditional threshold too. For example, unemployment would have to dip below 6 per cent before interest rates were to rise. These monetary policy innovations had been rejected by the Bank of England under Mervyn King. Mark Carney imposed his plans in Britain imme-diately. It did raise a question: given Chancellor Osborne had gone to great lengths to tempt Mr Carney into the job, was this a high-level form of political interference at the Bank of England, meant to keep interest rates as low as possible?

In Canada, Mr Carney had been a rare sight: a G7 central banker who had raised interest rates. He had acted independently of Canadian government wishes. At the same time, however, it was clear that his approach fitted with the UK government's desire for 'monetary activism'. As the chancellor told me: 'I've always thought that the macroeconomic debate about austerity was secondary to the monetary policy debate.' Would a Bank of England insider have pursued Carney-style innovations in monetary policy? Doubtful.

In Canada, Carney's many fans say that it is far too simplistic to suggest his policy is just 'lower for longer'. If the confidence coursing through the economy at the thought of low interest rates actually increases investment, jobs and house purchases, then rate rises could come sooner rather than later. In any event, the power of words and communications alone is limited. What about even more radical monetary policy options? A decade of near-zero rates is entirely feasible.

Why, it might be asked, did the Treasury or the Bank of England not just give £18,000 to each British household in a 'helicopter drop', rather than let that £375 billion stagnate in the murky, blocked intestines of British finance? The answer, officially, is that it would have created too much inflation, and would not have been reversible. The Bank needs its unconventional policies to at least appear as if they might be reversed at some point in the future, even if it turns out that this never happens.

And therein lies the rub. QE has been an invisible balm, but unwinding QE has displaced some pain of higher long-term interest rates, and higher deficits, to some point in the future. Is QE really consistent with Britain's 1997 anti-inflation macroeconomic settlement, by which the government gave the Bank of England independent control over interest rates? Is Britain's economic predicament credibly consistent with a target inflation exceeded for most of the past half-decade. Can the target be altered without igniting inflationary expectations? And does Bank of England independence really mean anything now it's the largest purchaser and holder of UK government debt? Fiscal dominance is in fact more the norm than full central bank independence. The independent central bank doggedly pursuing an inflation target may turn out to be a two-or-three decade fad.

QE is a policy that is massive, controversial, remarkably redistributive, uncertain in its effect, and is now resulting in a myriad unintended consequences. There are diplomatic and political impacts. Few can claim to understand it fully. QE might work. It might even be working. The jury is still out on its effect in Japan a decade ago. But given these imponderables, does it really make sense to rely on QE as the primary weapon for fighting a prolonged economic sluggishness? It did not and it does not, and now under new management, Britain will not. But the UK will soon discover, with its new experiments, if we really are at the limits of the power of monetary policy.

CHAPTER 10

THE RELUCTANT IMPERIUM

Dramatis personae

Zinedine Zidane, French footballer
Klaus Wowereit, mayor of Berlin (2001–)
Angela Merkel, German chancellor (2005–)
Gerhard Schröder, German chancellor (1998–2005)
Peter Hartz, former personnel director of Volkswagen
Otmar Issing, chief economist, European Central Bank
(1998–2006)
Tobias and Christoph, *Lederhosen*-sporting Bavarians
at Munich's Oktoberfest
Jens Zerkler, 17-year-old apprentice at a forklift truck factory
in Aschaffenburg, Bavaria
Thomas Mayer, chief economist, Deutsche Bank
Richard Walker, anchor, Deutsche Welle TV station
Hans-Werner Sinn, economist, Ifo Institute for Economic
Research, Munich
Horst Seehofer, leader of the Christian Social Union (CSU),
Bavarian sister party of the Christian Democratic Union (CDU)
Peter Altmaier, CDU chief whip
Martin Murtfeld, 76-year-old retired German banker
Frank Schäffler, backbench MP in the
Free Democratic Party (FDP)
Peer Steinbrück, former German finance minister, and Social
Democratic Party (SPD) candidate for chancellor

Berlin in the first decade of the Eurozone was like no other city in Europe. From the abandoned East German power station re-purposed as a gay techno club and the graffitied Tacheles squat populated by Bohemians and Faux-hemians, to the World Cup Final graced by Zidane's head-butt and the refounding of modern German footballing patriotism amid thousands of Schwarz-Rot-Gold tricolours in the Tiergarten. It was a city with space, pregnant with creative opportunity, but lacking any real industry, bar the re-emergence of national politics. Rents were cheap, jobs were scarce, and young creatives flocked to Mitte and Friedrichshain. 'Poor but sexy,' was the description by Berlin's mayor Klaus Wowereit of the new undivided city. Across Berlin, in the old West, something rather different was emerging.

The Bundeskanzleramt or Chancellery in Berlin, opened in 2001, is eight times the size of its American equivalent. By design, the new home of Germany's chancellor manages to evoke a calm, passive authority, in contrast to the executive potency of the White House. The no-nonsense Berliners have nicknamed the giant white cube with its massive round window the *Bundeswaschmaschine* ('federal washing machine'), or, even less respectfully, the *Elefantenklo* (elephant loo).

Inside the white cube, backing onto the River Spree, there are wide spaces, open walkways, glass and sculpture. The post-modern design was supposedly a conscious effort to avoid the pompous and the grandiose. Berlin's re-emergence as the seat of the German government for the first time since the war demanded a confident architectural statement. But it was a tightrope. German reunification was only tolerated by President Mitterrand of France because of the constraints imposed on German power by its membership of the European Union. As the German joke goes: 'France and Germany are in an authentic marriage. A mutual insurance pact, with occasionally some love. We love them, and the French love our money.'

The euro was the ultimate embodiment of that marriage, yet the euro crisis was to push Germany into an unchallengeable economic ascendancy. Berlin's post-reunification role in directing over a trillion euros into the impoverished former East Germany had created a certain reluctance to bail out any other countries in crisis. Not far from the city's gleaming political quarter could be found run-down districts full of the unemployed, the under-employed and the new poor. These were the results of new policies that had given Germany its great economic success, a success that was combined with social failure. This combination became Berlin's answer for the problems of an entire continent.

If the Bundeskanzleramt looks more like a seat of learning than one of the foremost citadels of global power, that is perhaps because there's a lot to take in, even in the immediate vicinity. The joyous destruction of the old Berlin Wall had led within two decades to an entire continent taking its economic cues from Germany. But Berlin's actions in the Eurozone crisis risked a whole new divide across the continent. The white cube has become the architectural embodiment of Germany as Europe's reluctant imperium.

'The temptation is always to relax,' says a senior German official. He was talking about the reform plans of the Eurozone problem nations, though he could have been referring to his surroundings in Berlin. At this time, in late 2012, crisis talk had abated a little. 'We don't want heightened stress, but we need to keep up the pressure. We need a combination of market pressure and peer pressure.'

This last sentence goes far in explaining Germany's often misunderstood position vis-à-vis the tumult sweeping across Europe. 'Need' refers to the notion that this is not just a crisis, but an opportunity for reform. 'Market pressure' shows that Berlin feels rather unmoved by occasional spikes or crashes in markets – indeed, it welcomes the incentives for 'good' behaviour. 'Peer pressure' is a little more controversial, involving as it does attempts to cajole smaller sovereign states in the Eurozone to make unpopular long-term market reforms, for their own good. It works best at the point where such countries ask for financial help to reduce their public debt or rescue their bankrupt banks. This is why more sceptical observers of Germany might refer to the Bundeskanzleramt as the Temple of Sado-Austerity. But that is not entirely fair. The core sentiment, though, is not entirely wrong. Earlier in 2012, a G7 finance minister had told me at Davos: 'The Germans feel the need to keep their feet on the neck of the small Eurozone countries, so we feel the need to keep our feet on theirs.'

Germany's weary domination of Europe in the twenty-first century is more by accident than by design. Berlin gets criticised by London and Washington for doing too little. And then protesters in Athens and Nicosia dress up in Nazi garb to protest against the 'Financial Fourth Reich' when Berlin does too much. Germany is often described as being trapped by its interwar history – the experience of hyperinflation and mass unemployment followed by the era of Nazism and territorial aggression. The clearest reasons for its approach to the Eurozone crisis are, however, a product of much more recent economic history.

In Berlin they claim they are inviting the troubled economic apprentices of Europe to learn from the economic template of the German master tradesman – a template that one might call *Vorsprung Durch Fiskalpolitik*. Germany's tough internal economic reforms that it carried through a decade ago took half a decade to bear fruit. As a key adviser to Chancellor Angela Merkel puts it, 'Perhaps it's very lucky for the European Union that Germany did its reforms earlier.'

How to flourish in a financial crisis: the new German *Wirtschaftswunder*

A peculiar pleasure awaits visitors – most of them German – to the five-star hotel at Autostadt, the automobile theme park smack bang in the middle of Germany, near Wolfsburg. After touring the Volkswagen factory, and collecting their brand new VW from a robot-operated conical glass tower, who could say '*Nein*' to a morning dip in an industrial canal? Most infinity pools offer the illusion of bathing in a sea or lake or glorious landscaped vista. At Autostadt, patrons relax in a heated pool that offers the illusion of swimming in a smoky brown-green canal built to service the towering 1930s chimneys of the Volkswagen Kraftwerk power station.

Efficiency, technology, an absurd obsession with cars, Nazi-era architecture: Autostadt ticks most of the boxes of the Teutonic stereotype. But VW was not just the quintessential German export. On this very site, the blueprint for the Beetle was developed. During the Second World War, the factory was diverted to manufacturing military vehicles and parts for V1 Doodlebug flying bombs and so became a target for Allied bombing. After the war the Beetle blueprints were found by the British military. Colonel Charles Radclyffe restarted production at a rebuilt factory after offering the plans to uninterested British manufacturers. Volkswagen went on to become the second biggest car company in the world, owning marques such as Audi, Bugatti, Bentley, Porsche, Skoda and Lamborghini. VW and the Deutschmark were the twin totems of the *Wirtschaftswunder* – Germany's postwar economic miracle. At the beginning of the twenty-first century, the plant also became the template for Germany's subsequent economic success, and eventually a blueprint for the Eurozone itself. But first, the orgies.

VW's spending at five-star hotels around Europe featured strongly in the 2005 Federal election campaign. Gerhard Schröder would lose this election narrowly, leaving Angela Merkel with the keys to Berlin's White House (although she chose to stay living in her modest flat). Executive entertainment billed to the company included high-class prostitutes, Viagra, and parties for middle-aged executives at a club in Hanover called 'Sexworld'. At the heart of these stories was the German model of industrial harmony and cooperation between shareholder, worker and the state. VW is a fifth-owned by the Lower Saxony government, of which Schröder himself had been prime minister. A special law essentially prevented its takeover. VW's personnel director Peter

Hartz was a close adviser to Chancellor Schröder, who in turn became known as the *Autokanzler*. Payments and 'bonuses', authorised by Peter Hartz, were made to VW worker representatives. Under Germany's *Mitbestimmung*, or co-determination laws, half the supervisory board of all major companies are made up of directly elected employees or union representatives. The workers and the owners would literally 'co-determine' large investment decisions, anathema to businessmen in the UK and USA. The model emerged out of. the industrial strife that erupted in West Germany in the mid-1970s. The laws minimised strikes and helped underpin the long march of Germany to usurp the USA as 'world export champion' in 2003 (China subsequently took the title in 2009). The VW scandal showed how the social cooperation model had become a little too social. Union bosses were being bribed to acquiesce in plans to limit wage rises or transfer car production to cheaper locations. For their parts in the scandal, some worker representatives were jailed, an MP resigned, and Hartz himself was given a suspended sentence and a large fine.

Export growth did not mean jobs and wage growth. The year 2005 witnessed a peak in Anglo-Saxon smugness at the economic stagnation of Germany, the new 'sick man of Europe'. Wage growth was non-existent, unemployment was at 11.5 per cent (over double the rate in the UK), and growth was down to a paltry 0.7 per cent – compared to Britain's credit-boom-fuelled 3.2 per cent. An entire nation of Teutonic losers still thought there was money to be made from making things that customers wanted to buy – or making things that helped other countries make things that customers wanted to buy. These Germans were austere depressives, preferring to eschew the accoutrements of modern life such as credit, store loyalty cards and owning houses. And then, to top it off, the epitome of their manufacturing miracle, the Volkswagen Group, appeared to be mired in corruption, sex parties and Viagra.

This gloating *Schadenfreude* was entirely misplaced. The seeds of a spectacular German revival had already been sown – in precisely the same place. Peter Hartz, the VW personnel director, was also the mastermind of Chancellor Schröder's wave of reforms to Germany's labour market and welfare system. At VW, Hartz had become known for innovative policies that avoided compulsory redundancies at the politically sensitive company. 'My experiences in the global corporation Volkswagen were very helpful,' Mr Hartz told me. 'We had already successfully implemented some of the proposals within the company. We also analysed all European systems, including Britain's. Good suggestions from all over Europe, including England, contributed to our deliberations.'

The 'Hartz IV' reforms for the country were focused more on hiring rather than firing. Generous welfare payments for the unemployed (three-fifths of last wage) were slashed to a basic flat rate of €345 per month. Massive tax incentives were created for 'mini-jobs' – low-paid, often temporary work. Hartz promised that unemployment would halve. Initially it went up, over the 5 million level only previously seen in the Weimar Republic. The reforms were deeply unpopular, and led to Schröder's narrow election defeat in 2005. Schröder was fired by the electorate – in part, for making his compatriots easier to fire.

Early in 2011 I travelled to Frankfurt to speak to Otmar Issing, the most influential German economic policymaker in the first years of the euro. 'These reforms came from Schröder, who might have lost the elections because of them, but they worked,' Issing told me. 'If you do it too late you're out of office before progress is visible. It took many, many years of wage constraint before Germany came out of the overvaluation in which it entered monetary union. Germany was the only larger country that didn't see an increase in unemployment during the crisis, [so] minor reforms in the labour market, in sum, led to flexibility... which made this result possible.'

Indeed, the numbers were remarkable. As the crisis began to engulf Portugal as well as Ireland and Greece at the beginning of 2011, I went to Germany to report on the locals I imagined would be fed up with writing cheques for the 'Club Med'. But the German economy was surging too much for anyone to care.

They are fond of pigs in Munich, as long as they are skewered and served up as a spit-roast. Business is booming in the tents that hold 10,000 revellers paying €9 a time for authentic Bavarian brews. The oompah band blares out Neil Diamond's 'Sweet Caroline' at high volume, and thousands of *Lederhosen-* and dirndl-sporting Germans cry out, 'Good times never seemed so good,' before clinking their glasses. I had flown in from a crisis-ridden Athens. It seemed scarcely possible that I was in the same currency bloc or even economic planet as the previous day. Bavaria is home to what they call a high-tech 'laptops and *Lederhosen*' boom. Tobias and Christoph are German electricians from a nearby town. 'There is no crisis here,' says Tobias. 'The problem is that we have to pay for every country in Europe. Where do the taxes to go? To Greece?' Christoph interjects: 'We make our good work here and then we have to solve the problem of the others.'

In the 1990s economics undergraduates were taught about 'sclerotic' Germany, with its structurally higher rate of unemployment than free-market Britain. It was an axiom of European economics. In mid-2005 Germany did indeed suffer from an unemployment rate of 11.5 per cent, compared with Britain's 4.5 per cent. Since May 2009, however, Germany has had a lower unemployment rate than Britain. By mid-2013, UK unemployment had nearly doubled in eight years to 8 per cent, while in Germany it had more than halved, to 5.4 per cent. German ministers talked of being on the 'expressway to full employment'. Employment broke new records.

In the Bavarian town of Aschaffenburg is the Linde forklift-truck factory. It is a classic German export niche. In any gold rush the fortunes are made selling shovels rather than actually finding gold. And in a global trade boom, fortunes are made in forklift trucks. Linde is the second biggest manufacturer after Japan's Toyota. When I visited the factory in early 2011, it was the essence of a growing economy, at a time when Britain was contracting. Experienced German engineers meticulously checked their precision engineering, successfully competing on quality grounds with cheaper competition from Asia. Every single one of the bright red trucks, lined up like toys in Hamleys, was sold out. The order book was full for months in advance, and the orders were mainly from Asia. I was particularly struck by my meeting with a 17-year-old apprentice called Jens Zerkler. He was genuinely delighted at his chance. 'I always wanted to do this,' he told me. 'It was clear after school that I would be an apprentice. It was my dream, my wish to come here.'

At the time, Germany was enjoying the fastest growth for twenty years. Germany was the China of Europe. And the crisis in the Eurozone? *Keine Krise hier* ('no crisis here'). For the then chief economist of Deutsche Bank, Thomas Mayer, it was a story of sacrifices rewarded, with Germany benefiting from the Asian recovery. 'During the earlier part of the past decade,' Mayer told me, 'Germany worked very hard to restructure companies, cut costs, look for new markets. At the same time the government did a number of reforms – tax, regulatory and welfare reforms. Everything came together in 2007, but then you have the Great Recession interrupting it. And with the world economy coming back now, the dividends of all this effort are paying out.'

The success in forklift trucks was replicated in other industries and across their supply chains. Germany has been brilliant at identifying and exploiting specialist high-quality export niches with a global market, and has spawned a range of medium-sized companies, the so-called Mittelstand, to supply these markets with items ranging from conveyor belts to industrial springs. One company has cornered the world market in antennae for skyscrapers. The top Mittelstand companies adhere to the '80 per cent model' – an 80 per cent global market share, and 80 per cent of production exported. Such products are rarely glamorous, but all, in retrospect, are rather obvious commercial bets as emerging economies develop. Rather brilliantly, whether China or India wins the global industrial race for cars, or motorbikes or missiles, German companies will be on hand to equip the factories. Linde's parent company is now part-owned by a Chinese enterprise, which is itself owned by the Chinese state. There is a long-run challenge, from China, for example in solar power, but Germany starts the G7 race to reindustrialise in rude health.

In German minds, their commercial success during the global financial crisis was a direct result of their acceptance of pain, suffering and tough medicine. Greece, Ireland, Spain, Portugal and Italy had done the reverse. They had enjoyed the good times arising from euro membership without paying the up-front price. This vaguely Faustian 'morality' notion has become baked into public discourse in Germany. 'It is linguistically unavoidable in Germany – "*Schuld*" means both debt and guilt – so it's automatic for Germans to see debt as something iniquitous (and it therefore takes a little more reflection to recognise the responsibility of the lender),' says Richard Walker, a German TV anchor. 'The media stokes this – referring to crisis countries as "*Schuldensünder*", debt sinners, often without differentiating between the countries' very different circumstances. Then the mix of austerity and reforms that Germany demands are referred to as "*Hausaufgaben*" – homework. That is of course virtuous – Germany has done it; countries that haven't deserve to be on the naughty step. And those that do gain favour – like Portugal and Ireland at some points – get referred to as "*Musterschüler*" – model pupils.'

As the financial crisis morphed into the Eurozone crisis, the Faustian pact would become Germany's next big export.

The euro crisis spreads

By autumn 2011 the euro crisis had spread to five nations. By then it was much more than just a financial matter. The crisis had reached a second phase, a remarkable, historic experiment in sovereignty. German 'peer pressure' demanded that the crisis nations make a sacrifice of sovereignty normally only seen in the case of countries conquered in war.

Germany's frontline at this time was in Luxembourg. The grand duchy hosted a nondescript building in its financial district, far away from the marble-floored palaces beloved of eurocrats. The offices of the European Financial Stability Facility had only been established a year previously, and were shared with a tractor finance company. The staff collect souvenirs, particularly fridge magnets, from Beijing, Abu Dhabi and Moscow, the places where they have attempted to raise loans to help Europe's indebted periphery. The EFSF was the focus of the debate on global financial diplomacy and German fears.

'The EFSF is too big,' says Hans-Werner Sinn, one of Germany's leading economists. 'Europe is not a nation-state, but it wants to socialise the debts. It's a big poker game between the markets and the stable European countries which in the end will result in a loss of credibility and creditworthiness in the latter.'

The EFSF is effectively an exercise in painting lipstick on the pigs. It offered troubled European nations a lower government-borrowing interest rate by effectively rolling these rotten debts in AAA gold dust. This was achieved using exactly the sort of structured financial wizardry that had turned subprime mortgage loans into fool's gold. Off-balance sheet. Tick. Structured investment vehicle. Tick. Based in Luxembourg. Tick. The very existence of the EFSF was the result of an early-hours compromise at a Brussels meeting in May 2010. As time ran out, Germany refused a French suggestion that these massive new powers go to the European Commission. Britain's only contribution to break the deadlock was to suggest a 'special purpose vehicle'. The funds were under the direct command of the Eurogroup, a committee of seventeen Eurozone finance ministers. The original thinking was that the fund would be so big, and would inject so much confidence, that it would never be required.

Horst Seehofer, the leader of the Bavarian Christian Social Union, Merkel's sister party, was unconvinced: 'It's not a euro crisis. It's a debt crisis. We are doing our bit with enormous debt guarantees. But the answer cannot be that we take national debts and socialise them into European debt, because we would then stop being a stability union and start becoming a debt union.'

The alchemy was achieved through €780 billion guarantees from Europe's remaining AAA nations, with the biggest chunk – €211 billion – coming from Germany. The US consulting firm McKinsey developed the idea, and senior staff at the EFSF were seconded from the firm. The EFSF accumulated a war chest of €440 billion to lend to Portugal, Ireland and Greece, and to prop up the banking systems of Italy and Spain, if required. The US Treasury secretary, Tim Geithner, believed these sums were insufficient, and suggested that the EFSF should be accorded bank status and then additionally leveraged up to an eye-watering €2 trillion. That would be ten times the annual budget of the European Union. The EFSF employed just fifteen people.

French president Nicolas Sarkozy was pretty keen on the IMF-conceived idea. The problem was that the funds still had to be found somewhere. The EFSF could be leveraged by licensing it as a bank, and giving it access to funding streams from the European Central Bank. Germany and the ECB were not at all keen. In Berlin they likened the €2 trillion number to 'multiplying money like bread in the Bible'. Any attempt at leveraging the fund would require help from the Sovereign Wealth Funds in the East. 'The problem was that the French wanted the Chinese to buy into these ill-conceived leverage models,' says a well-connected Eurozone diplomat. Indeed, in October 2011, President Sarkozy spoke to President Hu Jintao of China as the EFSF chief Klaus Regling was in Beijing to petition the Chinese leadership. A leading Western banker advising the Chinese told me that 'the whole idea of the Chinese bailing out the Eurozone was doomed'. For a Chinese leadership focused on maintaining its political legitimacy, it would have been 'just completely politically unsustainable' for a China with a per capita income of $5,000 to be bailing out Europe with a per capita income of $30,000.

This was around the time I met Jin Liqun, Chairman of the Supervisory Board of the China Investment Corporation (see Chapter 4, page 115) in Paris at a conference of Sovereign Wealth Funds at the American embassy. At one dinner, as representatives of funds controlling $9 trillion chomped away at the duck in the very place where the postwar Marshall Plan funds were disbursed, French officials came to do business with these vats of eastern capital. Mr Jin laughed out loud when I asked him if China's funds would bail out the Eurozone. The welfare system was the 'root cause of the Eurozone crisis', he said, and working harder and longer would solve its problems. 'The root cause of trouble is the overburdened welfare system, built up since the Second World War in Europe – the sloth-inducing, indolence-inducing labour laws,' he said, and added that China will only invest in Europe's crisis-ridden banking system if it can be sure 'there are no black holes'. To really reform the Eurozone, there needs to be greater productivity in the labour force, said Mr Jin. 'People need to work a bit harder, they need to work a bit longer, and they should be more innovative. We [the Chinese] work like crazy,' he added. 'The European countries enjoy a lot of advantages in science, technology, in managerial expertise. You just need to tap those advantages and you will be back on your feet.' The Chinese Communist leadership was telling Europe to dismantle its welfare state. And Germany agreed.

In private, Germany's leaders would invite Europeans in a job to consider the question: 'at what wage would a Chinese person do your job?' Germany had something of a special relationship with China: Berlin understood Beijing's need for real investments in the Eurozone – such as in Greek ports or Portuguese utilities – rather than grandiose French plans for transcontinental financial engineering.

To gain the approval of Germany's parliament, the Bundestag, for the expansion to €440 billion, various assurances were made that the fund would not be artificially increased into the trillions. The Bundestag did give the existing size and powers of the EFSF overwhelming backing, but the message from Chancellor Merkel's own government benches was that Germany was reaching the limits of its tolerance.

Chancellor Merkel's top political adviser, Peter Altmaier, then chief whip, told me that 'it was very tough indeed' to pass the vote without relying on support from the opposition, but signalled more was to come. 'I'm now looking forward to taking the next concrete step in reassuring the markets that we'll do everything we can to stabilise the euro and preserve the Eurozone.'

So the seeds of a government split had been sown. Chancellor Merkel would become increasingly dependent on the SPD opposition for the votes to pass the various bailouts. The tension reflects a split in Germany's two most-cherished postwar political axioms – a commitment to European integration, and an utter aversion to debt. As Altmaier told me, 'It is our aim to reconcile these two different objectives, on the one hand European solidarity and further commitment to European integration, and on the other hand a stronger impetus on budget deficit consolidation and a stability culture across Europe.' The euro crisis, specifically the EFSF, entangles these two factors in a difficult embrace between solidarity and stability.

Cautious does it: stable money, low inflation and low debt

'Finally money became so worthless that it was cheaper to burn it than to buy fuel. . . Germany could not even find the paper to print its worthless money on.' The message from the robotic voice emanating from the videoscreens at the Bundesbank museum could not be clearer if it was set to Kraftwerk and played on loudspeakers. Visiting the museum appeared to be a rite of passage, with German schoolkids initiated into the cult of stable money, low inflation and low debt. The Bundesbank steered Germany's postwar economic miracle after the ravages of hyperinflation in the 1920s, when you needed a wheelbarrow to carry the cash needed to buy a loaf of bread. And if you want to know why Germany hesitates over signing the cheque, launching the big bazooka to solve the euro crisis, then come here.

Remarkably, in a pull-out draw, you can see the 1920s German currency written on playing cards and on gift wrap. There is even embroidered currency, not to mention a trillion-mark note. It was the Bundesbank that permanently put an end to high inflation with a strong and stable Deutschmark. But now the euro, run by the European Central Bank, is in trouble, and again people are talking of trillions. In the gift shop you can buy bricks of shredded notes, Deutschmark fan memorabilia, pfennig cufflinks. The German obsession with currency stability at times becomes surreal. In 1996 the Bundesbank's then chief economist Otmar Issing wrote an essay for the *Frankfurter Allgemeine Zeitung* invoking the debts of the composer Richard Wagner, Freud's theories of anal eroticism, and religious guilt to explain what French philosopher André Glucksmann has called Germany's 'currency religion'. In Freudian terms, 'money replaces the function of excrement', in the end debasing everything that is noble and distinguished. A country's currency reflects its psychological disposition. Therefore, suggested Issing, sharing a currency between seventeen different countries would either make the currency a blend of psychological traits, or require the constituent nations to change their psychology. The latter is what was being referred to a decade and a half later as 'peer pressure' or 'spreading the stability culture'.

In Frankfurt I met a 76-year-old retired senior German banker called Martin Murtfeld. 'We want to ask our European friends to understand the hesitation of many Germans,' Murtfeld told me. This country is still deeply influenced by experiences over two or three generations. The incredible inflation of the 1920s caused the tragedy of the Nazi period and the Second World War. Our thinking since was that monetary stability is one of the preconditions for sound democracy, and avoiding social unrest. Until the euro was created, the philosophy was that if there is a problem with the banking system, it's up to the bankers to sort it out.'

At Deutsche Bank, Murtfeld was a member of committees of bankers that were obliged to write off the debts of Mexico and Bulgaria during the 1980s and 1990s. 'We solved the rescheduling case of Mexico, and we made a major discount to the Bulgarians, solved by the banks themselves, without too much noise.' Like many Germans, he felt the direction of Eurozone policy was for the banks to dump the price of bad lending onto the taxpayers of countries such as Germany. He was right. At the peak of boom-time lending to Spanish property developers, one senior German banker summed up his approach to an enquiring civil servant: 'Join the party. Dance near the door. Everybody knows it.' Mostly, that is exactly what the German bankers did. In Spain, the German investments in fuelling Spain's credit boom had been channelled via covered bonds, leaving the German bankers with the security of a legal ring fence on the best assets on bank and caja balance sheets (see page 249). In Greece (see page 19) they were at one point the most exposed, and then cunningly left that exposure to the French. In the US subprime debacle, the German banking system suffered horrific losses, having been lured by the AAA ratings given to toxic junk in a supposedly rules-based system. A large taxpayer bailout followed.

But debt and hyperinflation, and the social evils arising from overprinting money, do loom large in Germany's history. This is why a quietly spoken government MP called Frank Schäffler voted 'No' even to the expansion of the EFSF bailout. 'These rescue packages do not help, they add fuel to the fire,' he told me. The transfer union is the taboo. Hans-Werner Sinn, the influential economist, was telling Germany that it was a transfer union in the USA that led to the Civil War. In Berlin, they say Germany has already been pouring structural funds into Greece for thirty years. More money is available in EU stabilisation funds than the USA put into Europe after the Second World War under the Marshall Plan. And what did Germany do with a chunk of its Marshall Plan funds? It started KfW, the state-owned business bank that offers cheap long-term loans to growing businesses.

Germany's sensitivity about its history in the first half of the twentieth century does much to explain its reluctance to assume an imperium in Europe in the early years of the twenty-first. German government officials point out that the main player in the crisis, the European Central Bank, although based in Frankfurt, is independent, not an organ of the German state. 'We are not in the Troika,' they insist, when asked if they are fed up with Greece.

Ironically, no Germans today seem to remember the period of deflation and political extremism that accompanied Chancellor Brüning's austerity policies of 1929–32, although there is a small exhibit on this at the Bundesbank museum. Arguably, those last years of the Weimar Republic provide the most relevant parallel to what is happening today in countries such as Greece (see page 33). But one can only go so far in explaining Germany's approach to the crisis by invoking the shadow of the interwar period. It gives context, but not motivation. The 1970s experience – when Chancellor Helmut Schmidt famously said that 5 per cent inflation was better than 5 per cent unemployment, and promptly got both – probably does more to explain the current caution of Germany's political class.

The wages of restraint...

At the heart of Berlin's decision-making apparatus is a room on the third floor of the north wing of the Chancellery where a team monitors other European nations under the guidance of trusted Merkel adviser, the historian-diplomat Nikolaus Meyer-Landrut. He is the uncle of Lena Meyer-Landrut, who won the Eurovision song contest for Germany in 2010, just weeks into the Eurozone crisis. It seems unlikely Germany will win the contest for the next few years.

Meyer-Landrut is known for his collection of beautifully presented PowerPoint slides, occasionally deployed to ward off the many foreign do-gooders who try to persuade Germany to fire a silver bullet to kill the ravening werewolf that is the euro crisis. In just three slides, Meyer-Landrut presents the orthodox German account of the crisis, involving ten-year bond yields, labour-market competitiveness and deficits across the nations of the Eurozone.

Bond yields, showing the cost of borrowing, come first, and the graph stretches back not to before the crisis in 2005 or even the beginning of the euro in 2001, but all the way back to 1995, nearly two decades. The message is this. Before the euro, Italy, Spain, Greece and Ireland all used to borrow at interest rates much higher than the 7 per cent deemed a crisis in 2012. In 1995 Ireland was paying 10 per cent, Spain 12 per cent, Italy 14 per cent. High yields are not a crisis. In fact we are seeing a return of sensible bond-market discipline for fiscal wrongdoers. Germany had tried to insist on strict rules on government borrowing, known as the Stability and Growth Pact. These rules had not worked, partly because Germany itself abandoned the discipline. High bond yields were the real incentive against a lack of fiscal discipline. Another question arose from the same graph. What did the southern countries do with the windfall of long-term borrowing rates under 4 per cent, in a sense accessing credit lines with interest rates meant for Germany? The deficit graph, the second slide, showed that the problem nations had taken advantage of those low interest rates to ratchet up their borrowing, often unproductively, the money bleeding into extra public servants, higher wages, unneeded motorway networks and vanity projects rather than underpinning the economic modernisation of these countries. Even those such as Ireland and Spain that stuck to the fiscal rules would end up having to borrow thanks to their bankrupt banks. The banking systems of these nations certainly were taking advantage of these lower Eurozone borrowing rates.

The main event, though, the third slide in the show, is the competitiveness slide. For Berlin, the graph of 'unit labour costs', stretching back to the creation of the euro, shows that the windfalls granted to the problem nations were frittered away on pay rises, at a time when Germans, amid union restraint, were accepting effective pay cuts from the Hartz IV reforms. It is a graph that is close to the heart of many German economists. It invites the whole of Europe to copy Germany's reforms as their payback for the Faustian joy of the first decade or so of illusory rises in living standards caused by the adoption of the euro.

Otmar Issing showed me this graph in 2011. 'Unit labour costs were diverging from day one of monetary union,' Issing told me, 'so over time this must lead to a crisis. It was anything but unexpected. In the past it would have been corrected by a devaluation of the escudo for example, but this tool does not exist anymore.' He pointed out that Ireland at the time had higher GDP per capita living standards than Germany.

But how can Germany insist on Hartz IV for all? 'There may be no article in Maastricht about wage negotiations,' Issing responded, 'but once we have joined monetary union it has implications, and if you don't comply you get deficits and unemployment. I see people saying Germans want to impose a Teutonic regime. This is nonsense. It was the regime enshrined in Maastricht. What most politicians underestimated or didn't understand was that joining the euro has implications throughout the economy, well beyond the monetary sphere.' Germany's many years of wage restraint, Issing insisted, shows to the crisis countries that 'It can be done and it will be done in other cases'.

I got a similar view from a key figure in Merkel's government. 'This is what we forgot in the ten-year euro honeymoon,' he told me. 'The roots of the crisis are not in Europe. They are in policy areas that remain national.' The architect of Germany's reforms cautions against one-size-fits-all. 'The labour market reforms in Germany contributed to the reduction of unemployment. They were connected with an economic recovery, which was critical. . . Every country and every national economy has to follow its own path of reform', Peter Hartz reflected in summer 2013.

In Berlin they are painfully aware that it takes years to see the benefit of such reforms. A reduction in Ireland's labour costs was heralded as progress, but much of this was the simple arithmetic consequence of the collapse of its construction sector. A small uptick in the forecast for Germany's unit labour cost line causes concern about whether Germany 'needs to take some of its own medicine now'.

That is the simple morality play. Tough-minded pain-loving Germans made sacrifices and now reap the rewards. Crisis countries wasted their windfall, had a great party, and now face market disciplines, and should learn the German lessons. In fact, if they can't borrow money from the market, and need a bailout, they will be obliged to learn the lesson.

Except that is hardly the full story. Berlin seems to be bluffing.

Germany always writes the cheque in the end

As the crisis raged in the Mediterranean, record employment saw German tax revenues come in well over expectations. Debt interest payments also collapsed as German bond yields sank as a result of flows of safe-haven money. In autumn 2011 the German treasury was cancelling large chunks of its debt sales, at the very moment when the entire Eurozone looked close to collapse. In fact, so tax-rich was Germany's Bundesboom that on the day the Greek prime minister, George Papandreou, dined with Chancellor Merkel, Germany cancelled the same amount (€16 billion) from its debt sales in the next quarter as Greece's entire annual target budget deficit under Troika plans. Put another way, Germany could have just proceeded with its initial borrowing plans and funded Greece's entire annual fiscal imbalance at the drop of a hat, at interest rates of less than 2 per cent. It would have been a type of eurobond, and it was not on the cards. But Germany was on a different planet to Greece, and even Britain. Two different worlds in one single currency. Germany was not just immune from the Eurozone economic crisis – it directly benefited.

'This is French propaganda,' a German professor told me. He was worried about the direction of the Eurozone. Most of the German economic establishment suggest that this economic outperformance is a result of the tough reforms, not the single currency.

But German exports doubled under the euro. At the dawn of the euro in 2000, Germany had a balance of payments deficit, and a tiny trade surplus with the rest of the world of just €6.3 billion in 2012 prices. Just seven years later that surplus peaked at €170 billion, and was still €151 billion in 2012, the largest part of that with the rest of the Eurozone. The 2012 trade surplus with Spain alone was larger than the total surplus with the entire world in 2000. In 2011 Germany's net trade surplus with Greece and Portugal combined was just below its overall global trade surplus in 2000. It is difficult to escape the conclusion that when Berlin asks the crisis nations where all the money went, the answer is that an awful lot of it was spent on German imports. It was a case of an exporter offering potential customers loans at epically low interest rates, just so they could buy the vendor's goods – just as the Chinese had done for US consumers.

The euro meant that German industry had quadrupled the size of its domestic market to 329 million potential customers. Labour reforms clearly helped, but so did the creation of the Eurozone – the second biggest economic entity in the world, with no trade, labour or currency barriers or risks. On top of this, outside of the Eurozone, German industry was helped along by the gravitational pull that the crisis exerted on the value of the single currency. German exports were made cheaper than they would have been under the Deutschmark. Between 2009 and 2012 the euro depreciated by 10 per cent. German insurer Allianz calculate that in the euro crisis the boost to non-euro trade would make up for the decline in demand from the euro area. Indeed, by 2012 there had been a marked switch in German trade away from the Eurozone towards the rest of the world.

Allianz also attempted to tot up the savings in interest payments on Germany's debts that occurred during the crisis. Banks and companies were parking their money in safe German government debt, driving down the interest rates asked of Berlin. In 2012 it estimated €6.5 billion had been saved, and a total of €10 billion since the crisis began. Projecting this windfall forward, the insurer calculated that the German debt office would save a remarkable €67 billion from the crisis elsewhere in the Eurozone. All of which suggested that the Germans could contribute considerably more to solve the problems of the imbalanced Eurozone – either financially, in terms of fiscal transfers, or by easing the South's path to regaining competitiveness by tolerating higher prices in Germany. Around the table at the G7, the world's leading central bankers began to conclude that the Eurozone crisis, frustratingly sapping confidence from all their post-2008 recoveries, was something very well understood by economists. It was a simple balance-of-payments crisis made more complicated by the rigidity of the single currency. The onus of adjustment needed to be shared by surplus nations such as Germany, as well as the deficit nations such as Greece, Ireland and Spain.

Mervyn King, the former governor of the Bank of England, put it like this to me in 2011: 'We have to find a way of gradually disentangling these exposures, to make sure that countries that need to repay debt can earn their way in the world by being sufficiently competitive and other countries want to buy their exports. And that countries that have accumulated vast stocks of assets and reserves start to spend some of that in order to boost their spending, making it easier for us and the other indebted countries to export and repay our debts in turn.' I asked him if he feared a Eurozone collapse. 'I think the word collapse is not a well-defined phrase and I don't want to get into scenarios. I do not know what the future holds. Anyone who looks back at the history of financial and economic crises knows that it was never easy to know what would happen next. What I do know is that we have to be very clear on understanding what the underlying problems are. And the underlying problems are that some countries have too much debt, and other countries, because there is always a lender corresponding to a borrower, have lent too much, and we've got to find a way of disentangling this. It won't happen quickly, but we have to allow exchange rates to move to provide the incentives for households, businesses and others to be willing to buy exports from those countries that need export-led growth, and spend less in countries that need to reduce their exports and rely more on domestic spending.'

King was implicitly referring to China, but the arguments increasingly applied to Germany. When ministers from Berlin went to international meetings they were told that Germany had to make at least one of four choices: pool debts with crisis countries, make fiscal transfers of up to 5 per cent of GDP to the crisis nations, allow large inflation in Germany, or break up the euro. Their response: 'we will find a fifth way'. Back in Berlin, there is no doubt that the government was beginning to feel the international pressure, from the USA particularly. Domestically too, periods of acute eurostress were uncannily linked with drops in the poll lead for Chancellor Merkel, especially against her main challenger Peer Steinbrück of the SPD. An adviser spells out the current thinking on writing a large cheque to finish off the euro crisis: 'We don't think we need a big permanent transfer system. We need to provide incentives for national reforms. Did Italy manage to create the right business environment in the south of Italy with transfers from the north? The amount of money that Germany has put on the line is more than the federal budget of our country, and they say we are not showing solidarity. Ask a US congressman what he would say to making available guarantees, paid-in capital and loans more than the US federal budget for Argentina, Chile and Mexico. By this calculation I don't accept that Germany is lacking solidarity.'

Chancellor Merkel has been an exponent of the cautious approach. Her view is that you should not cross a bridge before you arrive. There is no big strategy. There are principles, but no prophetic judgements. 'If she just followed the euphoria and panic up and down each time, this would not be policy. Politics has to be steady,' says one of her senior diplomats. Expectations are being played down for a grand solution to the crisis on her watch.

Despite the tough rhetoric, for nearly three years a pattern developed in which the European debt crisis blew up every few months. The markets, the pesky Anglo-Saxons, Brussels and Paris meet stiff resistance from Berlin. And then, at the last minute, in a dark corner of a conference centre in Brussels or Wrocław or Marseille, Berlin capitulates. Germany always writes the cheque in the end, because the euro has been excellent for its domestic economy. The main fear in foreign central banks was that by pushing things until 'one minute to midnight', an accident might occur. US Treasury secretary Geithner turned up at one Eurozone meeting on his plane to warn of 'the threat of cascading default, bank runs and catastrophic risk'.

German leaders do have a habit of not quite matching their tough rhetoric with actions. In 2009 Steinbrück, Merkel's former finance minister and 2013 challenger for the chancellorship, accused the British prime minister, Gordon Brown, of 'crass Keynesianism'. At the same time, Steinbrück was enacting a fiscal stimulus measure double the size of Brown's, including trading in old cars for new ones (so-called 'cash for clunkers'), subsidies to keep workers in jobs, and tax cuts. Likewise, the tough rhetoric about cajoling the Eurozone's recalcitrant children to behave better belies the fact that Ireland, Portugal and Greece have all got progressively better deals on their bailout loans.

Indeed, it is difficult to find an ordinary German complaining about lazy Greeks. The only angry Germans in this respect seem to be economics professors. The one time a political party – Frank Schäffler's FDP (Free Democratic Party) – explicitly offered an anti-bailout platform, it did very badly, to the benefit of the centre-left and Greens, who promise even bigger bailouts. 'We started this campaign at a point when it was already far too late. Voters see it as a tactic and not a conviction,' Schäffler told me. Hans-Werner Sinn said 'it was a great mystery' why voters express their discontent with bailouts by voting for political parties that seem to accept even bigger bailouts. The answer could be much simpler: discontent with Eurozone bailouts is much overhyped for now. Germans aren't all cowering in fear at the return of the Weimar Republic. The second postwar axiom, a commitment to European solidarity, remains the best predictor of German instincts at those moments 'when push comes to shove'.

On the periphery, even bankers who say they have been on the receiving end of Germany's arbitrary economic justice hold their hands up. A former Cypriot finance minister told me in the middle of that nation's crisis: 'In a strange way the German hegemony, the total power of the Germans, irrespective of if you agree or disagree, is a more effective way of governing the euroblock. You have leadership and direction.'

Merkel's advisers echo this: 'Do not underestimate people in the crisis nations saying to us, "Please use the leverage that you have to change our countries."'

A more reasonable question concerns the broader social impact of the Hartz IV reforms on Germany itself. The impact on the unemployment numbers was miraculous. But Chancellor Merkel does not need to stroll far from the Bundeskanzleramt to see the highest levels of unemployment in Germany. The reforms pushed down wages for poorer Germans. Between 1997 and 2010, 5 million Germans were pushed out of its middle classes. The MiniJobs and 'one-euro' jobs created by the Hartz reforms were providing an escalator down rather than up for large swathes of German citizens. Social mobility was declining. Official measures of poverty reached all-time highs, with one in six Germans now beneath the poverty line. More than one in three children in Berlin relied on a Hartz IV payment. The German dream of 'prosperity for all' is fractured, even if there are plenty of jobs. Hartz IV recipients were becoming ghettoised. It's easy to see why southern Europe may not volunteer for a German blueprint that amounts to 'Get Paid Less'.

Hartz himself told me: 'The reforms needn't necessarily be accompanied by wage reductions.' Does he accept that some of the Hartz reforms have led to more poverty, less social mobility, and declining living standards? 'Absolutely not. The reforms opened up prospects for all so that no one should arrive at a dead-end situation. The long-term unemployed missed out when the reforms were actually implemented... Not everything labelled "Hartz" is actually "Hartz".'

Back at the Oktoberfest in Munich, Franz Kollman, a 72-year-old Bavarian, runs the dodgem ride, which he has named 'Euroskooter'. EU flags hang off every car, and there's even a plastic fresco of the Parthenon. 'I'm still a big fan of the euro,' he tells me as he dispenses plastic euros to the revellers to operate his ride. 'If one country backs another, in the end everything will work out.' In Berlin, however, a fundamental intellectual debate was emerging, sometimes between the finance ministry and the Chancellery. In the early summer of 2012 this debate centred on Greece. Was Greece domino or ballast? Would the fall of Greece from the Eurozone set off an uncontrollable domino effect in Spain, Italy and elsewhere? Or was Greece the ballast that needed to be ejected to steady the Eurozone ship? German finance minister Wolfgang Schäuble was at this moment a believer in the ballast theory. But he was not calling all the shots.

For now the German economy is still creating enough jobs and wealth for Germany to fall back on its traditional role of fostering solidarity across the European Union although that solidarity comes with strings attached. But with a new downturn, that collegiate spirit will be tested as much in Berlin as it has been in Athens, Dublin, Madrid, Lisbon and Nicosia. A backdoor solution to this conundrum lay on a patch of German territory that was becoming progressively less Germanic: Frankfurt.

CHAPTER 11

GROUND CONTROL TO EUROTOWER

Dramatis personae

Wim Duisenberg, first president of the European
Central Bank (ECB) (1998–2003)
Jean-Claude Trichet, ECB president (2003–11)
Silvio Berlusconi, Italian prime minister, periodically
Mario Draghi, ECB president (2011–)
Brian Lenihan, Jnr, Irish finance minister
(2008–11)
Patrick Honohan, governor of the Central Bank
of Ireland (2009–)
Axel Weber, Deutsche Bundesbank president (2004–11)
Jens Weidmann, Deutsche Bundesbank president (2011–)
Lee Buchheit, sovereign debt restructuring lawyer

On the thirty-fifth floor of the Eurotower, the 1970s HQ of the European Central Bank in Frankfurt, a member of Mario Draghi's team looked out towards the River Main docks. The construction of the ECB's new headquarters building had already begun: two slender towers in the shape of giant wedges linked by a gleaming glass atrium. 'When we move there, not only will the euro still exist, but there will be more than seventeen members,' he tells a guest sceptical of the euro's future. The words were carefully chosen. 'More than seventeen' still holds out the possibility of a shuffling of the membership pack. Perhaps a Latvia could be substituted for a Cyprus, for example. But the words were conveying an unusual confidence at that time in late 2011, a time when the whole euro project seemed to be falling apart. It was an early window into what in the Eurotower became known as 'conditional irreversibility'. This unspoken Draghi doctrine is designed to stop the markets betting on the Eurozone's collapse, while reassuring donor nations, such as Germany, that strings are attached to the rescues designed to keep crisis nations in the euro.

It sounds contradictory. The motivation to save the euro obviously went beyond a simple desire to move into a state-of-the-art HQ. Most central banks have steel-reinforced bomb-proof vaults in their basements. In those vaults are piles of gold bullion and ancient sovereigns, and probably secret underground tunnels. The Bank of Spain has Royal Steps and a room full of priceless Goyas. Not so the basement of the ECB's current HQ in Frankfurt. Its basement instead contains a bar-cum-nightclub called Living, which blasts out the German equivalent of Chas 'n' Dave, interspersed with the odd tune from Right Said Fred. In 2002, on the evening of the launch of the first euro notes and coins, Living's standards, at least musically, seemed rather low. By 2012, Living had begun advertising the fact that punters could eat a €12 steak lunch 'at the ECB'.

Back at the start of the euro's physical existence, the launch of the new currency on 1 January 2002 was generally regarded as a triumph. In a spectacularly choreographed operation, the new notes and coins came into circulation simultaneously across a great swathe of the planet, from the Aegean to the Caribbean, appearing in all twelve Eurozone countries and their overseas territories in the course of a single night. The Banque de France had insisted on three small boxed dots on the corner of the map on banknotes, to represent its Caribbean territories. Cyprus, not in the EU at the time, was not even on the map. To avoid arguments over which national landmarks would feature on the banknotes, they instead featured stylised bridges that did not actually exist (although later these fantasy bridges were actually constructed by an obsessive Dutch fan of the single currency). Crucially, on its launch, the new currency worked without any hitches – apart from a hike in inflation caused by a tendency to round up exchange rates.

At the Eurotower they noticed the tendency of euronotes to 'migrate' south from Germany and Holland as north Europeans went on holiday. No longer would marks and guilders swapped for holiday pesetas and lire need to be sent back by the truck-load. So great was the influx of northern euros that Spain, for example, had to print far fewer notes – it could simply recirculate migrating euros. In January 2013 the value of euros in circulation topped €900 billion. In 2006 the euro had already overtaken the dollar as the most circulated physical currency. Up to a quarter is circulated outside the Eurozone, most in tracked truckloads provided by commercial banks to their correspondent banks from Britain to Bulgaria. The demand for physical euros is seasonal: a large spike before Christmas, and a smaller one before the summer holidays. But there is a long-term upward trend. The impact of financial panics is clearly discernible. There have been local spikes in Greece and Cyprus, as described in Chapters 1 and 13 (see pages 2 and 386). In October 2008, just after Lehman Brothers collapsed, an extra €43 billion worth of euro banknotes appeared, and the entire circulation of the currency increased by an unheard of 6 per cent in just one month. The bulk of it comprised a 48 million (11 per cent) increase in the number of €500 notes, and these have remained in circulation to this day. As described in Chapter 1, it was a demand serviced by printing presses in Germany, Austria or Luxembourg. Only those nations had the plates for the world's most valuable banknote. Basically, this was caused by numerous Germans who, fearing the imminent collapse of global capitalism, marched on their banks. The notes were heading for safety deposit boxes and people's mattresses. In an era of ultra-low interest rates, where the opportunity cost of not putting money in a bank is tiny, one's mattress seems as good a place as any to stow one's savings. And under the mattress is where these bundles of the world's highest denomination banknote have remained.

In its other great task, monetary policy, the infant ECB was finding its feet. Its inaugural president, the Dutch economist and politician Wim Duisenberg, was rapidly christened 'Dim Wim' for a series of blunders. Officials would tell me, constantly, that central banking was about credibility, and while the Bank of England had had over three centuries to build it, the ECB had been in existence for just three years. Central bankers at the time were following the fashion for inflation-fighting credibility through strict independence from powerful finance ministers and other politicians. It was a script pioneered across town from the Eurotower, at the Bundesbank, and at that time this image of independence was also being developed by the Bank of England. The ECB was routinely under pressure to protect its independence from comments by the French, and then from the then German finance minister, Oskar Lafontaine.

Just a decade on, that challenge to the ECB's independence has been totally turned on its head. Now it was a question as to whether Europe's puny politicians were sufficiently credible to stand up to an all-conquering European Central Bank. The worm had turned. The ECB had become the second most powerful economic institution on the planet (after the Federal

Reserve) – or even, given its tacit political role, arguably *the* most powerful. And in a Europe dragging its feet over implementing the changes needed to end a damaging crisis, the ECB held all the cards. The ECB governing council could and did decide to pull the plug on the banking systems of smaller nations. Its president would pen stern letters to elected G7 leaders, demanding dozens of reforms. And the ECB had the power to take on – and beat – the bond vigilantes betting on euro collapse.

The price of pizzas and the incoherence of the Eurozone

'I watch pizzas,' says a senior Eurozone official. Perhaps this unusual interest stemmed from the inflation-wary German tabloid that greeted Mario Draghi's ECB appointment with the headline, 'Mamma mia, for Italians, inflation is a way of life, like pasta and sauce.'

The official's interest was tightly focused on the price of a freshly made 30-cm margherita in an ordinary restaurant. 'In Sicily, it is €12 or more,' he says. 'Here in Germany, more like €6. In some parts of Frankfurt near the ECB, maybe even less than €5. And the quality is high.' (My own unscientific online check of pizzeria menus in Frankfurt and Palermo did indeed yield prices around €4.50 versus €11.50.) The pizza was a product requiring the same flour, tomato and mozzarella, the same energy, and comparable minutes of labour throughout the continent.

The pizza test provided an intriguing lens on the incoherence of the Eurozone. There's no reason why pizza, or beer, or haircut prices should be exactly the same even within a country, let alone within a single currency zone. But in theory, after a decade of monetary union, the prices should have converged as the constituent economies of the Eurozone converged. Why were the costs so different? In the Eurozone, German food prices had fallen a little, and Italian prices had risen. On top of that, restaurant prices in Italy are higher than in Germany. To the man from the ECB, the high cost of a pizza in Italy illustrated the price to punters of high labour costs and an uncompetitive market. Cars and TVs were converging in price, as imports, and larger goods were produced and traded cross-continentally. The price of pizza was part of a wider puzzle of a Eurozone that had diverged rather than converged, a Eurozone in which existing imbalances had not rebalanced but become even more unbalanced. The ECB's big answer to this crisis was to force national economies back into line. But first they had to buy some time.

The view from 'Main-hattan': The ECB and the Eurozone crisis

On the floor above Draghi's office, on the thirty-sixth storey of the Eurotower, is the meeting room of the ECB governing council. This is the control room of the Eurozone. Against a panorama of skyscrapers cradling the River Main (a view sometimes dubbed 'Main-hattan'), the room is dominated by a doughnut-shaped wooden table. Two large projector screens and two plasma screens display presentations from ECB staff. A Reuters terminal with currency charts is immediately behind the president's chair. It is here, most crucially, that twenty-three men (and in 2013 it *was* all men) squeeze around the table to make the decisions on Eurozone interest rates, bond purchases and emergency bank funding. Twice a month on a Thursday, seventeen governors of the national central banks of each euro nation, and six executive board members led by Mr Draghi, hold a ponderous monetary seance. Intriguingly, the ex-Bundesbank president, Hans Tietmeyer, suggested the council sit in alphabetical order, not by nation but by surname. Perhaps he did not like sitting next to the Greeks, whose euro membership he had advised against.

The governing council members have to make decisions based on the entire currency area, not the vested interest of the nation-state they happen to come from. This room is the very place where old Europe traded sovereignty for its new currency. The twenty-three men who sit at this table check in their national baggage at the door, becoming post-national Europeans as soon as they enter the room. Minutes of their meetings are not due to be published for three decades, unlike the five years for the US Federal Reserve and two weeks for the Bank of England. This is supposed to help the council act in comparative secrecy without 'national' pressure over decisions and votes. So the council meeting room can be seen as the high temple of Europeanism. Recently, the quarrelsome German central bankers, with names like Weber, Weidmann and Welteke, tended to be alphabetically positioned almost next to the ECB president. On the presidential desk was Mr Draghi's golden chairman's bell. As the reluctant Bundesbank representatives around the table grew increasingly wary of the ECB's crisis interventions, bringing order to these secretive meetings may have required more than a spot of campanology from Mr Draghi and his predecessor, Jean-Claude Trichet.

The fear on the other side of Frankfurt, at the Bundesbank, was *Gelddrucken*, money printing. From the outset, Germany had been reassured that the euro was a reincarnation of the German currency, a 'euromark'. Anti-inflation discipline and targets had been inherited directly from the Bundesbank, and hardwired into the Maastricht Treaty. Bundesbank personnel such as Otmar Issing had been transplanted to the ECB. For the first few years, even the old-school German monetarist tradition of targeting monetary growth was included as part of the way that the ECB did business. The ECB successfully kept inflation below 2 per cent – at 1.97 per cent in its first decade or so – a better record of monetary stability than even the Bundesbank. Periodically the ECB would lambast its constituent nation-states for fiscal indiscipline. No one took much notice.

Then came the crisis: Greece, Ireland, Portugal, Italy, Spanish banks and then Cyprus. Europe was paralysed, given the choice between Germany's 'smallest loan possible, at the last possible moment' strategy, and the collapse of its periphery. Elsewhere, in the USA and UK, central bankers had used quantitative-easing programmes to lower long-term interest rates by gobbling up their own government's debt by the mountain-load. But the Eurozone was different. Only some smaller nations were in trouble, while the core nations were seeing their interest rates going down because of the crisis. It was like a spontaneous, naturally occurring quantitative easing for the rich Eurozone nations, caused by the collapse of the poorer ones. For many in Germany, this was the natural order of things – market discipline at work. An ECB intervention would be illegal under the Maastricht Treaty prohibition on 'monetary financing'. Maastricht anticipated and forbade governments funding them-selves using money magically created by their central bank. Even putting that aside, for the ECB to intervene in a manner routine in London and Washington would have required value judgements to be made and risks to be taken on Greek debt, Irish debt and Italian debt. In the year before Draghi's presidency began, two high-profile protectors of Germanic instincts on the governing council, Jürgen Stark and Axel Weber, resigned amid concern about the bank purchasing such debts. Their only answer was '*Nein*'.

Silvio versus the ECB

'The ECB is not here to bail out Silvio Berlusconi,' one leading ECB figure told me in private. The previous year, 2011, relations between the ECB and the mercurial Italian leader had been torrid. In the Italian budget crises of the 1960s and 70s, the Bank of Italy, the country's central bank, could be relied on and was legally obliged to buy up Italian government bonds – a form of monetary financing. In 1973 Governor Guido Carli wrote in the Bank of Italy's annual report that to abstain from buying his government's debt 'would be a seditious act. . . refusal would make it impossible for the government to pay the salaries of civil servants and the pensions of most citizens'. So Berlusconi's 2011 gambit that the ECB would buy up Italian bonds had a grounding in Italian history, even if it was entirely at odds with the German conception of what the bank should be doing. In May 2010, at the beginning of the Greek crisis, the ECB had created the Securities Markets Programme (SMP) to buy Greek government debt for about a month, with the aim of lowering effective borrowing rates and defusing the panic in bond markets.

A year on, the conflagration had spread to Italy, with its stagnant economy, its dysfunctional political system mired in sleaze and its giant mountain of public debt. Italian and Spanish bond yields were rising dangerously above 6 per cent against a backdrop of possible Greek euro exit. The gold price was surging, the USA was about to lose its AAA rating. At its August meeting in Frankfurt, the ECB governing council discussed Italy's problems, but no consensus was reached on whether or not to resume the purchase of Italian bonds.

The following day the ECB's then and future presidents, Trichet and Draghi, wrote an extraordinary secret letter, in English, to Berlusconi, outlining steps they required the Italian government to take in order 'to urgently underpin the standing of its sovereign signature'. Existing budget plans were 'important steps, but not sufficient'. Large-scale privatisations, reform of wage bargaining, a review of hiring and firing laws, and a speeding up of spending cuts were all specified as 'essential' for something – implicitly the ECB's purchase of Italian bonds – though that was left unsaid. For good measure the letter also specified the legal method through which Berlusconi should make the changes: 'as soon as possible with decree-laws, followed by parliamentary ratification by end September 2011'. The letter concluded with a terse sign-off: 'We trust that the government will take all appropriate actions. Mario Draghi, Jean-Claude Trichet'. On the same day Berlusconi announced at a press conference that Italy would balance its budget one year early, by 2013, a key demand of the ECB letter. Italy's economic sovereignty seemed at a low ebb at this point. (Three months later the European Commission's Olli Rehn would outdo even Draghi and Trichet when he sent Berlusconi a thirty-nine-point questionnaire about his reform plans, with a request that the Italian leader append his answers and send them back to Brussels by return.)

When questioned about their intrusions into national sovereignty, the executive members of the ECB's governing council are rather defensive. 'I don't accept the premise of your question,' one told me. 'We were not aiming to interfere in any way with the political process of any country. We were, as we should be, providing advice. We were saying what could be useful for the countries themselves to improve their situation in markets. Our role is to provide advice, so we could not impose anything.' His words seemed rather inconsistent with the tone of the peremptory letter sent to Berlusconi.

At the IMF, officials looked on with interest. 'The ECB made desperate attempts to solve the problem by relaunching the SMP for Italy, with some "conditionality" being negotiated directly,' one of them reflected. 'Of course Berlusconi would say yes to everything, the ECB would buy the bonds, and then suddenly the next day [he] would renege on all his promises.' The ECB at that point was effectively underwriting Berlusconi in office. He had survived a budget vote after a month, but had severe trouble over other elements of Italian economic reform, and then began backtracking on unpopular elements of the package. The ECB essentially stopped buying Italian bonds.

On 19 October 2011, 200,000 Greeks protested outside the Greek parliament, amidst Molotov cocktails, tear gas and riot police. In Paris on the same day, President Sarkozy's wife Carla Bruni went into labour, while the president himself was attempting to give birth to a new European order. The unwieldy management of the euro crisis was to be replaced with an executive 'economic government'. Sarkozy flew straight from Carla Bruni's maternity ward in Paris to a meeting at Frankfurt's Old Opera House. The day had been set aside as a formal farewell to the departing ECB president, his fellow countryman Jean-Claude Trichet. Some 1,800 guests, including a host of luminaries, paid various degrees of tribute. The former German chancellor, Helmut Schmidt, warned of the 'dramatic failure up until now of the European Union's political bodies to contain the dangerous turbulence and uncertainty'. He continued: 'What we have, in fact, is a crisis of the ability of the European Union's political bodies to act. This glaring weakness of action is a much greater threat to the future of Europe than the excessive debt levels of individual euro area countries.' The incumbent German chancellor, Angela Merkel, put it like this: 'If the euro fails, then Europe fails. But we will not allow that, for the future of Germany was, is and remains for us connected with the future of Europe.' The celebration ended with a ceremonial handing over of the ECB chairman's bell from Jean-Claude Trichet to Mario Draghi.

In the evening the ECB had arranged the opening gala of a month of Italian cultural events, ironically coinciding with the moment that Italian political dysfunction seemed on the verge of bringing down the entire project. The Treaty of Rome created the European project, yet in Rome that project now floundered. In the programme notes, Mario Draghi reminded concert-goers that 'one of the first seeds of the idea of a united, federal Europe was the Ventotene Manifesto, drafted in 1941 by Ernesto Rossi and Altiero Spinelli, two ardent Italian anti-fascists who were confined by the regime to the little island of Ventotene'. He reminded his listeners that 2011 was also the 150th anniversary of Italian political unity, 'after a lengthy process that led to the formation of a single conscience'.

At a more private leaving party for ECB president Trichet, the sound of Claudio Abbado conducting Rossini's *Barber of Seville* floated through the Old Opera House. President Sarkozy, obsessed with the notion of 'economic government' for Europe, developed the concept of the 'Groupe de Francfort' (GdF), a tight executive of elected leaders and unelected eurocrats to drive forward decisive action to end the crisis. It would be a political and fiscal foil to the European Central Bank. However, Sarkozy faced strong resistance to his plan to give Europe's bailout fund, the EFSF, a banking licence and therefore access to ECB funding, a move that would have increased the bailout fund's firepower into the trillions. Undeterred, at a subsequent summit Sarkozy arranged for GdF pin badges to be distributed to his selected crisis A-team. President Obama dropped in on one meeting. The GdF also seemed to take against Berlusconi, who was publicly laughed at by Merkel and Sarkozy at a summit meeting. In Brussels, they joked that the 'Groupe' existed mainly in Sarkozy's head. Financial markets continued to test Europe's capacity to provide rescues for too-big-to-fail Spain and too-big-to-bail Italy.

After the ECB reduced its bond purchases, Italian yields shot back up to an even less sustainable 7 per cent. In a steamy and chaotic frenzy of plots and intrigue, Berlusconi eventually resigned. It seemed to be a direct result of the ECB. Senior figures in Italy say that this is an exaggeration, and that Berlusconi had already lost his coalition. Either way, Berlusconi would never forget the behaviour of the central bankers in Frankfurt. Evidently, refusing to buy Italian government bonds was no longer 'seditious'. And at the ECB and in Berlin they would not forget the difficulty of enforcing conditionality on big European states. When asked if Italy had effectively taken the money and run, senior Berlin officials are clear: 'Very nakedly it was this. It's a clear expression that if you don't have a system with reliable conditionality, you can't give them the money.'

The ECB, Ireland's bailout and the world's worst bank

There are analogous stories about the power exercised by the ECB in Ireland, Spain and Cyprus. A former member of the Eurogroup of finance ministers estimates that 70 per cent of what is decided at their summits has been written in advance by the European Central Bank. Ireland thought it had done everything right. In the lead-up to the crisis it had mainly kept to its Brussels borrowing limits. Post-crisis, in its dealings with other members of the Troika, the Irish were lionised: 'The Irish government was a delight,' a senior Troika figure told me. 'The Irish were extremely pragmatic, they wanted to put an agreement in place quickly. We never had to twist their arm or anything. And they always wanted to do the toughest stuff up-front, and they wanted to cut wages by 20 per cent across the board, which is unbelievable. So Ireland was not a problem at all.'

Across a table in Merrion Street, Dublin, in early 2011, the officials of Ireland's department of finance debated with nego-tiators from the Troika. There was not much to negotiate, because there were 190 conditions laid down by the Troika, all of which the Irish government wanted to implement in any case. All the unpopular ones could now be blamed on 'overlords' from the IMF and ECB. It was political cover for a reboot of Ireland. But there was one giant cloud: its rotten banks – in particular, Anglo Irish Bank. It was a cloud that had lingered from the start of Ireland's descent into the bailout club.

Anglo Irish was a basket-case bank, an all-encompassing bet on a never-ending Irish property bubble. Once awarded the title of 'world's best bank', it was fairly close to being the worst, in a competitive field. The skeleton of Anglo's flashy unfinished headquarters in the Dublin docklands, with a Ferrari dealership next door, is the symbol of Ireland's excess. Still, that excess would have been a matter for Ireland's coterie of corrupt, prop-erty-addled bankers, were it not for a disastrous decision made in 2008. That year the Irish government guaranteed all deposits, and then all lending, including the financial market bondholders who funded Ireland's lending binge. Unlike ordinary depositors, they would have expected to reap the consequences of their commercial bets. No more. Free-market capitalism had been put on hold amidst the global financial panic. The bondholder bankers, most of them foreign, were guaranteed too – a blanket guarantee of €440 billion, about three times the size of Ireland's entire annual economic output. It was, at first, an inexpensive way of stemming a bank run, as it cost little up-front. The late finance minister Brian Lenihan called it 'the cheapest bank bailout in history'. In the UK it provoked official panic, as massive flows of deposits went west across the Irish Sea, in pursuit of those generous guarantees. But two years on, when the guarantees were called, the cheap talk proved to be fatally expensive.

'If you knew it was going to cost €30 billion, the sensible thing for the Irish government to do would have been to have closed it down to depositors and for bondholders to have to taken a hit,' one of Ireland's most senior policymakers told me. 'For the Irish authorities in retrospect, I think it was a very bad mistake.' Anglo Irish did not have cash machines, and could not be considered systemic for the functioning of ordinary deposits or the payments system.

The first guarantee of September 2008 was an Irish sovereign decision. Indeed, the 'Anglo Tapes' of internal conversations of its bankers from just before this decision showed the contempt Anglo Irish had for Irish taxpayers. Not only was an initial negotiation of €7 billion a number 'picked out of my arse', but the senior bankers also plotted to lure a small amount of taxpayer funding, knowing that the government would never be able to stop and would not get its money back. It is true that it was in keeping with European policy that 'no bank should fail' after the Lehman Brothers crash, but the decision was made on flawed grounds, by Irish politicians. The second guarantee, made in November 2010, is more complex.

For the previous few weeks, the Irish government had been reluctant to embark on a Troika programme. The 'two Brians' (finance minister Lenihan and Taioseach Cowen) felt that having funded their sovereign borrowing requirements until mid-2011 there was no need for the dead hand of the inspectors. If a programme was needed, they felt they had maximum bargaining power to limit their loss of sovereignty. That seemed to be mainly defined by keeping Ireland's 12.5 per cent rate of corporation tax, the lowest in the Eurozone, and a totem of the Celtic Tiger. The policy had attracted tech giants such as Apple, Google and

Microsoft, as well as Europe's bankers. 'Corporation tax had to be got off the agenda before we'd even start talking,' said one Dublin official. 'We made no bones about talking about being fully funded in mid-2011. With a bank run on, it wasn't really in our interests to prolong it, but we could hold out for longer.' Secret, plausibly deniable, negotiations had started with Brussels commissioner Olli Rehn in September 2010.

Frankfurt was the ultimate determinant of Dublin's fate in three ways. First there was the intervention in Irish government bonds under the SMP (in the same manner that was to occur in Italy a year later). As market interest rates for Irish government debt spiked to nearly 9 per cent, Lenihan requested that Frankfurt continue purchases, eventually revealed at €14 billion. The ECB's fiscal hawks wanted to see that Ireland's deficits were under control, and proposed even bigger spending cuts and tax rises. Ireland had not had a property tax since Fianna Fáil's Jack Lynch won a thumping landslide in 1977 after promising to abolish rates. Ireland managed to vote itself into a tax system where half its citizens paid no income tax. Irish people paid no direct charges for their water and sewerage. Ireland had raised entitlements, for example offering €535 a month in child benefit for families with three children, over double the level in the UK (£185). The Troika was puzzled to discover that neutral Ireland paid its military chief more than militarily busy Britain. All of this was made possible on the rotten fruit of an unsustainable property boom.

Second, and more importantly, was the question of Ireland's 'addict' banks. The 2008 guarantee for Anglo Irish and other rescued Irish banks merely gave the opportunity for depositors and market funding to exit stage left. How did the banks pay for the real and electronic cash being withdrawn, given withered funding and apparent insolvency? Principally by recourse to funding from Ireland's central bank, part of the eurosystem, and increasingly via ELA emergency funding ('emergency liquidity assistance' is the official name, although in Ireland officials rebranded ELA as 'exceptional' or 'extraordinary' after realising that the assistance was not going anywhere). In total the ECB funding was worth more than Ireland's entire €160 billion GDP. The Irish economy made up less than 2 per cent of the Eurozone, but Ireland received 25 per cent of all loans made by central banks within the Eurozone. Emergency funds were designed to be advanced to solvent banks facing a liquidity problem under the centuries-old doctrine of 'lender of last resort'. The precise parameters of solvency were, however, unclear under the policy of 'constructive ambiguity' designed to prevent moral hazard by banks. In other words, the central bankers would not identify in advance how they would rescue troubled banks, because, rightly, they feared bankers would abuse the privilege and indulge in risky funding, knowing they would be supported by their central bank. Unfortunately, the ambiguity was more destructive than constructive.

In October 2010 the ECB tightened its risk control framework (its rules on emergency funding), seemingly with Ireland in mind, which brings us to the third way in which Frankfurt defined Ireland's fate. A series of letters, phone calls and faxes were sent from Frankfurt to Dublin expressing concern at the level of ECB funding. The ECB 'were a little coy' – there were no defined threats to withdraw funding, but the Irish Department of Finance was left with the clear impression that life could be made difficult, through changes to charges and collateral rules. In a secret letter Trichet let it be known that the ECB was exposed and Ireland needed to shape up. The general tone of the letter, one member of the ECB governing council told me, was 'There's got to be a programme or there's going to be trouble.' Two and a half years later, in Cyprus, the ECB were not so shy, and directly threatened to withdraw the emergency bank support in terse public declarations, following a Cypriot parliamentary vote against a Troika programme (see Chapter 13, page 398).

In Dublin back in November 2010, obliging a nation to take a 'voluntary' bailout was proving rather tricky. The crisis was beginning to affect other nations. Major financial news-wires were briefed that Ireland was negotiating a bailout. Irish ministers insisted that this was 'a fiction'. The by-lines of these reports tended to be Frankfurt. Other powerful European finance ministries, when asked about the source of the Irish bailout rumours, suggested 'Try a city in Germany that is not Berlin.' It wasn't Leipzig either. Nor was it just Frankfurt. In a radio interview with the *Irish Times* journalist Dan O'Brien just a few weeks before his death, Brian Lenihan described arriving at a Eurogroup finance ministers meeting late on account of Brussels fog. The ministers proclaimed that 'the functioning of the single currency was at stake'. At that point German finance minister Wolfgang Schäuble asked Lenihan to leave the meeting and announce that Ireland was seeking a bailout. Lenihan refused, saying he had no authority. Still Ireland resisted. At that Brussels meeting Irish journalists were asking German journalists what was happening in Ireland.

Two days later, something remarkable happened. Ireland's central bank governor, Patrick Honohan, also a member of that ECB governing council, rang up Ireland's main morning radio show and invited himself on air from Frankfurt. He revealed the likelihood of a bailout worth 'tens of billions of euros', and that teams from the ECB, IMF and EU were already in Dublin. In fact, Honohan was to chair a meeting with the officials within the hour. Honohan had consulted neither of the two Brians. It felt like a monetary coup d'état. He explained that he had been texted about a *Financial Times* leader article entitled 'Europe heads back into the storm', which suggested that preparations should be made 'for a run on the Irish banks spreading'. The governor was talking in his financial-stability capacity to prevent concern about such media commentary resulting in actual bank runs. Ireland's elected government felt that it was being bounced into applying for a bailout by the ECB's man in Dublin. A large swathe of the Irish public felt that the truth was finally being revealed about what they regarded as a duplicitous and incompetent government. Indeed, days later the government collapsed. Senior Frankfurt figures say it is 'absolutely not true' that the ECB pushed Ireland. Yet the crucial letter remains secret. And in Cyprus, very nakedly, this is exactly what happened. In both cases, however, the ECB argues that the *really* extraordinary intervention was their toleration of huge emergency liquidity funding for months on end in the first place. Bankrupt banks should not get life support. The Troika programmes ensured that the ECB would be repaid.

Frankfurt undeniably *did* intervene in one matter. The Irish government was minded to burn those bondholders who held now unguaranteed Anglo Irish debt in late 2010. The IMF agreed that losses should not just be nationalised, but shared with bankers. 'And at that stage,' a senior Irish policymaker told me, 'their hand was stayed by Europe and particularly by the European Central Bank. It made the cost-benefit analysis and said "This is not a good idea."' The ECB believed that fully honouring the outstanding debts of Anglo Irish was 'the least damaging course'. The Irish government made the same cost-benefit analysis and concluded that it could not afford to throw around €5 billion or 3 per cent of GDP away. 'So at that stage,' my informant went on, 'clearly Ireland did take a hit for Europe.' The burden of paying Ireland's bank debt, particularly the ECB emergency funds, (not just Anglo Irish, also the bankrupt Irish Nationwide) was transferred to the Irish state through a €31 billion promissory note. It always had the sniff of an accounting fiddle. The stream of annual payments of €3.1 billion or 2 per cent of Ireland's GDP, was, however very real. It was to last a decade, with smaller payments afterwards, essentially to pay interest.

It was Ireland's misfortune that it was the subject of the first experiment with a formal bailout facility. There was no form book, manual or real precedent. Much of the documentation developed by the Troika for Ireland was emailed over for a name-change and deployed again for Portugal six months later. Some of the experimental mistakes were later unwound. Brian

Lenihan would remind his staff that 'Every time you issue debt you lose sovereignty.' But the island's sovereignty was dripping away towards Frankfurt more than any Irish politician could have appreciated. Every time a decision needed to be made, it seemed to emphasise that it would be Irish taxpayers and their children and grandchildren who would pay the bill for obscene banking excess, rather than the international funders of the guilty banks. The ECB was a driving force behind this. And this was just the first instance of the ECB stepping into areas where it had little mandate.

'It's true the ECB was involving itself in things it never planned to do,' one Eurozone central bank governor told me. 'Anything it lends to a bank in a certain country, there's a risk of default. That risk of default will be passed back to all seventeen other member countries. If it buys bonds of a government, same thing. Any losses will be carried by the taxpayers of those member states, who are otherwise expecting dividends from the central bank. So this is not something that is written into the mandate of the ECB. Nor did we ever imagine there would be issues of this type. So it gets drawn deeper and deeper into other types of policies.'

Putting specific conditionalities at a high level of its policy action 'is way beyond what the ECB was imagined to do'. But not just that, now it is involved directly in the Troika teams devising the conditionality. Why? Because it has large teams of trained financial economists. The ECB is very close to the action and has been asked by the rest of Europe to get involved. So for all these reasons the ECB is getting into territory that it wasn't designed for.

The Irish government and central banker Patrick Honohan did, in 2013, lighten the burden of the promissory note. By liquidating the company holding the remnants of Anglo Irish and Irish Nationwide, essentially the promissory note was swapped for a series of long-term government bonds of up to forty years. The principal, the stock of the loan, would essentially not be repaid until the 2040s. An odious debt had become merely abominable. However, the net burden on the Irish state had been slashed from €25 billion to €1.4 billion over the next decade. The net present value of the repayments had been cut by 35 per cent according to University College Dublin economics professor Karl Whelan. The flipside was that the costs of the debt crisis would still be being paid half a century on. Still, the Bundesbank was concerned that the deal violated Article 123 of the Maastricht Treaty, the famed prohibition on monetary financing. The ECB neither stopped, nor endorsed the deal, but released a neutral statement saying the Irish decision had been 'noted'. The Bundesbank and other northern central banks vowed to check each year that the Irish deal was not a backdoor version of printing money.

There was one amusing, even bitter, irony at the end of all this. The shell of the totemic uncompleted headquarters of Anglo Irish on the Dublin dockside was eventually sold to a wealthy new tenant for a knockdown price. In the crazy years, it had been valued at €250 million. The new purchasers bought it off the National Asset Management Agency (NAMA) – Ireland's 'bad bank' – for €7 million. From 2015 it will be the new head-quarters of the Central Bank of Ireland, and, effectively, the embassy of the ECB in Dublin.

Back in the Eurotower, teams of economists run the slide rule over the economic metrics of existing and potential member states. Staff at the ECB – like northern donor-nation finance ministers and some officials in Brussels – describe the policies that programme nations are obliged to pursue as 'homework'. (The word features in internal ECB presentations.) Latvia is held up as the poster boy of how 'internal devaluation' can work. In 2012, just three years after its austerity programme, the Latvian economy grew by 5 per cent. Latvia retained its peg to the euro, rather than devalue its currency. Yet it endured a brutal collapse, a 20 per cent shrinkage in the size of its economy. 'Austerity' does not really work as a description for a programme in which nearly a third of public-sector staff were fired, and the salaries of the lucky majority that kept their jobs were cut by 40 per cent. Taxes were hiked, and benefits slashed. One in ten Latvians have left the country since 2000, half of them after 2008. Yet in the Eurotower, Latvia is considered a grand success. The principal difference between it and, say, Greece, is that Latvia began the 'adjustment' with a debt that represented only 7 per cent of GDP, an extraordinarily low level. The programme left it with a merely normal debt level. The Latvian lessons may be rather limited. At the Eurotower, they at least now focus on the institutional structure of a nation. Latvia's capacity for self-flagellation, and its acceptance of punishment from others, rather sets it apart.

Refinancing the Eurozone banking system

As he started his new job in 2011, Mario Draghi was learning much larger lessons about the Eurozone. He set about managing the ECB's unique political economy. He lavished praise on the Bundesbank, at the same time as cutting interest rates and pumping hundreds of billions of euros into the Eurozone banking system. The cut in Eurozone interest rates – at his second governing council meeting – was the first time that the ECB's German chief economist, Jürgen Stark, had effectively been overruled. With inflation at 3 per cent, already well above the target level of 2 per cent, Stark had suggested waiting to see the impact of price pressures. For the German economic establishment, the euromark was turning into the eurolira. Every few days Draghi would offer a rhetorical sacrifice at the Teutonic monetary altar. Yet he was doing something rather less in keeping with German sensibilities. After that meeting in December 2011, I asked him why he did not simply do what was standard practice in London and Washington and 'print money' by buying government debt on a massive scale?

'We have a treaty,' he replied, 'and the treaty states what our primary mandate is, namely to maintain price stability. Also, the treaty prohibits monetary financing. I am old enough to remember that, when this treaty was written in the early 1990s, some of the countries around that table were actually doing what you suggest doing now, namely some of the central banks of these countries were financing the government expenditure of their governments through money creation, and the consequences were there for all of us to see. That is why, in a sense, this treaty embodies the best tradition of the Deutsche Bundesbank, whereby monetary financing has always been prohibited.'

Yet at the same time, one trillion euros were being ploughed into the Eurozone banking system via the LTRO (long-term refinancing operations). Some of this found its way back into government bond markets, through the banking system. This was not so far off the *verboten* quantitative easing. But it spectacularly calmed the worst excesses of Eurozone bank panic. Dollar funding that had basically stopped for French banks, for example, restarted. This echoed an earlier inconsistency under Jean-Claude Trichet. Direct sovereign bond purchases from governments were prohibited, and instead were bought from the financial markets. The purchases were 'sterilised' with offsetting 'sales' – essentially one-week deposits. The idea was that the inflationary impact of bond purchases would be neutralised. When it came to private debt held by banks, secured by property, then no such safeguards were required. The ECB launched two programmes for 'covered bonds', the German-designed instrument that had seen no defaults since its creation by Frederick the Great in the mid-eighteenth century. Was the €400 billion of covered bonds that were secured on Spanish real estate really less risky than a sovereign bond? (See Chapter 8, pages 247–49.) Is there any reason why it is any more moral to fund a private bank's credit excess and yet absolutely prohibit direct funding of a nation's fiscal excess? In a tight squeeze, the ECB programme did help maintain, against the odds, the incredible historical record of Frederick the Great's creation.

At Axel Weber's farewell in May 2011, following his resignation, Trichet, in a manner described as 'poisonous' by the

Frankfurter Allgemeine Zeitung, politely omitted any mention of the bitter public debate over ECB purchases of government bonds. Trichet instead 'delightfully' explained that the ECB had 'followed Axel's advice' in deciding to support the 'German innovation' of covered bonds from May 2009. It was the 'most notable' contribution of Bundesbank expertise to the ECB's crisis-fighting weaponry, Trichet said. Put slightly differently, in other respects the Bundesbank was far from helpful.

'The Bundesbank has this habit of following up what has been decided after a governing council agreement. This is not correct,' another central bank governor suggested to me. 'The idea is that [Jens] Weidmann [Bundesbank president and a member of the governing council] is speaking for himself. He is not there on behalf of the Bundesbank. It helps him form an idea, but these are not country or [national] central bank-backed decisions. It is the ECB council's decision.'

The de facto president of Europe

It is July 2012, the eve of the London Olympics. Around the Eurozone, Greece has managed to stay in the club, Cyprus has just begun its game of trying to stave off a bailout for a few months, and Italy, Spain and Europe's banks are still borrowing at disastrous rates. Indecisive political summitry has left the dangerous doom loop between sovereign and banking debt intact and reinforced. It is going to take an Olympian effort to douse the Eurozone's flames. Mario Draghi arrived at a conference nakedly designed by the British government to promote investment and trade on the back of the Olympic opening ceremony. Cookies dusted with icing sugar and formed in the shape of the Olympic rings tempt delegates. Mayor Boris Johnson entertains CEOs from across the world with jokes about how London has more Michelin-starred restaurants than Paris and less rain than Rome. The setting is Lancaster House, a mansion owned by the UK Foreign and Commonwealth Office. The place has seen some history – including the birth of new nation-states such as Malaysia, South Africa and Zimbabwe. And before that, in 1944, it was in Lancaster House that the European Advisory Committee of the UK, USA and the Soviet Union first recommended the postwar partition of Germany and its capital, Berlin.

Whether it was history, bonhomie or the inspiration of competitive sport, Mario Draghi pushed the ECB and Europe further than it had gone before. In off-the-cuff remarks, he at first likened the euro to a bumble bee that 'should not fly', one that was in the process of 'graduating into becoming a real bee'. He rambled on about how the Eurozone's employment, debt and deficit numbers were better than those of the USA and Japan, and how Europe had a 'degree of social cohesion you would not find in those two countries'. It raised the odd eyebrow amongst the highbrow audience. But he had a central message to the world: 'The euro is irreversible.' This was because of the political capital invested by Europe in the project.

Then, with the shuffle of an actor about to deliver the killer line of a play, he looked down at his notes. 'There is another message I want to tell you today. Within our mandate, the ECB is ready to do whatever it takes to preserve the euro.' He paused for dramatic effect, before continuing, 'And, believe me, it will be enough.'

The remarks were prepared, but unscripted. Confusion reigned outside. Had Draghi finally announced the 'bazooka'? Or was he just riffing? One of his G7 colleagues felt that the ECB president had genuinely believed that he simply could not do UK-style bond purchases, and the trillion-euro LTRO bank-funding operation would solve the Eurozone problem. 'No one off operation can do that, though,' one of Europe's most senior central bankers told me. 'A current account deficit needs perpetual flows to fund it.' The Draghi speech was not planned, it had no formal text, but after seeing that the LTRO was no longer working, my informant opined that 'Draghi saw no point in presiding over the sinking of the euro'.

The markets gave a rapturous reception to Mario's musings. But the remarks had not been cleared with other members of the governing council, nor, it appeared, with members of his own staff. He spent the next few weeks working hard to get around the objections of the Bundesbank. Draghi did not actually have the authority to promise 'whatever it takes'. Like Mo Farah running the 10,000 metres at the Olympic Park, Draghi was bouncing the Germans into running at his pace.

In August the blueprint was outlined, and by September the details of the programme known as Outright Monetary Transactions (OMT) had been fleshed out. The Bundesbank briefed against the plan, and Jens Weidmann never voted for it. But Merkel and the new French president, François Hollande, did back the approach, despite German critiques of Draghi.

In Berlin, Chancellor Merkel had entertained Chinese investors and the leaders of smaller EU nations. All warned her of the impact of jettisoning Greece from the Eurozone – the ballast theory. She went with the domino concept, and backed Draghi's efforts. As one influential observer of the Eurozone put it: '[Before July 2012] The ECB seemed to detach itself from an interest in the survival of the currency of which it was the central bank, which I think was totally disastrous. . . it was like a priest arguing against the existence of God.' Draghi had changed that, and he had brought Merkel with him.

OMT was a lifeline as Europe squabbled over new rules for fiscal and banking union. The clever part was designed to avoid the Berlusconi-style run-around of the year before. Unlimited bond purchases were on offer, but only for governments with agreed EU bailout programmes, inspections and conditionalities. The idea was that the elevated interest rates charged by markets to borrowing Eurozone nations could be decomposed into a part due to the fiscal profligacy of that nation, and a part due to the existential fear about the collapse of the Eurozone. As Ignazio Visco, governor of the Italian central bank, explained to Italian newspapers in Rome, two-fifths of the spread between Italian and German borrowing rates was fair. The other 300 basis points, the additional 3 per cent interest rate premium charged to the Italians, was down to the redenomination risk of a euro collapse and the return of the lira. The point of OMTs was to shrink the interest premium charged because of fear of euro collapse, while maintaining the tough conditionality required to shrink interest charged to cover domestic fiscal risks. Draghi called it 'a fully effective backstop to prevent potentially destructive scenarios'. A colleague of his on the governing council said, 'It is a bridge that basically shows you cannot grow Europe by monetary means, but it is a bridge that makes the euro irreversible.'

The very clever thing about the OMT was the sheer cunning of its game theory. For the first year, OMT achieved the Holy Grail: it offered a theoretically unlimited intervention to scare markets off, but was sufficiently credible to be believed – so much so that it was not actually required. It was a magic trick, or perhaps more precisely a confidence trick. Not a cent was spent, but confidence returned and interest spreads collapsed. Draghi had killed the doomsday scenario. The euro was here to stay.

This was 'conditional irreversibility', which sounded like a fundamental internal contradiction. Others in Germany felt that Draghi had cunningly limbo-danced under an important red line. The natural result of this would surely be the weakening of 'market pressure' on the programme nations for economic reforms and borrowing discipline.

The OMT is essentially an ambulance with doors that will not open if the injuries are self-inflicted. In reality, if tested, the distinction would prove rather arbitrary. If a country qualified, and then reneged on the conditions, then the ECB is supposed to sell bonds, in a mildly punitive manner. This would go well beyond the 'seditious' and connote effective control. It would be unthinkable for, say, the US Federal Reserve to do this to a bankrupt California. 'Does the ECB pull the plug and cause another crisis in this case?' asks one leading central banker. 'The Bundesbank can see this. The German people were promised that the ECB was a Bundesbank for Europe. It's not.' There is no difficulty seeing why the Germans felt OMT was a pathway to a more straightforward form of monetary financing, and likened it to a narcotic.

The key question, however, is this: why did Jens Weidmann, president of the Bundesbank, not resign? Two German predecessors resigned over similar versions of the same policy. Equally, it is difficult to imagine how this scheme would have survived without the tacit backing of Chancellor Merkel. She was already taking a considerable domestic political risk in backing an Italian to head the ECB. Trichet went as far as he could, given there was no explicit transfer union (the promise to transfer funds from wealthy and fast-growing parts of the EU to the poorer parts, a fundamental practical and theoretical feature of any currency union, but not the Eurozone). The ECB is becoming the backdoor mechanism for an implicit transfer union that most economists feel is necessary for the euro's long-term survival. Nobody has told the German public that it is their historic duty to fund the Eurozone, just as Spanish, Greek and Italian politicians are unwilling, explicitly, to tell their public that the price of euro membership is lower wages. The default line runs straight through the middle of the doughnut-shaped table in the ECB's governing council meeting room.

There are two democratic deficits in the whole way that the European Central Bank is seeking to save the euro. For crisis nations the ECB is stepping beyond its mandate in inflicting conditionalities upon sovereign states. For donor nations, the ECB is beyond its mandate in its role as a backdoor transfer union.

'The way we designed OMT was exactly to address this point,' says one of the architects of Draghi's plan. 'To make sure that our action is being complemented by clear political decisions by the national governments, coping with their own problems. If we had done this like we did it two years ago with the SMP, which was formally, officially unconditional, I think we would have been much less effective.' Yet, I ask him, is this not just fudging the issue of lack of democratic accountability, whereby Germany is obliged to pay up, and the crisis nations are obliged to endure more pain? 'The democratic legitimacy of this is guaranteed,' he responds, 'because the debtor countries have to go to their parliaments to legislate for fiscal consolidation or structural reforms. The creditor nations too, when they use the European Stability Mechanism have to go to their parliaments in Germany, or the Netherlands. So all in all the OMT has improved democratic accountability.'

Alternatively, one might say that the policy had bought a year's space and relative calm ahead of Germany's 2013 federal elections. In the meantime, however, the European Central Bank had a fundamental change of view about how to make economic and monetary union function. A fiscal pact was now necessary but insufficient for the euro. The experience of Spain and Ireland showed that the euro required oversight of the continent's banking systems too. Both nations had descended into financial bedlam, despite mainly sticking to the euro's Stability Pact. The problems had come in the banking system. The ECB was willing to step up. Yet it had absolutely no experience of banking supervision.

Suddenly the ECB's democratic deficit threatens to turn into a chasm. The origins of the need for central-bank independence over monetary policy have strong foundations. But is a strong political independence appropriate when the central bank is the driving force behind labour-reform policies, fiscal plans, and now continent-wide banking policy?

By 2014, the ECB will face its first of a series of huge new tests. Lee Buchheit, the lawyer who helped Greece renegotiate its private sector debts (see pages 16–20), feels it is going only one way: Official Sector Involvement. Again the instinct to acronymise a problem remains strong. OSI really means that the official sector, and the taxpayers that fund the official sector, will be asked to provide debt relief to the countries whose private creditors have been paid out using official sector loans. Basically Germany and friends face a cruel choice in 2014.

'This could be accomplished through a haircut to the principal of official-sector loans, but that is unlikely to be politically palatable in northern Europe,' says Buchheit. 'The alternative is a long-term stretch-out of the maturity date of the loans. A stretch-out would allow northern European politicians the dignity of saying to their taxpayers: "Citizens, we shall get every euro back that we lent to those countries, perhaps not in our lifetimes, but sometime down the road."'

There is an amazing contrast with how the Americans, Europeans and Japanese dealt with the Latin American debt crisis of the 1980s and 1990s. During that crisis also, it was publicly denied that there would be write-offs. Quietly, though, banks were padded up, accountants pressured and loan-loss provisions made, all of which meant that, after a few years, the banks that lent the defaulters the cash ended up bearing the losses. But the banks survived. In the euro crisis, instead, governments and central banks stepped into the firing line instead of the banks. So taxpayers face taking the hit that their banks did not.

'It's the equivalent of the guys in the tumbrel watching the folks going to the guillotine and right at the last moment saying: "Why don't we change places?" Then you hop into the tumbrel and then they get out,' Lee Buchheit told me.

'Those who so fiercely opposed any form of sovereign-debt restructuring in Europe, and the senior management of the ECB was probably the epicentre of this sentiment, did so in the belief that such a step would threaten the very existence of the European monetary union. Far better, they argued, to monetise every sovereign-debt instrument south of the Rhine than to risk the demolition of the euro itself.'

Frankfurt absolutely does not say this, even privately. No German politician was really saying this either, at the opportune moment to win a mandate, in the run-up to Germany's 2013 federal election. The decision to bail out banks funding the Eurozone periphery, and then haggle later on about who would pay for the fact that the banks did not, was the fundamental judgement call. No one has been held to account on this. The ECB does, however, quietly seem to be preparing the ground for a massive centralisation of power.

If the ECB has its way, the Eurozone will have essentially a single banking system, a single currency, and a strict straitjacket on the capacity of its member-states to borrow. Right now, however, it takes credit for cunning manoeuvres that temporarily calm the storm, while blaming the acute social problems that have emerged on individual nations.

In December 2012, in the ECB's ground-floor conference centre, I asked Mr Draghi if record Eurozone unemployment was a 'price worth paying' for saving the euro. 'It is hard to say whether it is a price worth paying,' he replied. 'This question should rather be addressed to the policy-makers that created this situation to begin with. Let us not forget that we are in this situation... because of the poor policy-making, or the lack of policy-making, in the years before the crisis. The crisis has simply highlighted these disequilibria that already existed. It has high-lighted that our banks were not properly capitalised. It has highlighted that the budgetary and debt positions of our govern-ments were not sustainable, and, finally, it has highlighted that our euro area governance ought to be vastly improved. What is happening now is the direct outcome of the policy decisions that have been implemented in order to respond to these disequilibria that were unsustainable. I agree that it is a very hard price to pay, but it is unavoidable.' Journalists do not normally ask him about unemployment.

Frankfurt, like Berlin, blamed the scourge of youth unem-ployment on national governments. Even prime ministers elected on the slogan 'Austerity is killing us', would turn a little coy when asked who was doing the killing. Germany? The ECB? Enrico Letta, Italian prime minister from April 2013, responded to the question thus: 'Of course, it was the debt. Italy made enormous mistakes in the past raising the debt and now we need to have structural reforms, reduce the debt, but at the European level we need growth policies, not the austerity poli-cies of the last three years.'

Draghi felt the contractionary impact of budget cuts could be mitigated by German-style structural reforms to increase export competitiveness and create jobs and growth. But basically, yes, unemployment was a price worth paying for the policies designed to save the euro. It won't be the only price. Draghi faces a rollercoaster ride of persuading European politicians to set up some sort of permanent transfer system, essential to mitigate these types of problems in parts of the Eurozone. The perennial debate about whether Greece will leave will be the least of the worries of those who move into the new Eurotower. They are planning a novel architecture for Europe to deal with fiscal excess, banking mania and rampant unemployment – as well as over-priced pizzas.

Mario Draghi is 'a solutions-orientated guy' according to one of his colleagues around the doughnut-shaped table. But he has a lot of solutions to find. And Draghi is not just president of the European Central Bank. In the absence of any leadership elsewhere, Draghi is the de facto president of Europe.

CHAPTER 12

THE GREAT CARBON WARS

Dramatis personae

Jake Ulrich, 'the Carbon King'
Magne Normann, a hydrocarbon general
Dr Ashti Hawrami, oil minister of the Kurdistan Regional
Government (KRG) in northern Iraq
Tariq Shafiq, a co-author of the Iraqi central
government draft oil law
Sheikh Yamani, former Saudi oil minister (1962–86)
Jim Covert, developer
Anatoly Paramonov, Gazprom official who runs the
control room of the Central Operations and Dispatch
Department of Gazprom
Alexander Medvedov, Gazprom official
Yana Sukhushina, editor, Gazprom TV Project 24
Dmitri Nureyev, manager at Pestovoy number 16
Andrus Ansip, prime minister of Estonia (2005–)
Palan Halder, farmer in West Bengal
Jairam Ramesh, former Indian minister for power
Rahul Bajaj, Indian industrialist
Arthur Tait, carbon trader working for Gazprom
Andris Piebalgs, former European Commissioner for Energy
Professor Paul Klemperer, UK government adviser on
auctions, and Oxford University academic
Ed Miliband, UK energy secretary (2008–10)

Jake Ulrich is the Carbon King. He is the hydrocarbon version of the Man from Del Monte, a bounty hunter traversing the world's hot and cold spots trying to find fresh sources of warmth. Up until the financial crisis that meant the natural gas that heated most of Britain's homes and fuelled its cookers. Britain and Europe's North Sea reserves had peaked, and Ulrich's problem these days is that there aren't too many of the world's suppliers of gas and oil that like to say 'Yes'.

Ulrich's job is part geopolitical negotiator, part businessman, part financier. When I met him in 2008, crude oil prices had just reached $100 a barrel for the first time. Although he had seen at least two oil-rich presidents in the previous week, it was Jimmy Carter, US president during the 1970s oil crisis, that he invoked in our interview. In 1977, he reminded me, a cardigan-clad President Carter famously told Americans to wear a sweater and turn their thermostats down to save energy. Ulrich's message? High-cost energy is here to stay and people should adjust. 'I do think we will see people change their behaviour,' he said. 'I think people will use less energy. I hate to go back to the Jimmy Carter days in the USA, but maybe it's two jumpers instead of one.'

So, three decades after Carter's speech, one of the two leading figures at Centrica, Britain's biggest energy-supply company, was giving out the same message. 'I think people will change the temperature they keep the house,' Ulrich told me. 'They'll be more cognisant of energy waste, they'll buy better appliances.'

The message went down badly in the popular press. Ulrich's house was besieged by journalists, and the details of his executive pay package were splashed across the pages of the tabloids. People resented the fact that they were being told to adopt a more Spartan lifestyle by a multimillionaire. But his predictions were, of course, quite right.

A leaked industry report suggested that UK domestic gas prices could surge by 70 per cent, and then remain there, if oil prices stayed at $100. Ulrich's efforts to source alternatives to North Sea oil were being hampered by rampant resource nationalism

– the escalating tendency for countries with significant energy reserves to use their position as a geopolitical bargaining tool. By far the easiest, cheapest and greenest way to counter this tendency is for consumer countries to pursue energy efficiency on a national scale. The average internal temperature of a British house is 18 degrees – 5 degrees higher than in 1970. So it is clear that we have been spoiling ourselves. What Ulrich was signalling was the necessity of changing our behaviour – what economists might call 'demand destruction'. In simple terms, we need to turn down the national thermostat, and face the fact that we are entering a 'two jumpers' era, an era that marks the end of cheap, easy energy. But there is no sign yet that we are prepared to give up on the pursuit of hydrocarbons in the earth, even while carbon dioxide accumulates in the atmosphere.

So it's a global battle to acquire the carbon under us and clean up the carbon over us, too.

In the land of black gold

The oilman they call 'the General' surveys the terrain from Fishkhabour, a remote village at the northwestern tip of Iraq. A Turkish army observation post is visible on the other side of the River Khabur, the tributary of the Euphrates that marks the tense frontier between Iraq and Turkey. Turkish fighter jets can sometimes be heard in the skies above. Kurdish PKK rebels lurk in the nearby hills. Welcome to black gold's very last land frontier.

To the west of Fishkhabour lies Syria. But the General's interest is not in borderlines, but pipelines. Two pipelines, to be precise: one large, one somewhat smaller. The large one, which serves as Iraq's main northern oil artery, can be seen snaking its way north into Turkey. It is now gushing with black gold after years of routine sabotage by Kurdish insurgents. And then there's the General's own gutter-sized mini-pipeline. At this moment, in 2008, it just falls short of merging with its larger cousin. The gap is no more than 10 metres. 'We do not have approval to link into that pipeline at present,' says the General. 'We have been producing oil for a few months now, it's test production, but we intend to have a tie-in with the existing infrastructure through Iraq and into Turkey.'

The General, despite his nickname and his aviator glasses, is not a military man. Nor is he a Kurd, a Sunni or a Shia. His name is Magne Normann, and he is the first foreigner to hit new oil in Iraq, not just since the fall of Saddam in 2003, but since the late 1970s. A geologist, expert driller and occasional diplomat, Normann works for DNO, a tiny Norwegian oil company. The General and his band of local Kurds, expats and hired Chinese drillers struck oil at their first attempt, and there is more than a hint of *There Will Be Blood* about their quest to export it.

An area of natural oil seepage lies a few hundred metres from the Norwegian and Kurdish flags that mark the entrance to DNO's £150 million facility at Tawke, in Iraqi Kurdistan. It's littered with jerry cans used by local villagers to collect free fuel supplies. 'This is plain crude oil straight from the ground. It's engine quality,' says Normann as he stirs a stick through the slimy warm sludge bubbling to the surface.

He has reason to be elated. This brand-new field has 800 million barrels of oil in reservoirs deep underground. Officially Tawke ranks as a 'giant' field, but by Iraqi standards it is a tiddler. As the price of oil settles at around $100 per barrel, it should make a handsome profit for DNO and the Kurdish and Iraqi governments. And DNO has beaten even the reserve-hungry major oil companies to the prize.

'Nobody else wanted to go here,' says Norman with some pride. 'We were the first international oil company that had the guts to go to northern Iraq, and we made a discovery on the first exploration well we drilled. So far we can say we have been very successful.'

But there is a hitch. The DNO deal has been reached with the Kurdish Regional Government (KRG), and is yet to be signed off by Iraq's central government Ministry of Oil. In Baghdad the oil minister has threatened to blacklist any company signing oil concessions with the Kurds. For the General this means that the new oil discovery cannot yet be exported through his pipeline. The KRG oil minister Dr Ashti Hawrami says, ominously, that Baghdad's approach smacks of 'former regime tactics'. 'This is new oil for Iraq. We are doing our bit for Iraq. I just wish my colleagues in Baghdad would do the same,' says Hawrami.

Making the deal with the Norwegians and co-opting their expertise has helped the KRG bypass Baghdad entirely. The Kurds passed their own regional oil law after squabbling in the federal parliament in Baghdad over the terms of a proposed national oil law. The physical reality of DNO's ready-to-pump pipeline is now an audacious bargaining chip for the KRG. The Kurdish leadership is now dropping strong hints that it will soon announce unilateral export of oil.

Tariq Shafiq, a co-author of the central government's draft oil law and a veteran Iraqi oil engineer, says that this action could bring about the disintegration of Iraq. 'What Kurdistan gets will have to be given to others,' he says. 'It will create the envy of those who do not have oil. Oil is not distributed evenly throughout Iraq. They are really trespassing on Iraq's property and that is going to create damage beyond repair if they don't stop.'

The flags of Kurdistan and Norway flutter in the gusts of wind that swoop down the Tawke valley. The General does not want to talk politics, but he is confident he will soon get the export licence he needs to start earning hard currency for the $80 billion of oil stuck in the rock beneath his feet.

The basic technology of drilling, he tells me, hasn't changed since Colonel Drake first drilled for oil in Pennsylvania back in 1858: rock samples are flushed out by a white drilling fluid poured through the exploration drill. 'We look for the stain of oil in the drill cuttings,' Normann says. Fortunes ride on specks of viscous brown in the milky white fluid. The 'we' here is actually the Great Wall Drilling Company, owned by the Chinese government, which shipped over two of its biggest rigs and a few dozen drillers and geologists. Normann has no qualms about employing a company owned by a state that doesn't hide its hunger for hydrocarbon. US officials in Baghdad are rather relieved that it is a Norwegian oil company, albeit using Chinese drills, that is poised to become the first exporter of the new oil.

While pipeline politics keeps his pumps idle, the black-gold buccaneer back in Tawke has not been twiddling his thumbs. Normann has piped drinking water to the local village, and imported hospital equipment from Norway. 'Hearts and minds,' he declares. But he's also come up with an ingenious way to get his crude oil to local markets. Four tankers line up on top of one of his oil wells and are simultaneously filled with 200 barrels of warm crude oil spurting directly from three kilometres below ground. It must be the world's biggest fuel stop.

Iraq's potential wealth is staggering. Crude is even easier to extract in the south of the country, where the fields are so-called super-giants. Hawrami calculates that, with concerted investment, the nation's oil earnings could increase fivefold, to $200–$300 billion per year, creating 'five new Dubais' in Iraq's major cities and 'more money than the nation could ever spend'. Under Saddam, says Hawrami, Iraq's oil was a curse, used to buy weapons to kill the Kurdish people. Iraq, he says, should be planning its own sovereign wealth fund, to deal with the problem of having too much money.

Iraq could have chosen a more centralised state-run oil industry, keeping prices high by only slowly releasing its oil bounty onto world markets. Officially the plan is to rejoin OPEC's system of quotas for oil production, designed to keep the price high. However, Iraq's allegiance to the OPEC cartel could be somewhat compromised by the existence of a privatised, fragmented, competitive and market-driven industry in the north of the country.

For Iraq as a whole, one might argue that it would have been better to leave the oil in the ground. The country has been a victim of a particularly vicious form of the 'oil curse' – that frequently observed phenomenon whereby the existence of extensive hydrocarbon resources in a country serves to underpin bad, often dictatorial, governance. Even Sheikh Yamani, the Saudi politician, fears it for his own country. Yamani was Saudi oil minister from 1962 to 1986, and as such became the public face of the 1970s oil embargo ('Yamani or your life') by which the Arab oil producers hiked up prices and restricted supplies in retaliation for the perceived support by the West of Israel. When I asked him in 2001 whether oil had proved to be a blessing or a curse for oil-producing countries, the Sheikh smiled enigmatically: 'I am worried about the future. If you get money so easily, you relax and you lose your muscles.'

He believes that the oil age will end not for lack of oil, but because technology will replace the need for oil. So in the very long term the oil prices would fall with declining demand. 'The Stone Age did not come to an end because we had a lack of stones, and the oil age will not come to an end because we have a lack of oil,' he said. Yet the oil price has more than trebled since this prediction of underlying falls in crude oil prices, at the behest and to the benefit of a number of badly run non-democratic governments.

Memories of Saddam's chemical assault on the Kurds have not faded in the north of Iraq, and the Kurdistan regional government is leaving nothing to chance. Kurdish Peshmerga paramilitaries patrol what is effectively an international border between Iraqi Kurdistan and the rest of Iraq. And that border marks an economic boundary as well as an ethnic one. The Kurdish regional government have encouraged US property tycoons to construct massive gated property developments such as 'the American Village'. This lies to the north of Erbil, on the arid rocky road to the oil fields, and comprises a development of 400 homes featuring green lawns, picket fences, a shopping centre and an artificial lake.

I met with one of the developers, Jim Covert, who proudly

points out to me some of the key features of this showpiece of Americana: 'a typical American garage, with automatic door. We measured it to fit the biggest cars available on the market, so your Hummer will fit in here,' he tells me. Dozens of houses were sold off plan, before they had even been built, for as much as half a million dollars each. The money is here, even if the banking system is not. Some of the six-figure dollar deposits were paid in bags of cash. 'This is like the Wild West,' Covert tells me enthusiastically. 'Now is the time to get in here to get established and make money because there's so much money coming from oil.'

Iraqi Kurdistan alone could have more oil than Nigeria. Saddam Hussein's ban on oil development in the region has left a legacy of exploration opportunities for DNO and for seventeen other small oil companies from Canada, Turkey, Iraq, the USA and a number of Asian countries. But Kurdistan's reserves are dwarfed by untapped reserves in the Shia south of Iraq, and strong potential reserves in the unexplored desert in the west of the country.

By 2008, Iraq's main oil artery from the north of the country to the Turkish border was again gushing with black gold. Half a million barrels of oil a day now flows from the Kirkuk field to the Turkish port of Ceyhan. At times they pump through 1.6 million barrels in four hours. That's the time they have before hot crude oil pumped from underneath the massive Kirkuk field starts to warm up the earth above the pipeline route, alerting insurgents that the oil is flowing. Further south, the Ministry of Oil has built a 10-metre wall around the pipeline to protect it from attacks. The measures seem to be working. A relatively uninterrupted flow of crude through this pipeline has boosted Iraq's oil exports back up to pre-Saddam levels.

By 2011, the Kurdish government's gambit – inviting new exploration under better terms than those offered by the central government – was starting to pay huge dividends. Tensions with the central government in Baghdad flared up, but Baghdad repeatedly backed down. Major oil firms such as ExxonMobil were now favouring new developments in the Kurdish areas, at the expense of their deals struck in Baghdad. The General was at last able to connect his small gutter pipeline to the main export pipeline, and was starting to be repaid for his investment. But by December 2012, that route out was cut off over a dispute between the KRG and Baghdad. The Kurds announced a deal with Turkey for their own separate export pipeline, bypassing Baghdad's pipeline at Fishkhabour. This would give Iraqi Kurdistan de facto oil independence from the rest of Iraq.

In theory, these developments could help break OPEC in our lifetime, lowering global oil prices and thereby helping Western economies by raising living standards. But the disagreement over Kurdistan's right to invite prospectors to drill for oil is part of a wider argument about the stability of Iraq. There is a violent dispute within Iraq about the status of the oil-rich city of Kirkuk. This city lies at the heart of an ethnically mixed area (Arabs, Kurds, Turkmen and Assyrians all live here), and the dispute concerns the question whether Kirkuk should become part of Iraqi Kurdistan. By 2013 BP was eyeing deals with Baghdad over dilapidated giant oil fields in Kirkuk – a sensitive issue with the Kurds. Turkey watches on, doing deals with the Kurdish administration, whilst nervous of the impact of KRG assertiveness on its own Kurdish minority, which for many years has been agitating, sometimes violently, for independence. In 2013, Turkey signed a peace deal with its own Kurds, opening up the possibility of Kurdish oil pouring into Turkey.

Security in Iraqi Kurdistan depends on that militarily policed internal border with the rest of Iraq. Syrian Kurds are rising up against their leaders. Iraqi Kurdistan may be the Wild West of the Middle East. But that does not mean it's going to end up like California.

Pipelines remain a fault line. Iraq's oil curse is yet to turn into a blessing.

Gazprom: a new breed of energy giant

Three thousand kilometres to the north, in southern Moscow, there is a thirty-five-storey building shaped like a giant phallus – or, officially, a 'large pencil'. Within this angular Russian precursor of London's Gherkin, there is what appears to be a war room. The room is dominated by a 6-metre plasma screen displaying a map of western Europe, as if plotting a re-run of old Soviet invasion plans. Rendsburg, Tilburg, Aachen, Fos-sur-Mer and other apparently random small towns are marked in Cyrillic characters. They are connected by a series of luminous green lines. But these are not planned attack paths. They are pipelines – not for oil, but for gas. This is just the start of the ambitions of Russia's hydrocarbon giant Gazprom, one of a new breed of state-owned energy giants that are trying to reshape the energy map of the world.

Gazprom is the direct descendant of the old Soviet Ministry of Gas, which turned itself into a state corporation in 1989, retaining its assets and later being part-privatised (under Yeltsin) and then being brought back under Russian state control as part of Putin's drive against the oligarchs. Gazprom may be a 'new breed of energy giant', but its institutional roots are buried deep in Russia's Communist past.

'This is where the life of Gazprom is centralised and managed,' says Anatoly Paramonov, who runs this control room of the Central Operations and Dispatch Department, the 'heart' of Gazprom. 'Here we set out what the gas supply should be, where it should go, and to which customers.'

Of particular concern are weather forecasts. Every Friday, the meteorological outlook up to 3,000 kilometres away will determine how much gas he will allow to flow from pipelines in Siberia. Over the seven days it takes gas to flow to Germany, or the nine days it could take to get to Great Britain, small fortunes can be made and lost. Russia's Unified Gas Supply System is controlled from this room twenty-four hours a day. Paramonov takes out a small remote control and the screen fills with a map of the UK, with small towns such as Moffat, Peterborough, Carlisle and Bacton marked in Cyrillic script.

At the time I visited, in June 2006, Gazprom was already the largest single provider of Europe's fuel for central heating and power, and it was doing little to quell suggestions that it wanted to buy Britain's entire gas distribution network, part of an ambitious strategy to connect the world's biggest gas supplier directly into the homes of western Europe, 'from drill to grill'. The plan was exciting the world's markets, leading the majority state-owned Russian company to trade on the Russian stock exchange at a value of $300 billion, making it the third biggest company in the world. As Alexander Medvedev, the official in charge of Gazprom's expansion strategy, told me at the time: 'If we are being realistic in the long term, then we should dream not about $300 billion but about a one trillion market capitalisation. It will not be a fairy tale, it's a real target which could be probably given to the company in the next three to five years.' 'The biggest company in the world?' I ask. 'Yes,' he replies, with a villainous smile.

Back at HQ, Anatoly Paramonov spots a cold snap in the Rhineland or the West Midlands, and from his war room instructs the chief dispatcher to flick some computer switches to send gas molecules flowing west from Siberia. Deals are thrashed out with executives from gas-hungry energy consumers in a glass pyramid at the top of the building. Gazprom remains the largest single provider of Europe's fuel for central heating and power. A straightforward trading relationship is the theory. The practice has been a little more complicated. A clue to this complexity is in the marble sculpture of a tsar-like figure wrapped in a giant gas flame that welcomes visitors to Gazprom HQ. The bigger clues lie further east.

Midnight in Novi Urengoy

It's midnight in the sleepy Siberian backwater of Novi Urengoy, a town carved out of nothing by the Soviet Union's gas ministry, now Gazprom. Novi Urengoy is home to 100,000 people, packed into row after row of concrete Soviet-era apartment blocks. Red-faced gasworkers stumble drunkenly through the midnight daylight groaning like zombies in a horror film. It's not surprising the workers enjoy a drink or two during the all-too brief summer, when for two months the sky never goes dark. We are only a few dozen kilometres south of the Arctic Circle, and the rest of the year, apart from the shortest of springs and autumns, is one long winter, in which for many months the sun barely peeps above the horizon, and temperatures drop as low as −55 degrees Celsius. In the indigenous Nenets language, Urengoy means 'godforsaken rotten place' – and that was before the construction of those grim apartment blocks. As a wind-up, our hosts have only supplied us with one-way plane tickets. Despite the unremitting bleakness of the place, thousands of workers come to live here, attracted by relatively high wages. Novi Urengoy came into being four decades ago when seismologists accidentally stumbled upon huge gas reserves in the area. A pioneering team, living in tiny cabins, braved the harsh Siberian winter to build the pipeline network that would carry Urengoy's treasure across the Soviet Union. The reindeer-herding Siberian tribes long ago abandoned the area, leaving it to the hunters of hydrocarbon.

Here, in Russia's sub-polar regions, the winter snows melt away briefly each year to reveal a relentless expanse of tundra. Dotted around this Arctic desert are drills sucking gas from the Urengoy field, which lies beneath a thick layer of permafrost nearly 2 kilometres deep. It's the second biggest gas field in the world, the largest field in one country – 10 trillion cubic metres of gas, enough to meet all of Britain's needs for an entire century.

Twice in the past decade, in 2006 and 2009, spats between Russia and Ukraine over the price of natural gas have led Russia to turn off the tap, which has also affected gas supplies to other European countries. 'Energy security is a complicated matter and it's a two-way street,' says Alexander Medvedev. 'We are as dependent upon our customers as they are on us,' he says. I ask him if Gazprom is threatening western Europe. 'We are not threatening anyone, we are simply saying that to call for the role of Russian gas to be artificially diminished is a very dangerous thing.' That sounded threatening enough to me.

There is a manufactured bleakness to Novi Urengoy. Here, all aspects of life – accommodation, healthcare, the local TV channel, banking – are run by Gazprom. The old Soviet-style propaganda has been replaced by Gazprom TV, which broadcasts the company's message into Urengoy's homes every day. A Gazprom 'chef' explains the company's recipe for success: Urengoy's gas is filtered, dried and compressed before being pumped into pipelines going west. But why does a gas company need a TV station?

'Gazprom TV has existed for fifteen years – the leadership of the company has never questioned why we exist,' Yana Sukhushina, the editor of Gazprom TV Project 24 tells me. 'We are fulfilling our function to tell as many people as possible what we do and why the company is needed. This is Gazprom town. If the company wasn't here, the town wouldn't be here. So there's no question we need Gazprom TV,' she says.

There is even a Gazprom matron, who offers the gasworkers hydrotherapy. In Novi Urengoy, everything is driven by the gas giant. It is almost impossible to get beyond the airport without an official invitation. The Gazprom standard has replaced the hammer and sickle. This really is Gazpromgrad.

Gazpromland: from state socialism to Kremlin-commanded capitalism

And what goes for Novi Urengoy goes for Russia. Under President Vladimir Putin's careful watch, this unified state-owned gas super-monopoly was shaped to drive Russia's economy. Lucrative assets of private-sector energy companies such as Yukos were seized and sold to Gazprom. The Russian Duma (parliament) voted to pass a law protecting Gazprom's monopoly from all competition.

Dmitry Medvedev, Putin's deputy PM from 2005 to 2008 and temporary successor as president (2008–12) doubled up as Gazprom's chairman. In some years, Gazprom has been responsible for over a quarter of all taxes paid in Russia, and for a tenth of Russia's GDP. Gazprom bought banks, TV stations formerly critical of the Putin regime, and even anchored a successful bid for the 2014 Winter Olympics in the Black Sea city of Sochi, close to the president's holiday residence. The Sochi games look likely to be the most expensive Games ever. The rise and rise of Gazprom is no accident. The subject of Putin's doctoral thesis at the St Petersburg Mining Institute was 'The Strategic Planning of Regional Resources Under the Formation of Market Relations'. In it, he argued for the creation of an organisation that would champion Russia's national energy reserves. Two decades on, President Putin regularly expresses his pride in having constructed Gazprom from the chaotic and mainly corrupt privatisations that followed the collapse of the Soviet Union. Gazprom controls a fifth of total world reserves of gas. If Novi Urengoy is Gazpromgrad, then Russia itself is Gazpromland.

So the state socialism of the Soviet era was simply replaced by a new brand of Kremlin-commanded capitalism. At first Putin played his cards well. During the world boom, he used Russia's gas and oil revenues to pay off almost its entire national debt. Indeed, he also paid off, early, all the lingering bad debts from the Soviet Union. By 2008, Russia's national debt (the entire stock of accumulated deficits throughout its history) was just 8.5 per cent, a smaller proportion of its economy than the UK's deficit in just that one year. All of this came from selling Russia's hydrocarbons to the world. But just trading hydrocarbon was not enough. Gazprom pursued a strategy of trading gas concessions for access to higher-profit businesses further down Europe's gas-supply chain.

The paradox is that, much as Western governments fear Gazprom's long-term strategy, Gazprom needs Western capital to reach the deeper-lying gas. Russia has launched a charm offensive to show off the brand-new facilities it has built in the most inhospitable of environments.

Energy becomes power: Russia as petrostate

Almost pure methane hisses out of the ground at remarkable pressure at the Pestovoy sub-field, north of the Arctic Circle and the most remote of sixteen stations at Urengoy. 'Here we can do it ourselves,' Dmitri Nureyev, one of the managers at Pestovoy number 16, told me. 'We've started producing gas and we've almost reached our target. But for some of the deep-lying deposits, if we had foreign partners to help with development and production, we'd welcome that.'

For years German industrial strategy has been to reserve their spot of this resource real estate. Russia fuels German industry with a flow of gas that was uninterrupted even during the Cold War. Russia and German companies have been trading Europe's energy system like schoolboys playing Top Trumps. Chunks of Germany's internal energy-delivery system have been swapped for access to the hydrocarbon-rich deep deposits near Urengoy. This gas from the Achimov Formation of western Siberia is particularly hard to get at, existing as it does in high-pressure reservoirs in Jurassic rock formations over 3 kilometres underground. After marrying German deep-drilling expertise with Russian knowledge of operating in the permafrost, the German company BASF swapped its entire gas-storage business and also its gas-trading business for access to more Achimov exploration blocks. Thus Gazprom gained ownership of the largest gas-storage facility in western Europe.

In 2005, just before he left office, Chancellor Gerhard Schröder of Germany signed a deal with Gazprom to build the controversial Nord Stream pipeline, which connects Russia directly to Germany underneath the Baltic Sea. With a length of 1,222 kilometres, Nord Stream is the longest undersea pipeline in the world and thus its construction was a major undertaking – but it helped Russia bypass troublesome transit countries such as the Ukraine. Shortly after leaving politics, Mr Schröder became chairman of the same Gazprom pipeline project. Gazprom even sponsored one of his local football teams.

In Estonia, one of Russia's small Baltic neighbours, Prime Minister Andrus Ansip warns against depending on Russia for one's energy supplies. His nation, the wealthiest of the ex-Soviet republics, is 100 per cent reliant on Gazprom's gas. As he shows me around the high-tech Cabinet room, he points briefly to paintings of the numerous Estonian victims of Nazi occupation. But he takes more time in showing me portraits of leading Estonians jailed and killed under the years of Soviet rule. 'We know that Russia is using its gas as an argument in foreign policy,' he tells me, '[the 2006 Ukraine cut-off] wasn't a wake-up call for Estonia because we had those conflicts already in 1992'. Since breaking away from the Soviet Union, Estonia has moved closer and closer to the West, eventually joining both the EU and NATO. At the same time, relations with Russia deteriorated, and among the many bones of contention has been the impact of the Nord Stream pipeline on the sensitive environment of the Baltic Sea. For its part, Russia has from time to time tightened the screws on Estonia, for example launching a crippling cyberwar campaign against its small neighbour in April 2007 in retaliation for the relocation of a Soviet war memorial.

The thrust of Putin's policies, since his accession to the Russian presidency in 2000, shows how energy becomes power. For Russia, the strategy stretches well beyond gas. Gazprom is just one string to Putin's bow. In 2004 domestic and foreign oil businesses were subsumed into the state-owned company Rosneft, which by 2012 had become the biggest oil company in the world. And it is not just hydrocarbon that Putin is interested in. Russia has also cornered the market for enriched uranium, crucial to the boom in nuclear power that many see on the horizon.

Russia, it would seen, has all the cards. Its confidence in the power bestowed upon it by its energy resources was reflected in comments made to me by Gazprom's Alexander Medvedev just months after the first cut-off of gas to Ukraine in 2006. 'If they want to attack the system of long-term contracts or artificially diminish the role of Gazprom, there is a question,' he said. 'Exactly how will the objective demand be met? Where are the major sources in the long run? There's no substitute for Russian, Iranian and Qatari gas in the long term.'

Events were to show, however, that Russia has overplayed its hand. The threatening noises emerging from Moscow were noted and acted upon by Russia's main energy customers in western Europe. After 2007, Europe diversified its supplies, sucking in more gas from Norwegian pipelines and on ships from Qatar, undermining the fixed prices being charged by Russia. Gazprom's customers began to hit back, renegotiating $8 billion of price cuts in 2012. Western energy executives who visited the thirty-fifth-floor glass pyramid in Moscow described Gazprom as a 'wounded Russian bear' – one that was in 'a bad way'. As for Gazprom's ambition to become a trillion-dollar company – well, at the end of 2012 it weighed in at just one-tenth of that, fourteen places off the top spot of global corporations.

But Russia had flexed its muscles; in its own mind, it had regained world attention and respect. Western economies are as addicted to carbon as ever, and the emerging economies of the East are developing the habit. Russia continues to push for co-ordination of global gas suppliers in an embryonic price-and-quota-setting gas cartel modelled on OPEC. Gazprom's Medvedev once threatened that such a cartel would be more powerful than OPEC itself. The members of the Gas Exporting Countries Forum (GECF), including Russia, Iran and Algeria, together control three-quarters of the world's reserves of natural gas and are responsible for more than two-fifths of its production. Their efforts are undermined by Qatar pouring its tankers full of gas onto world markets. The GECF's ambitions have been further thwarted by American exploitation of substantial US reserves of shale gas, which are providing the world's biggest gas consumer with its own degree of energy independence. In the Gulf of Mexico and on America's western seaboard, terminals built for liquefied natural gas imports, are now being converted to handle potential gas exports. Manufacturing is being reshored to America, with the promise of cheaper indigenous energy. The US actually overtook Russia as a producer of gas.

But the GECF may take comfort from the fact that OPEC itself did not acquire global reach overnight, being largely ignored for over a decade following its birth in Baghdad in 1960, after efforts from the powerful 'Seven Sisters' (the cartel of Western oil companies that dominated the global oil industry from the mid-1940s to the 1970s) to drive down crude oil prices. Gas molecules are, however, less fungible, and so less tradable than barrels of oil.

And what about OPEC itself? Russia periodically flirts with joining – or at least likes to give that impression. A leading Russian oil executive, who did not wish to be named, believes an OPEC that included Russia would control 51 per cent of the crude oil market and 'define the oil price'. But at Rosneft, the state-owned giant, they say they are still waiting for an offer from OPEC that would compensate for the risks of cutting production. After a crash in world oil prices in 2008, Russia even hinted it might limit oil production to help OPEC. Russia has clearly benefited from OPEC's decision in 2005 to abandon its policy of keeping oil prices around $25 per barrel, a policy it had maintained for half a decade. In the years after the financial crisis, that price has been volatile, but typically closer to $100 a barrel.

Some say the power and influence of Gazprom and Rosneft shows Russia is becoming a shady petrostate. The Kremlin retorts that supplies of gas have never stopped flowing to western Europe. It's all just part of the hard bargain the New Russia is driving with the West. Why, the Kremlin argues, should Russia not use its natural resources to usher in a new golden age for the country?

From the Kurdish mountains to deep below Siberia economic currents are flowing that will determine how much extra western European households will pay just to keep warm: in Norway, Qatar, off the Falkland Islands, and in the shale deposits underneath the USA and eastern Europe.

Further east the global energy battle is claiming a different type of Western victim: the fight against climate change.

India's power surge and the global debate about climate change

In the eastern Indian state of West Bengal they call electricity 'current' – and that current is flowing to entirely new places, with consequences well beyond India's poor. Purandar village in the Ganges Delta is the frontier of India's expanding electricity grid. When I came here in January 2010, just six months after the main power line reached the village, I witnessed another household being connected to the grid for the first time. Palan Halder and his family were joining the ranks of 500 million Indians with access to electricity – but there remain another 500 million who are still without.

In this part of the world, electricity is still enough of a novelty to warrant a Hindu blessing, involving the scattering of petals and religious chanting. For Palan Halder and his family it has been a two-year wait. Now their household will be lit by light bulbs, cooled by a fan, entertained by a television. Palan's wife will have the chance to earn extra money by stitching saris using an electric sewing machine. His pride, though, is tempered by the thought of the half billion Indians still without power. 'I don't like that,' he says. 'I want to see that everyone has electricity.'

The pylons continue along the roads into the Sundarbans, a vast wilderness of rivers, creeks and mangrove forest that straddles the border with Bangladesh. Yet even beyond the point where the roads and the pylons stop, on the forested islands of the Ganges Delta, the energy revolution is still visible. Farmer

Rabindranath Mondal has shelled out 14,000 rupees (around £200) for a subsidised solar panel. 'There's no electricity here,' he tells me. 'You can only have solar power here, though it's very costly. But,' he proudly adds, 'we do have a TV set.' Mondal's household is just one of 20 million that the Indian government hopes to provide with solar power over the next decade. But it won't be enough for everybody.

Most people come to the Sundarbans hoping to catch a glimpse of the increasingly rare – and sometimes man-eating – tigers that lurk in this mosaic of forest and water. When I visited, I was hunting for another big beast, a politician and economist called Jairam Ramesh. Ramesh was at the time India's environment minister, and thus the man at the fault line between the country's push for economic growth, and the impact that push is having on the environment. A former power minister, he was India's chief negotiator at the failed climate-change talks in Copenhagen in 2009. 'We want to be an *affluent* society,' he told me when I tracked him down, wandering through the Project Tiger reserve. 'We don't want to be an *effluent* society, which is what the Western countries are.' I ask him if half a billion Indians will get access to electricity. 'Absolutely. Not half a billion. One billion Indians must have access to the modern standards of living – you can't condemn half a billion Indians to the Stone Age.' And how exactly will all this electricity be provided? 'Even with all the nuclear, with all the hydro, with all the solar and all the wind and other wonderful sources of energy that we will have, 50 per cent of the power that we generate will still have to come from coal,' he asserts, thumping the side of the Tiger watchtower to emphasise each word.

Follow the electricity pylons back inland and you can see why. The importance of coal to India's future power needs is clearly visible on India's National Highway 2 on the way out of Kolkata into the heart of eastern India's coal belt. In the neighbouring state of Jharkhand lie India's biggest coal mines.

And around the city of Dhanbad, known as 'the Coal Capital of India', hangs the acrid smoke of burning coal. Incredibly, many coal seams have been on fire since the days of the British Raj. At dusk, innumerable fires can be seen flickering across a scarred and scorched valley. The flames are fed from beneath the surface of the earth, and as the fires burn away the coal under the ground, gaping holes appear on the surface, sometimes swallowing whole houses and families. The villagers took me to one such hole, over 3 metres deep, that appeared just eight days ago. The locals call it 'Satan's Womb'. Lax standards in the coal industry over decades have meant that many homes have been built directly above where coal fires burn underground. 'Our children can't live well here,' says a local resident called Nagasur. 'How can we live here? I am only 34 years old, but look at my face. I look like I'm 50, don't I?'

It's hot and sulphurous here – the land is literally on fire and you can see why the locals call it hell. But, despite these appalling conditions, everyone – including young children – is collecting coal (a basket of the so-called black diamonds can fetch 30 rupees, about 40 pence). India's coal reserves are vast: four to five hundred years' worth lie beneath its soil. So even the fires that crack open the land with deadly molten chasms won't slow its use. Coal India was the most valuable company on the Indian stock market in 2011. Many Indians regard the environmental impact of coal as a necessary evil, not just to connect half a billion Indians to the electricity grid for the first time, but also to power the export industries of the future. India shining means India burning.

India's power surge is not just to connect up its poor, but also to fuel the energy-rich tastes of its 200 million-strong middle class, who are flying more, and buying more.

Evidence for this can be found in the city of Pune, on the other side of India. Bajaj, long known as the iconic manufacturer of auto-rickshaws and cheap scooters, has switched its factories to the production of motorbikes. Richer Indians are demanding more for their rupees. The company also has ambitious plans to export Indian motorbikes into Europe.

Rahul Bajaj is one of the elder statesman of Indian industry: 'The world watch out. We are not just going to conquer the market by exporting but we are conquering the market by buying other companies,' he says, referring to Tata's purchase of Jaguar Cars and Land Rover. Bajaj has already snapped up a third of KTM, a leading Austrian motorbike manufacturer. And he is now manufacturing KTM bikes in India. But there are constraints at home. 'I would say this: I need infrastructure – I need roads, I need power. How can you go without power? We are short of power.'

Back on the Bengali expressway towards Kolkata, you pass through Durgapur, the steel capital of Bengal. The National Highway 2 is littered with slow-moving Tata lorries dragging massive irregular chunks of steel shaped into two-tonne cylinders, counterweights and pipes. The industrial thirst for energy is barely met by the construction of giant new 'supercritical' thermal power stations capable of supplying 1.2 gigawatts. Right now India's total electricity supply is equivalent to 200 of these power plants, still well short of demand. India says it needs the equivalent of 900 of these by 2030. . . but at what cost?

India appears oblivious to the current environmental dangers caused by its coal industry – dangers that are literally swallowing up its own citizens. So it may well be too much to expect them to do anything to avert the dangers of climate change, dangers that may not impact the world for another few decades. Anyway, climate change, they insist, is a problem caused by the rich nations.

Already, back in the Sunderbans, they're seeing changes in the weather. Four islands have been submerged by the sea. Some attribute this to global climate change. I came across one family who had to leave their land after their rice fields and fish ponds were flooded in a cyclone, forcing them to fish for crabs. 'Yes, the level of the water is rising,' a boatman told me, 'and the river is also becoming very silty. There is no future for our children on this island.'

Few places are more vulnerable to rising sea levels than the highly populated, low-lying plains of Bengal. Bengal – which encompasses Indian West Bengal and the whole of Bangladesh – is humanity's Ground Zero for climate change. In the years to come, changing weather patterns are likely kill tens of thousands, and to leave millions more homeless, vulnerable to famine and disease. Already India has tried to build a fence to keep out refugees. Rising sea levels are making themselves felt in other ways. The disappearance of some islands has disrupted the tigers' habitat, leading to a marked increase in their willingness to enter local villages. At one point two villagers were being killed per week.

Our visit to the Sunderbans coincided with that of India's environment minister Jairam Ramesh, who had come to release back into the wild a tiger cub that had wandered into a village. Despite the vulnerability of human lives and of the environment that Jairam Ramesh witnessed here, India is proving immune to international pressure on carbon emissions. The country is understandably more concerned with growth than climate change. 'We have to factor climate change into economic growth,' Mr Ramesh tells me. 'Clearly our priority is economic growth. Clearly we have to grow a country like India with its massive challenge of poverty and employment, we have to grow at 8 to 9 per cent a year. Indian emissions are survival emissions. In the West they are lifestyle emissions, so I would tell my environmentalist friends to change their lifestyles before they preach to us as to what our development strategy should be.'

He is echoed by Indian industrialist Rahul Bajaj, who thunders warnings that Indian industry will not be held back by Western concerns about climate change. Plenty of leading Indian businessmen treat climate change as if it was a neo-colonialist conspiracy to keep the BRICS countries down. Mr Ramesh had an especially blunt message for the British negotiator at the failed Copenhagen climate talks, now the leader of the Opposition at Westminster. 'This constant preaching from Ed Miliband, for example. On India and China he became an evangelical, you know, but I can tell you that Ed Miliband's carbon footprint is probably twenty times my carbon footprint.'

The global debate about climate change becomes tangible in India. Should all its people be connected to the electricity grid? Should Indians who want to travel from Mumbai to Kolkata have to catch a twenty-six-hour train, or should they be able to fly?

The growing assertiveness of India and of China in recent years has caused the collapse of negotiations on both world trade and on the environment. It is difficult enough to establish a global consensus on trade. Yet trade is an area where, in theory, the challenge is to share out the benefits fairly. For climate change, the global negotiation centres on finding an equitable method to share out down-payments and costs, with uncertain returns, in decades to come, for future generations. It requires an unlikely alignment of interests across a complex matrix of intergenerational and international perspectives. Should young Indians be stopped from flying so as to prevent London and Manhattan being swamped by the waves? Did Western youth in the twentieth century pause to consider the impact of their insatiable consumption of carbon fuels on the islands of the Ganges Delta?

Put simply, if the world really is concerned about climate change, then people in rich countries will have to turn down their thermostats and pull on a couple of jumpers when the weather turns cold. If we in the West readjust our lifestyles, then the carbon in that Iraqi oil field, in that Siberian gas field, in that Indian coalfield, might just remain under the ground – and not end up in the atmosphere.

The carbon traders of Kingston upon Thames

Europe did come up with a method of trying to restrict carbon output, a method dreamt up by the high priests of high finance.

It was called carbon trading. Greed can never have been so good. At one point, because 'almost everything has a carbon footprint', the proponents of carbon trading believed that carbon could one day become the most traded commodity on the globe. Half the current trading comes through London, and the City of London is emerging as the world centre for carbon capitalism.

Kingston upon Thames is an unlikely hub for anything, but nestled in the greenery beside the River Thames lies a futuristic office block designed to accommodate a small army of planet-saving, carbon-dioxide-sapping capitalists. Arthur Tait is in charge here, and his ambition is clear: to become the number one trader of carbon in the world. It is 2008, the heyday of trading carbon.

I asked Tait whether ambition such as this – the profit motive itself – can really be the saviour of the planet. 'Effectively, yes,' he replies. 'I think it'll save it a lot more efficiently than a carbon tax would, or forcing draconian measures on countries that wouldn't take those measures. So a market-driven force is probably the only way we're going to save the planet.'

That, in part, is the point of this nascent market. Put a price on emitting carbon and then someone, somewhere, will take the money not to emit it. At the same time there are a whole load of brokers, traders, bankers, fund managers and lawyers trying to match supply with demand – making a packet, while retaining a planet-saving afterglow.

But guess who Mr Tait works for? A company whose other ambition is to be the world's biggest supplier of hydrocarbon energy: Gazprom.

In the background, Tait's team of traders are barking into their trading phones, hustling deals, watching variables as diverse as temperature charts in Europe, the escalating price of crude oil and the negotiating position of the awkward Czechs over the allocation of the right to emit carbon in Europe. There are no pinstripes or strangely coloured blazers. The traders are casually dressed but utterly focused on the latest information coming through their Reuters terminals.

'From a standing start a few months ago,' says Tait, 'the people here will aim next year either to sell into the market or trade eight million tonnes of carbon reductions, but within the next three years grow that up to 80 to 85 million tonnes.'

Tait's team has just signed a deal to buy up 1.3 million tonnes of CO_2 emissions savings made through upgrades to a polluting manufacturer in South Korea. The reductions have been certified to the United Nations standard. But that's just the start of the wheeler-dealing. Tait takes me over to another floor of the building. 'On Susan's desk, what we'll do instantaneously is sell on the bulk of those savings into the Japanese market,' he says, as from her desk in Kingston upon Thames Susan flogs a million tonnes of finest-quality, un-emitted Korean carbon to Korea's near-neighbours in Japan. 'Japan is very short of carbon,' Tait remarks. Of the 300,000 tonnes remaining, 70,000 is handed over to the trading desk to do smaller deals in the carbon market, while 230,000 tonnes worth of carbon permits are sold to Gazprom's commercial gas customers in the UK – in this instance, a major supermarket. It's a remarkable 'dual-fuel' deal. Gazprom provides the supermarket with hydrocarbon-rich gas, and it also supplies the permits to offset the consequent emission of CO_2 from burning the fuel. Carbon-neutral gas is, apparently, a popular new product.

'Zero-carbon oil' is probably being developed, somewhere in the world, right now (the brand name could be 'Conscious Crude'). For detractors, carbon-neutral gas is a startling symbol of carbon trading's false dawn. The detractors included one rather unlikely man: a Latvian politician called Andris Piebalgs. Between 2004 and 2009 this straight-from-the-hip Baltic bruiser served as the European Commissioner for Energy, and so shares responsibility for Europe's pioneering emissions-trading scheme. It's known, in the jargon, as a 'cap-and-trade' scheme.

The scheme works as follows. Countries, together with certain industries and companies, have their emissions of carbon dioxide capped at a specific negotiated level. The right to emit that carbon is then handed out by the government in the form of a permit. Polluters emitting carbon require a credit for every tonne put out into the air. Emit less than your allocated permit allows and you can sell the surplus credits on the market – so polluters are paid to emit less carbon. Emit more than your allocation and you need to buy new credits, a financial punishment for over-polluters. The price is then set by the interaction of supply and demand for the credits. If all traders are emitting too much carbon, the price of permits will skyrocket. The higher the price of carbon credits, the greater the incentive for polluting industries to rein in their emissions. That is the theory that drives the carbon traders of Kingston upon Thames. Gazprom's vision is to marry its unrivalled supply of hydrocarbon gas from Siberia to Russia's highly inefficient industrial base, ripe for carbon-saving technology. Russia could be the OPEC of the carbon market.

'We'll instigate projects in Russia,' says Arthur Tait. 'Those projects will reduce emissions. We'll get certificates for those and trade those here too.' Gazprom would thus become a one-stop shop for 'low-carbon' gas. It is complicated, but it isn't rocket science. The real difficulty, however, is in setting up the system in the first place – which brings us back to Mr Piebalgs. The trailblazing European Trading Scheme (ETS) tripped over itself in Phase 1. The price of carbon crashed from an effective €30 per tonne to a pointless price of €0.63 (about 50p). But when I cheekily asked him if the ETS had been a failure, I did not expect him to say 'Yes'. But he did. 'Yes, I would describe it as a failure,' he told me. 'And we also know the reasons.' Commissioner Piebalgs went on to say that the price of carbon needed to be at least €20 to €30 per tonne. 'If you want to create a market you shouldn't make too many compromises – and the mistakes were obvious. If you give allowances for free, on a not very clear basis, you can expect that you will have too many allowances – and that's what happened.'

Yet even after governments began charging for carbon permits, the carbon price still slumped to new record lows. The net result was rather depressing: massive multibillion windfalls to the very worst polluters. Anyone angry about the bank bail-outs should perhaps pause to consider the impact of the carbon market. Not only were far too many permits handed out, all but 7 per cent were handed out completely free, to the worst polluters.

'Giving out permits free is like giving out money free,' says Professor Paul Klemperer, a British government adviser on auctions from Oxford University. 'Having any system of emissions permits will raise consumer prices, and those price rises automatically compensate the companies for the costs of the permits. If you then give out the permits free, you're compensating the companies twice. There is no need to give them extra windfall profits by giving away the permits.'

The result was predictable. Carbon trading forced up the price paid for electricity in Europe, benefiting power companies at the expense of consumers. Yet for the polluters, the cost of being part of the trading scheme was precisely nothing. In fact, the ETS was routinely mentioned by City analysts as a reason to buy shares in power companies and other heavy carbon polluters. In the end, a scheme designed to provide incentives to cut carbon emissions only succeeded in handing over billions to the worst offenders.

Precise numbers are hard to come by. A report for WWF (the World Wide Fund for Nature) by analysts Point Carbon puts the windfalls to power generators in Phase 2 of the ETS up until 2012 at an incredible £50 billion. Ofgem, the UK energy regulator, sees windfall profits at £9 billion in Britain alone, but billions have already been made in the first phase of the trading scheme, which ended in 2008.

It is no surprise, then, that major US polluters and power companies are lobbying hard for the same helping hand, the same multibillion-dollar windfalls, from embryonic US emissions-trading schemes. The surest sign of disaster was that the oil supermajors began to feel a little left out of this bonanza. The largest oil firms in the world lobbied for a system of 'upstream cap-and-trade' in the USA, in which carbon credits are earned and traded by the companies actually physically removing hydrocarbons from the ground, rather than those who actually burn the oil, gas and coal.

For economists such as Paul Klemperer, this jackpot for the supermajors was utterly predictable. 'An emissions-permits system that's implemented this way makes even the most polluting firms better off,' he says. Carbon trading in and of itself should reward clean companies, punish dirty companies, and channel the world's investment to those parts of the world where £1 can save the emission of the largest volume of carbon dioxide.

'A tonne of carbon saved above Beijing is the same as a tonne saved above Birmingham,' is a carbon market mantra, but free permits have, in essence, been a rather expensive bribe to get power companies to participate in the scheme. It's an entire field of juicy carrots, with little threat of a stick.

In effect, consumers paid for a bailout of an industry on the grounds of environmentalism, which ended up rewarding the worst polluters most of all. Yet unlike the banks, those companies did not even need a bailout in the first place. It was the perfect example of the impact of complex 'financialisation' combined with vested-interest lobbying. The emergence of carbon trading was a clear effort to avoid the more straightforward solution: the imposition of a tax on carbon.

In the end, carbon emissions did go down in Europe, but this had almost nothing to with emissions trading, and everything to do with the economic collapses wrought by the financial crisis. Will a single barrel of Kurdish oil, a single therm of Siberian gas, a single basket of Indian coal remain unburnt as a result of the scheme so far? Brutally put, no. And that failure has been noticed elsewhere.

As Jairam Ramesh, India's climate change Dr No, puts it: 'It was certainly hypocritical of the Western world not to recognise that climate changes call for fundamental lifestyle changes in Western society.' And so, in the very place where climate change could cause most damage to human beings, the Indian environment minister is clear: the climate change crisis is a matter for the West and its profligate lifestyles. He has an energy-supply crisis to address.

CHAPTER 13

LENT IN LARNACA: THE CYPRIOT JOB

Dramatis personae

Anonymous Cypriot government adviser
Rebecca, a teacher concerned about the fate of her daughter
Michael Sarris, finance minister of Cyprus for five weeks
(28 February–2 April 2013)
Chris Pavlou, vice chairman, Laiki Bank
Andreas, an angry Cypriot pensioner
Nicos Anastasiades, president of Cyprus (2013–), and a lawyer
Andros Kyprianou, leader of AKEL, Cypriot
opposition Party (2009–)
İrsen Küçük, leader of the Turkish Republic of
Northern Cyprus (2010–13)
Jeroen Dijsselbloem, Eurogroup president,
Dutch finance minister (2012–)
Stolla, distraught Bank of Cyprus worker
Gabriel Sterne, former International Monetary Fund (IMF)
official, and economist

'There is no business going on in Cyprus right now.' I am speeding through the suburbs of Nicosia in the back of a taxi, and the man talking to me is a key adviser to the country's embattled president. Cyprus is on the cusp of capitulating to an ambush on the newly elected government by the more powerful nations in the Eurozone.

'People are just buying necessities and our banks are today being sold at fire-sale prices,' the rattled adviser tells me. He struggles to contain his bewilderment at the way his country is being treated. 'The Troika has caused a problem here, and they won't give any money unless we go and tax deposits, which is unheard of. Most frustrating of all is that they just would not listen to us as equal citizens.'

Ultimatums from central bankers and threats from fellow finance ministers are a risk for any debtor country requiring a rescue loan – especially a small debtor country with no bargaining power. Like many of Cyprus's elite, the adviser had entrusted his six-figure savings to a Cypriot bank. Incredibly, within days, he would end up losing a large chunk of his own personal wealth to pay for a new approach to bailouts determined by the Eurozone's powers. A European bank deposit would never be the same again.

The island laboratory

The people of Cyprus had been looking forward to the spring of 2013. A fluke of the calendar had lined up three bank-holiday weekends in a row, to celebrate Green Day, Greek National Day and Cypriot National Day. For the devout, this was also the period of Lent, a time of self-reflection, piety, fasting and repentance. For everyone else, the holidays presented at the very least some extra time to enjoy life and the eastern Mediterranean sun. Cyprus was not Greece. Sure, the property bubble had burst. And, yes, unemployment had risen, but not to Greek or Spanish levels. Standards of living and pay were still, on average, high. International negotiations on Cyprus's economy lurked in the background, as they had for a year, but no one was too worried. Cyprus was a relatively liberal market economy with few of the structural problems of the Eurozone's Club Med.

Then, halfway through March, the crisis blew up in everyone's faces. Suddenly, the island was turned into a laboratory for dysfunctional Eurozone economics. The reasons for – and consequences of – Cyprus's collapse went beyond economics and well beyond the rim of the choppy Mediterranean. The Cypriot economy was deliberately made to suffer a heart attack, as its banking system was closed down. Amidst acrimonious and botched international negotiations, the country ended up with draconian controls on capital, and with essentially one foot outside the Eurozone. And the people of Cyprus, not surprisingly, were left bewildered and upset. In 2013, Lent in Larnaca reached well beyond fasting and the giving of alms.

All of the drama of Cyprus's fortnight from hell could have been witnessed from the airport town of Larnaca. The arrival hall was packed with offshore savers. Flights in were full of expatriates. Private jets lined up on the tarmac with foreign billionaires facing ruin for trusting the safety of a Eurozone nation's banking system. Eventually Euro Force One, aka the cargo plane full of banknotes sent by the European Central Bank, would be obliged to make a flying visit even more precarious than the Athens Airlifts of previous years. In the meantime, the citizens of Larnaca, like all the people of Cyprus, found themselves threatened with a Eurozone-sponsored electronic mugging, before being locked out of their bank accounts. The cash machines rationed the amounts they were prepared to dispense, strictly and methodically. Queues began to form. Small businesses could not fund their payrolls, or pay their suppliers. For those who did get their cash, or who had thought ahead and withdrawn their savings in time, there was still a problem. If they had ideas about taking their money abroad for safety, they were obliged to think again, because at Larnaca airport, Cypriot customs officials were enforcing the first ever controls on the movement of currency within the Eurozone – or, indeed, within the European Union. Euros in Cyprus were now physically trapped on the island – and essentially worth less than euros elsewhere. For Cypriots, the single currency was looking rather binary.

While schoolchildren paraded through Larnaca on one of the national holidays, a teacher stopped me on the street. 'I don't think the parade should be taking place today,' she told me, in tears. 'These children should stand in front of parliament to tell them about their ruined futures. Our lives are ruined.' The teacher's name was Rebecca. She had saved for years to send her daughter to medical school in Germany, but now she feared for her savings – and for her job. 'The people of Cyprus,' she continued, 'are beginning to realise that from a prosperous country we are going to be the beggars of Europe.'

The first move made by the government of Cyprus at the behest of the Eurogroup (the committee of Eurozone finance ministers) turned out to be a fatal blunder. They attempted to grab a portion of the bank deposits of the entire population, including the life savings of mothers, grandmothers and widows. Overnight, just under 10 per cent of balances above €100,000, and nearly 7 per cent of balances below €100,000, would be seized electronically before the banks reopened after the Monday bank holiday. International transfers were frozen. The deal was wearily brokered in the early hours of the previous Saturday morning in Brussels. At the meeting, the Cypriot president, Nicos Anastasiades, and his finance minster, Michael Sarris, had been effectively ambushed by their fellow Eurogroup ministers. Sarris was filmed at the meeting looking lonely and shell-shocked, scratching the back of his neck. He and his president were just weeks into their jobs. Their predecessors had stalled through a year of ultimately fruitless negotiations, aimed at plugging a gap in the island's finances. The total required before the country's economic cardiac arrest was €17 billion – an irrelevant sum for the Eurozone as a whole, no more than the acceptable level of error on German quarterly fiscal forecasts. Nonetheless, Cyprus was to become a testing ground, a show of strength, a statement of intent in Germany's election year. Cyprus itself would have to find €7 billion internally, while northern European taxpayers would only be on the hook for €10 billion. With Cyprus, the euro's overlords decided to take a different approach from the one they had taken with Greece. Cyprus's financial system was mostly funded from small and large bank deposits. So the depositors were going to take a hit. Rather than being bailed out, they were, so to speak, going to be 'bailed in'.

Neither the Irish nor the Greek banks were 'bailed in' like this in their first bail-outs. The market attacks on the Eurozone had eased up after the ECB's Mario Draghi's promise to do 'whatever it takes'. The euro's overlords had some space to try something new. The essential reason for this was political. In the case of Cyprus, there was a different balance of terror. Unlike Greece, Cyprus did not have the strong negotiating position of the mugger-addict with a syringe. Cyprus was *too small to bail*. Or, strictly speaking, it was too small to *have* to bail out. The finance minister Sarris was told this very clearly in the early hours of that fatal Saturday morning by several of his counterparts, notably the German finance minister, Wolfgang Schäuble. Sarris was told that Cyprus had no bargaining power because financial chaos in an economy that made up just 0.2 per cent of the total Eurozone had not and would not spread to Spain, Italy, Greece or anywhere else. Indeed, Cyprus's impact on other countries' bond yields had been carefully watched for ninety days. After all, even the strong election performance in Italy of 'two clowns' (as the former German finance minister Peer Steinbrück called politician-billionaire Silvio Berlusconi and politician-comedian Beppe Grillo) had barely interrupted the europhoria prompted by Mario Draghi's actions the previous September. So what threat could little Cyprus present?

Therefore Sarris was told that the incredibly harsh medicine offered by Germany and friends was a take-it-or-leave-it offer.

Chris Pavlou, one of Cyprus's most senior bankers and a veteran of the City of London, was in the room for some of the preparatory meetings in Nicosia between newly elected President Anastasiades and the young economists and bureaucrats representing the Troika of the EU, the ECB and the IMF. I asked him whether the Cypriot leaders had really been told that they had no negotiating power and did not matter. 'Unfortunately that's what they said, yes,' Mr Pavlou replied. 'And it's not very nice actually to see two or three people half your age, clever people, coming over there and shaking their [fingers at] the president and saying "You have to do this, otherwise we'll bring you down." They were 30- to 35-year-olds. It is very painful for somebody who's just been elected to actually face that.' 'Humiliating?' I asked. 'At best,' Pavlou said.

Pavlou was vice president of Laiki Bank, Cyprus's second biggest, which when we spoke was only days from liquidation. He said he had witnessed the worst two or three days that he'd ever had to experience. 'And I've seen through crises in many, many countries,' he continued. 'This one – it was devastating, because you can see your own people, your own country going into the abyss without any end. . . It's traumatic and scary.'

Over the long bank holiday weekend, the bankers kept the cash machines supplied with money. There had been an immediate run on the savings banks that had tried to open on the Saturday morning. Cash was being rationed through the cash machines. 'I even went around and spoke to people in the queues,' Pavlou told me, 'and fortunately or unfortunately I convinced a few people to turn around and go home. Some machines ran out and we needed another half an hour, people were very patient, they were waiting, and the money, it came.' Pavlou was there on one of the occasions that the money was delivered. He warned the people waiting by the cash machine that the money could run out in the next hour, because the banks were only covered by their insurance to transport so much money in one go. 'People, actually I admire them,' Pavlou continued. 'They were patient, they were standing. Clearly you could see there was a lot of anxiety. And fear, if you like – a little bit. But there was no trouble.'

In the coastal city of Limassol, a roundabout had been decked for Carnival by a slightly sinister circus merry-go-round. It is also the site of ten cash machines. Methodically, cars would slowly whirr around the roundabout, as passengers checked out cash levels at each machine. Some alerted their friends via text or Twitter if they found a working cash machine. Others kept the information close to their chests. 'Maybe the savings that will be cut will be returned to us,' one wondered. 'We are not happy, but what can we do? We don't have a choice. We thought the EU would be better friends to us.' Another shrugged his shoulders at an empty ATM and vowed to find a working one. One woman queuing outside a savings bank told Reuters that she had drawn a €12,000 loan to support her daughter's studies, deposited the money back in the bank – and so would lose nearly 7 per cent of it. British nationals were warned by diplomats to bring different currencies and forms of payment if visiting Cyprus. The RAF flew in €1 million in notes for British military personnel at the island's two UK bases. In Nicosia an angry Cypriot left a bulldozer outside an empty cash machine. Most Cypriots, oblivious to what was about to hit, had disappeared to the mountains, as is traditional for the Green Day bank holiday. There was general incredulity that Cyprus, not at all the most 'badly behaved' of the crisis countries, was clearly being treated as the very worst.

In Nicosia, officials from the European Central Bank arrived immediately after the Eurogroup decision and sought meetings with the country's president and the president of the Cypriot parliament. The Cypriots had become somewhat standoffish. The feeling on the Cypriot side was that the ECB was attempting to ram through changes in parliament in the hours before the markets reopened on the Sunday night, or at the very least by Monday night. For their part, the Cypriots were looking to buy more time for their parliament and government officials to reconsider the drastic 'bail in'. Cyprus was trying to wriggle free – or, from the northern European perspective, to renege on commitments made only hours before. Cypriot MPs were rebelling against the deal, trading stories about how, at the crucial Brussels meeting, northern European delegates high-fived each other when Cyprus caved in. The Central Bank of Cyprus summarily announced two unplanned bank holidays. This was in itself a remarkable development. Not since the Great Depression of the 1930s had any Western nation declared a bank holiday for the sole reason of propping up its own financial stability. And it was to get much worse.

A cesspit of money laundering?

Some backstory is worthwhile at this point. Although the Cypriots themselves were largely taken by surprise, anybody moving in government circles in Berlin in the previous months could not have failed to notice that, as far as Cyprus was concerned, a new type of solution was being considered. Chancellor Merkel was, it was reported, much more concerned about Cyprus than Greece. Germany's intelligence service, the BND, had written a report for parliamentarians picturing the island as a cesspit of money laundering. The clear message was that any bailout of Cyprus – which would largely be paid for by the German taxpayer – would in the end be of much less net benefit to the Eurozone than to a bunch of wealthy Russian gangsters.

Senior MPs from Chancellor Merkel's own CDU party, thus briefed by the BND, toured the capitals of Europe, warning that Cyprus was 'a very special case' because of enormous money laundering, 'especially of course by Russians'. For Germany to help Cyprus, the MPs stated, certain preconditions had to be met concerning banking transparency. Above all, the 'criminal structures' woven into the Cypriot economy had to be unthreaded.

A low-level propaganda war broke out between Berlin and Nicosia over these issues. Cyprus issued independent research showing it was even more compliant with anti-money-laundering legislation than Germany itself. The message was pushed by a London-based consultancy made up of economists who used to work for the UK government. For its part, the Troika commissioned the bond trader PIMCO to research the funding requirements of the Cypriot banks. Nicosia in turn employed BlackRock to research PIMCO's research.

The motivation for the German approach was partly economic, but also hugely political. Germany's official opposition had chosen to pick an election fight with Chancellor Merkel over 'a bailout of the Russian mafia'. The reality was that the opposition SPD (Social Democratic Party) had been broadly supportive of Chancellor Merkel's approach to the euro crisis at the time of crucial votes on bailout funds. But when it came to Cyprus, the SPD – which wielded considerable influence in the upper house, the Bundesrat – saw an opportunity to make political capital. So it was abundantly clear to observers of the political scene in Berlin that Germany was going to play hardball with Cyprus, and that the Russian connection was going to loom large.

Muscovites on the Med: the Russian connection

The huge new marina at Limassol was built to accommodate Russia's de facto Sixth Fleet. Massive berths had been constructed to service an armada of super-yachts owned by Russian oligarchs. 'Limagrad', as it had become known, offered all the home comforts favoured by the Russian elite, alongside almost permanent sunshine. The city hosted Russian restaurants, Russian radio stations, and even a Russian strip club. The Cyrillic alphabet was everywhere. And the city also sheltered a large chunk – around €24 billion – of Russia's offshore money. Russian money accounted for half of all foreign deposits in Cypriot banks, and up to a quarter of total deposits. There is no doubt that a proportion of that money was dubiously made in the 'Wild West' era that followed the collapse of the Soviet Union.

But the full story was more nuanced than the suggestion made in Berlin that Cyprus was being kept afloat by laundering Russian mafia money. When international audits were conducted on compliance with anti-money laundering rules, Cyprus *did* actually come out cleaner than either Austria or Germany. That said, even a former Cypriot finance minister admitted to me that 'on balance, while we do have rules and regulations against money laundering, the way they are implemented may be more relaxed than [in] other countries'. But the Russia–Cyprus nexus was not just about sheltering money. For a start, the country's rate of corporation tax was only 10 per cent. Cyprus also had a system of international treaties designed to make the island a channel for investment into Russia and other countries. On top of that, a stable legal system, a shared Orthodox Christianity, and longstanding ties dating from the Soviet era cemented Cyprus's position. The Cypriots had done the opposite of the banking systems of countries such as Ireland, the UK and the USA. Lending was almost fully funded by deposits, rather than hotter flows of bondholder money. In theory this should have been a strength: deposits are the most stable form of funding. But the reliance on Russian deposits – while partly a consequence of tax competition, and largely perfectly legal – did become a systemic fragility.

Pavlou, chairman of the audit committee, said that while he was there Laiki Bank was clean. 'I saw no signs anywhere that money laundering was part of any business at all,' he told me. 'In Cyprus we are paying 4.5 per cent interest rate. Nowhere in Europe can you get a 4.5 per cent interest rate in euros. We have a tax treaty, we have very good weather, we have the same religion, do I need to give you any more? And the people from Russia, with very cold winters, they come to lovely Cyprus for their holiday and they happen to buy a house in Limassol or Larnaca as well.'

But the dependence on Russian deposits, and their deployment in long-term lending, turned out to be a core problem.

'Looking back,' Pavlou admitted, 'looking back, maybe we should have been more careful in taking so many deposits. What was happening was one of the cardinal sins of the bank. We were lending for one year, two years, three years, in some cases in Greece fifteen years, and we were funding it with funds that were very hot. At some stage the central bank had actually conditions that only 30 per cent of those funds were allowed to lend to the market. And suddenly I came in and saw that that regulation was blown out of the window. And nobody went to say to them "Listen, you broke the rule."'

So why the emphasis on Cypriot banking dodginess? Cypriot leaders describe how they have long been aware of a negative feeling from other EU finance ministers 'on principle' regarding the low corporate tax rate in Cyprus. They also report the distaste expressed by those ministers regarding the 'disproportionate presence of Russian money' in the Cypriot economy. The problem for Europe's bigger nations was that all these features were signed off as acceptable when Cyprus joined the European Union in 2004, and again when it joined the Eurozone in 2008. It was certainly odd that these features were highlighted as reasons for treating Cyprus more harshly than all other Eurozone nations, given no objections had been raised during the accessions, and not much had changed since.

During the island's initial hour of need in late 2011, the then-president, Demetris Christofias – a Communist who had been educated in Moscow – turned to Russia for a €2.5 billion loan on friendly terms. Cyprus had run a big 6 per cent deficit in the first two years of his presidency. Reaching out to Moscow had been an early effort to avoid the indignity of EU bailouts and the tuttings of those thirty-somethings from the Troika.

A senior G7 official had been in Moscow as the Cypriot crisis of March 2013 erupted with the 'bail-in' of depositors. He flew from Moscow to Larnaca on a plane that was full to the brim with passengers, even though it was not yet the holiday season. On the plane there were several strangely shaped metal briefcases stuffed into the overhead lockers. On the tarmac at Larnaca Airport, in addition to a number of other packed commercial flights, there were a dozen or so private jets. Some were chartered, others were registered to Russia. Taxi drivers at Larnaca reported that during those hectic days their clientele were almost exclusively Russian. Limousines ferried Russians from Limassol to long meetings with their lawyers in Nicosia. The Muscovites had come to get their money.

The really shocking thing about that moment in mid-March 2013 was that it wasn't just the money of the Russians that was threatened. Cypriot depositors themselves were also at considerable risk. The banks were still officially shut pending the passage into law of the EU deposit-raid agreement. In central Nicosia the first victims were the elderly, many of whom had never had to use a cash machine before. The mood on the island was febrile, if not yet panicked. Ordinary Cypriots queued at ATMs for money replenished once a day by the nation's new emergency service: security vans full of euros run by British contractor G4S.

On the streets, Cypriots were broadly consistent in their view as to who was to blame: Germany. Germany, they insisted, was trying to drive Russian deposits off the island, with the intention of gaining primacy in the race for Cyprus's abundant gas reserves. Before the parliamentary vote, protestors surrounded the German embassy and tore down the German flag. Credit and debit card payments were working only fitfully, as merchants feared having to pay the deposit tax on such transactions. Cyprus was starting to turn into a cash economy, albeit one that was running out of cash. Outside a branch of Laiki I met an elderly man called Andreas. He had no luck in getting money out of the ATM. I then watched as he rang the bell on the door of the branch to complain. A bank clerk briefly opened the door, only for another clerk to stick a handwritten sign on the outside. The sign said 'Closed'. It was a scene which, in nearly two decades of studying and reporting economics, I never thought I would actually witness. Andreas was furious, 'Angela Merkel has taken my money,' he shouted, before entering into an angry debate with a fellow ATM victim. This other man told me he was willing to accept the deposit levy of 7 per cent if it meant keeping Cyprus out of the crisis. Half an hour later I found Andreas clutching five €50 notes. He had in fact been putting his debit card in the machine the wrong way around, because he had never used it before, always choosing to get his money from the branch instead. Now, clutching his notes, he told me it was his money, neither Merkel's nor Schäuble's. When I challenged another protesting Cypriot about the presence of Russian money, he was indignant. 'What about the City?' he shot back. 'What about London? What about Chelsea?' Everybody knew that Chelsea Football Club was owned by Roman Abramovich, one of the richest men in Russia, who made billions selling his Siberian oil company in 2006. This man's indignation was shared by many of his fellow-countrymen.

In parliament it was becoming clear that Cypriot politicians were not going to push the deposit tax through against the wishes of their citizens. Perhaps in a small country, the political elite were too close to their electors to impose the proposed deposit grab – after all, they would personally know dozens of friends and relatives who would be affected. It was touch and go. As in Greece, those politicians who believed there was no alternative to swallowing the bitter pill conjured visions of Armageddon if the country refused to take its medicine. President Anastasiades himself said the country faced a choice of 'catastrophic disorderly bankruptcy' or 'painful but controlled crisis management'. The former would lead to the failure of Laiki and eventually of the Bank of Cyprus (BoC), the country's largest bank, along with the complete collapse of Cyprus's service sector and a possible exit from the euro. These were the big guns. This was the imperfect economic union at play. The brinkmanship went as far as a threat to withdraw provision of lender-of-last-resort liquidity from the European Central Bank (known as Emergency Liquidity Assistance or ELA). When other nations needing a bailout had been subjected to this threat, their parliaments had tended to vote the 'right' way. President Anastasiades phoned Chancellor Merkel in her limousine, pleading 'I need more solidarity,' reported the *Wall Street Journal*. Her reply was brief and to the point. 'I won't negotiate with you,' she said. 'You need to talk to the Troika.'

Yet Cyprus said *Oxi* – No. In the end, not only did the measure fail, but not one MP dared vote for it. Even those government MPs who wanted to vote for it were told to abstain. Cyprus was jubilant. Protesters partied in the streets outside parliament. Little Cyprus, a mere five-hundredth of the total Eurozone economy, had stood up to Berlin and Frankfurt.

I spoke to Andros Kyprianou, leader of the opposition AKEL party, as he triumphantly walked out of parliament after the vote. He was dismissive of the Troika. 'They went much too far,' he told me. 'And according not just to us, but to international opinion, what they did was unjust and unfair.' He insisted that Cyprus's newly discovered gas deposits meant that it had 'very big wealth', a factor that had been completely ignored by the Eurogroup. I asked if the Troika should learn its lesson. 'That's what I believe,' he replied, 'and I hope that they will change their policies, because you cannot solve the problems of the economic crisis with the same prescription that lead to the crisis.'

Parliamentary democracy reigned supreme in Euroland, at least for a day or two.

The three broad stages of Cyprus's attempt to escape the Eurozone's particularly harsh adjustment programme might be characterised as: (1) Extend and Pretend, (2) Befriend (Russia), and then (3) Depend (on gas). The Cypriot government pondered a €3 billion raid on the pension funds of the public sector, and also on those of the banks and the state enterprises, to be repaid when needed by the proceeds from gas finds. This strategy entailed some heroic assumptions about a patch of the Mediterranean lying 160 kilometres south of the island. The results of one test drill on the Aphrodite Field, 1,500 metres below the surface of the sea, led the prospector concerned to claim that it had found €30 billion worth total Cypriot gas reserves – double what Cyprus needed for its bailout. Some external experts suggested that total Cypriot gas reserves could be worth as much as €300 billion, while others estimated that the commercially recoverable reserves were worth no more than €2 billion.

The Cypriot leadership hoped that the likelihood of some billions' worth of gas reserves would change the equations on its debt sustainability. A sufficiently optimistic assessment might obviate entirely the need for a bailout. Certainly, all sorts of gas-backed warrants and bonds were considered as an alternative to borrowing from the EU. Even after it was clear depositors were going to be hit, Cyprus pondered offering long-term gas-backed IOUs as compensation. A hydrocarbon treasure trove undoubtedly lay in Cyprus's territorial waters, but there were bigger issues at play. The major oil and gas companies were not putting in large bids for exploration. After all, Cyprus had been something of a trouble spot, and who was to say when trouble might blow up again. The 1960s had seen bloody fighting between the Turkish and Greek communities on the island. And then in 1974, a coup by Greek nationalists intent on union with Greece prompted a Turkish invasion. The result was the partition of the island, with the Turks proclaiming the internationally unrecognised Turkish Republic of Northern Cyprus, and the Greeks concentrating in the south. The line of partition – the so-called Green Line – runs right through the capital, Nicosia.

Northern Cyprus: the Turkish connection

Across the rooftops of Nicosia you can see the different flags, the monuments and the minarets that symbolise the split. At street level, it's difficult to detect the divide –until you stumble into the border guards. Off limits for nearly four decades, some streets are still deserted. This no man's land – the UN buffer zone – contains an airport terminal, car dealerships, and even an Avro Shackleton aeroplane; everything here is frozen in time. From the Turkish-controlled side, on top of a casino with views across both sides of the divide, a senior official points south. 'They used to come here for their gambling,' he tells me. 'Now their entire economy is a casino.'

Cyprus had forged a close relationship with Israel, which also had an interest in the prospects of extracting natural gas in the eastern Mediterranean, and in developing its export capacity. Relations between Israel and Turkey, the ultimate bogeyman for Greek Cypriots, had been frosty since 2010, when the Israelis had used armed force to intercept a Turkish relief convoy heading for Gaza. But now, just at the very same moment as Cyprus's financial fortunes hit rock-bottom, relations between Israel and Turkey began to thaw. Turkey had also announced a peace deal with separatists in its Kurdish areas. Turkey was securing allies, extending its influence in the region, and looking for energy to fuel its booming economy. In ordinary circumstances, Turkey's pipeline network would offer the perfect export route for Cypriot gas. Turkish ministers make the point regularly. But since the Turkish invasion of 1974 and the proclamation of the Turkish Republic of Northern Cyprus, the internationally recognised, Greek-dominated Republic of Cyprus in the southern half of the island has snubbed all overtures from Turkey.

In the north they felt that they had done all that they could to restore harmony on the island. Under the Annan Plan, the UN sponsored a vote on the establishment of a federation of two states as the 'United Republic of Cyprus'. Separate referenda were held in the north and the south in April 2004. The vast majority of northern Cypriots (65 per cent) voted for the plan, but in the south, only a minority (24 per cent) were in favour. The European Union felt a little tricked, as during the negotiations on Cypriot membership of the EU, solving the divide had been one of the EU's conditions for allowing Cyprus to accede – which it formally did in May 2004, just a week after the referenda. The EU began to allocate aid to northern Cyprus, even though it was still occupied. At the time, Cyprus was booming and Turkey was suffering in the aftermath of an IMF rescue. Nearly a decade on, the view from the north was that the boot was firmly on the other foot. Turkish officials struggled to balance concern about the prospects in the south with outright *Schadenfreude*. İrsen Küçük, who is the leader of the Turkish Cypriots and calls himself prime minister (though this title is disputed in the south), said, 'Of course, I see this as the accumulated effect of many years [of their system]. I can say that the juncture they now find themselves at, has not come as a surprise to us.'

By 2013, Turkey's economy was booming, pumping extra aid, tourism and investment into the north. Students from Turkey and developing countries, finding the West increasingly inhospitable, flocked to northern Cyprus to study. The economy was growing at 2 to 3 per cent per year, and the government set a target for 5 per cent. When I drove through the north, I found myself on brand-new motorways, speeding past numerous luxurious villas built for Turkey's new elite. When I arrived at the north coast, I stumbled across something extraordinary on the beach: piles of giant steel pipes, made in China. They were for an 80-kilometre pipeline that was to pump drinking water from a reservoir on the mainland of Turkey directly into the homes of northern Cyprus. A young graduate engineer called Fatima was overseeing the project. A dam and a pumping station were being built too, and these would also produce hydroelectricity. When finished, the north will benefit from 75 million cubic metres of water per year for drinking and irrigation, sourced from the rains falling on the plateau of Anatolia. The south will have its gas. The Turkish Cypriots think their water wealth will be a crucial bargaining chip in any reunification talks.

'Natural resources belong to both communities – Turkish Cypriots and Greek Cypriots,' İrsen Küçük told me. 'Looking at Cyprus as a whole, there are two important economic opportunities here: gas and water. The gas needs to be utilised in the most economic way possible and conveyed to Europe through

Turkey.' On the one hand, Turkey made it clear that it would not countenance the south using its gas as a security to pay the debts of its banking system. On the other, it felt that the south's predicament had created better conditions for unity and a lasting peace. 'My opinion is, thinking logically, and considering the people in both countries and caring for their livelihoods and welfare, this could lead to relatively more positive developments,' Küçük told me.

Perhaps that's why Küçük told me that depositors were welcome to put money in the banks in the north, which were 'safe, stable, very healthy and strong'. Finance minister Ersin Tatar took me on a walkabout of Nicosia's Old Town. At the Ledra border crossing he peered over no man's land, noting that in the Turkish part of town the banks were open and the economy was growing, while in the south there were plans for capital controls. The Green Line felt like the Default Line between 'western Europe' and the fast-growing emerging economies. It has to be said that Mr Tatar did not actually know at the time how much deposit protection existed for this prospective tidal wave of safe-haven deposits flooding into his breakaway republic. Still, at that moment, foreign deposits in the banking system of an internationally unrecognised sovereign entity did appear safer than those in the European Union banks a few hundred metres away.

Bank Holiday Island's man-made disasters

Back in the south, the calm response of Cypriots gave way to panic when local media reported that Laiki Bank was about to be wound down after the parliamentary *Oxi*. Long queues formed outside Laiki's cash machines. The branches were still not open. The banks started to limit the size of daily cash withdrawals, previously over €600. The limit eventually came down to €120. At Limassol port the cargo terminal began to back up with stranded containers full of imports that could not be paid for. Retail supply chains stopped functioning. Shops and restaurants accepted credit-card transactions at their own risk. Exporters of halloumi cheese could not pay their suppliers. Economists normally say an economy has 'stalled' if it has stopped growing. In Cyprus the economy had stalled in the truest sense of the word. It had stopped. It had suffered a heart attack.

Contingencies were being drawn up for capital controls in Cyprus, as they had been in Greece the year before. In essence Cyprus already had temporary capital controls with the announcement of multiple impromptu bank holidays. These six days of unplanned and two planned bank shutdowns – making for twelve consecutive days when the banks were closed, including weekends – were already an extraordinary development. The last time bank holidays had been announced in a European country in order to restore financial stability was in the wake of the collapse of the Austrian bank Creditanstalt in July 1933. (Latvia in 2008 was the only event in Europe that gets close, but that principally involved just one bank.) In the USA, such bank holidays had not been called since the Great Depression of the 1930s.

I wondered if the Eurogroup geniuses who had set the Cypriot bank run in motion had ever read Roosevelt's 'fireside chat', delivered on the radio in similar circumstances exactly eighty years previously: 'It needs no prophet to tell you that when the people find that they can get their money – that they can get it when they want it for all legitimate purposes – the phantom of fear will soon be laid.' Thus, in a statesmanlike way, Roosevelt used the broadcast media to boost confidence and douse the flames of financial panic. Sadly, no statesman of similar stature emerged in Europe during the Eurozone crisis. In 1933 Roosevelt stopped bank runs by creating deposit insurance. In 2013 the Troika created pent-up demand for a bank run by stopping deposit insurance.

From big bang to basket case

It should not be forgotten that Cyprus, two years before its financial collapse, was largely untroubled, fairly wealthy, and certainly not a basket case. A measure of this is the fact that after the financial crisis began to unravel in Greece in 2009, Greek depositors transferred €5 billion into the Cypriot banking system, believing it to be a safe haven. But then, on 11 July 2011, the Cypriot economy was hit by something entirely unexpected – a massive explosion.

In January 2009 the US Navy had intercepted a Cypriot-flagged, Russian-owned vessel in the Red Sea. It turned out to be carrying ninety-eight containers of explosives from Iran to Syria. The vessel was escorted to Cyprus, and the US government leaned on the Cypriots to confiscate the cargo. The explosives were transferred to the Evangelos Florakis naval base between Limassol and Larnaca on the south coast of the island, where they remained for two years in what turned out to be entirely unsafe conditions. In the early hours of 11 July 2011, several of the containers caught fire, resulting in an explosion so huge that it created a crater some 600 metres wide, destroying virtually the entire naval base, and killing thirteen people, including the commander-in-chief of the Cypriot navy.

The explosion also knocked out the nearby Vasilikos power station, responsible for generating half the nation's electricity. The country was hit by blackouts, and in Nicosia, in the height of summer, the air conditioning was off for several weeks. Cyprus had to import power from the Turkish north. The losses incurred amounted to 12.5 per cent of Cyprus's total economy, punching a large hole in the nation's public finances.

Cyprus's prospects were being determined by random man-made disasters, with their roots in the squabbles of larger powers. And an equally damaging version of the same story was playing out in Cyprus's banks.

A Big Fat Greek Shredding

When, in relation to Greece's financial crisis, Chancellor Merkel of Germany insisted on her policy of 'Private Sector Involvement'

(PSI; see page 17), Greece's subsequent effective default on its sovereign bonds cost Cyprus's banks, such as Laiki, almost the same amount as had been raised in deposits: in 2011 Laiki lost €2.3 billion on its holding of Greek bonds of €3.1 billion, while BoC lost €1.9 billion. So the losses made on a single trade by two banks cost the nation nearly a quarter of its annual economic output.

As a former Cypriot finance minister told me, 'This was not a natural disaster. It was obvious, it should have been very clear to bankers and the central bank. For Greek bonds for the two years before PSI [2009–11] – you could see a daily and weekly fall in their value. The signals were there. This is where the Central Bank [of Cyprus] is at fault. It let the bankers here gamble safety and soundness on a single bet where the risk was clear.' The former government blamed the then governor of the Central Bank, Anastasios Orphanides, for a familiar trait of central bankers during the boom: an obsession with monetary economics and interest rates, and a neglect of prudential regulation of banks. Orphanides in turn blamed the old government for its persistent deficits.

In April 2011 Orphanides gave an interview to Reuters. 'I am puzzled by the continuing questioning of the sustainability of the Greek debt,' he said. 'In my mind, restructuring of the Greek debt is not necessary as long as Greece continues to implement the programme… Even in the highly unlikely situation… of imposing losses on the holdings of Greek debt, our banks would manage to weather that.' Despite sitting, around that doughnut-shaped table, on the governing council of the European Central Bank, Orphanides called this wrongly. Greek debt restructuring was agreed within three months, and with each new negotiation the restructuring became more drastic. And, as it turned out, Cyprus's private banks could *not* weather the storm.

The pattern of lending to Greece by Bank of Cyprus, the country's largest, was truly astonishing. On the morning of 10

December 2009, BoC officially had negligible exposure to loans to the Greek government, after cutting back from a previous peak of €1.8 billion. According to an independent investigation, BoC then chose to take its lending to record highs, *after* Greece revealed its full woes, and eventually lost the bulk of the money in the Greek bond haircut. On the eve of the decision to burn Greece's bondholders, BoC had built its holding back up to €2.4 billion. The bank was effectively using €3 billion of European Central Bank low-interest one-year loans not for the usual purpose of propping up the bank's existing balance sheet, but instead to lend more money to near-bankrupt Greece at a higher interest rate. Traders call it a 'carry trade'. It was a bet that Greece would never default on its bankers. That happened to be the public view of Governor Orphanides, perhaps influenced by the views of his colleagues on the European Central Bank governing board, who at the time believed in the inflexible honour of the Eurozone 'sovereign signature'. BoC had in fact placed its head in the guillotine in the months leading up to the blade falling. For a time it earned a handsome profit. After a year and a half, it was a total disaster. What Cypriot banks suffered was not so much a haircut as a lobotomy.

At Laiki, Chris Pavlou spotted the problem. 'There's nothing wrong with buying government bonds, provided it is 10 to 15 per cent of one's capital,' he told me. 'But what happened at our bank at the time, the Greek government bonds, instead of being 10 to 15 per cent of the capital, it was 150 per cent of the capital.' He shook his head. 'If you lose so much, then you cut it. Thus I understand that once or twice it was suggested to the top that they should sell this and just take the losses, 300 to 400 million euros, whatever.' As it turned out, the loss came to €2.3 billion.

Effectively, Greek government debts worth €4.2 billion – about half the cost of the Athens Olympics – were shunted on to depositors at Cyprus's big two banks. But the helping hand given by the Greek Cypriots to their big brothers and sisters in Greece went well beyond that.

After the losses incurred by the big two, I received an email from a leading Greek investment banker. 'There's a convenient story that Cyprus suffers from its investment in Greek bonds,' he wrote, 'and Greece is responsible for the plight of Cyprus. This is not the case, not even partially.' He pointed to massive lending losses at Laiki, and a tangled web linking Cyprus, Greece and a bank called Marfin.

The strange case of the monks and the bankers

It was not the monks of Vatopaidi who brought down Greece. The Holy and Great Monastery of Vatopaidi is one of many monasteries on Mount Athos, a remote peninsula in the northeast of the country from which all women are banned. The only female animals allowed are cats.

But the Holy and Great Monastery of Vatopaidi *was* involved in a wider scandal concerning questionable land investments, a scandal that helped to bring down the conservative-led Greek government in 2009. It then led to the landslide election of George Papandreou, the revelation of cooked government borrowing books, and the start of the all-consuming Greek crisis. So the monks of Vatopaidi did play an inadvertent role in revealing Greece's problems. The scandal, which was to see Abbot Ephraim serving a brief term in prison, concerned political pressure on Greek ministers over a dubious land swap. The abbot's incarceration prompted diplomatic complaints from the government of Vladimir Putin in Russia, now strongly allied to the Orthodox Church. The Vatopaidi also had particularly strong connections to Cyprus. Their bankers for the deal were Marfin. In 2006 Marfin had effectively merged with Laiki and another Greek bank called Egnatia. An investigation by Reuters journalist Stephen Grey showed that the Vatopaidi land deal was also emblematic of wider questionable lending in Greece that would cause huge losses at Cypriot banks. In October 2010 a Greek parliamentary inquiry into the Vatopaidi deal suggested 'serious conflicts of interest', and that some Marfin loans to the monastery ended up benefiting bank shareholders and executives in a 'heap of violations, perjury and possibly falsification of documents'. Deals like those done by Marfin with the Vatopaidi – involving questionable, opaque lending in Greece – were in fact more relevant for the calamities of Cyprus than for those of Greece, and were raised in June 2013 at a Cypriot investigation into its banking crisis. Marfin's former owner told Reuters that the bank was cleared of wrongdoing by the Bank of Greece after an audit in 2009, and 'nothing was substantiated' by other investigators.

The wider problem for Laiki, now merged with Marfin, was a web of lending to connected parties by the latter. Chris Pavlou, then the just-resigned Chair of the bank's Audit Committee, described to me how 'a big party started' after the UK bank HSBC was rebuffed from buying Laiki by the government of Cyprus in 2005. HSBC had held a 25 per cent stake since 1972, but sold to Greek investors. Laiki set out extraordinary ambitions to become the biggest bank in southern Europe, aiming to overtake BoC and to buy up banks across the Mediterranean. 'It's very sad having to think about it, but everything to do with governance was destroyed. When I got in the bank, in late 2011, in December 2011, I walked in on a Saturday morning and I couldn't believe what I saw in front of me. I couldn't find a balance sheet of the bank, I couldn't see any governance whatsoever, I couldn't see any lending limits. They were from the Greek subsidiary... In some of the loans in Greece, there was absolutely nothing behind it. Collateral was almost zero, and very low interest rates.' I asked Pavlou about sketchy connections, maybe, between the bankers and the loan recipients? 'One could find evidence of some connections there, yes. A conflict of interest. I think some of the lending there, some of the practices were very dodgy,' Pavlou told me.

The original intention in 2006 was for the merged bank to be headquartered in Athens alongside the bulk of its operations.

Political concern in Cyprus saw the HQ transfer to Nicosia – and the liabilities from Greece would effectively transfer to Cyprus too. The merger deal closed in March 2011. The larger Greek unit, replete with rotting government bonds and dodgy loans, was now a mere branch of a smaller Cypriot bank.

'Troika go home!': the deal at gun-point

Back to Lent 2013. The Hilton Nicosia played host to a bizarre mix of international journalists, thirty-something Troika officials, accountants, management consultants and beefy Russians with their stillettoed girlfriends. There was also a crack team of Greeks working for Piraeus Bank. Piraeus knew a thing or two about bailouts. In the previous year it had received €7 billion from the European bailout funds allocated to Greece. All in all, more than a third of this Luxembourg-based bailout fund, the European Financial Stability Fund (EFSF), had been used to help the Greek banking system. Less than a year before the collapse of its own banks, Cyprus had been one of the guarantors of the bailout for the banks of its larger neighbour.

The banks in Cyprus were never offered the same deal, either by the EFSF or by its permanent successor, the European Stability Mechanism. In addition, the Eurogroup's approach to Cyprus prioritised the protection of the Greek units of Cypriot banks. Effectively, the €5 billion of Greek deposits in Cypriot banks were ring-fenced and guaranteed for Greeks, even though the bulk of the losses were incurred in Greece. So Greece would keep the deposits, the Cypriots would get an even more drastic haircut, and Cyprus would get the rotten liabilities. The Greek units of both Laiki and BoC would be sold to the Piraeus bankers waiting at the Hilton at a fraction of their book value. Not only had Piraeus itself been saved by EU bailout money partly funded by Cyprus, but the actual fire-sale purchase of the Greek units of Laiki and the Bank of Cyprus was funded by the Hellenic Financial Stability Fund, itself entirely funded by EU bailout cash. The Eurogroup was willing to give Greece bailout cash (partly backed by Cyprus) to support its parts of the Cypriot system. But it was not willing to bail out Cyprus itself.

At best, there was a staggering inequity in the treatment of Cypriot and Greek banks. At worst, the EU specifically intervened to protect Greece, and to export part of its own dodgy loan default over the sea to Cyprus. As a by-product, Cyprus was destroyed as an offshore financial centre. Certainly at the height of fevered negotiations, the issue of the treatment of the Greek units was at the very top of the concerns being expressed from Brussels about laws being passed in Nicosia. Bank queues could be tolerated in Nicosia. But not in Athens.

On the middle Monday of that nightmare Lent, there was a planned bank holiday in Cyprus, to celebrate Greek Independence Day. Most Cypriots felt there was little to celebrate, and much to bemoan – primarily, their country's rotten dependence on an EU with uncertain motives and questionable competence. On Greek Independence Day, teenagers marched through Nicosia representing the city's schools, youth groups and sports teams – including those from across the Green Line. The march finished near the European Union house, resplendent with large banners celebrating the EU's recent receipt of the Nobel Peace Prize. But the parents lining the route were pensive. Inside, their feelings of national pride were replaced by a sense of emptiness, of loss or anxiety for the future. The tail end of the march was joined by protesters shouting 'Wake up Cyprus!' The next day, at 11 a.m., most of the same teenagers emptied out of Nicosia's classrooms and rushed onto the streets, marching in their thousands on the presidential palace to vent their anger at Cyprus's financial collapse and against the Troika bailout deal. '*Exo i Troika tora!*' ('Troika go home now!') they chanted to the tune of the White Stripes' 'Seven Nation Army'. Banners declared

Your mistakes
Our future.

Schoolkids and students, organising themselves through Facebook and Twitter, really did think that the European Union and the IMF were stealing their future. 'We can no longer afford to take loans to study,' said Christina, a student at a private English school. 'Fight on, with all your voice until you can't shout anymore,' she says. 'For your country, for your parents!' shouts another young girl protester. In Nicosia there was none of the violence seen in Athens. The police were relaxed, chatting with the kids. The riot squad kept out of sight behind the trees. But there was the same anger.

A second bailout, not a second chance

President Anastasiades had returned to Brussels for a second negotiation, after finance minister Michael Sarris's talks in Russia had collapsed without even a meeting with President Putin. At one point during his negotiations in Brussels, an emotional Anastasiades threatened to resign and to call a referendum on the deal – as Greece had briefly suggested in 2011. He also threatened to block the sale of the Greek branches of Laiki and BoC to Piraeus. Ultimately, however, Cyprus had even less bargaining power than the week before. Not only did the Cypriot mess cause no financial contagion to Eurozone bonds, but there was scant evidence of human contagion, of people in other countries rushing to their banks to withdraw their money. Cyprus came closer to euro exit than any other nation. Some EU finance ministers were entirely prepared for that eventuality, should it arise. However, Chancellor Merkel, unlike her finance minister, believed there was a geopolitical rationale for keeping Cyprus in the euro.

Eventually a compromise was reached. All deposits under €100,000 would be protected, but larger deposits in Laiki and BoC were now to take a stratospheric hit of 40 per cent to 80 per cent. Laiki was to be wound down, and BoC self-capitalised by raiding large deposits. The government was desperate to protect BoC and so preserve some residue of Cyprus's international financial services industry. The fact that many MPs had their savings in BoC may also have concentrated minds. In the end, many thousands of Cypriots were to lose hundreds of thousands of euros. From the Eurogroup perspective, it became clear that the first deal – involving raids on even the smallest depositors – had been an unmitigated disaster. Now, one week later, the Eurogroup finance ministers said that the first deal they'd signed off was 'against European principles'. The president of the European Central Bank had not been present at the first negotiation, and described the initial decision to hit small deposits as 'not smart, to say the least', but insisted this mistake was quickly corrected the following day in a teleconference of Eurogroup ministers.

A few weeks later I spoke to the new Eurogroup president, Dutch finance minister Jeroen Dijsselbloem. He was unrepentant. 'The way we dealt with Cyprus,' he told me, 'especially in the second outcome, was inevitable. It dealt with problems in Cyprus in a very direct way, focusing on the banks where the main problems have arisen.' He said that the debt burden imposed on Cyprus by the second deal was not more than they could afford. 'So debt sustainability is guaranteed,' he continued, 'and it's dealing with the problems in a way that deals with the source of the problem.'

Throughout the EU, however, those anti-European parties that had previously been on the fringe of politics were now cock-a-hoop at the attempted deposit grab. In their wildest fantasies, they could never have imagined Brussels actually sanctioning the seizure of the money of ordinary citizens – even temporarily.

A former finance minister of Cyprus told me that for his country the second deal was 'a complete cock-up', even worse than the first offer. After the parliament rejected the first deal, the Cypriot newspapers screamed that David had defeated Goliath and that Cyprus had taught Merkel a lesson. When he saw these headlines, he told me, he thought, 'My God, this is our end. There is no way in an election year she would let Cypriots humiliate her. For me it was clear that it made her stance very very tough.' Ex-banker Pavlou also said that the second deal was 'three or four times' worse than the first deal. The depositors who would no longer lose 7 per cent of their money probably felt differently. Cyprus's main industry, however, had been destroyed.

Various bank board members were fired. Bank workers led the protests outside the Central Bank of Cyprus and the parliament. Graffiti appeared on the walls of bank branches. In Limassol, one branch was attacked with a Molotov cocktail. BoC workers massed in the spectacular white atrium at the centre of its HQ. I sneaked in. Workers cried as they explained they just wanted a chance to work and put things right. 'We are protesting because we do not understand why they are closing us down,' Stella told me, with tears in her eyes. 'We have children, we have families, and we are willing to work. Our debts are too big, yes, but we will work to repay it. But they don't give us a chance.'

This was no ordinary demonstration. Workers held placards saying 'Traitor', 'Shame' and 'Go home Demetriades' (a reference to the governor of the Central Bank). One of the placards was carved out of a sign for the 'Harvard Club of Cyprus'. In the foyer a selection of BoC's 'Bank of the Year' awards were on display. The workers then marched on the Central Bank – effectively the embassy of the ECB in Cyprus. It was the Central Bank that had sold off BoC's Greek unit for a song, and it was the Central Bank which, that very morning, had dismissed the BoC's bosses. Hundreds of bankers mounting a sit-down protest at their country's central bank – had the world turned upside down?

Even after ordinary depositors were spared, there was little lessening in the mood of moral outrage. Plenty of ordinary Cypriot retirees lost their life savings. House-sellers were caught mid-sale. The Orthodox Church was preparing food parcels. Businesses had closed. The banks had still not opened. Electronic transfers were blocked. The shutdown was the longest recorded by the IMF. Capital controls were being prepared, in contravention of the very point of the European Union single market.

The Cypriot parliament had little choice. The ECB was holding a gun to its head. After a majority on the ECB governing council voted for a public threat, Frankfurt issued a statement announcing it would cut off Emergency Liquidity Assistance to Cypriot banks if a deal was not agreed with the EU and IMF within four days.

On Day 12 of the crisis, plans were finally put in place to reopen the banks the following morning – subject to draconian new capital controls. And then, as dusk fell over Nicosia, the shouts of the increasingly irate protestors were drowned out as the air filled with the angry buzzing of helicopters and the deafening wail of police sirens. The uproar seemed to be converging on the Central Bank. Had the previous day's sit-down protest by the bank workers turned into a riot?

The truth was even more extraordinary. At the Central Bank itself, tense meetings between international financiers, American management consultants, British Treasury advisers and Cypriot bankers suddenly broke off. Four very large green juggernauts laden with euros had arrived from the European Central Bank, just hours before Cyprus's banks were due to reopen. An historic just-in-time delivery.

That afternoon a Boeing 767 cargo plane in the livery of Maersk Star Air had been spotted amidst a crowd of smaller private jets parked at the end of the runway at Larnaca airport. Flight logs record that the Boeing 767, registration OY-SRH, had flown from Cologne to Munich in the early hours, and then, via Athens, to Larnaca. Its cargo? Five billion euros in notes. The cash had been transferred from the Bundesbank logistical reserve at the request of the ECB. After the notes had been loaded onto the four huge trucks, their onward journey to Nicosia was accompanied by squads of police cars, while overhead the helicopters of the island's security force kept a wary eye on the convoy's progress. It was not quite 'helicopter money' – but almost.

In ordinary circumstances the extension of the ECB's emergency liquidity would be an almost entirely electronic matter. In the case of Cyprus, given the public distrust of banks, the restoration of liquidity required a cargo plane full of actual euro notes. They had come courtesy of Cyprus's *real* central bank, the one based in Frankfurt, 2,500 kilometres away – the European Central Bank. Effectively, the ECB's threat made a week before to pull emergency liquidity funding to the island's main banks, was a threat to withhold the cash that arrived on this plane. The consequences would have been dire. Maersk Star Air OY-SRH was what passed for a printing press in a nation that had ceded its monetary sovereignty.

A magnet for dodgy money?

Elsewhere at Larnaca Airport, at the customs desk between security and passport control, a new sign appeared. It said: 'Movement of currency up to one thousand euro per passenger only.' And this applied even to passengers flying within the EU. It was just one of a number of decrees restricting the movement of currency in and out of bank accounts, cash machines and off the island.

Meanwhile, fanning out from the Central Bank in Nicosia, G4S security vans sped across the island, shadowed by police cars. Their task? To deliver the cash before the reopening of bank branches at noon. In Larnaca there were queues of two or three dozen people waiting outside each branch. It was an orderly affair. At a BoC branch, names of clients had been placed on a list in arrival order, enabling people to sit in the shade of a nearby tree. At a branch of the Cooperative Bank, the elderly were ushered to the front of the queue. At a branch of Laiki, one businessman was furiously knocking on the window. He didn't want to withdraw cash; he wanted to make a deposit. This was not the feared bank run, because capital controls rendered that pointless. It was controlled transactional demand for cash. Maria, a travel agent, told me that she was making a deposit 'so that my cheques will clear'. Eventually the branch opened, twenty-five minutes later than advertised, twelve days after its last opening. Customers were invited in two at a time. A novel form of capital control.

Blame was being spread liberally – and correctly. The European Union and Germany were blamed for allowing the deposit bedlam. Cypriot regulators were blamed for allowing banks to destroy themselves on Greek gambles. Politicians were blamed for being outfoxed in negotiations. The previous Christofias government was blamed for failing to agree a deal on better terms. Bankers were blamed for taking Cypriot capital and international deposits, and allowing it to disappear into a black hole in Greece. The Greeks were blamed for palming off their fiscal and banking losses onto their Cypriot brethren. And Turkey was blamed – for being Turkey. The Troika authorities basically got away with not explaining their disastrous decision-making.

Economic forecasts for the official Cyprus aid programme played down the impact on growth and the deficit of the botched bailout. One IMF executive board member asked to approve Cyprus's loan complained two months later: 'This huge fiscal effort would be quite difficult to materialise in any country, but even more in Cyprus that needs to find a new business model in the midst of the deepest crisis it has ever had, in an unfavourable international environment and while its Eurozone partners are themselves striving for more fiscal adjustment. Every programme needs a pinch of optimism but in this one the required dose of goodwill – or suspension of disbelief, if you will – goes way beyond the average. The two pillars of the economy in Cyprus are banks and tourism. The two biggest banks are insolvent. One will be liquidated and the survival of the other cannot be taken for granted.' The Eurozone is built on the premise of sharing sovereignty and decision-making for the greater good. Cyprus raises serious questions about competence and cluelessness.

By a complete fluke, the branch of Laiki I chose to film turned out to be the very branch that Slobodan Milošević used to help fund his wars in the Balkans. Private jets with bags of Milošević Deutschmarks arrived weekly at Larnaca in 1993 and 1994, defying UN sanctions. Billions were laundered in this way, according to a report by Morten Torkildsen of the United Nations war crimes prosecutor's office, helping Mr Milošević's pariah government pay for fuel and weapons to pursue wars in Bosnia and Kosovo. At the time, bank workers complained that they were not paid enough to count the mystery inflow of banknotes. It was a vivid reminder that there had been many things wrong with the Cypriot financial system. Something of a pattern had emerged, a pattern in which controversial foreign billionaires had become the clients of Cypriot law firms, whose senior partners had then become politicians. Perhaps German intelligence was right after all about Cyprus being a magnet for dodgy money.

If German intelligence *was* right, why was Cyprus allowed to join the EU in 2004, then the euro system in July 2007? Cyprus adopted the euro as its legal tender on 1 January 2008, after the financial crisis began. There was a balloon-filled party to celebrate, at which a beaming Cypriot EU commissioner Markos Kyprianou (later to resign as Cypriot foreign minister and face charges after the fatal naval base explosion of 2011) withdrew the first euro notes from a Cypriot ATM at the stroke of midnight. At the time Cyprus had been invited to join the club, Brussels, Frankfurt and Berlin knew all about the large Russian deposits in the country's banks, and about the latter's questionable activities in the 1990s. They were also aware that Cyprus's banking sector was unusually large for such a small country.

Nothing much had changed in the intervening years. Between December 2007 and mid-2012, Russian deposits in Cyprus remained pretty stable. Although during this period the deposit base of Cyprus's banks rose from €52 billion to nearly €71 billion, the great bulk of this was due to an €11 billion rise in deposits from Cypriot residents. The biggest foreign rise was not Russian, but the €5 billion increase of 'safe haven' deposits from Greece, after the crisis there.

Lose-lose for everyone

Even on its own terms, Germany will probably end up shelling out more than it would have had it just simply shelled out for the bailout, says former IMF official Gabriel Sterne: 'Basically the Troika had to choose between a bunch of unpalatable options and they went for the one that was worst according to sensible analytical criteria but more palatable to Germany. The Troika could have chosen to lend to Cyprus at low interest rates, and then take the gas revenues when they came in. Everyone would have been better off; Cyprus, Germany, Russia, the IMF. And the Troika could have haircut Cypriot government debt but they were scared of legal action and they had [promised that] Greece was "unique and exceptional".'

The 'justice' meted out to Cyprus by the Eurozone was somewhat arbitrary. Arguments deployed in northern Europe to explain what had been done to Cyprus could have equally applied to Malta, or to Luxembourg. On the one hand, yes, taxpayers across the EU were being spared the brunt of the crisis. But across Europe depositors were now being told to treat a large deposit in a peripheral Eurozone bank as if it was a junk bond. Jeroen Dijsselbloem, president of the Eurogroup, made matters even more uncertain by implying that Cyprus was a model for future 'bail-ins'. European bank shares slumped, as at this point it made no sense to have more than €100,000 in any periphery banks. Dijsselbloem was publicly slapped down, and was obliged to issue a 'clarification' of his remarks. But the doubt about the sanctity of a European bank deposit remained. Cyprus itself had been treated demonstrably worse than other Eurozone countries. Its main industry had been destroyed, its people had been starved of cash. The banking heart attack also destroyed the growth figures, miring Cyprus even more deeply in a man-made fiscal crisis.

There seemed to be some method in this madness. UK officials were surprised that Berlin never asked for a contribution to the bailout of an old outpost of the British Empire. 'There was a lot of discussion over whether to help Cyprus: not only a large number of expats, lots of Cypriots in Britain, and two sovereign military bases, so we did consider it several times,' George Osborne told me.

Cyprus did ask for help directly from other nations, but Berlin said that this would not reduce the amount of Cyprus› €7 billion 'bail-in'. The UK assisted in other ways. Key UK Treasury officials helped Cyprus› negotiations with the Troika, and even to mediate between the Cypriot government and its central bank.

Faced with the fiscal crisis, the idea of a return to the Cypriot pound was privately gaining popularity amongst the island's establishment – many of whom had lost large amounts of money. The country has only been in the Eurozone for half a decade, and there is a willingness – undetectable in other bailout countries – to consider, in the medium term, a complete exit. Alternatively, Cyprus may be pushed into a rapprochement with Turkey, which would be the quickest way for it to export its new-found gas. The development of real estate in the no man's land along the Green Line could also spur growth. Cyprus is now suffering the aftermath of a crisis, under the shadow of the IMF. Turkey is booming. The rejection of the Annan Plan in 2005, when Cyprus was strong and Turkey weak, seems a world away. Many Greek Cypriots said to me that what happened to them in the spring of 2013 was punishment for how they had voted in 2005.

Above all, Cyprus was plainly unlucky that its banks required a bailout in the run-up to a German election, during a period already full of planned bank holidays. A year earlier, and like Ireland, Spain and Greece, its banks would have been bailed out in full, with no losses to any creditors. Instead it became a laboratory and an example to other countries. And the experiment is not yet over. Bank accounts are still difficult to open, and capital controls remained in place months after their 'temporary' imposition. Neither the country's elite nor its highly educated youth are likely to forget the Lent of 2013. And what happened to them then will never be forgiven.

EPILOGUE: NEW DEFAULT LINES

If there is any point to economics, and the pursuit of growth, it should be the advancement of ordinary people. In the years of easy growth before the credit bust, the rising tide lifted most vessels, from the superyachts to the rowing boats. But the promise of rising living standards for everyone has stalled. The boom in credit masked this for around a decade. In some countries, such as Britain, the United States and the nations of the Eurozone periphery, the argument right now is not so much about who shares the proceeds of growth, but rather who bears the burden of paying the cost for the decade of excess.

In Rhode Island I met some of America's 48 million recipients of food stamps: working pensioners who cannot earn enough to buy the food they need. Here, on the 1st of every month, the supermarkets are swarming with food stamps users. The same aisles empty from the third week, as the so-called 'Gold Cards' (formally state-funded Electronic Benefit Transfer cards) run out of federal government dollars. 'I hoped to qualify for a platinum,' jokes an unemployed carpenter, before explaining to me how he runs out of the $200 monthly allocation of food stamps in week three. For one in six Americans – more than the population of Spain – food stamps are an alternative currency, and the number of US citizens reliant on them has nearly trebled since the turn of the century. These are not generous benefits by European standards, about £40 a week, but you don't expect to see this sort of dependency in the USA. A pensioner and her son in Bristol, Rhode Island, describe how many working families rely on the Gold Card, but few want to talk about it openly. There is a stigma. The government prevents the card being used for the purchase of hot food, pet food, alcohol and cigarettes. One user says she feels the stigma and the shame if shoppers in line see her buying ice cream with the Gold Card. The cards are presented fleetingly at tills, and quickly hidden in wallets. In wealthy towns and across this nation, struggling, working Middle America seems to want to pretend that it is getting by without government handouts. After food stamps run out, the food banks kick in for the last week or so of the month. If a family runs out of food stamps at the start of a school holiday, it can push them over the edge into hunger, as parents need to find the money for extra daily children's meals. 'Poverty in America used to be isolated in urban and rural settings that most people didn't see. Now it's more public, much closer to home,' says Andrew Schiff, who runs the logistical backbone for Rhode Island's food banks.

In Cyprus the Orthodox Church was also preparing food banks, after the collapse of businesses starved of working capital and bank funding. The Cypriot debacle was an extreme example of a boundary being tested. Ordinary depositors were lined up to pay the price for a nation's banking excess with a chunk of their savings. We are now entering a bail-in world. The banks were bailed out, and now ordinary people are being bailed in. And not just in Cyprus. Bail-ins are going global.

This leads me to a first big conclusion. Those who breathlessly declared that, in the aftermath of the financial crisis, we were seeing the end of capitalism, were spectacularly incorrect.

Let's focus on the UK for the moment. If you look through the lens of Marx, then it's pretty clear that, right now, capital has never been so ascendant over labour. Capital is capturing the returns to growth, and labour is losing them.

The best example of this is the basic refusal of Britain's workers to ask for pay rises. The inflationary price-wage spiral has completely failed to fire. The bargaining power of British workers has never been so weak. It's not just about low levels of unionisation, it seems that the British worker now internalises the idea that their job can be done more cheaply in China, or by an eager foreign worker. So that means when inflation has hit above 3, 4 or even 5 per cent, wages fail to keep up, growing by just 1.8 per cent. When inflation fell below 3 per cent in 2013, wage growth fell below 1 per cent. This trend is predicted to continue until 2015. In the public sector there were massive strikes over pensions. But at the end of it all, millions of workers ultimately accepted paying more, even after a real pay cut, for a palpably worse pension provision.

In November 2012, the then governor of the Bank of England, Sir Mervyn King, went as far as to publicly exclaim his pride in such real pay cuts, in the face of a slumping pound: 'Wage inflation has been remarkably low at around 2 per cent a year. That's a real test of whether we have allowed domestically generated inflation to pick up. We haven't. This is the first time since the Second World War that the United Kingdom has been able to absorb a very large depreciation of its currency without domestically generated inflation wage costs picking up. I think that's an achievement for monetary policy and I think the MPC [Monetary Policy Committee of the Bank of England] can be rightly proud of that.'

I first saw this dynamic at first hand at the Honda factory in Swindon in 2009. Japanese just in-time delivery stretched to their employment practices. A collapse in demand for cars was transmitted immediately around the world and led to them cutting down on working time as much as on steel. Workers accepted a 3 per cent pay cut for workers and 5 per cent for management in the place of compulsory redundancies, to cope with the slump in world trade after the Lehman collapse. It was the new 'Honda Effect'. So there is no wage-price spiral. Workers have been tamed; labour is mute.

Something similar is happening with savings. To support their economies, nation-states such as Britain are printing money by the truckload. At least with interest-rate cuts, one can see directly how borrowers or companies could benefit. The transfer of savers' returns to borrowers has been a form of macroeconomic bail-in. But £375 billion of quantitative easing (QE) is crushing the pensions of current retirees, alongside savings income. Yet at the same time, QE has also inflated the price of accumulated wealth even further – monetary policy for the wealthy (see Chapter 9, page 285). And there can be no doubt that it has benefited large corporations and big banks disproportionately.

The euro crisis has got nothing to do with a crisis in capitalism. It is basically political. The single currency could, and would, work if German voters felt comfortable with spending their buoyant tax revenues on supporting the comparably trivial problems in Greece or Ireland. If Germany and Brussels can persuade Rome and Madrid to increase their economic competitiveness, it could even be something of a success. But this is a diplomatic game, not a fundamental problem with the economic system.

I have seen this on the streets of Athens and even at the Occupy protests I visited in New York, London and Frankfurt. It's very tempting to see all this as a global insurrection as TV cameras skip from riot to protest. What I find remarkable is that protests like this aren't much much bigger, given the crunching of living standards. Again, despite the rise of radical parties, protests and riots, the internal devaluation strategies insisted on by Brussels and Frankfurt have, when push comes to shove, been endorsed in elections. Centre-right parties that are broadly more comfortable with market-based reforms are now in office across the periphery. The backlash of the workers and unemployed of the periphery has not happened yet. Even in China, nominally Communist, the largest migration of humans on the planet, that of migrant workers from rural China to its factories, is testament to the bargaining power of managed state capitalism over its people.

Of course, there is a notable exception to this hegemony of capital over labour, and that is the industry where workers capture far more of the returns as wages and bonuses than the shareholders. Even as the UK economy slumped, even as some of their employers were bankrupt, three-quarters of workers in this industry expected higher or the same bonuses. Even when their bonuses were hosed down, fixed pay was simply adjusted up. As one British bank chief executive told me during the crisis: 'Marx would have been proud of the triumph of labour in the banks.'

Everywhere else capital is most definitely in the ascendant. Right now it's game, set and match to capitalism.

DEFAULT LINE #1: Living standards and working wages

'It is true that Manchester people stress this when their attention is drawn to the revolting character of this hell upon earth.'

These were the words used in 1844 by Friedrich Engels to describe his visit to the textile mills near the centre of a Manchester booming during Britain's Industrial Revolution, and home to waves of migrant workers from Ireland.

In 2012, a plan was hatched to lure them back. The promise was no less than the return of Manchester's rag trade, but in a form less dark and less satanic than its nineteenth-century predecessor. Reshoring, rebalancing and reindustrialising Manchester's textile industry was the call – the rag trade returning to its historic home. In theory, this was the reverse of offshoring, imbalances, and deindustrialisation: just what George Osborne said he wanted for the UK economy.

At Headen & Quarmby in Middleton, the retail guru Mary Portas commissioned a range of upscale women's underwear called 'Kinky Knickers'. They started hand-making them in north Manchester this year, and the results have been incredible. 'Lovingly Made in Britain' is the label stitched into each pair of knickers. The company's MD David Moore says that they have increased their staff fivefold, and they could increase by another tenfold again, such is the demand for homespun underwear. He wants to turn what was a warehouse for imports into another manufacturing facility: high-street retailers are on the phone; Headen & Quarmby are going to expand their range.

So far so good for this, the niche of the upscale manufacturer. But this is just the start. The local councils, politicians, businessmen and industrialist Lord David Alliance have got together to form an initiative to test the ground for a much more substantial return of mass manufacturing to the area. Lorna Fitzsimons, the affable former Labour MP for Rochdale, runs it and has commissioned a series of consulting reports on what parts of the textile supply chain could return. The answer is: almost all of it – even weaving and spinning.

Brands such as ASOS, Pacific White and Boohoo.com explain why this can happen. Boohoo's offices are housed in a former mill right in the centre of Manchester. As with ASOS and Pacific White, it is internet-based fast fashion that is changing the economics of offshore clothes manufacturing. There are bags of product in the basement, high-end design and sample production on one floor, and a catwalk, studios and models for online catalogues, filming and photography on another. Under the 'made in China' model right now, a firm would have to put in their whole order for spring 2015 by October 2014. They'd have to second-guess emerging trends, the sizes, the colours. They'd have to discount 80 per cent of stock from full price because that equation would inevitably be wrong.

Well, nearshoring and reshoring changes all that. The company can get the clothes on the shelves quicker. They can do a test run of, say, 500, and then swiftly reorder. They can shout at somebody in person if the colour is wrong. Reshoring takes huge amounts of risk out of the supply chain. Boohoo's CEO Chris Bale told me that eighteen months previously 75 per cent of his product came from China. Now over half of it is made in the UK. One million 'skater' dresses were made and sold in Britain in this way. He says there isn't enough textile manufacturing capacity to service the demand. Another Boohoo boss tells me all of his friends are starting factories. Seven years after start-up Boohoo is already profitable and revenues are booming.

In this instance Boohoo's supplier's factories are in Leicester, and they employ some of the women laid off when local textile mills closed in the 1980s. Other brands have clothes factories in Manchester. Go down the road past Oldham to Delph and you will see that not all the mills died. At Mallalieu's of Delph, the trademark 40-foot chimney is still attached to a working mill that weaves high-quality fabrics for Barbour jackets. Some of their cloth featured in the 2012 James Bond movie *Skyfall*. The factory buzzes with whirring needles turning thread into tartan and other fabrics. There always was a niche for luxury. What is amazing, perhaps, is that MD David Mallalieu is now starting to export cloth to the Chinese. Selling cloth to China, from Britain. There *is* a market.

And if that was not enough, then I was told than even basic spinning could be about to return. It seems to break most of the rules of economics. A German industrialist told me that they were 'in discussions' and ready to supply new factories designed for mass textile manufacturing in the Greater Manchester area. 'If we don't do it, the Chinese will do it for themselves. They're already doing that in Italy,' said one new member of Manchester's prospective rag trade mafia.

The re-industrialists of Britain's northwest want and need much more infrastructure: ports, roads, high-speed rail. At peak times, the trams of Manchester's Metrolink light railway are full. In Delph, says David Mallalieu, there is an amazing opportunity, but the skills aren't there. Fitzsimons tells me that there are just five training places in the entire country for skilled textile machinists. In Middleton, David Moore suggests that less employment red tape would allow him to open more factories. This is a vexed question. But it is clear that in an industry that is becoming ever more just-in-time, and ever more flexible in demand and supply, there is a case to be made for trading jobs for labour-market flexibility.

The tens of thousands of jobs created from this vision of a return of Cottonopolis will not necessarily be highly paid. If they do return, they may well do so on the basis of highly unpredictable patterns of internet-based demand. If Britain wants these jobs back onshore, then there may have to be a trade on pay or conditions, or the prices people pay in clothes shops and online. There is a choice. The vision of Chinese-owned manufacturing and assembly on the docks in the Wirral described in Chapter 4 (see pages 116–17) will, for many, represent a dark dystopia. But with youth unemployment hovering near record levels, it would be a brave local politician who turns down such job opportunities. As David Moore at Headen & Quarmby told me: 'not everyone can be Ph.Ds or invent medicines.'

This is another sign of the pressures on British living standards, and the realisation that jobs are being prioritised instead of pay. It is a choice that has already been made in the UK car industry. Despite industrial gloom about manufacturing, British car assembly, manufacturing and exports have boomed recently. Factories that might have closed were kept open, in a series of high-wire negotiations over their future with foreign owners. 'The unions were absolutely brilliant,' a coalition government minister told me. Government offered the car industry R&D support and some sparse funding. The unions traded more demanding patterns of shift-working for the preservation of jobs. The argument that they urged on more hard-line worker representatives was that 'our kids need to have access to employment in the industry'. German unions were much more inflexible and entrenched. The minister said of the conduct of the unions in the period 2010–13, 'Whatever their rhetoric and reputation, they were pragmatic, and ultimately this is very typical of what has happened in Britain and in industry generally, and even in the public sector. The unions fought hard on pensions, but accepted the need for reform, and showed a remarkable degree of maturity on pay policy.'

Exports from the UK car industry reached a record in figures released in January 2013. But jobs in the industry were not surging. The rearguard action over factories had merely maintained the larger units, not staunched wider haemorrhaging of jobs. In fact, everywhere I film new factories in Britain there is the haunting silence of large manufacturing spaces with not many people. In Chepstow, a company famous for building Brunel's bridges in the nineteenth century anticipated cuts to public transport budgets in the twenty-first by diversifying into green growth. Mabey Bridge invested £38 million in a facility for manufacturing highly engineered 120-metre-long steel towers for wind turbines. The 25,000-square-metre state-of-the-art factory could produce 100 towers per year. But the number of jobs worked out at a modest 240 skilled posts. The factory was highly automated. And even that number of jobs was cut as the government scaled back its support for wind power.

Robots are winning over people. Manufacturing is changing in other ways too. At the Chinese-owned MG factory in Longbridge in Birmingham, the promise is 300 jobs next-door in research, design and marketing. The sight of the process of assembly is rather sobering. A small part of an old assembly line transports ready-made car kits shipped in 80 per cent complete from a factory in Lingang, near Shanghai. The cars, already painted, glide past the several dozen stops on the line suspended on metal hooks. Each stop used to represent two or three jobs for a very specialised stage on the line. Now they are all empty, apart from the last three. At this last stage, another assembled unit containing the engine and some of the front suspension is 'stuffed up' into the body, some wires are connected, wheels are added, and that's it. It would be harder for some people to assemble an Airfix model aeroplane.

Robots, competition from China, limited wage bargaining power and an underemployed army of young workers: it's a heady cocktail and one that limits the returns to labour. Credit filled the gap during the boom. In America and in Britain, tax credits also helped bridge the gap between low-paid work and living standards. The state and especially central bankers are trying to cushion the decline now, though rather imperfectly, by boosting asset prices artificially. This cannot last. A fundamental question, therefore, is whether the state will have a larger role rather than a smaller one in the next decade. Tax credits are being pared back amid deficit worries. In the times of plenty, tax credits were focused on pensioners and families, but childless workers missed out. In more austere times the support for pensioners has been maintained, and tax credits for working families reduced. This is the reality of politics of an ageing electorate. It perhaps makes little economic sense. The minimum wage could be an important policy lever to bridge the gap. But large rises in the minimum wage could also imperil some forms of reshoring and reindustrialisation. More local discretion over minimum wage levels is probably worth exploring.

DEFAULT LINE #2: Housing and intergenerational equity

A different form of state action on living standards could be this: an all-encompassing strategy to make things cheaper: housing, education, transport, energy and food. Housing obviously has a rather bizarre status in the inflationary firmament. It is the only basic material need for which a price increase is supposed to be a cause of celebration. Why isn't this ringing alarm bells? It is difficult to elicit an answer from a politician on the question of whether more balanced house prices are a good thing or a bad thing.

Clearly, a massive programme of house-building makes sense economically and in terms of young people's living standards. The current attempt to preserve household net worth by propping up house prices is leading to an ossified housing stock, impinging on labour and social mobility and impacting upon productivity. Housing benefit is an extraordinary cost to the state. About £24 billion a year is being spent in real terms, much of it going directly to landlords. Britain will spend a staggering £120 billion on housing benefit in the next half-decade, and that is after cuts. For context, that would pay for the construction, though not the land costs, of 1.2 million actual houses. In fact the £120 billion in real spending on housing benefits contrasts with just £40 billion spending on actual houses. Spending on housing increases jobs and growth and creates family living space. Spending on housing benefit subsidises landlords, creates poverty traps and adds nothing to the housing stock. It's not difficult to be bewildered that successive governments prefer to fund failure rather than invest in the future.

The large number of second homes and the number of homes bought by non-Britons as investments have resulted in large swathes of the UK housing stock, particularly in the southeast, effectively being removed from the domestic housing market, and often even being unused. They've basically been exported. London is becoming like a giant hotel. Tracking the number of second homes, and the number of homes bought by non-Britons as investments, would help inform the government's ambitions for new house-building. One out, one in, would make some sense.

Apart from that, 'freedom to build' is a great German concept, one that is good for the economy, the construction industry, the environment, living standards, living space and avoiding property bubbles. Essentially, in the German constitution, anyone can build on their property as long as there is no law against it. The burden of proof over planning changes fundamentally. Planning law in Britain is an extraordinary constraint on the ambitions of future generations. The same system was copied in Ireland and Australia, to no good effect. Without a fundamental shift in planning, young British workers face a daft dependence on their parents for access to ever smaller properties, in places they don't want to live. The forces opposed to changes to current UK planning law are extremely powerful. This does not mean that they are right.

Housing dysfunction is compounded by the tax system. Successive governments are too scared to tax wealth and property relative to labour and other forms of consumption. In Britain, for example, the flawed council tax, the UK's only real tax on property, has been frozen for six years, whereas VAT on sales has been hiked. Demographically, the great fiscal challenge will be paying for an ageing society. Yet wealth everywhere is concentrated in older hands. However unpopular they may be, wealth taxes across Europe are on their way in the coming decades.

Right now, austerity programmes are typified by a grand diminution of expectations for the retirement of a current generation of twenty- and thirty-somethings, set against the absolute protection of the retirement rights of a current generation of retirees. Does that make sense? Is that generationally fair? Should a government prioritise unaffordable retirement payments over investing in future productivity, and in educational opportunities that will actually yield growth and tax revenue.

Lastly, a very dark thought. The chief executive of one of Britain's most important financial services firms, with access to millions of points of actuarial data, told me that the widespread strategy to deal with the growing retirement costs arising from lengthening life expectancy – i.e. working longer – 'does not work'. Continuously delaying the retirement age only works for three to four years, not ten years. 'What has driven the extension of life expectancy? It is fewer coronary accidents. It does not mean they'll be able to work for decades longer.' So the spread of cholesterol-controlling statins, blood-pressure-controlling antihypertensive drugs and technologies to unblock arteries, is keeping people alive for longer. But it does not necessarily follow that their health will permit them to work for longer. If he is only half right, Europe's fiscal fate is grim indeed.

Something similar happens in healthcare. Politicians are promising every expensive healthcare development to everyone, even in state-run heath systems like the NHS. Either taxes go up, expectations of the NHS are managed, politicians rein in their promises, or some health user charges will have to be introduced.

DEFAULT LINE #3: Austerity and spending

Public-spending restraint in one form or another will be required beyond the end of this decade. In the light of this, and accepting that the British and European economies will be suffering a

Japanese-style post-bubble deleveraging hangover at the same time, a change of spending priorities might make sense.

'Brutal austerity' in Britain was in fact far better described as patchy austerity. Overall spending went up in cash terms over three years of Mr Osborne's chancellorship from 2010. This is nothing like the 15 per cent cash cuts in public spending in Greece and 12 per cent cash cuts in Ireland from 2009 to 2012. 'Doing a Greece' would have left British spending at more like £569 billion in 2012. 'Doing an Ireland' would have left it at £589 billion. In fact, on the like-for-like Eurostat measure, total government cash spending in the UK was 4 per cent up at £747 billion in 2012. Inflation in the UK and deflation in Ireland explains some but not all of the difference in the percentages.

On the government's own spending measures, total spending went from £669 billion in the last years of Labour to £701 billion in 2012/13 in cash terms, although that was flat in real terms. Tax forecasts were pencilled in to go from £515 billion to £622 billion. In fact only £580 billion was raised. As with his predecessor in 11 Downing Street, Mr Osborne's borrowing numbers were off-target and remained stubbornly high because of a sluggish tax take and moribund economy, not because of spending. Meanwhile 'annually managed expenditure', the other chunk of public spending on benefits, pensions and interest that is less planned, surged 20 per cent from £290 billion to £350 billion. This was brutal austerity applied in patches to spending that was not protected or 'ring-fenced' for political reasons. House-building was massacred, as was other infrastructure investment and regional business support funds. Spending on government investment, the best type of spending for fostering future growth, was halved from £49.5 billion to £24 billion. By the end of 2012/13 the coalition's cuts (i.e. those implemented in 2010/11, 2011/12 and 2012/13) had taken 20p out of every £1 in investment spending, compared to 4p in every £1 of day-to-day spending. If you are going to spend money, is it better to spend it on capital or current? Houses or housing benefit?

Reflecting in 2013 on the decision to cut capital spending, Mr Osborne said it was necessary, despite the weak economy: 'To be frank I was bequeathed some cuts by Darling, capital cuts principally. I banked those cuts because we had so much else to do. But I don't agree it was a mistake to cut capital: we also had to raises taxes and cut current spending.'

Despite the flat economy, the chancellor remained rhetorically true to austerity. In an interview at the IMF meeting in Washington DC he went as far as to say to me: 'When it comes to Britain, I think that argument is now completely won, in other words the argument that we had to deal with our debts. Those who say Britain should ease off on dealing with its debt, I think, are now on the margins of the debate.' Mr Osborne made this remark at a time when his party had slumped in the polls after the disastrous 2012 Budget following the scrapping of the 50p tax rate. The poor performance of the economy, he said, was all down to the overhang of debt in the private sector, and the drawn-out 'balance sheet recession' that followed. So why did he follow the advice of his forecasters that the economy would be enjoying strong growth through this time? Britain was enduring the worst recovery in GDP terms on record. All of its main economic counterparts had regained the ground lost in the recession with 'V-shaped' recoveries. Britain's recovery was not quite a sluggish 'L-shape', but had been a sunlounger-shape with a flattening footrest since 2010.

But the chancellor was also far more flexible than he would let on in public. He reacted to disappointing tax revenues by delaying the deadline for reaching his fiscal targets. He would never go as far as championing a borrowing-funded stimulus, but his targets had been designed to be extremely flexible. In fact by 2013 Gordon Brown's plan to halve the deficit, which was passed into British law, would have been broken by Mr Osborne, had he not quietly rescinded it. It was, however, unclear what the punishment for breaking this law would have entailed. Mr Osborne did not respond to disappointing tax revenues by demanding more cuts, as happened in the Eurozone periphery, perhaps the definition of true fiscal brutality. Osborne even started to talk the language of stimulus and infrastructure spending, despite having inflicted large cuts on infrastructure. In his media interviews he was rarely seen without a hard hat or high-visibility jacket. In mid-2012, at one of his visits to a taxpayer-funded construction site, on this occasion a giant shaft for the Crossrail project near London's Bond Street, the chancellor boasted about his capital spending record, claiming that while it included large cuts, those cuts were smaller ones than Labour had planned. With his Liberal Democrat deputy Danny Alexander by his side, he said: 'We are the people who sat around the table eighteen months ago and gave the go-ahead to this [Crossrail] project that we are standing in today. We are actually spending more on capital investment than the Labour Party planned, more on our roads and railways than they spent in the boom years. We have had to take some very difficult decisions, but if you look at the alternative, which was to allow Britain to turn into a basket case in Europe, I think that would have been a disastrous path.'

Osborne's original hope was that the confidence garnered by low long-term interest rates and fiscal credibility would be enough to excite the animal spirit of investment in jobs-rich infrastructure (Actually, the model infrastructure procurement in Britain tends to focus on a few dozen massive multinational construction companies, with large finance and legal departments. The money does not trickle down to local economies providing the Keynesian boost often cited.) It did not work, and probably never was going to. He then hoped that foreign sovereign wealth funds would fund a wave of power stations, rail links and broadband networks. Again, despite one or two successes, it didn't work. Pension funds were tapped up, but little money was forthcoming. He then offered up the Treasury balance sheet for contingent guarantees to private companies. Again there was the odd success, such as an extension to the London Tube network. After March 2011, the OBR reported that Mr Osborne had announced contingent guarantees worth

£95 billion, that do not count as public borrowing, but might do. One might call it 'contingent Keynesianism'. But he would not cross his red line of planning to borrow more in order to provide a Keynesian boost to the economy, despite the cheapest borrowing costs in British history. Happening to borrow more because the economy was weak and tax revenues down was fine; planning to borrow more was a fiscal sin that would be punished by the fiery anger of the bond vigilantes.

Even that line was fudged in 2012, when borrowed money was directed to house-builders in return for stakes in homeowners' new-build property. This 'Help to Buy' scheme involved borrowed money, but in accounting terms – rather handily – did not count as increasing the deficit, because the state 'owned' 20 per cent of each of the houses bought, as loan collateral. Detractors were withering about Help to Buy, calling it 'dangerous' and 'moronic'.

More broadly, the path taken by Mr Osborne was not greatly different from the one that would have been taken by Mr Darling or by Ed Balls. 'Osballism' was the order of the day: the political debate about fiscal policy was a particularly extreme tale of the narcissism of small differences.

There are three things going on in Britain that are obvious but little acknowledged in the fiscal Punch-and-Judy show that has dominated the UK economic debate:

1. Deleveraging is dragging the economy and is far from over.
2. Fiscal policy is being used to accommodate failure rather than to plan and strategise for long-term growth.
3. A large chunk of our economy and our tax base has essentially disappeared for good.

The last point reflects the fact that the City of London was a production house for toxic derivatives and the capital of the shadow banking system. Some of the losses booked by big multinational banks mean that corporation tax will not be paid by those banks for a decade. A choice will be required about whether to replace that missing tax base with a different one (e.g. wealth taxes), or whether the state needs to shrink back.

DEFAULT LINE #4: Banking and the sovereign doom loop

In the Eurozone, attempts to break the link between oversized banking systems and government support for those systems have been haphazard and often entirely counterproductive. In Britain, such links were not the fundamental problem to begin with.

In Britain, there were broadly two separate financial crises. A conventional consumer and corporate credit bubble, fuelled by lightly regulated demutualised building societies, such as Halifax, Northern Rock, Bradford & Bingley, tapping global flows of hot money in the shadow banking system. But the City of London also had a massive role in creating and mediating these flows, through opaque derivative technology developed, sold and traded by investment banks. Britain consumed the credit madness, but was also the site of its main factory. Reform has been based on some sort of separation between or ring-fencing of these two worlds. London was a production centre, the foremost factory for toxic derivative waste. Understanding and accepting that reality is not to be anti-banker but to recognise the truth. We could have constructed much better solutions to Britain's banking problems by acknowledging what had gone wrong and not trying to sweep it under the carpet.

Recognising these truths about London banking is intellectually liberating: it helps explain why growth is sluggish, tax revenues are weak and business credit is slow. In future, governments should not rely on such unreliable sources of tax revenue. The Golden Goose is dead.

At the heart of the banking system is the Basel system of formulaic self-regulation. My chapter on the formulae behind the shadow banking system (see pages 200–34), I hope, begins to show that the formulae are not based on science, and, in the round, skew the credit-creation system towards reinforcing the dysfunctional relationship with property. If governments and taxpayers are to implicitly backstop the banking system, why not skew the formulae in favour of growth and job creation and away from property?

How much longer can monetary and financial policy help put off a necessary cleansing of UK and European bank balance sheets? Losses are not being realised, which might have helped employment by keeping doomed companies alive. The understandable pain-alleviating forbearance has turned not just into endless extend-and-pretend, but now also into household and corporate zombification. Ultimately there are tens of thousands of companies and households with misallocated capital, arising from prolonged lows in interest rates. 'Eventually interest rates will have to rise, because capitalism requires capital,' said one important UK finance chief executive to me. Even more important will be a proper clear-out of the UK bank balance sheets. The risk is that Britain follows Japan's zombified path and not that of, say, Sweden, where the banks painfully cleansed their balance sheets and fostered new growth.

State-run banks is one thing; a bank-run state is quite another. Alistair Darling recalls the series of identical phone calls received at Number 11 Downing Street from bank chief executives after he dared to introduce a bonus tax on the largely illusory bank windfalls arising out of the 2008–09 bank rescue. In his book *Back from the Brink* (2011), amazingly, Darling describes how the chief executive of J. P. Morgan angrily raised question marks about buying UK government bonds in response to the policy. He wasn't the only chief executive to make such threats to a finance minister. Banks should fit the state, not the other way round.

DEFAULT LINE #5: Superstates and city-states

The euro crisis is not, essentially an economic crisis. It is a crisis of democracy, diplomacy, legitimacy and burden-sharing. In the economic jargon, the Eurozone is not an optimal currency area. Tax transfers, debt pooling and a transfer union are inevitable to make the union work properly. The move towards banking union could begin this by stealth. As Mr Osborne has said, if the euro is to survive, the inescapable logic is fiscal union and eurobonds. Berlin will decide the speed of this. In the words spoken to me by one leading European financier: 'it will cost €500 billion [in transfers] to solve the Eurozone crisis. It will cost at least €3 trillion not to solve it from a break-up of the Eurozone. Logic dictates that they know what they have to do.'

The opposition SPD and Green Party at least partially endorse eurobonds, or forms of debt-pooling, ahead of the 2013 federal election. Germany is much more than the economic hawks, inflation aversion and a reluctant Merkel.

Huge strides need to be made on youth unemployment. Enrico Letta, the Italian prime minister, told me in July 2013 about how he had devoted scarce fiscal resources to a massive tax cut for employing young people. 'We say to the young people: "your problem is our problem". We want to bring more hope for the youth and more hope for the country.'

Mark Carney suggested an interesting plan in his last speech before becoming Bank of England governor. 'In the medium term, one of the building blocks of European fiscal federalism could be a pan-European employment insurance scheme built on a common European labour market. This would reduce impediments for those looking across the continent for work, while providing a cross-country automatic stabilizer.' It was an idea rooted in the experience of a monetary union that works: Canada. Note to Berlin: Canadian monetary union works because of fiscal transfers worth 8 per cent of GDP.

Peter Hartz, the German jobs miracle architect, also told me about a similar new plan for youth unemployment: all European young people would have their talents diagnosed, with unemployed youth sent on a temporary basis to another EU member-state financed with EU funds for training and work. The German labour minister, Ursula von der Leyen, is already planning to offer apprenticeships to young Greeks, Spaniards and Irish. Europe's youth may need to learn German.

The UK will also renegotiate its relationship with this new, euro-centric and more centralised European Union in a referendum. There are some win-wins available in the renegotiation. Germany might try to leverage the threat of UK exit to galvanise a more dynamic Eurozone, more focused on physics than with farming. France is probably willing to give very little. However, can it really be credible that UK national interest will again be defined by what is good for financial services?

There is another – intriguing – aspect to the fiscal crisis. It is applying acute pressure on Europe's traditional member-states. In Britain we will see this with the autumn 2014 referendum on Scottish independence. Scottish nationalists feel fiscal autonomy will serve Scotland's interests and its economy better, but it is difficult to imagine how an Edinburgh-based central bank would or could have coped with the collapse of RBS, HBoS and the Dunfermline Building Society. In Spain, clearly, Catalunya – as the nation's main economic hub – is even more attracted to greater fiscal autonomy. Spain's constitutional settlement is up for grabs in its fiscal crisis. If Catalunya or Scotland start the process of national fragmentation, then what chance Belgium – or even Italy – splitting?

In a globalising economy fighting for multinational investment and a tax base, it is often suggested that a larger superstate is the natural response. Over decades, the opposite may be true. 'City regions' could become the natural unit of government. In the UK, for example, the rest of the country has to cope with the benefits and disbenefits of hosting the world's capital city nearby. A Manchester or a Leeds could eventually need taxvarying powers in order to compete. Already plans are afoot to devolve spending powers away from Whitehall towards the city experts who know best how to get young people off benefits in their localities.

DEFAULT LINE #6: The role of economics

Economics has developed into something of a state-backed theology in public policy. It is social science that has become a language for the calculation of costs and benefits. Its magical powers have been overstated, however. Many of these economic analyses are just extrapolations and the only accurate analysis is provided with hindsight.

Conventional market-clearing equilibrium economics inculcates a mindset of econofatalism: a belief that nothing can be done to change the inevitable financial fate of a nation's economy. Milton Friedman developed the concept of the 'superneutrality' of money. Superneutrality is an apt description of the approach to public policy that arises out of the overuse of economics. I know enough about economics to appreciate its flaws. It is a useful and occasionally wonderful lens on the world, and provides some principles to follow. But as a guide to how to create a sustainable society that works? No chance. Politicians need to show some spine and some vision, some competence and some bold daring. The theory of laissez-faire has been substantially undermined by the successful strategising of emerging economies and indeed the economic history of the developed world. We need, humbly, to learn from these emerging economies. The most successful ones have smashed most of what they were told by the IMF, bond markets, media-friendly PIMCO analysts and the like. The supposed bastions of the free market, such as financial services and the housing market, have proven nothing of the sort, and were largely parasitic upon government balance sheets.

I would call myself basically a new Manchester liberal. I believe in fundamental market principles (as Nobel prize-winning economist Amartya Sen once suggested, to be against the free exchange of goods and services is as absurd as being against the free exchange of words in a conversation), but few markets are truly free. Convoluted attempts to create them in railways, in British toll motorways, in toxic mortgage finance, in infrastructure and in carbon, have failed utterly – and expensively. When I visit parts of the world that are growing fast and see companies that are thriving there, more often than not, a smart and subtle hand of the state is never far away. Politicians have hypnotised themselves into believing the economic fates and meteorology are so immutable, that they dare not even think they can change things. They have become superneutral.

Central bankers have been key to the use of economics. As the crisis raged in 2008, I got the chance to put it to Alan Greenspan, chairman of the US Federal Reserve from 1987 to 2006, that it was basically his fault. He told me: 'The housing bubble in the US is fully explained by global forces, and indeed we at the Fed could not control long-term rates, which are the rates that effectively drive mortgage rates, which essentially said to us that our power to affect the forces driving the bubble were *de minimis*. And we tried but we failed. And every other central bank failed because the international markets took long-term rates out of the hands of central banks. It's essentially a problem of bubbles emerging periodically half a generation at a time – and I think we're learning that it's very difficult to stop these from occuring and the best thing we can do is to focus on how we prevent them from having catastrophic effects.'

British politics meanwhile is still trapped in an absurd 1980s culture war between Thatcherites and unionistas. By contrast, in 2009, Angela Merkel responded to the collapse in world trade by spending two days in a hotel with union and business leaders, thrashing out a balanced engineered response to maintain employment and demand. It combined 'right-wing' policies on wage restraint with 'left-wing' policies on borrowed stimulus. The result was an economy that powered back to health, regaining all of the lost ground in one of the sharpest V-shaped recoveries in modern history. Germany engineers finances towards productive industry and innovation. Britain has financialised our engineers towards useless financial innovation. In the 1990s and noughties, the latter approach appeared to conquer all. However, financialising the housing market does not an economic strategy make. The German government sees a house and considers it a home. Successive British governments see a house and consider it a piggybank. Now Britain needs a broader economic plan, one that stretches beyond deficit reduction and financialisation. To begin with, the generation of politicians that failed their nations need to reflect on, to account for and learn from their mistakes. This is a massive political opportunity.

The collateral damage that I have seen on my journey around the world economy, a flawed banking system and crisis Europe is almost always young and asset-poor. What should be the rational response of a young person of talent to the way Britain is being run economically? Leave the country. And that is what many are doing. Of the 3.6 million emigrants from Britain in the past decade, 2 million were aged 25 to 44. Large tuition fees have contracted the deficit, yes, but will increase the incentive to emigrate. Not being able to buy even a modest house to bring up a family will also increase that incentive. Britain is not so different from the countries of the Eurozone, from Ireland or Spain. I see a generational shafting of epic proportions, and the young whom we are relying on to create growth, jobs and tax revenues are starting to vote with their feet. They have choices, and so do we all.

Ten ideas to chew on

Books are often accused of being impractical. So, to end on a practical note, I offer ten ideas to chew on. They are all flawed, but they arise as part-solutions to some of the problems I have seen around the world. They are drawn from a trawl of what I identified above as the world's new default lines. Most of them would not emerge out of our insidery UK political system. They are a little random, perhaps, but I believe them to be worthy of discussion in the present economic context, as I write this in the summer of 2013.

#1. Shift the burden of taxation away from labour taxes towards wealth taxes.
#2. Abolish housing benefit in pre-announced phases, and...
#3. Switch tens of billions of pounds of funding to mass building of houses, and new working communities. Track changes in the available housing stock, i.e. minus houses bought for investment, rarely lived in, and basically 'exported'.
#4. Move most of government out of London to northern England.
#5. Ban any financial product that a bank chief executive cannot explain to their regulator.
#6. Scrap MPs' mortgage subsidies and raise their pay.
#7. Make stamp duty payable by sellers who benefited from the boom, not buyers.
#8. Allow different city regions in the UK to impose their own rates of corporation tax and minimum wage levels.
#9. Use EU renegotiation to phase out farmer subsidies and refocus EU policies towards clean energy and hi-tech research.
#10. Cut the voting age to 15.

Details of some of the numbers and references in this book will be available at www.thedefaultline.com.
Or you can contact me via Twitter @TheDefaultLine

ACKNOWLEDGEMENTS

Thanks to my *Channel 4 News* colleagues for allowing and encouraging me to pursue the writing of this book. My editor Ben de Pear and deputy Shaminder Nahal, alongside Dorothy Byrne at Channel 4, created some space for me to finish the book as it grew like a European sovereign debt. My former colleagues who sent me across the globe on the hunt for answers to the credit crisis: Ben Monro-Davies, Jim Gray, Martin Fewell, and Deborah Rayner.

Neil Macdonald, my occasionally suffering and brilliant producer, has held the fort amazingly in regular crises, and while I've been trying to finish writing the book. Former producers Rachel Jupp, Ben King, Job Rabkin, Girish Juneja, Emily Wilson, Julie O'Connor, Andrew McFadyen, Victoria Eastwood and Bessie Du, have flowed with creative juices in trying to help explain some the complexities of these roller-coaster economic crises. Bob in the Garage for fixing my tape deck.

Some of these stories have been filmed, captured and researched by artisan cameramen and editors such as Ray Queally, Stewart Webb, Graeme Heslop, Dai Baker, Chris Shlemon, Soren Munk, Philippa Collins and numerous others I have forgotten. Siobhan Kennedy and Sarah Smith continued and probably improved *Channel 4 News*'s excellent financial broadcasting while I was away.

It should be said that none of the opinions expressed here are that of my employer ITN, nor of *Channel 4 News*, nor of Channel 4. They are mine and mine alone.

Thanks again to Ben King for research help on the housing

chapter, David Cheal for research and fact-checking, Lachlan Cartwright for journalistic consultancy, and James Conway for German translations.

Emily Bell, Roger Alton, Jamie Doward and Will Hutton got my career in journalism rolling at the *Observer*.

I have had access to some top-level bankers, central bankers, and finance ministers in the course of my work and in the course of writing this book. Alistair Darling and George Osborne are both British chancellors who have had to make tough and unpopular decisions, but who recognise, accept and encourage the questioning role of the economic media. Numerous central bankers have helped me with the book. On-the-record broadcast interviews with Sir Mervyn King, Christian Noyer, and some thoughtful answers at press conferences from Mario Draghi, have all helped inform the economic story I tell here. In the banks and financial services industry, there are four or five chief executives who were so candid they would prefer to remain below the radar. The German embassy in London, the European Central Bank and the German finance ministry were very helpful. Anyone interested in European economics should make a visit to the Bundesbank museum in Frankfurt. At the UK Treasury, Jonathan Black, Jean-Christophe Gray, Rupert Harrison, Geoffrey Spence, and others have always been very helpful. At the Bank of England, Nils Blythe, Jenny Scott, Charles Bean, Paul Fisher, Martin Weale and many others have always been open to probing journalism.

On my travels, I have been the subject of amazing hospitality in Athens, Lisbon, Nicosia, Dublin, Berlin and Frankfurt.

Special thanks must go for the expert knowledge occasionally lent to me by a team of geniuses in the economic twittersphere and beyond. Matina Stevis, Janine Louloudi, Toby Nangle, Danny Gabay, Erik Britton, Gabriel Sterne, Richard Walker, Felix Salmon, Lorcan Roche Kelly, Brian Lucey, Theo Phanos, Lee Buchheit, Sigrún Davíðsdóttir, Shirley Beglinger, Luis Garicano, Oldrich Vasicek, Carl Emmerson, James Anwyl, David Curtis,

Toby Seth, George Pyper, Tom Seibre and Sony Kapoor. Social media means that there are a tonne of others who have unknowingly helped me too. Thanks to Otmar Issing for explaining unit labour costs right at the beginning of the crisis. Some of these people kindly read through first drafts of this book, and corrected mistakes, and improved the argument. All the mistakes are mine and mine alone.

On Greece, *Greece's 'Odious' Debt*, by Jason Manolopoulos is worth reading, as is anything by Matina Stevis or Stephen Grey. For austerity and bond trading, obviously follow the work of the Institute for Fiscal Studies, and Jim Reid, economic historian at Deutsche Bank. On Iceland, Sigrún's Icenews blog, and *On Thin Ice – A Modern Viking Saga About Corruption, Deception and the Collapse of a Nation* (2011), by Icelandic economist Jón F. Thoroddsen is the best book. On China, Stephen King's books *Losing Control* and *When the Money Runs Out*, alongside Justin Yifu Lin's *Demystifying the Chinese Economy* and *The Quest for Prosperity*, are must-reads. Brad Setser's blogs at the Council for Foreign Relations are still an excellent account of the geoeconomic build-up to the crisis. Ray Perman's *Hubris* about the HBoS debacle is a remarkable read, as is Alistair Darling's book on the crisis, *Back from the Brink*. I would watch out for the forthcoming book on RBS by the irrepressible Ian Fraser called *Shredded*. Andrew Tyrie's parliamentary report into the HBoS collapse is also a remarkable read. On the formulae that broke Wall Street I'd recommend Felix Salmon's seminal article on David Li for *Wired*. Nick Dunbar's *The Devil's Derivatives* is a must-read. I drew heavily on both of these and on Donald Mackenzie's and Taylor Spears' paper 'The Formula That Killed Wall Street' to set up Oldrich Vasicek's story. On the ECB, there is a book called *The Bank* (1999) by Matt Marshall that has some of the deep history behind the then slightly hapless institution.

Thanks to Lord Eatwell, Amartya Sen, and Rupert Gatti at Trinity College, Cambridge, for teaching me immense amounts about economics, yet at the same time engendering a healthy scepticism of its foundational axioms. Thanks to Joe and Anya Stiglitz for getting me to chair a dinner of Sovereign Wealth Funds that led to the interview with Jin Liqun. My agent Georgina Capel, publisher Anthony Cheetham, and the close attention of the wonderful Richard Milbank and the rest of the team at Head of Zeus have enabled me to get these thoughts onto the page.

Lastly, the capacity for fevered and argumentative debate fostered around the typically Mancunian, Bengali-Indian dinner table propelled me into journalism. Thanks to Farah, Farhad, Omar, Fatima, Mum and Dad. And most of all, my lovely, and rather patient wife, Verity.